Early Stages

Edited by ANN SADDLEMYER

Early Stages:
Theatre in Ontario
1800–1914

A project of the
Ontario Historical Studies Series
for the Government of Ontario
Published by University of Toronto Press
Toronto Buffalo London

ISBN 0-8020-2738-5 (cloth)
ISBN 0-8020-6779-4 (paper)

Printed on acid-free paper

Canadian Cataloguing in Publication Data

Main entry under title:

Early stages: theatre in Ontario, 1800–1914

(Ontario historical studies series)
ISBN 0-8020-2738-5 (bound). – ISBN 0-8020-6779-4 (pbk.)

1. Theater – Ontario – History. I. Saddlemyer, Ann,
1932–   . II. Series.

PN2305.05E27 1990   792'.09713   C90-094368-8

This book has been published with the assistance of funds provided by the
Government of Ontario through the Ministry of Culture and Communications.

Contents

The Ontario Historical Studies Series
Goldwin French, Peter Oliver, Jeanne Beck, and
J.M.S. Careless *vii*

Acknowledgments *ix*

Contributors *xi*

1 Introduction
Ann Saddlemyer *3*

2 The Cultural Setting: Ontario Society to 1914
J.M.S. Careless *18*

3 Amateurs of the Regiment, 1815–1870
Leslie O'Dell *52*

4 The Nineteenth-Century Repertoire
Robertson Davies *90*

5 Entertainers of the Road
Mary M. Brown *123*

6 Variety Theatre
Gerald Lenton-Young *166*

7 Theatres and Performance Halls
Robert Fairfield *214*

8 Chronology: Theatre in Ontario to 1914
   Richard Plant *288*   .

Select Bibliography
   Richard Plant *347* ·

Illustration Credits *355*

Index *357*

The Ontario Historical Studies Series

For many years the principal theme in English-Canadian historical writing has been the emergence and the consolidation of the Canadian nation. This theme has been developed in uneasy awareness of the persistence and importance of regional interests and identities, but because of the central role of Ontario in the growth of Canada, Ontario has not been seen as a region. Almost unconsciously, historians have equated the history of the province with that of the nation and have depicted the interests of other regions as obstacles to the unity and welfare of Canada.

The creation of the province of Ontario in 1867 was the visible embodiment of a formidable reality, the existence at the core of the new nation of a powerful if disjointed society whose traditions and characteristics differed in many respects from those of the other British North American colonies. The intervening century has not witnessed the assimilation of Ontario to the other regions in Canada; on the contrary it has become a more clearly articulated entity. Within the formal geographical and institutional framework defined so assiduously by Ontario's political leaders, an increasingly intricate web of economic and social interests has been woven and shaped by the dynamic interplay between Toronto and its hinterland. The character of this regional community has been formed in the tension between a rapid adaptation to the processes of modernization and industrialization in modern western society and a reluctance to modify or discard traditional attitudes and values. Not surprisingly, the Ontario outlook is a compound of aggressiveness, conservatism, and the conviction that its values should be the model for the rest of Canada.

From the outset the objective of the Board of Trustees of the series has been to describe and analyse the historical development of Ontario as a distinct region within Canada. The series as planned will include thirty-two volumes covering many aspects of the life and work of the province from its original establishment in 1791 as Upper Canada to our own time. Among these will be biographies of several premiers, numerous works on the growth of the provincial economy, educational institutions, minority groups, and the arts, and a synthesis of the history of Ontario, based upon the contributions of the biographies and thematic studies.

In planning this project, the editors and the board have endeavoured to maintain a reasonable balance between different kinds and areas of historical research, and to appoint authors ready to ask new questions about the past and to answer them in accordance with the canons of contemporary scholarship. *Early Stages: Theatre in Ontario, 1800–1914* is the eighth theme study to be published. In it, Ann Saddlemyer and her collaborators have described several aspects of the development of 'show business in nineteenth-century Ontario' – a period in which 'a small company of courageous, even foolhardy itinerant entertainers' grew in number and competence, 'reaching finally the Golden Age of melodrama, "The Road," variety, and the cinema.' By 1914, theatre in all its forms was an accepted and prosperous part of Ontario culture, but its Golden Age was 'slipping away.'

Ann Saddlemyer and her colleagues have written a fascinating and scholarly account, which will be a significant contribution to our understanding of the cultural history of this province. We hope that it will stimulate further exploration of the intricate relationship between society and culture.

The editors and the Board of Trustees are grateful to Ann Saddlemyer and her collaborators for undertaking this task.

GOLDWIN FRENCH
PETER OLIVER
JEANNE BECK
J.M.S. CARELESS, Chairman of the Board of Trustees

Toronto
20 June 1990

Acknowledgments

A study such as this could be undertaken only with the assistance not only of those who have been thanked by the authors of individual chapters or included in the bibliography, but of a great many scholars whose efforts, often unacknowledged, frequently unknown, have provided the foundation on which theatre and social historians can build. This volume itself has been almost ten years in the making and over that period has drawn upon the enthusiasm and expertise of most members of the Association for Canadian Theatre History / l'Association d'histoire du théâtre au Canada, as well as archivists throughout Ontario. Special thanks must go to Joan Fairfield, Dr Kathleen Fraser, Sarah Gibson, Linda Peake, and Dr Natalie Rewa for their careful research. But most of all, we are grateful for the wise advice and editorial skills of Dr Goldwin French, Dr Peter Oliver, and Dr Jeanne Beck and the patient faith of the Board of Trustees of the Ontario Historical Studies Series.

Contributors

Before taking a position with the Department of English at the University of Western Ontario, **Mary M. Brown** had been a producer for the CBC and was for many years an actress, director, and designer in the London Little Theatre. Her publications include articles and books on nineteenth-century Canadian drama and fiction, and at the time of her death in 1982 she was writing a history of grand opera houses in Ontario, 1880–1919, and a book on the C.J. Whitney–Ambrose Small Circuit, 1875–1919.

University professor and Senior Fellow of Massey College and former chairman of the Department of History at the University of Toronto, **J.M.S. Careless** has received many awards for his books and articles on the history of Canada, including the Governor General's Award for 1954 and 1964. His many public offices include service as director of the Ontario Heritage Foundation, chairman of the Historic Sites and Monuments Board of Canada, and chairman of the Multicultural History Society of Ontario. He has been co-editor of the *Canadian Historical Review* and has acted as consultant to various film, radio, and television historical series.

Novelist, essayist, playwright, and sometime actor **Robertson Davies** was born in 1913 in a household in which theatre was mentioned and discussed every day; he became a theatre-goer himself at the age of four, after seeing a play by the Canadian Marks family, and from them he progressed to players who now seem legendary, such as Mrs Fiske, Henrietta Crossman, Otis Skinner, and William Gillette. These experiences and his years as a teacher of theatre history and drama at the University of Toronto when he was the first Master of Massey College inform not only his chapter for this book but his novel *World of Wonders.*

Awarded the 1958 Massey Gold Medal for design of the Stratford Festival Theatre, **Robert Fairfield** has practised architecture in Toronto since 1945. His firm's commissions have included the Province of Ontario Pavilion at Expo '67, the Canadian ambassador's residence in Ankara, a new town at Frobisher Bay, New College at the University of Toronto, and design of a theatre complex in Ithaca, New York. His theatre consulting work has also included new theatres at Kenyon College and in Cleveland, Ohio. A former member of the Board of Trustees of the Art Gallery of Ontario, he is currently a member of the Advisory Board of the Architectural Conservancy of Ontario.

A professional actor and director and a teacher, **Gerald Lenton-Young** received his doctorate from the Graduate Centre for Study of Drama, University of Toronto, for his thesis on vaudeville in Toronto of 1899 to 1915. In addition, he was co-founder of Winnipeg's comedy Theatre, an improvisational company experimenting with scenarios from the Italian *commedia dell'arte*. While remaining a member of Canadian Actor's Equity and ACTRA, he teaches theatre at the University of Regina.

Artistic director of Theatre Laurier and teacher of drama and theatre at Wilfrid Laurier University, **Leslie O'Dell** received her doctorate from the Graduate Centre for Study of Drama, University of Toronto, for a thesis on theatre in Kingston during the nineteenth century. She has acted on stage, film, radio, and television and had sixteen original plays produced. Her current research is on performance theory and theatre for the disabled.

Co-founder and co-editor of *Theatre History in Canada / Histoire du théâtre au Canada* and former president of the Association for Canadian Theatre History, **Richard Plant** has published extensively as a bibliographer, drama critic, and editor. Also a director and sometime actor, he teaches in the drama department at Queen's University and as visiting professor to the Graduate Centre for Study of Drama at the University of Toronto. He is currently completing a new edition of the *Bibliography of Canadian Theatre History* and a book on twentieth-century Canadian drama.

Master of Massey College and professor of English and drama at the University of Toronto, **Ann Saddlemyer** has published on twentieth-century theatre and drama, especially that of Canada and Ireland. She was founding president of the Association for Canadian Theatre History and, with Richard Plant, co-founder and co-editor of *Theatre History in Canada*. She serves on numerous editorial boards, has lectured extensively both in Canada and elsewhere, and occasionally reviews theatre for the CBC.

Early Stages

1
Introduction

ANN SADDLEMYER

There were Christians and Heathens, Menonists and Tunkards, Quakers and Universalists, Presbyterians and Baptists, Roman Catholics and American Methodists; there were Frenchmen and Yankees, Irishmen and Mulattoes, Scotchmen and Indians, Englishmen, Canadians, Americans, and Negroes, Dutchmen and Germans, Welshmen and Swedes, Highlanders and Lowlanders, poetical as well as most prosaical phizes, horsemen and footmen, fiddlers and dancers, honourables and reverends, captains and colonels, beaux and belles, waggons and tilburies, coaches and chaises, gigs and carts; in short, Europe, Asia, Africa, and America had there each its representative among the loyal subjects and servants of our good King George, the fourth of the name.[1]

When William Lyon Mackenzie, that quintessential stage manager of the political arena, thus surveyed an election crowd at Niagara in the late 1820s, the population of Upper Canada was 237,000, less than half that of Lower Canada. It was more than 140 years since Frontenac had established the first permanent European settlement at Fort Cataraqui, where Kingston now stands, and less than twenty since the Battle of Waterloo had opened the floodgates to British immigrants who would join the large numbers of Loyalists and other Americans already come up from the south. Despite Mackenzie's rhetoric, the population of the territory that would become Ontario was primarily English speaking, decidedly Protestant, and culturally rooted in British traditions – as it would remain throughout the period covered by this volume. But Mackenzie also had a keen eye and good ear for what was unique to this motley crowd of farmers, gentry, frontiersmen and traders; for this volatile, interested, and willing audience knew what it wanted and was prepared to go to great lengths (sometime hundreds of miles) to get it. As John Godley reported while visiting Toronto in 1842,

Ottawa, Rideau Hall, theatricals in the ballroom

Ottawa, Rideau Hall, audience for private theatrical, 1873

In this country all the world is in a whirl and fizz, and one must be in the fashion; every thing and every body seem to go by steam; if you meet an acquaintance in the street he is sure to have just arrived from some place three or four hundred miles off, and to be just starting upon a similar expedition in some other direction. After a short experience of this mode of life one quite forgets that there is such a thing as repose or absence of noise, and begins to think that the blowing of steam is a necessary accompaniment and consequence of the ordinary operation of the elements – a Yankee music of the spheres.[2]

Although politics and politicians would endure as the most engrossing entertainment for Canadians – some of the earliest indigenous dramas were barely disguised political pamphlets – other pastimes flourished in Upper Canada. The first racetrack was operating at Niagara by the 1790s, and, at the other end of the social scale, the Toronto Hunt would soon be established (to remain active within the city boundaries until after the First World War). Nor, given the frontiersman's taste for strong liquor, is it surprising that taverns – as ubiquitous then as banks are today – were among the first to offer shelter and temporary stages for the many itinerant performers who made their way from Lower Canada or New York state even before the Erie Canal was completed in the 1820s. A newspaper was published in Niagara in 1793, by which time the first masonic lodge – surely one of the most theatrical of the province's many partisan organizations – was in full operation. By 1800 the first library had appeared (supported by private subscription), and reading aloud became even more of a common drawing-room entertainment with the serial reprinting of contemporary novels in local journals. Visitors from Montreal doubtless reported the establishment there in 1797 of Ricketts's circus with its added attractions of stage performances. But during the first years of the nineteenth century York, population 600, had been treated not only to the excitement of a 'learned pig,' but to performances of Sheridan's *The School for Scandal* (by a troupe of New York 'gentry'), Home's *Douglas*, and Macready's *The Village Lawyer* (on tour from Montreal), and to an evening of 'Songs, Recitations and Ventriloquisms' (by two gentlemen from London, England). Thus a pattern of dependence on touring companies from the United States and Britain supplemented by visitors from elsewhere in Canada, all with a marked preference for the familiar repertoire, was established. However, with the performance during 1816–17 of close to thirty plays and as many farces by the Kingston Amateur Theatre on a fitted-up stage complete with painted scenery (a drop curtain featured the nearby Falls of Chaudière), stage lights, and costumes, an accompanying strong tradition of amateur productions was introduced. The first publication of indigenous drama, in the Niagara *Gleaner* one year later, completed a picture familiar to this day.

Even before Mackenzie's political gathering at Niagara, York had its own resident circus, 'Columbus' the elephant (a separate excitement), and a literary and debating society. Kingston could entertain visiting performers from Montreal in a 'small but comfortable theatre erected in the rear of the hotel,' Hamilton boasted its own local performances, and Ancaster had its own amateur society. But 1833 is also the year that the Kembles did *not* visit York for want of a proper theatre building. When within months of the snub one was created in a converted Wesleyan church, the city fathers established a new custom by immediately passing a by-law requiring performance licences. As the railway developed in the 1850s, so too did theatre buildings, encouraging further and more lavish touring circuits interspersed with resident stock companies and determined amateur societies, which spawned discriminating audiences who could – and did – demand both variety and standards. Theatre must provide something for everyone – and so it did. By the late nineteenth century there were about 250 touring companies on 'The Road,' Ontario's capital had at least three handsome major theatres in continuous operation in addition to many smaller establishments, while as far west as Rat Portage (present-day Kenora) prosperous towns established more permanent companies in handsome 'opera houses,' well-fitted town halls, mechanics' institutes, and market buildings.

Although the garrisons of Upper Canada provided the earliest and perhaps most organized enthusiasm for theatrical entertainment and frequently assisted local townspeople in building the first stages, amateur and professional theatre co-existed alongside garrison performances throughout the nineteenth century. Encouraged by social patronage, notably Lady Dufferin's New Year entertainments on the specially fitted stage of Rideau Hall in the 1870s and the establishment of Governor-General Earl Grey's Musical and Dramatic Competition in the early years of this century, the amateur tradition has always been strong, developing intelligent performance and discriminating audiences. We might well wonder how the picture of Canadian theatre would have changed had the first lieutenant-governor of Upper Canada, John Graves Simcoe, enjoyed theatre as much as some of his successors. But the military influence did not cease when British troops withdrew in 1869: during the First World War some thirty or forty Canadian entertainment troupes – including the popular 'Dumbells' – toured France, and rare is the Canadian who has not seen the Mounties' famous musical ride.

Amateur theatre also provided a forum for those local playwrights who were not satisfied with only a reading public. For it will be obvious from

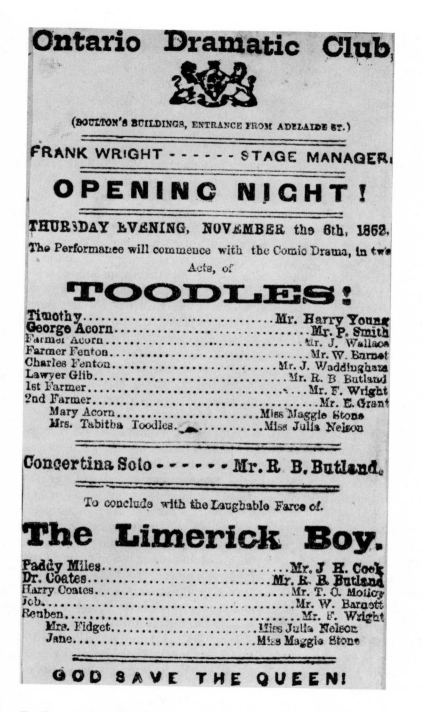

Ontario Dramatic Club,

(BOULTON'S BUILDINGS, ENTRANCE FROM ADELAIDE ST.)

FRANK WRIGHT - - - - - - STAGE MANAGER.

OPENING NIGHT!

THURSDAY EVENING, NOVEMBER the 6th, 1862,

The Performance will commence with the Comic Drama, in two Acts, of

TOODLES!

Timothy............................Mr. Harry Young
George Acorn.........................Mr. P. Smith
Farmer Acorn.........................Mr. J. Wallace
Farmer Fenton........................Mr. W. Barnet
Charles Fenton.......................Mr. J. Waddingham
Lawyer Glib..........................Mr. R. B Butland
1st Farmer...........................Mr. F. Wright
2nd Farmer...........................Mr. E. Grant
Mary Acorn.......................Miss Maggie Stone
Mrs. Tabitha Toodles............Miss Julia Nelson

Concertina Solo - - - - - - Mr. R. B. Butland.

To conclude with the Laughable Farce of.

The Limerick Boy.

Paddy Miles..........................Mr. J H. Cook
Dr. Coates...........................Mr. R. B. Butland
Harry Coates.........................Mr. T. C. Molloy
Job.................................Mr. W. Barnett
Reuben..............................Mr. F. Wright
Mrs. Fidget......................Miss Julia Nelson
Jane.............................Miss Maggie Stone

GOD SAVE THE QUEEN!

Toodles as performed by the Ontario Dramatic Club, 6 November 1862

this history that the most important missing ingredient is indigenous drama. True to their British-American roots, Ontarians preferred to pay for the established culture they inherited rather than risk their money on the untried or unknown (the theatre has always required ready cash on both sides of the curtain). Then, as now, acceptance at home was achieved only after success abroad. In the years before 1918 those native playwrights whose work received more than one professional performance number no more than half a dozen, and of these the most enduring – notably McKee Rankin and W.A. Tremayne – tended to have connections with American producers. Although there were the usual 'adapters' among a company's entourage, resident playwrights were rare; however, Graves Simcoe Lee (perhaps Ontario's first native playwright), an actor at the Royal Lyceum, was promoted by his manager John Nickinson, and Frederick A. Dixon had Rideau Hall for his workshop.

Another way of reaching one's audience was, of course, through the reading public. In addition to closet dramatists such as Thomas Bush, John Richardson, Charles Sangster, Charles Mair, William Wilfred Campbell, and Robert Norwood, who followed the strong nineteenth-century British tradition of publishing in book form, there were a remarkable number of politically active theatrical pamphleteers, many of whom did have their works produced. The authors of playlets printed in the satirical newspaper *Grip*, for example, saw their works reach the Ottawa stage, as did the anonymous author of 'Prince John John or Specific Scandal.' But only William Henry Fuller achieved national recognition, when the popular American actor–manager Eugene A. McDowell toured *H.M.S. Parliament* between Winnipeg and Halifax in 1880. Fuller took advantage of the contemporary rage for Gilbert and Sullivan to publicize his attitude towards policies – 'national,' new, and old – originating in Ottawa; in addition to that other Canadian favourite, *Uncle Tom's Cabin*, there were hundreds of companies, ranging from dual casts to juvenile players, touring their own adaptations of *Pinafore*. But lack of a stage did not deter critics in Ontario and Quebec[3] from continuing to chastise Ottawa (and sometimes Toronto) or from airing more personal grievances through dramatic dialogue. Many parliamentary and assembly 'scenes' were published in *Grip*; the *British Colonist* contributed *Provincial Drama Called the Family Compact* in 1839 by 'Chrononhotonthologos' (Hugh Scobie); W.H. Fuller's *The Unspecific Scandal* was twice registered (i.e., copyrighted), in 1868 and 1874; and John Simpson of Niagara had published two wittily allusive socio-political commentaries, *Captain Plume's Courtship* and *A Dramatic Sketch*, in his *The Canadian Forget Me Not for 1837*. Meanwhile, in 1876 journalist and patriot Nicholas Flood Davin bitterly satirized fellow

'"Toodles" as performed at the Provincial Hall, Toronto'; this political cartoon illustrates the way people thought in dramatic metaphors about politics (*Canadian Illustrated News*, 29 March 1873)

politicians in *The Fair Grit*, a fine medley of styles ranging from comedy of manners to sentimental musical comedy, and Sarah Anne Curzon publicized sexual discrimination at the University of Toronto in *The Sweet Girl Graduate* as early as 1882. Curzon later turned her attention to establishing the claims of real-life heroine Laura Secord in poetic drama (1887), but surely the most intriguing of 'poetical' defences came from the pen of 'Caroli Candidus,' who attacked religious and social hypocrisy in the bitter satire *The Female Consistory of Brockville* (1856).

Although these publications doubtless achieved a relatively wide readership, few seem intended for the public stage.[4] However, some authors did receive local production, most notably those calling upon the talents of the many musical organizations that had grown up alongside amateur theatre groups. John Wilson Bengough, for example, saw his Gilbert and Sullivan parody, *Bunthorne Abroad, or the Lass That Loved a Pirate*, performed by the Templeton Star Opera Company in Hamilton in 1886, and Jean Newton McIlwraith had a hit with her musical comedy on the subject of national identity, *Ptarmigan* (music by J.E.P. Aldous), at the Hamilton Grand Opera House in 1895. What must be the most consistently popular of Canadian light operas originated in Kingston in 1889, where *Leo, the Royal Cadet* by George Frederick Cameron (music by Oscar Telgmann) received the first of many productions which would continue until after the First World War and ceased then only because the scenery was destroyed during a local flood.

Masques and pageants have also been popular in Canada, ever since Marc Lescarbot organized a marine masque in honour of the return to Port-Royal of his commander, Sieur de Poutrincourt, in 1606 – one of the first recorded events by our European ancestors in Canadian theatre history. Although the contribution of military bands to travelling companies regularly provided instant local colour,[5] and there were many pageants based on historical subjects, the best-known Ontario pageant is that prepared by Dixon to greet the Marquess of Lorne and Princess Louise at Ottawa's Grand Opera House in 1879. An equally colourful and arguably more 'ethnic' spectacle greeted the twentieth century in Sault Ste Marie, when seventy-five Ojibway Indians from the Shingwauk band performed in L.O. Armstrong's *Hiawatha* on the Garden River Reserve.

Before the First World War Ontario remained staunchly British in temperament and taste. Even the influence of American theatre was suspect, despite – perhaps because of – the grip held by variety syndicates on the extensive network of theatres throughout the province. In 1911 editor B.K. Sandwell was to bemoan the 'annexation of Canadian theatre' by U.S. theatre chains, and the following year the British Canadian Theatrical Organization Society was founded to organize tours

Sarah Anne Curzon, playwright

Kingston, stage of Grand Opera House with cast of revival of *Leo, the Royal Cadet*, 1915

by British actors. There had always been a strong element of distrust concerning American influence, waxing and waning (as it does to this day) with political issues affecting economic, immigration, and military policies. Nor did Ontario audiences – although admittedly less restive than those in other parts of Canada – always remain passive over issues political *or* moral: twice in 1836, for example, the British flag was destroyed in rowdy protest over government policies. There were many public objections when, in 1851, the Dean family introduced the 'New York Bloomer' costume in Toronto, and houses were also noticeably small when Matilda Heron appeared as a 'fallen woman' with John Nickinson's resident company a few years later. The appointment of an official censor was not deemed necessary until 1913 in Toronto, however, partly because until then religious disapproval of public entertainment had provided an effective restraint, and the major variety syndicates shrewdly prided themselves on offering 'a clean show.'

Emphasis on respectable family fare with a moral has always been a familiar ploy for drawing an audience, from the 'travelling flea circuses' of the 1830s, to the early 'dime museums' and 'opera houses' which followed hard on the completion of the network of railway lines across the province, to the later performances of 'little theatre' groups established in major cities of the province, such as the Arts and Letters Players

Sault Ste Marie, 'The most important members of the cast,' *Hiawatha*, c. 1920

of Toronto (1910) and the Ottawa Drama League (1913). Indeed, there was serious public debate over the advisability of allowing certain circuses in 1856 because of their lack of educational content.

Whether influenced by their Scottish forbears or the peripatetic teachers (ironically, many of them American) who staffed many of the province's early public schools, metropolitan Ontarians were, as they still are, inveterate educators and organizers. When the St Lawrence Market and Hall was completed in Toronto in 1851, it was opened with a lecture on slavery; dancing classes were advertised in Kingston's *Upper Canada Herald* as early as 1825; and by the following year Mr Dwyer was sufficiently established as an elocution teacher in York to receive a benefit performance. Doubtless many of these early educators were aspiring, unsuccessful, or 'resting' performers, but there can be no doubt about the authenticity and earnestness of the many mechanics' institutes and literary and debating clubs established in the 1830s and 1840s, the dramatic readings and 'entertainments' sponsored by Victoria College in Cobourg by mid-century and later by the young University of Toronto, or the performances of temperance societies throughout the latter half of the century. As Ontario achieved 'High Victorian' seriousness, training in the arts became an even more essential asset to well-born young ladies and gentlemen. Amateur theatrical groups and reading societies also re-established ties among disparate immigrant groups and preserved social mores, just as the multicultural organizations of the twentieth century have served to unite and remind ethnic communities of their common tradition. In 1849, for example, the Toronto Coloured Young Men's Amateur Theatrical Society rented the Royal Lyceum for three nights, perhaps in response to the Toronto Council, which in three successive years had rejected the black community's petition for censorship of travelling circuses and menageries that performed 'certain acts, and songs, such as Jim Crow and what they call other Negro characters.'

It was only a matter of time before elocution would become established in the education curriculum, and although there would not be general acceptance of drama as a school subject until well after the Second World War (and then most notably in the western provinces), it was not uncommon to have student productions in Latin and Greek, and a School of Elocution was attached to the Toronto Conservatory of Music in 1892 with Harold Nelson Shaw as its principal until 1898. Shaw's program became increasingly oriented towards theatrical skills until he succumbed entirely to the profession himself and toured Ontario and Manitoba with the Harold Nelson Stock Company. In 1899 he joined the conservatory's rival institution, Toronto's College of Music, to serve as principal of its School of Elocution and continued to develop the theatre program until he once more gave in to the call of 'The Road' in 1902. Local 'stars' gained their glitter most often in the United States, occasionally in Britain. Even when, like Ida Van Cortland and Albert Tavernier or the admirable Mrs Morrison, they spent most of their careers in Canada, they received much of their early training and experience elsewhere.[6]

Although many of the early newspaper notices of theatre productions tended to be more puffery than appraisal, dramatic criticism was not unknown even during the early years. Leslie O'Dell records the frank comments of the anonymous reporter of the London *Free Press* concerning the standard of garrison entertainments in the 1860s, and even before that, regular reviews of the Toronto theatre scene were being published by the editor of the *Daily Leader*. Admittedly Daniel Morrison may have been a biased enthusiast – he was to marry Charlotte Nickinson of the Royal Lyceum – but there is plenty of evidence in local newspapers to indicate a lively interest in standards and techniques. Critics were quick to applaud new scenic and technical contributions. There was gaslight on stage in Toronto by 1842, while as early as 1863 audiences of the Grand Opera House in Hamilton were enthralled by the famous 'Pepper's Ghost' illusion made possible by better lighting and a judicious use of plate glass. Similarly Ottawa had electricity on stage in 1885. Costumes were of course regularly remarked upon, but stage setting and machinery became

Sault Ste Marie, 'Hiawatha, in the drama of 1904'

increasingly lavish as variety theatres promised more and more delights
to larger and larger audiences. But not until the introduction of Hector
Charlesworth's columns in *Saturday Night* and the Toronto *World* in the
1890s was theatre criticism accorded a consistently high profile.

If the history of a people and a nation is the reorganization of what we
choose to remember, the history of the theatre might be considered a
painstaking recollection of those brief moments more frequently
forgotten. For the theatre is perhaps the most ephemeral of all the arts and
its pressured practitioners the most careless of custodians. Too frequently
even today we are left with scattered facts from which to weave a
consistent narrative of performance – all the more difficult then to
recapture the productions of past centuries, when we must depend upon
the few scrapbooks, account books, playbooks, and posters that have
been hidden in attic trunks and forgotten drawers. Again and again in the
following pages you will read the scholar's lament that frequently we
have only newspaper accounts – themselves highly selective – to rely
upon. Occasionally memoirs that go beyond mere ego serving will
surface; old photographs, sketches, and drawings are eagerly sought and
anxiously scanned for telling details. Yet Ontario has been fortunate in its
early historians and diarists such as Henry Scadding, James Young,
George Harrington, Pelham Mulvany, John Ross Robertson, and C.C.
Taylor; and there were many more lesser known or anonymous recorders
of regional entertainment.

Since this project was first mooted, two remarkable and dedicated
scholars have died: John Spurr and Mary M. Brown. Building on their
solid foundations, a new generation of theatre historians has arisen who
are slowly and painstakingly filling in the interstices of our cultural past.
But the topics chosen for inclusion in this volume indicate that many
aspects of our theatre history still beg attention and archival support, most
notably the activity of non-English-speaking theatre. This first volume of
history of the theatre of Ontario, then, can be considered only a beginning.

But what a picture emerges, despite the blank spots! Of a small
company of courageous, even foolhardy, itinerant entertainers swelling
in ranks until they cover the province, reaching finally the Golden Age of
melodrama, 'The Road,' variety, and the cinema. Of local enthusiasts
devoting precious energy, time, and money to encourage the preservation
of a way of life remembered 'back home' while preparing the way for the
establishment of a colourful new culture recognizably their own. From
the 'various curiosities' at O'Keefe's Assembly Room in York and the
humble but enterprising entertainments of Mr and Mrs Emmanuel Judah
in the rear of the Kingston Hotel to the 'British Blondes' of Shea's

Hippodrome and the opening of yet more elegant 'opera houses' throughout the province, this was show business in nineteenth-century Ontario. Then suddenly in the autumn of 1914 Ontarians and their entertainers alike began to follow the beat of a different drum. The Golden Age began slipping away. What followed belongs to another story, which will be told in the second volume of this history.

NOTES

1 William Lyon Mackenzie, *Sketches of Canada and the United States* (London: J. Murray 1833), 89

2 John R. Godley, *Letters from America* (London: E. Wilson 1844), vol. I, 199–200

3 cf L.E. Doucette's articles, '*Les Comédies du statu quo* (1834): Political Theatre and Para-theatre in French Canada,' parts I and II, *Theatre History in Canada / Histoire du théâtre au Canada* 2:2, 83–92 and 3:1, 21–42

4 At least 115 Ontario plays were published during this period, but relatively few were produced; see Richard Plant's chronology for a complete listing.

5 McDowell's production of the popular *Rosedale*, for example, always required the assistance of the resident battalion and sometimes a child actor.

6 Another early educator, whose career will be discussed more fully in the next volume, was Dora Mavor Moore, who received her first training with the Margaret Eaton School of Literature and Expression from 1909 to 1911, subsequently becoming the first Canadian student to be accepted at the Royal Academy of Dramatic Art and a few years later the first to perform at London's Old Vic Theatre.

2 The Cultural Setting: Ontario Society to 1914

J.M.S. CARELESS

I

Ontario effectively emerged from the nineteenth century. So did the theatre in Ontario. The development of theatre in this setting, however, involved some fairly obvious pre-conditions: sufficient concentrations of population to offer potential audiences, adequate means of communication so that players could reach them, and enough public demand to bring actors to perform – and at times be paid. These rather basic prerequisites barely existed in the thinly peopled, isolated Ontario community of the early nineteenth century, its life and interests deep in bond to the relentless toil of pioneering settlement. But they appeared increasingly as the century proceeded.

During its course, in fact, four major, interrelated processes worked to shape an Ontario society in which the theatre could root and thrive: the growth of settlement itself, the rise of towns and cities, constant improvements in communications by land and water, and the sweep of technological advance which brought industrialization, along with mounting wealth for some and increased amenities of life and leisure for many more. By 1914 all four processes together had produced the twentieth-century Ontario of crowded cities and throbbing factories, close-knit southern countryside, and far-spread northern resource domains. Whatever the magnitude of changes since, the outlines of the modern province were firmly set by that time; for they had steadily emerged across the nineteenth century onward to the First World War. This then, was the founding, forming age of the provincial community and of the theatre in its midst.

The surging growth in settlement, from around 100,000 inhabitants in 1812 to over two and a half million a century later, produced an Ontario population substantially able to establish and support theatres. And since this population throughout the nineteenth century was overwhelmingly drawn from British and American sources, it readily looked to the powerful tradition of the English-speaking stage. The rise of major urban centres, moreover, supplied prime focuses for theatrical audiences and enterprises, while the coming of steamboats, canals, and above all railways made those places increasingly accessible to American road companies or touring transatlantic stars – and in due course also to indigenous touring groups. Still further, a society advancing in wealth and attainments as well as numbers displayed a growing interest in the arts, performing or otherwise. Finally, the process of technological and industrial change massed large working forces in the leading towns, people who had both the time and the need for organized public recreation: for the collective, regular kinds of entertainment that theatre could provide.

So much, in broad terms, for the material content of theatrical development in nineteenth-century Ontario. Yet it might be felt that this brief introductory approach is altogether too materialist in its perspective, paying insufficient heed to non-material, cultural factors no less inherent in the growth of the theatre. One could respond that lumber has loomed larger than literature in Ontario history, mines and machinery larger than music, or city drains and debentures larger than drama. Nevertheless there need be no argument, since plainly throughout that history the cultural-cum-intellectual and the social-cum-economic have bridged and blended at myriad points. Certainly it is not possible to examine the context of theatrical activity in the formative age of the province without making reference to ethnocultural patterns among its inhabitants; to the state of literature, architecture, and learning; to public tastes and communications media; and, in general, to the outlook and behaviour of a society expanding through a century and more.

To include such elements in a closer study, however, it is necessary to treat the growth of the Ontario community within several main successive periods. The first was the era of frontier migration and occupation, from the late eighteenth century through the 1830s. Theatrical beginnings were small and often transitory in this opening era; yet during it were laid supremely important foundations for the structuring of Ontario's social and cultural life: a wide basis of rural settlement, emergent towns, a well-established farming and lumbering economy, and a provincial population closely linked to both Britain and the United States in its origins, institutions, and interests. All this early development set basic terms for the appearance of theatrical activities of various levels and kinds. Whatever their subsequent course in the community, they cannot be divorced from the historic settings in which they initially took shape – within the pioneering period to be examined first.

II

Settled Ontario essentially began with the migration of the United Empire Loyalists in the 1780s. Until their arrival, it was an inland wilderness ranged by Indians and fur traders, with British garrisons placed at key points such as Niagara, a tiny French-Canadian farm community on the Detroit River, and little more. But when, at the close of the American Revolution, some 6,000 loyal adherents to the British cause in the old colonies moved into this interior territory, they laid a base for lasting settlement in the lands that fronted on the upper St Lawrence and the lower Great Lakes. The newcomers – soldiers, farmers, and artisans, with their wives and families – were largely drawn from the back-country population of New York and Pennsylvania and included German and Highland Scottish immigrants and Mohawk Indian allies. In any case, most Loyalists were well adapted to the rigours of clearing pioneer farms, and many also shared the cohesion derived from years of regimental service together. They survived and grew in numbers, as other Loyalists came to join them, shaping a new community west of the long-established French-Canadian holdings in the main St Lawrence valley. Hence the province of Upper Canada was established in 1791, giving this rising society of the Great Lakes region its own pattern of British government and law, distinct from that of the predominantly French-speaking region to the east, which was constituted the province of Lower Canada at the same time.

The American Loyalists were the veritable founders of Upper Canada, the future Ontario. As such, they originated for it a strong historic tradition: of prizing and conserving British ties and institutions, especially as guarantees against absorption by the republican United States. Soon, however, rising in the 1790s and running on into the new century, another, much larger influx of American settlers began. They were typical frontiersmen, who came, not from sentiments of British loyalty, but simply because they were attracted by the abundant, fertile, and freely granted Upper Canadian wild lands. These post-Loyalist Americans filled in gaps in settlement on the fronts of Lakes Ontario and Erie and pushed on inland. They moved up Yonge Street and cut through the woods north of the new provincial capital of York on Lake Ontario. They travelled into the Grand and Thames valleys to the west, and along the Ottawa to the east, where lumbering particularly developed in the giant pine forests of that area. The patterns of their backwoods farm life, their rough-and-ready social democracy, and the Methodist circuits (based in New York State) that spread with them, all pointed to the fact that the post-Loyalist migrants had tied Upper Canada fully into the whole, vast, westward-moving American frontier.

In contrast, only a trickle of British immigrants arrived during this time of the Napoleonic Wars in Europe, when Britain needed its manpower at home, shipping was scarce, and the high seas were perilous. The results were plain by the time the War of 1812 broke out in America and effectively ended the post-Loyalist migration. In a notably enlarged Upper Canadian population – risen from 14,000 in 1791 to some 100,000 in 1812 – only one-fifth was of British origin to four-fifths American, while Loyalists formed but a quarter of the latter group.[1] The province was largely developing as one more segment of an expanding, flourishing, American Great Lakes world, dealing freely and constantly with the very similar peoples of the neighbouring states across the border. Their modes of living, social attitudes, and democratic proclivities continued to find close counterparts in Upper Canada itself. In fact, the common socio-cultural and physical aspects of this Great Lakes realm would, in time, make it as natural for stage entertainments to move across its borders as it was for its inhabitants to do so themselves. The speech of New York State, Ohio, or Michigan was no more foreign in the Upper Canadian province than the English theatrical traditions on which all would draw. In a sense, the ultimate flow of theatre around the Great Lakes basin was simply one expression of shared affinities and interests in the entire lakeland region.

Nevertheless, the province was not to become just another Great Lakes state. The British and Loyalist elements within it remained influential well beyond their numbers. While Loyalists were very much Americans themselves, except in political feeling, their loyalism was a special mark of imperial service, suffering, and distinction. They held most of the local magistrate posts; some were large land-owners; others shared in leading circles of government and business. A number in older settled districts built handsome houses in the Georgian or the developing 'Loyalist' style ('Federal' in the United States), signifying that they had advanced in comfort and gentility far beyond the crude log cabins of the backwoods. But above all, Loyalists constituted a firm core in a still half-shaped frontier community which looked to British links and power for the very survival of Upper Canada.

As for British influences, the immigrants who actually had arrived from Britain included most of those in the colony with superior education, social standing, and positions of authority. They bulked large in whatever little 'towns' there were. In the capital, York – still a mere hamlet of government and garrison – the provincial officials, the military command, the clerics of the state-supported Anglican Church, and virtually all the notables in law and commerce were strong upholders of British imperial ties. The same was true in other centres of commercial and garrison life such as Kingston and Niagara, both of which had been gathering points as well for original Loyalist settlers. The garrisons themselves not only embodied Britain's supremacy, but also provided valuable cash markets for rising farm districts in their vicinity. Soon Britain itself would furnish far larger overseas markets for the colony's expanding grain and wood production. In addition, the British parliamentary and legal systems were integral to Upper Canada. So too in their own way were the British models (and pretensions) of polite society in York and other controlling centres. Such learning as there was, such cultivation, looked earnestly to Britain as the true source of enlightenment and taste.

While little of this influence might directly affect the daily lives of the American backwoods majority, these British factors were no less potent in shaping early Upper Canadian development. In short, emerging Ontario contained its own distinctive mixture of American, Loyalist, and British ingredients. It would make its own place in North America – but not within the United States. The War of 1812 was to confirm that point decisively.

From 1812 to 1815 invading American armies strove to take Upper Canada by force into the United States. Undoubtedly, before the conflict American settlers in the province had widely assumed that it would one day become part of the union. They had no strong grievances against British rule; yet neither were they eager to take up arms against their former compatriots. Nevertheless, the professional skill of British regulars, the forest craft of Indian allies, and the growing effectiveness of loyal militia managed to withstand the invaders. And by the war's end the bulk of the post-Loyalist Americans had definitely committed themselves to an Upper Canada still under British control. At the start, they might have felt constrained to do militia service only for fear that their land grants would be annulled. Increasingly they came instead to fight willingly, to drive off attackers who had brought on the shooting, who were destroying their crops and buildings and threatening the very livelihoods they had been working to build. The war left far keener anti-republican sentiments and suspicions behind it in the province; but it also left a much more self-aware and coherent Upper Canadian community, whose members had shared in defending their own soil.

With widening community consciousness, political activity grew vigorously in the post-war province. Enduring party groups appeared, liberal and radical reformers opposed by Tory-conservatives. In part this polarization reflected a sharpening clash between American and British elements, between advocates of change on conceivably American democratic lines and defenders of British institutions against new Yankee menaces. Many reformers, however, found their inspiration in the spreading Liberal movement within Britain itself. Moreover, to a great extent the heating up of the political climate through the 1820s and 1830s expressed the strains and problems of an increasingly complex, fast-enlarging society. For this era also brought a new pace of economic development to Upper Canada and a fresh wave of immigration, each of which strongly fostered the other.

The introduction of steamboats on lakes and rivers and the ventures into costly canal building on the main waterways were important aspects of the new economic growth. Still more significant were the demands of an industrializing, urbanizing Britain for colonial raw materials and foodstuffs. Upper Canada's grain and timber exports flourished, as did the provincial merchants who sent the produce outward by the St Lawrence River and distributed returning imports to a prosperous countryside. There was work, ample land, and timber resources for many more settlers. And now there was a swelling pool of people in the British Isles who wanted to emigrate: those in old occupations hard hit by the new factory industries, in overpopulated and impoverished rural areas, and industrial workers themselves, huddled in ill-built factory towns. From the end of the Napoleonic Wars in 1815 a flood of migrants began to pour from the British islands across the peacetime seas. Upper Canada first felt the surge with the settlement of disbanded soldiers after the war; but the tide ran on – with fluctuating ebbs and peaks – well into the 1850s. The results were profound; this was an inundation. It made the province's society far more fully British in membership and culture than it had been before.

Even into the 1840s the immigrant influx was so extensive that one can only make some generalizations here about the spread of the Anglo-Celtic newcomers in Upper Canada. They pushed the settlement frontier northward beyond its previous post-Loyalist limits, from the uplands between Kingston and the Ottawa River to the Peterborough district, the Lake Simcoe area, and across the wide Huron Tract that fronted on Lake Huron. English immigrants figured notably in the rising towns, not only among the upper classes but as shopkeepers and craftsmen besides. Many English also settled in the countryside, as in the London district; but unless they were retired officers on half-pay or would-be landed gentry – persons of local authority and standing – they usually blended fairly quickly into the existing Anglo-American rural population. Protestant Irish, Ulstermen, were especially numerous and ubiquitous; in the towns as merchants or skilled artisans, but equally in strongly 'Orange' blocks in rural areas, as in Leeds or Simcoe counties. Catholic Irish opened the Peterborough district to farming in the 1820s, settled in western counties above Lake Erie and elsewhere, yet particularly flocked into the Ottawa

Valley, or clustered in urban centres as unskilled labourers. As for the Scots, to the east they made Glengarry county almost a Highland clanship, largely occupied Lanark and Renfrew, and gave Kingston a strongly Scottish flavour. To the west they were plentiful in the Guelph region, in Oxford and throughout the Huron Tract; and all across the province Scots prominently appeared in the developing business and professional middle classes.

By 1841, in consequence, Upper Canada's population had reached some 480,000; of which less than 14,000 were French Canadians (chiefly along the Ottawa) and only 6,500 of continental European origin (mostly Germans centred in Waterloo County), while of the rest, virtually half were immigrants from the British Isles.[2] Among the last group, Irish, preponderantly Protestant Ulstermen, formed the largest element, followed by English, then Scots. The Irish, moreover, had a distinctive impact: not only through their almost tribal presence in areas such as western Middlesex County, where the murderous feuds surrounding the 'Black Donnellys' of Lucan came later to be celebrated in legend, literature, and drama, but also through the popularity of 'stage Irishmen' in nineteenth-century theatre, readily received figures of boisterous comedy or sharp folk wit alike. Yet in any case, the whole provincial community was overwhelmingly English speaking, strongly now of British origin, and decidedly Protestant in its religious character as well. And religious patterns were highly influential in this enlarged society.

Anglicanism had been reinforced by English settlers, along with Anglo-Irish adherents and some Scots Episcopalians; but the two largest denominations were the Presbyterians, much expanded by the Scottish influx, and the Methodists, long firmly rooted in the province and notably increased by the many Wesleyans among the British immigrants. There were sectarian divisions in Methodism and Presbyterianism; indeed, sectarian splits and alignments played a prominent part in the social and political life of Upper Canada. None the less, the broad, underlying strains of Methodism and Calvinism exerted powerful influences upon the community as a whole. It was hard working, self-reliant, and determined. It could also be rigorous, dour, and puritanical. Card-playing, dancing, unedifying music, and certainly theatrical amusements, were illicit, dangerous indulgences to staunch Calvinists and Methodists – not that some might not succumb to sin in varying degrees. Hence in a society that was both severely practical in interests and considerably disposed against sensual, immoral entertainment, the development of an art form and public recreation such as the theatre could be severely affected. In sum, more than the unremitting labour and the rude state of pioneer existence inhibited theatrical beginnings in such a milieu.

At the same time, however, there was a development far more favourable to theatre in the rise of urban communities which accompanied economic growth and immigration. As settlement advanced, little service-and-supply villages emerged inland. In serving and supplying them in turn, places on the fronts became busy commercial towns: from Cornwall, Kingston, and Belleville to Hamilton and Niagara. Bytown (later Ottawa) sprang up in the 1830s as the focus of the Ottawa Valley lumber domain; London coalesced in the midst of the swift settling of the western peninsula. Such towns as these were often rudimentary by later standards, but they sustained increasing activities and drew people, money, and building enterprises. York especially burgeoned, to become Toronto, the province's first city, in 1834 with a population of over 9,000. Earlier, it had been surpassed as a commercial centre by Kingston, which stood at the head of the St Lawrence River, commanding outward trade by that historic transport route. But Toronto was more centrally located in respect to major areas of advancing settlement, had advantages already through its position as the seat of government, and could make good use of an alternative trade route to the outside world, once the Erie Canal opened a through waterway from the Great Lakes to New York City in 1825.

These rising Upper Canadian centres, particularly Toronto and Kingston, could now supply positive pre-conditions for theatrical developments; concentrations of potential audiences with cash money (not backwoods barter), upper-class patrons with some interest in and knowledge of the theatre, and locations accessible to visiting players on major traffic lanes – whether upriver from Montreal, or across New York state by the Erie Canal and on by steamboat over Lake Ontario. Moreover, in towns that also held imperial garrisons a tradition of amateur theatricals was fostered by the British officer group, whiling away the tedium of peacetime garrison duty with something other than field sports or horse racing. In Kingston especially, which from the War of 1812 became the main military stronghold of Upper Canada, garrison theatre developed. Immediately after the war, Kingston's first theatre was set up in an empty brewery by army and navy officers, aided by a few gentlemen from the town.[3] Leslie O'Dell will tell us more.

As for York/Toronto, here the earliest performances recorded occurred in 1809 and 1810; but they were fleeting, almost chance affairs, given the size of the place and the state of travel at that time.[4] According to Mary Brown, it was not until the burgeoning mid-1820s that little American touring companies began to include York on their seasonal circuits around Great Lakes towns, a practice much aided by the opening of the Erie Canal. This touring theatre continued intermittently – there still were years when no professionals came to York at all – and as yet it had to perform on makeshift stages in hotels, inns, and assembly rooms, where 'the one-eyed fiddler Maxwell' supplied a limited musical accompaniment.[5] On one celebrated occasion, indeed, the stage even got entangled in the ardent Upper Canadian politics of the day. On 31 December 1825 a touring company from Rochester gave a special New Year's Eve performance of *Richard III* before a well-wined audience of members of the provincial parliament. During the musical prelude, as the convivial crowd called for songs, Captain John Matthews, a retired British officer and an active radical reformer, demanded 'Yankee Doodle,' and then 'hats off' for the American anthem, 'Hail Columbia,' following renditions of national British airs by the cast.[6] The incident brought on a furore of loyal outrage, hot partisan clashes in parliament, and Matthews's own recall to Britain to justify his army pension. Here was a teapot tempest; but it also indicated that if the American stage was reaching into Upper Canada, it yet had to pass through a screen of sharply pro-British sensitivities. Still, at this point it is fair to recall the war of little more than a decade earlier, when in 1813 York had twice been raided, seized, and sacked by American forces. A German patriotic anthem might have been equally unwelcome in a London theatre for some years after 1940.

At any rate, the stage at least found regular quarters in York with the appearance of the Theatre Royal, then in the early 1830s offering a resident base for visiting players or local amateurs alike; by 1836 it had gained seeming permanence, housed in its own frame building. Unfortunately this structure burned in 1840 – effectively coinciding with the close of an era in Ontario's development.[7] Yet, however limited was the growth of theatre within this initial pioneer period, some roots had been put down, and, especially in the young city of Toronto, these roots would grow a good deal thicker in the era to follow.

III

In the late 1830s, the settlement boom in Upper Canada was sharply checked by world depression and the disruptive Rebellion of 1837. Trade collapsed; immigration all but halted. The rebellion itself, launched by a radical element exasperated with Tory government road-blocks in the path of change, was brief, localized, and easily put down. But it left an aftermath of bitterness and strain, heightened by raids from American radical sympathizers. Not till 1840 did the dark years end, as border violence faded, trade began to revive, and immigration started to flow again. The next year, moreover, marked the end of the old province of Upper Canada. In 1841 it was combined with its Lower Canadian neighbour to form a single United Province of Canada, in an imperial effort both to provide a broader trading unit for economic growth, and to submerge possibly rebellious French Canadians within an over-all English-speaking provincial majority. Yet the two halves of the new United Province remained widely different, and they held equal representation in its parliament, so that the two old Canadas largely persisted as sectional blocs within the structure of union. Hence Upper Canada, now termed Canada West (or often, indeed, Upper Canada still), went on growing in its own right. The union of the Canadas would achieve considerable economic success. But until Confederation in 1867 at length replaced it with a more extensive and effective federal form of union, it stayed divided into two sectional communities, socially, culturally, and politically.

Thus Upper Canada / Canada West certainly survived as an entity, to be recognized once more in 1867, when it became the province of Ontario within the new Canadian dominion created by Confederation. And in the intervening period, from the 1840s through the 1860s, a far more solid, closely occupied, and organized regional community developed in the Ontario setting. The renewed influx of settlers occupied remaining agricultural lands below the enormous and inhospitable rock mass of the Precambrian Shield: opening up the Bruce Peninsula, spreading through the 'Queen's Bush' to the shores of Georgian Bay, and dotting rough little farms that fed the lumber camps all across the back country to Pembroke on the upper Ottawa. Of course, pioneering aspects still endured, especially in areas of low-level, lumber-supporting agriculture. But generally, even during the 1840s, the main gaps in continuous settlement were filled in; and in the 1850s the settlement frontier virtually came to a halt, up against the limits of the Shield.

At the same time, immigration from the British Isles subsided during the 1850s, partly because there was no longer such inviting wild land in Upper Canada, partly because Britain had largely now adjusted to the dislocations of industrialism at home. Yet before this great migration had ended, it reached new heights in the late 1840s with an influx of mainly Roman Catholic Irish settlers. Whereas the earlier years of the decade had brought reasonably well-prepared, healthy (and often notably successful) immigrants, in fair balance from England, Scotland, and Ireland, during the years after 1846 there was a rush of ill-prepared, starving, and fever-ridden Irish, fleeing the disastrous potato famine in their homeland. Many died in tight-packed 'coffin ships,' in quarantine camps on the St Lawrence or in the back alleys of Upper Canadian towns. The sick, the dying, the broken survivors, posed a desperate social problem. But many did survive: to work in lumbering, on the upper St Lawrence canals or on the new railways that began to be built in the increasingly prosperous

1850s. In any case, they greatly enlarged the Irish Catholic ingredient in Upper Canadian life. They also provided numbers behind a rising demand for state-supported Catholic separate schools in Canada West, heightened historical clashes of 'Orange and Green' stemming from Ireland, and roused anti-Catholic prejudices among the still-dominant Protestant majority, which indeed often viewed poor Catholic Irish immigrants as agents of disorder, violence, and crime.

In any event, growth in Upper Canada became increasingly intensive, not extensive, as a filling society knit itself together and built up its institutional framework. Improved through roads linked many rural neighbourhoods, where frame and brick dwellings were replacing log structures. Newspapers rose in numbers and readership with the development of better communications outward from the towns. The electric telegraph by the late 1840s brought quick news overland from Montreal and New York. The same decade produced both the provincial public school system, promising far greater mass literacy, and the beginnings of higher education: at Anglican King's College, which became the provincial, non-denominational University of Toronto in 1849; at Presbyterian Queen's in Kingston; and at Methodist Victoria in Cobourg. Municipal governments arose in towns; and further, a comprehensive municipal system for both rural and urban areas was set up in 1849. Still further, responsible self-government was established for the province as a whole in the 1840s; so that its people now controlled their own political affairs through cabinets and parliaments chiefly dominated by moderate liberals and conservatives – the earlier extremes of both radicalism and Toryism having dwindled considerably. In effect, the Upper Canadian community had acquired a new variety of instruments for shaping and directing a much more integrated social and political life.

The railway appeared as a particularly powerful integrating force. In the earlier 1850s, years of prosperous export trade, a soaring railway boom began, fed by lavish, optimistic expenditure on the new means of transport. Lines were laid from the upper St Lawrence northward to the Ottawa, to carry its lumber wealth down to rising American markets. From Toronto the Northern Railway reached the upper Great Lakes at Georgian Bay; and the Great Western was built from the Niagara River via Hamilton to the Detroit River, connecting with American main lines at either end. When in 1855 track was extended from Hamilton to Toronto, the latter city thereby gained rail contact right through to New York.

In 1856 the transprovincial Grand Trunk Railway, the world's longest line in its day, was extended to Toronto from Montreal and Quebec. Its construction continued westward to Sarnia on Lake Huron, while other lines were also thrust across the western peninsula. Though in the late

1850s another trade depression brought a swift winding down of these construction projects, the railway boom, before it ended, profoundly altered Upper Canada. It decreased isolation in inland districts, opened new through traffic routes across the Great Lakes' heartland to St Lawrence and Atlantic ports, and provided year-round transport for heavy goods as well as far swifter and more certain travel for passengers. The broad-stacked, wood-burning locomotives that clanked and swayed through the countryside brought a veritable revolution to the Ontario community – social no less than economic.

Major urban places were especially affected. The thriving port of Hamilton, a city since 1846, grew further as a rail and industrial centre, with foundries, machine shops, and car-building works. Bytown, to become the city of Ottawa in 1854, expanded not only as the focus of big saw mills to cut lumber for export by rail to the United States, but also as the home of related wood-working industries, from door-and-sash plants to match factories. Niagara Falls and Windsor shot up at either end of the Great Western line. Inland towns such as London, Guelph, or Berlin (later Kitchener) advanced with their new rail access to the outside world. Kingston and some other towns along the older St Lawrence water route, did less well, however, since much of the trade no longer flowed to their harbours but bypassed them by rail to the larger centres with more facilities. In that respect, Toronto was the greatest gainer of all. It had become the heart of a radiating rail network, to east, west, and north; and it would add more strands to its web when railway projects revived in the later 1860s. Toronto's dominant wholesale firms and leading retail stores, its rail-rolling mills, its clothing and printing industries, its busy banks and stock exchange, all owed greatly to the command the city had acquired as the hub of the Ontario transport system. In fact, Toronto was evolving as a regional metropolis, a role enhanced when it became a political capital again in 1867, as seat of government for what was now the province of Ontario.

The population of Toronto grew from 30,000 in 1851 to 56,000 in 1871, as that of the province mounted from 952,000 to 1,620,000.[8] The city's rising affluence in this mid-century era was displayed in abundant building – only temporarily checked by depression when the railway boom collapsed, until prosperity began anew in the mid-1860s. The first wave of civic construction in the 1850s produced distinguished edifices such as St Lawrence Hall, Torontonians' chief public auditorium for years to follow, University College, St James' Cathedral, and the neoclassical mass of Osgoode Hall. The second phase, extending onward into the 1870s, brought imposing new office blocks, stations, and hotels, the tall 'French Renaissance' Grand Opera House begun in 1873, and much more (Toronto *Globe*, 21 September 1874). Residential building was equally active. Styles for public structures varied from pilastered and ornamented classical forms to Victorian Decorated Gothic; fashionable private houses no longer favoured the British-inspired Regency cottages or American-derived classic revival models of a previous generation but proclaimed themselves Italianate, with round-arched windows and would-be Tuscan towers. (On a lesser scale, the same could be said of buildings in other Ontario towns.) Moreover, in the fast-growing provincial metropolis the horse-drawn street car arrived in 1861, running up Yonge Street to the little suburban village of Yorkville, as Toronto's residential reach spread northward. The central city streets and homes now were gas-lit and on a public water supply, though both gas and water systems were run as major private businesses.

City newspapers became major businesses also, maintaining large plants and work forces to provide editions for both town and country. The Toronto *Globe*, for instance, which claimed the largest circulation in British North America, installed a 'giant' steam-drive rotary press in the early 1850s and another in the early 1860s, to turn out its dailies, weeklies, and farm journals, not to mention handbills and all kinds of job printing. These press developments assuredly impinged on that of the theatre. There were ample facilities now for announcing and advertising (unlike the infrequent mentions in earlier scanty little papers) and soon for reviews or social news concerning theatrical events. Altogether, increasing ease of communication and transport and growing urban size and affluence significantly improved the setting for theatre in this mid-century period.

No less significant were rising cultural standards and creative attainments in provincial society as a whole. Certainly the journeying mountebanks, dubious wonders, and mangy menageries (described in more detail by Gerald Lenton-Young), which from time to time had provided a low level of public entertainment even in pioneer days, were still broadly in evidence: visiting the agricultural fairs, for instance, which spread in better-developed rural areas from the 1840s onward. Moreover, while Kingston in 1841 had trooped to gawk at the 'camel leopard,' allegedly the first giraffe in captivity, by the 1860s 'European' circuses with sets of trained lions and a host of glittering attractions were bringing in the town crowds (Kingston *Chronicle and Gazette*, 7 August 1841; Toronto *Globe*, 16, 17 July 1866). On higher levels of entertainment, however, musical and choral societies were springing up across the province and performing in public or masonic halls. Jenny Lind and other professional singers and musicians came to Toronto's St Lawrence Hall from the early 1850s. And lecture series, often held in the proliferating mechanics' institutes but patronized by the best society, featured prize names of the period such

Playbill: Toronto Dramatic Society, 3 January 1859

as Ralph Waldo Emerson and Horace Greeley.[9] Clearly, too, the emergence of university communities and growth of learned professions fostered an advance in cultivated tastes and interest. Finally, a culturally maturing society now produced a distinctive body of its own literature, from the prose of Susanna Moodie and Catharine Parr Traill to the poems of William Kirby and Charles Sangster, or the poetic drama of Eliza Cushing – who also published 'dramatic sketches' in the *Literary Garland* of Montreal, journal of the pioneering illuminati through the 1840s.

Of note as well was the publication of *The Female Consistory of Brockville* in 1856, an indigenous play, a satire of petty social politics in a small Upper Canadian town, written under a pseudonym, Caroli Candidus, but probably written by the local Presbyterian minister, who had suffered from charges of misconduct set forth by ladies of his congregation. This early 'native' drama was not to be presented on stage for 125 years.[10] Yet actual dramatic performances in the era markedly expanded, still – as Robertson Davies reminds us – offering fairly standard imports of British and American plays, from Shakespeare classics to popular nineteenth-century melodrama and farce. Music, song, and dance were also integral to this theatre, whether performed by amateurs or professionals. Unquestionably, the hostile currents of Calvinism and Methodism remained strongly manifest. Still, not only could 'good' theatre be more widely accepted among well-to-do social élites aspiring to cultivated tastes, but theatrical entertainments of whatever level might also find substantial audiences among the enlarging urban trading and working classes. Garrison theatre flourished as well during the era (tending still to keep alive Sheridan and other works of eighteenth-century English drama) until the withdrawal of British imperial troops from the Canadian dominion by 1871 brought its inescapable impact. Some later officers of the military nevertheless maintained the British garrison tradition, while in the new federal capital of Ottawa, from 1867, an increasing civil garrison of administrative and political functionaries provided a further base.

Important also were the proud new halls, which now began to appear, with auditoriums or 'opera houses' built in. Joint products of the railway prosperity and the municipal development of the era, they offered ready facilities for either local performers or touring companies. Cobourg's stately Town Hall, opened in 1860 and described in detail by Robert Fairfield, was an early prime example, not only in the splendour of its Opera House, but also as part of a grand railway vision – to befit a new rail gateway to the great interior beyond. Cobourg's line inward, however, had been built only as far as Peterborough, when its causeway

Toronto, playbill: Royal Lyceum, 25 March 1856

across Rice Lake collapsed, and the grand vision faded in financial ruin.[11]

But there is room here to give some detail on theatrical activities over the period only in Ontario's largest centre, Toronto. There they were desultory at first, and back in makeshift quarters following the loss of the Theatre Royal by fire in 1840. At last, in 1846, the Toronto Lyceum opened in the unused stable of the former Government House of Upper Canada.[12] It attracted both amateur and touring professional groups for two seasons, until the government took the building back for other purposes. In 1848, however, a new permanent theatre, the Royal Lyceum, was designed and built, to be first used for a concert at the end of the year.[13] Centrally located, gaslit, and reasonably well appointed (if rather amateurish in design), it seemed to promise great things to producers and city theatre-goers alike. But the Royal Lyceum's early years were full of disappointments, until the good times of the 1850s. Then, notably, a successful stock company was established by John Nickinson, a capable English actor-manager with much American experience, who took over the theatre in 1853.[14] He and his competent leading actors, including members of his own family, brought a new era of resident professional theatre to Toronto. A regular clientele profitably patronized the Royal Lyceum to see plays ranging from those of Shakespeare or Sheridan to *Uncle Tom's Cabin* and *The Lady of Lyons*, together with visiting stars and opera companies and the always popular travelling minstrel shows. *Uncle Tom's Cabin* was a perennial favourite, reflecting, perhaps, the strong abolitionist sympathies among Upper Canadians of the period that were expressed in institutions such as the Toronto Anti-Slavery Society and philanthropic schemes to aid and settle fugitive American slaves.

Ontario's advancing metropolis was obviously growing as its most prominent theatrical centre as well. Unfortunately the sharp depression of the late 1850s led to diminishing Toronto audiences, and to financial failure for Nickinson in 1859. A succession of maladroit managers tried to keep the Royal Lyceum going through the doldrums of the early 1860s, with periodic closings and revivals but generally a decline in both the quantity and quality of productions. Only in 1867, when good times had returned and a skilled new manager, George Holman, had taken over, did the theatre regain its earlier popularity and success. In fact, it now reached its peak years, enjoying sound direction, a well-qualified resident company, and full houses, while performing a good deal of opera in English as well as current new plays from the New York and London stages. This happy era ended in 1872, when an unwisely grasping owner transferred Holman's lease to other bidders. They were not destined to succeed.[15] But by then, the mid-century period was passing, and broad new developments overtook Ontario.

IV

One signal change that had taken place in the Ontario community was that by 1871 the great majority of its members were native-born Canadians: the inevitable result of declining immigration, of time, and of natural increase. Immigrants continued to arrive in more limited numbers, chiefly from Britain and northern Europe, and there were some Americans who entered, usually into business or professional life. But however significant these newcomers might turn out to be individually or qualitatively, they did not affect the widening quantitative lead of the native born. Not till late in the century would there again be sweeping immigration. Until then, what might be termed High Victorian Ontario set itself more firmly in an Anglo-Canadian mould. Its people still were greatly influenced by their British values and imperial ties, and by their American neighbourhood and the continual flow of material and cultural goods from over the border. Yet, none the less, they also evinced a growing sense of Canadian nationalism in quest of an identity.

The rising national sentiment was intimately connected with the achievement of Canadian Confederation in 1867. By 1871 the nation truly stretched from ocean to ocean, British Columbia having joined it in that year, the great northwestern plains region in the year before. Ontarians were proud – perhaps too eagerly proud – of their prominent role in founding this vast transcontinental state. Some were migrating westward to settle the plains; most were looking expectantly for the Pacific railway that would open up the west and bind the country together. All seemed to share a confident vision of a new nationality destined to rise in North America within the proud membership of the British Empire. Indeed, in many ways this was nationalism and imperialism combined.

But nationality would not come easily. The hopes of Confederation were soon strained by the re-emergence of Anglo-French sectional disputes within the young dominion. The Pacific railway project foundered in a mire of political scandal in 1873, not to be revived till 1880 or completed, finally, till 1885. The prosperous immediate post-Confederation years were followed by a long cycle of world price deflation, which extended with few breaks from the mid-1870s well on into the 1890s. In consequence, the west was slow to settle and develop, while disillusion and regional discord increasingly wracked the Canadian union. And the Red River Rising of 1870, the North-West Rebellion of 1885, twice took Ontario militia westward to deal with these angry disturbances to the national dream. Nevertheless, signs of aspiring nationalism continued to be plain.

The Canada First movement arose in the 1870s. Essentially Ontario based, it sought to bring on the realization of nationhood by both patriotic literary appeals and political action. Its ardent young idealists did not get far in mundane politics; but they struck respondent chords and roused opinion, and their writings contributed to the growth of a self-consciously Canadian literary tradition, from the poetry and drama of Charles Mair to the pamphlets and editorials of William Foster. The national tradition grew onward through the 1880s, without the strongly political emphasis of the Canada Firsters, in the poems of Isabella Valancy Crawford, George Frederick Cameron, and Archibald Lampman; in the prose of William Kirby, Graeme Mercer Adam, Sarah Jeannette Duncan, and others. Furthermore, critical literary reviews blossomed: The *Canadian Monthly* (1872–82) and *The Week* (1883–96), both of which promoted Anglo-Canadian cultural self-awareness as well as setting discriminating standards for intellectual tastes. These periodicals, published in Toronto, drew widely on Ontario contributors, even while they reached beyond the limits of the province. And manifestly that province was now exhibiting a new level in cultural development, a new stage in perceiving and expressing Canadian concerns.

Material developments in High Victorian Ontario equally expressed a new stage. In the countryside a well-established rural society was turning to more specialized and capitalized farming, in a movement away from the general, often indiscriminate wheat raising (or wheat mining) of earlier years. Partly this change occurred because indifferent pioneer farming methods had depreciated wheat crop yields, leaving Ontario agriculture less able to compete with the rich, opening grain fields of the American, and later the Canadian, western plains. But it was also true that there were valuable markets to be found in raising foodstuffs for Ontario's swelling urban population, in producing bacon for Britain, barley for American brewers, or in dairy-farming, fruit and tobacco growing, and still other locally specialized, more intensive kinds of agriculture. Farmers widely took to agricultural machinery (while its manufacture became an important Ontario urban activity) and put money in land drainage, substantial barns and stables, fertilizers, and improved stock. The consequences seemed well displayed in the series of shining Ontario pictorial county atlases produced in the 1870s which illustrated a long succession of fine farm estates: tall, ample, brick, frame, and stuccoed houses, sleek animals in neatly fenced fields, and glossy buggies rolling along gravelled drives.[16] In various respects, certainly in nostalgia, this High Victorian era appears as the golden age of rural Ontario, healthily stable and solidly productive; not yet seriously dislocated by urban pulls and power, or feeling its full subjection to mounting capital costs, mortgages, and market vagaries.

Yet even then there were indications that all was not golden on the farms. In some areas, especially in older eastern districts or on the rugged inland fringe of lumbering, the thinness of the local soil was becoming evident, now that its initial virgin fertility had been used up. Abandoned fields or future rural slums were threatening here. Generally speaking, too, those on poorer farms everywhere were feeling the pinch of mounting land and production costs. Not every farmer had a fine estate. Nor was there more good land available: thus the movements to the north west plains, into the United States, or simply to the nearby city. Rural depopulation had already begun in less advantaged areas of the province by the 1870s, off the lands of an overflowing agrarian society. The trickle would grow to a stream in the 1880s, steadily enlarging the urban social segment at the cost of the rural in Ontario. Conscious, indeed, that they were being thrown increasingly on the defensive, as early as 1872 farmers began to organize themselves in the fraternal Grange movement, which sought to instil among the countryside community appreciation of the values of farming life and to foster rural education and co-operative supplying or marketing. Granges spread widely across the province in the depression years of the later 1870s that affected even better-off sectors of agriculture. Moreover, in the 1880s farmers turned to political action, voicing their protests against exploiting external forces, and seeking 'farmers' policies' through the Patrons of Industry, which sent seventeen agrarian members to the Ontario legislature in the elections of 1894.[17]

But the plain fact was that the social and industrial power of the city was inexorably advancing through the High Victorian period in Ontario, despite the stretches of depression, and was scarcely slowed by them. With respect to industrial growth, much emphasis is usually laid on the National Policy of 1879, which established a decisively protective tariff to foster Canadian home manufacturing. Without doubt, tariff protection did much to encourage the development of industry in Canada, patently so in Ontario; but it is important to recognize that this was already well under way – especially in Ontario – and that the National Policy was an effect, no less than a cause, of the growth of the industrial interest that successfully pursued protectionism.

At least since the 1860s, manufacturing had been markedly expanding in the main Ontario centres, stimulated by the railways that focused industrial activities in well-located places on their routes. But railways themselves were expressions of advances in steam and iron technology which brought new potentialities and demands to industrial production. The results appeared on through the earlier 1870s in multiplying factories: farm-machinery plants; engine, boiler, and stove works; textile and knitting mills; carriage and furniture manufactories. As usual, Toronto showed the greatest range of enterprises; but Hamilton, Brantford, Guelph, London, Belleville, Kingston, and Ottawa, along with other towns, took important shares in the spreading industrialism. Some factory ventures failed in the later 1870s' depression; others endured and grew. Then the National Policy encouraged a strong upsurge of manufacturing well into the 1880s, while the opening of the Canadian Pacific Railway across the continent gave promise of new western markets for Ontario plants, once a line had been extended to meet it near North Bay in 1886. Thus, despite more business failures in a renewed harsh depression of the early 1890s, Ontario's industrialization activity continued, becoming by that time more and more strongly concentrated in larger factory units in the leading towns, as smaller firms in lesser places found themselves hard put to compete. Smoking factory chimneys – then proud symbols of progress – rose above the High Victorian cities, while 'surplus' farm dwellers flocked there to find their fortunes – or at any rate a job.

In the absence of major immigration, city populaces in the period mainly grew through the inflow from the countryside. Close-built, working-class quarters sprang up to serve the factories. Here life might be drab, hard, and monotonous for industrial workers, although at least they did not encounter the same sort of language and cultural barriers that subsequent non-English-speaking immigrants would experience in cities – or even the shock of a primeval land, such as earlier British settlers had known. And while there certainly were sweat-shops, long factory hours, insecure employment, and inadequate housing for many in the expanding labour force, workers could and did organize trades unions in an effort to improve their lot. With skilled labour in the van, as in the great Toronto printing strike of 1872, they gradually gained factory legislation and workplace inspection; and in 1883 a convention of delegates drawn widely from Ontario unions established an enduring Trades and Labour Congress. Though the depression cycle still kept wages low into the 1890s, the organized labour movement was a firmly rooted feature of industrial Ontario by that time.

Meanwhile the pace of technological change was also ameliorating urban working and living conditions to some significant extent. An increasingly productive industrial system turned out more and cheaper goods to offset limited wages. The advent of the telephone in the late 1870s heralded a new stage in technology, which continued over the next decade to electric lighting and soon to the electric street car. By the mid-1890s the city dweller had arc lamps to brighten his roadways and incandescent bulbs in his house and places of work or recreation; electric motors to pump the civic water mains or drive the latest, clean factories;

and effective streetcar service to take him from his employment to more congenial home surroundings in outlying areas of town. Electric power companies from Toronto to Sault Ste Marie, from Ottawa to Niagara, now joined the business hierarchy of banks, investment corporations, railways, and major industrial enterprises that dominated much of the Ontario community.

Urban residents had constituted 20 per cent of the province's population in 1871. By 1891 they represented 35 per cent of its more than 2 million inhabitants – a striking increase in proportion largely to be attributed to industrial development.[18] Hamilton's population had risen from 26,000 to 49,000 in the same period, London's from 16,000 to 32,000, and Ottawa's from 21,000 to 44,000.[19] As for Toronto, it had grown more than threefold, from 56,000 to 181,000[20] – though the annexation of erstwhile suburbs such as Yorkville and Parkdale contributed to the city's total.[21] In any event, the Ontario metropolis had particularly expanded during the 1880s, depression or no, and its financial houses, wholesale firms, and department stores transacted a dominant share of the province's business. Walt Whitman then had found Toronto 'a lively dashing place ...[with] long elegant streets of semi-rural residences, many of them costly and beautiful.'[22] It was also vaunted as the 'City of Churches,' themselves a tribute to wealth, as well as godliness, with their towering Gothic spires or massive Romanesque façades.

In such a place – and similarly and proportionately in smaller Ontario centres – theatre could scarcely help but grow during this High Victorian era. Despite the constraints of depression incomes or continued pious prejudices, there were massed urban dwellers seeking organized entertainment, people who could no longer readily escape into the unplanned leisures of the countryside, now that cities had become large and confining and rural areas correspondingly more remote. Some instead might try summer 'picnic trains' or steamboat excursions and always the age-old refuge of the tavern. But for those who wanted other recreations besides social drinking, those who could not afford regular train or water journeys outward, those who sought brief escapes to brighter realms than dingy offices, regimented factories, or cramped cottages, the theatre offered prompt and easy relief. So for the civic masses as for the urban classes, leisured or cultivated enjoyment, critical appreciation in some circumstances, the social duty to see and be seen in other cases, might also be effective purposes behind theatre-going. At any rate, the context for theatre was now well developed in a rapidly urbanizing society, and its presence rose in size and scope accordingly.

The building of theatres indeed became a feature of the period, along

Illustration from *Canadian Illustrated News* (28 February 1880) of W.H. Fuller's national success, *H.M.S. Parliament*

with music pavilions and more public halls of various kinds. By 1875 Hamilton and Ottawa each had an opera house, and there were two in Toronto, the Royal and the Grand. In smaller places they continued primarily to be incorporated in new municipal buildings, such as the fine example in Petrolia, opened in 1889 and later restored in all its Victorian eclectic charm. Touring companies made good use of these expanding facilities, on regular circuits across eastern, central, and southwestern Ontario, carried by rail and linked by telegraph and telephone. Local theatre continued as well, and evinced some native Canadian content. In Ottawa, for instance, W.H. Fuller wrote his musical satires, *The Unspecific Scandal* (1874; an arch reference to the Pacific Scandal) and *H.M.S. Parliament* (1880), though only the latter was staged. There was now more Canadian-made drama to draw on also, such as Charles Mair's *Tecumseh* (1886), plays by the novelist Gilbert Parker, or the light-hearted whimsies and parodies of Frederick Augustus Dixon, another civil servant, whose work was notably performed at Government House in Ottawa. Dramatic clubs or musical groups kept amateur theatre alive, supported by university and professional circles in an Ontario community of extending cultural consciousness.

Again, however, only theatrical developments in the chief metropolis can be exemplified to any degree for this High Victorian period. In Toronto the era might seem to have opened inauspiciously, with a Royal Lyceum, past its prime and floundering in ineptitude and poor quality productions, which in any case burned down early in 1874. Actually, this theatre had been outlived; it was too small and inadequate to suit the new day of theatrical activity that was dawning in a much larger city. In the fall of 1874 the Grand Opera House opened a commodious and comfortable replacement with 1,300 seats (compared with 700), a big, well-designed stage, and a handsomely appointed, domed auditorium.[23] The Queen's Theatre, too, which had provided some alternative to the old Royal Lyceum in its last phase, continued; though when the new Grand collected the cream of the trade, the Queen's sank to 'a low-class variety show,' according to a contemporary, 'of which it can only be said that the audience was more debased than the stage performers.'[24] The Royal Opera House provided popular competition also, until it burned down in 1883; fires were a frequent hazard in the theatres of the day. But the Grand prevailed, despite occasional rivals – and despite its own fire in 1879, which was followed by rapid reconstruction with still more seating, space and elegance, graced by a magnificent drop scene of the Temple of Jupiter in Athens.

Over the years the Grand's productions ranged from W.S. Gilbert's *Charity* in 1874, *Twelfth Night*, *Jane Eyre*, and *East Lynne* (all 1877) to

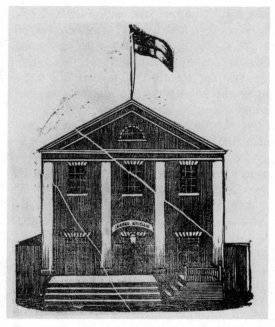

Toronto, Royal Lyceum depicted in a woodcut for the *Boy's Times*, 21 July 1858

Romeo and Juliet and *As You Like It* with Madam Modjeska in 1884.[26] Often as well, there were evanescent comedies, featuring sensational 'effects,' presented by visiting companies: hackneyed fare of vulgar farce and cheap spectacle, according to the censorious *Week* in 1885, but no doubt necessary to satisfy audiences and keep the books balanced.[27] The fact was still that the Grand Opera House could and did offer professional drama of sound quality, if regularly copying that on the New York and London stage. This was not makeshift frontier theatre. And if the audiences – and the Grand's competitors – frequently preferred minstrel shows and melodrama, these too were essential parts of the active contemporary theatre. Onward into the 1890s the Grand still held its place as a leading institution in what was now the solidly established theatrical life of Ontario.

V

Through the earlier 1890s the recurrent cycles of depression still dragged at the province, until in 1896 world recovery began. The year marked the onset of a great new era of prosperity, one that would extend into the new century, with only brief interruptions, almost to the First World War.

This was a transforming time for Canada, and for Ontario as a sizeable part of that domain. Immigration rose steeply once again, as fresh tides poured in from Britain, the United States, and now from continental Europe. The west at last was effectively occupied, and the burgeoning western farm community provided ever-larger markets for Ontario industry. Not only was the CPR used to capacity, but new transcontinental lines were under construction, in another railway boom that saw widespread building within Ontario itself. Its cities grew apace in the bustling times. The mineral and forest resources of the northern areas of the province were brought into production; towns developed on these northern frontiers as well. Rural southern Ontario also prospered, thanks to high local and export demands for agricultural produce, although the drain to the cities continued, and farmers organized themselves for politics with renewed fervour as the balance in Ontario society continued to shift against them.

By 1914 the province's population had reached 2.7 million, over 50 per cent of it urban.[28] In spite of the influx of immigrants during the period, however, the native-born Anglo-Canadians still predominated in Ontario, since the bulk of the new arrivals went on to the west. Nevertheless, considerable numbers of British migrants stayed in Ontario cities as office and store workers or factory hands, in a virtual transfer from one urbanized environment to another. Many continental Europeans also settled in the cities, particularly Toronto, largely turning to semi-skilled trades, small crafts, or pick-and-shovel labour. Some of these non-English-speaking immigrants moved as well to scattered rural areas; but especially they went to Ontario's opening north, finding work in lumber camps and mines, on railway construction gangs, or at smelters and pulp mills. They became a major ingredient in a northern society that centred in the mine, mill, and rail headquarters towns rising in the rugged wilderness.

In the cities and towns of the south, the 'non-British foreign born' added their own distinctly new note to the community. Here they were not yet a major element; they offered just a foretaste of later multiculturalism in Ontario. Even in Toronto by 1914 the foreign born constituted less than 12 per cent of the city's inhabitants.[29] But inevitably they stood out in their strangeness, breaching the former widespread English-speaking homogeneity of the urban population. Inevitably, also, they clustered in ethnic neighbourhoods within the towns – driven by strong social and economic imperatives amid these alien surroundings – and so stood out more plainly in localities of their own. But in time they made their way against barriers of language and prejudice, low pay, poor housing, and bewildering differences in social customs. They learned, adapted, and began to thrive in Anglo-Canadian settings, while keeping alive their Mediterranean, Jewish, or Slavic heritages, which promised much for the future cultural enrichment of Ontario. Yiddish theatre, for example, began in Toronto in this era.

In the north, Finns, Italians, Germans, and Hungarians, Slavs from Poles to Serbians, and other ethnic groups set strong and varied multicultural stamps on each main centre of settlement, although the northern population in total was only a small part of that of the province as a whole. Yet the growth of the north was such a major aspect of the whole period from the 1890s to the First World War, markedly influencing the life of southern Ontario as well, that it demands special attention. Again, it was but a foretaste of a good deal more to follow after 1914; but even by that date extensive northern developments had gone far to complete the basic structure of the present province.

It would be hard to fix precisely on their beginnings. By the 1860s, at least, lumbermen were cutting steadily northward into the margins of the Laurentian Shield, particularly up the Ottawa River Valley. In the 1870s and 1880s they were heavily exploiting Muskoka and Manitoulin forests and northern shores of Georgian Bay and Lake Huron, and were reaching as far as Kenora beyond Lake Superior. Meanwhile, in 1884 the building of the Canadian Pacific Railway across the rock mass of Algoma had opened the immense copper and nickel resources of the Sudbury Basin, where by the early 1890s the mining town of Sudbury was already pouring out its fumes. Yet, however consequential were these earlier activities, the whole pace of northern growth did not rise to a crescendo until after 1896, when good times started, and new resource processes and markets gave rapid impetus to the lumbering and mining northlands.

The new technology of making wood pulp and the international demand of big city dailies for cheap newsprint added more large-scale enterprises to lumbering – the cutting of pulpwood and the production of pulp and paper. The new technology of hydroelectricity provided power for these operations, bringing generating plants and mill sites to rushing northern rivers. Sault Ste Marie rose first as a power and pulp-milling centre in the 1890s and soon developed as a steel-making town thanks to the opening of iron mines in the vicinity. New methods of refining nickel, vital to hardening steel, turned a busy Sudbury increasingly to nickel production, especially in response to the world armaments race that led up to the First World War. And while Port Arthur and Fort William chiefly flourished as rail outlets for the ever-growing western wheat traffic, here and in many smaller communities dotted along the rail lines of the North resource-processing enterprises multiplied through the noontide years of boom.

There were specific mining booms as well. In 1903 the construction of the Temiskaming and Northern Ontario Railway beyond North Bay to open the more fertile 'clay belts' of the northeast to settlement uncovered rich silver deposits at Cobalt en route. A hectic rush to stake them followed, reminiscent of the Klondike Trail of '98; though this time the eager prospectors could get directly to the mining claims by train out of Toronto. The Cobalt finds, which in a few years changed a ramshackle campsite into a solid town of some 10,000, were succeeded in 1909 by massive gold discoveries further on in the Porcupine district, where the town of Timmins was to emerge, and in 1911 by a big new gold strike at Kirkland Lake. The mining frontiers continued to expand, building up Ontario's northern resource empire, and no less benefitting the industrial south as well: providing materials, markets, and enterprises to southern factory owners, wholesalers, and financiers. Toronto, as usual, especially gained, as the ruling centre of stock exchanges, mine promotions, and investment and supply houses, and as seat of the provincial government which controlled mineral, timber, and power rights. Northern development mean southern development, pre-eminently for the city business élites.

The wealth-engrossing major cities launched into another building spree, while their populations zoomed – Toronto's from 208,000 in 1901 to 376,000 in 1911, Hamilton's from 52,000 to 81,000 in the same period, and Ottawa's from 60,000 to 87,000.[30] New bank head offices, controlling branches spread out across the west as well as over northern and rural Ontario, arose in columned, classical magnificence. Massive insurance company headquarters and spacious department stores: these too were symbols of Ontario's urban financial and commercial power in the new century. And the age of the skyscraper had arrived in the cities, thanks to the steel-framed building, the electric elevator, and soaring downtown land prices. Toronto, now looming as a national, not merely a regional, metropolis, had inevitably the greatest concentration of this large-scale office building in its central business district. But big factories were also being added from Windsor to Ottawa, while Hamilton in particular built up its basic steel plants. Apartment blocks appeared on more central residential city streets. Bungalow suburbs spread on the margins, and, in between, contractors turned out long, verandahed rows of working-class houses. For the homes of the well-to-do, the picturesque exuberance of the so-called Queen Anne style of the late nineteenth century was increasingly replaced by the ordered, heavy dignity of the Edwardian period, primarily for the new magnates of corporate finance and industrial combines.

The vertical rise and the horizontal spread of the early twentieth-century city were greatly aided by the means of mass transit supplied by the electric streetcar, which now came fully into its own in serving both the sprawling urban fringes and the concentrating cores. The automobile increasingly manifested itself on city streets in the decade before 1914, but as yet it was either a rich man's indulgence or a special express vehicle, not a general, basic carrier. Even into the countryside a network of fast electric 'radial' railways fanned out from the towns, tying rural areas still more closely to major urban centres – at a time when primitive motor cars and highways designed for horses made country motoring perhaps a sport, but scarcely a convenience.

The expanding reliance on city streetcars and interurban radials was itself dependent on an increasing supply of cheap electricity. Such a supply rapidly became available, once the Hydro-Electric Power Commission was set up by the provincial government in 1906 to transmit power generated from the teeming energy of Niagara Falls across the industrial heartland of Ontario. Subsequently this major public utility extended its operations to eastern and northern areas, but well within the pre-war period it greatly affected industrial growth as well as electric transit. For in a province that had to import its coal, the abundant provision of flexible power drawn from its own vast water resources profoundly aided Ontario's manufacturing. The electrical age that had now arrived only increased the prosperity and pace of the community life, while further advancing industrialization and urbanization.

Yet life was by no means halcyon for all the inhabitants of booming Ontario. There were the marginal farms on misused lands, bush dwellers eking out existence where lumber frontiers had passed onward, leaving gaunt stumps and scrub wastes in their wake. There were neglected, impoverished native peoples, the harsh and hazardous world of mines and lumber camps, the callous exploitation of 'bunkhouse men,' largely foreign immigrants, on northern construction crews. The cities had their own slum-dwelling poor and miserable, and ethnic ghettos where families of newcomers were often herded into flimsy, unsanitary backstreet shacks.[31] Behind the façade of 'Toronto the Good,' moreover, there was ugly vagrancy, child neglect, ruffianism, and a variety of other social ills. Even city workers with fairly adequate employment (say, in factories more substantial than basement shoe plants or upstairs clothing workshops) had to face the ingrained hostility of owner-managers to union bargaining; thus, in a time of high rents and sharp inflation, the period saw recurrent waves of strikes and lock-outs, with intimidation and violence on either side.

Nevertheless, general working conditions did continue to improve: government industrial regulation and public social services did make more headway, as did the immigrant groups themselves. It was still a harsh age by later standards, yet no less vigorous and hopefully assertive in spirit. And for much of Ontario society, certainly for its confident upper and middle classes, that positive, assertive spirit was amply expressed in the cultural activity of the new century – which indeed was held to belong to Canada itself.

There was a fresh surge of national awareness; in literature displayed, for instance, through the launching of major studies in Canadian history such as the *Makers of Canada* series of biographies, or the multi-volume scholarly work, *Canada and Its Provinces*. Once more Ontario authors took a leading part in these enterprises. In fiction, Ralph Connor (Charles William Gordon) in 1898 published the first of his many highly popular novels set in Canada, often strongly evoking the eastern Ontario of his boyhood, as in his *Glengarry School Days* (1902). Gilbert Parker, Ontario born and educated, though writing in England, began a long succession of Canadian historical romances during the 1890s and produced the bulk of these best-selling costume pieces up to the First World War. Sarah Jeannette Duncan was active throughout the period; her book of 1904, *The Imperialist*, deftly epitomized her native Brantford's sense of both Ontario's British past and its North American present. E. Pauline Johnson conveyed her Ontario Iroquois heritage through sensitive poems; Wilfred Campbell, born in Berlin (Kitchener) and working largely in Ottawa, also wrote lyric nature poetry and complex verse dramas, collected in his *Poetical Tragedies* of 1908. And Stephen Leacock, in 1911, brought out *Sunshine Sketches of a Little Town*, full of sly humour and destined to become a classic of Ontario small-town life that would ultimately be presented on the stage as well.

Other literary forms served a growing reading public during the period, from *Queen's Quarterly* to Toronto's *Saturday Night* and *Maclean's Magazine*. In the area of music, the Toronto Conservatory of Music, the Mendelssohn Choir, and the Toronto Symphony Orchestra, established in 1908, responded to active cultural demands. So did increasing local dramatic, literary, and artistic clubs or university societies. In painting and related fields, the Royal Canadian Academy, Ontario College of Art, and the Ontario Arts Student League all fostered the rising artistic community; while painters like Tom Thomson and J.E.H. Macdonald opened new national visions as they portrayed the wild stark beauty of Ontario's north, thus leading the way to the subsequent achievements of the celebrated Group of Seven. Drama boasted Gilbert Parker's stage pieces, Connor's *Sky Pilot* of 1902, and the rather exotic plays of Wilfred Campbell (based primarily on Arthurian legend, though one had a Canadian theme). The works of expatriates such as McKee Rankin, James

Forbes, and Edgar Selwyn were also prominent, but they belonged more to the American theatre.

The fact remained, however, that in general the Ontario community still looked for its professional theatre to greater realms outside, and especially to the New York stage. This deep-rooted derivative attitude, as Mary Brown and Gerald Lenton-Young point out, and the ever-increasing flow of through communications essentially meant that resident stock companies, where they had existed, had been considerably supplanted by big touring professional enterprises that operated out of American metropolitan centres or imported travelling British companies. They played the New York successes, or London ones largely endorsed in New York, along with the older British-American standard fare. Another rooted influence was the continuing Methodist-Calvinist suspicion of the immoral tendencies of theatre. The combined effect of this attitude and the dominant practical conservatism of Ontario did not incline local managers and backers to try risky experiments with 'advanced,' convention-shaking dramas, any more than to invest in unheralded Canadian playwrights.[34] Social censorship indeed remained a powerful force in the pre-war province, and even imported successes still had to pass through the psychological and moral screen of the border.[35]

Within these qualifications, none the less, theatrical activities multiplied in a prosperous Ontario, on stages both amateur and professional, in plays from solemn tragedy to tinkling musical comedies. Furthermore, local summer stock, along with some touring Canadian companies, drew quite wide audiences. The aptly named George Summers successfully ran a stock venture based in Hamilton from 1902 to 1914, writing some of his own melodramas and building his reputation as a leading Canadian comedian. The seven companies of the Marks Brothers conducted another successful Ontario stock enterprise from 1879 to 1922. Vaudeville also became increasingly popular, enlarging on the still-active variety tradition of the minstrel show with its song-and-dance men, patter comedians, and balladeers, and bringing in the acrobats, jugglers, and animal acts besides. Still further, vaudeville's ultimate nemesis, the moving-picture show, had appeared as well; and small movie houses sprang up throughout the province from the last years of the nineteenth century. Other chapters will offer a fuller picture; here, there is space left only to specify some of the major developments within the focal city of Toronto.

Amateur theatre in particular prospered in Toronto over the period, in expenditure and quality as well as in quantity, thus testifying to the affluence, taste, and leisure of the upper ranks in the metropolis.

Moreover, it did offer a field for performing Canadian plays, such as were available. The South African War of 1899–1902 brought about a flurry of imperial patriotic presentations by amateurs, which led to more serious work thereafter, since acting, staging, and audience reception all improved with experience. The ever-present inhibitions of public morality still restrained ventures into the drama of new realism; but fresh departures were none the less more possible on the amateur than on the commercial stage. Then from 1907 to 1911 the first national amateur dramatic festivals under the auspices of the governor-general, Earl Grey, gave widespread stimulus towards excellence and attempts at innovation. By 1914, at any rate, various modern drama – not just current superficial hits – was receiving growing attention, and a transition to a more sophisticated and venturesome little theatre was under way.[34]

In Toronto's commercial theatre, the Grand still figured prominently, presenting international stars of the late Victorian or Edwardian years such as Ellen Terry, Henry Irving, Lillian Russell, and Sarah Bernhardt – the last having survived keen local newspaper discussions as to her moral worth.[35] Newer theatres, however, offered more competition. The big Massey Hall, product of the philanthropy of one of Toronto's wealthiest industrial families, had been open since 1894. This ungainly red-brick pile with a faintly Moorish interior (but excellent acoustics) did not perhaps compete directly, in its concentration on concerts or brief stands. But, among others, the Royal Alexandra Theatre became a strong contender, an Edwardian Beaux Arts masterpiece completed in 1907. For all its small site, it could compactly hold an audience of 1,500, thanks to the steep rake of its seating. More important, the Alexandra and the Princess (opened in 1895) established close ties with major American and British touring companies, leaving melodrama, musicals, and magicians increasingly to the Grand. Furthermore, on this level of the not-so-legitimate theatre, vaudeville and cinema continued to make inroads. Both the opening of Shea's Victoria Music Hall for vaudeville towards the close of the period in Toronto and then the beautiful Winter Garden, completed in 1914, and the rise of larger, specifically designed moving-picture houses, forerunners of the movie 'palaces' that were to follow, pointed to the eventual demise of the once-pre-eminent Grand.

Nevertheless, theatre itself had gone on expanding in Ontario, the amateur stage by looking in new directions. And if the professional stage was still chiefly regarded in terms of popular entertainment and high-salaried stars rather than as an art form, the influence of keen-minded amateurs might yet have a beneficial effect. True, the comparative dearth of Canadian-made drama had continued; but the historic circumstances of theatre in Ontario before 1914 gave good reason for the relatively slow development of playwriting, virtually the last native literary form to appear in any sizeable degree.[36] Aside from the constraining background of moral and religious prejudice and the sheer passage of time before a reasonably cultivated, large, urbanized community arose, the dominating power of older parent British and American cultures over this provincial society continued: the inbred deference to imperial British and the close communication with the neighbouring giant United States which had so habituated Ontarians to import theatrical offerings rather than to look to their own. Yet, as a result, if they remained tied to a larger stage beyond, they also knew its quality well and in time might add to that quality themselves. The once rudimentary frontier community had become fully part of a metropolitan world. That, in fact, was the essential meaning of the whole nineteenth and early twentieth-century course of development for Ontario – and the context for its emergent theatre.

NOTES

1 R.C. Harris and J. Warkentin, *Canada before Confederation* (Toronto: Oxford University Press 1974), 116

2 J.M.S. Careless, *The Union of the Canadas, 1841–1857* (Toronto: McClelland and Stewart 1967), 27

3 J.W. Spurr, 'Garrison and Community,' in G. Tulchinsky, ed., *To Preserve and Defend: Essays on Kingston in the Nineteenth Century* (Montreal: McGill-Queen's University Press 1976), 117

4 Mary Shortt, 'From *Douglas* to *The Black Crook*: A History of Toronto Theatre, 1809–1874,' MA thesis, University of Toronto 1977, 2–4. See Richard Plant's chronology.

5 C.P. Mulvany, *Toronto: Past and Present; A Handbook of the City* (Toronto: Caiger 1884), 117

6 Shortt, 'From *Douglas*,' 16–17; Edith Firth, *The Town of York, 1815–1834* (Toronto: Champlain Society 1966), 312–13

7 Shortt, 'From *Douglas*,' 32, 34, 42

8 *Census of Canada, 1871*, vol I (Ottawa: Queen's Printer), 420

9 J.M.S. Careless, *Brown of the Globe* vol. II (Toronto: Macmillan 1963), 4

10 Dorothy Sedgwick, *A Bibliography of English-Language Theatre and Drama in Canada, 1800–1914* (Edmonton: Nineteenth Century Theatre Research 1976), 15

11 P. Ennals, 'Cobourg and Port Hope,' in J.D. Wood, ed., *Perspectives on Landscape and Settlement in Nineteenth Century Ontario* (Toronto: McClelland and Stewart 1975), 188–90

12 Shortt, 'From *Douglas*,' 48

13 Ibid., 62–3

14 Ibid., 83–4
15 Ibid., 153–5
16 For example, see *Illustrated Historical Atlas, County of York* (Toronto: Peter Martin Associates 1969; reprint of 1878 edition).
17 Joseph Schull, *Ontario since 1867* (Toronto: McClelland and Stewart 1978), 54–5
18 L.O. Stone, *Urban Development in Canada* (Dominion Bureau of Statistics 1967), 29
19 *Census of Canada, 1891*, vol. I, 370
20 Ibid.
21 D.C. Masters, *The Rise of Toronto, 1850–1890* (Toronto: University of Toronto Press 1947), 165
22 Ibid., 169
23 William Dendy, *Lost Toronto* (Toronto: Oxford University Press 1978), 100. See James R. Aikens, 'Rival Operas: Toronto Theatre, 1874–1884,' PH D thesis, University of Toronto 1975, for activities of the Grand and its competitors.
24 Mulvany, *Toronto: Past and Present*, 119
25 Ibid.
26 Masters, *The Rise of Toronto, 1850–1890*, 205
27 Ibid., 206
28 Schull, *Ontario since 1867*, 186–7
29 *Census of Canada, 1911*, vol. II, 372; figures extrapolated to 1914
30 G.A. Nader, *Cities of Canada*, vol. II (Toronto: Macmillan 1976), 166, 203, 250
31 Schull, *Ontario since 1867*, 307
32 Murray D. Edwards, 'The English-Speaking Theatre in Canada, 1820–1914,' PH D thesis, Columbia University 1963, 299
33 Ibid., 75. See, for example, Leonard W. Conolly, 'The Man in the Green Goggles: Clergymen and Theatre Censorship (Toronto 1912–13)' *Theatre History in Canada / Histoire du théâtre au Canada* 1:2 (Fall 1980), 111–23.
34 See Robert B. Scott, 'A Study of Amateur Theatre in Toronto, 1900–1930,' MA thesis, University of New Brunswick 1966, for this paragraph.
35 See John Hare and Ramon Hathorn, 'Sarah Bernhardt's Visits to Canada: Dates and Repertory,' *Theatre History in Canada / Histoire du théâtre au Canada* 2:2 (Fall 1981), 93–116.
36 See Stanley Asher, 'Play-Writing in Canada: A Historical Survey,' MA thesis, University of Montreal 1962.

3 Amateurs of the Regiment, 1815–1870

LESLIE O'DELL

British Garrisons in Ontario

The British regiments stationed in Ontario following the War of 1812 until their withdrawal in 1871 represented not only the security of trained defenders of the empire but also the sophistication of upper-class British society. As members of the 'gentry élite,'[1] the officers set the standards of cultured behaviour and encouraged the local élite in 'keep[ing] barbarism at bay' through self-initiated cultural activities.[2] The tradition of amateur theatre among the British military, when combined with the social and cultural aspirations of the élite of Ontario communities of the nineteenth century, made a significant contribution to early theatre in Ontario. Garrison theatricals, mounted primarily for the leisure pastime of the participants and receiving enthusiastic local support, appeared at different times and places throughout the period of regimental postings in Ontario. The tradition of military theatricals was passed on to the Canadian army, which absorbed British regimental traditions whole-heartedly,[3] and it helped lay the foundation of amateur theatrical activity which continues as a vital form of entertainment in Ontario to the present day.

Kingston, London, and Toronto, the three major garrison cities, provide the clearest patterns of garrison amateur theatre. The chronological record of the British presence in these communities falls readily into three periods: 1815–37, 1839–54, and 1861–71. The first period extends from the end of the War of 1812 to the civil unrest in 1836–7. During these years in York, the contribution of the military to theatrical activity was limited to the patronage of amateur events and the use of the regimental band for certain of these performances. Kingston saw a variety of military theatricals, which were virtually the only such entertainment available to the public. One obvious reason for the noteworthy activities in Kingston was the number of troops stationed in the city. York had a single unit of one regiment, but Kingston had at least one line regiment, the right wing of the regiments stationed in York (i.e., the headquarters and the regimental band), and officers and men of the Royal Navy.[4] It is not surprising that among such a significant group of officers there would be a number interested in amateur theatricals.

Theatrical activities ceased during the Mackenzie-Papineau rebellions of 1837. But these events indirectly contributed to the emergence of theatre in Ontario, since troops were rushed to London in order to stave off what authorities felt might be a serious revolutionary uprising and realignment with the United States. The garrison in York, now named Toronto, was also upgraded, and, once the emergency ended, the officers stationed in London and Toronto had the leisure time to pursue a variety of cultural activities.

The Crimean War resulted in the removal of the troops stationed in London and the decimation of the ranks left in Toronto and Kingston. The loss of the military had an adverse economic impact on the three cities, but there was also a consistent growth in population from 1854 to 1861. The troops were brought back to London, Toronto, and Kingston after the Trent affair, when it appeared that England and the United States might enter into military conflict. The returning British officers discovered cities of significant size, with a corresponding change in their cultural life. With development of the railroads had come increasing numbers of American touring theatre troupes, and all three cities were now on established circuits; the pattern of local theatre companies with long seasonal engagements gave way to more intense periods of several weeks' activity. Regimental theatricals did not cease, however, with the emergence of alternatives to amateur performances. In Toronto, which supported a resident stock company throughout the final period, British regiments continued to entertain the public regularly.

The Social and Cultural Elite

Nineteenth-century Ontarians saw themselves as British subjects and looked to England for their social and cultural standards. Those towns and cities that boasted officers from 'home' could also claim a direct line to the latest fashions in conversation, culture, and respectable behaviour. And those mothers who could refer to a son-in-law in uniform acquired an instant cachet in society. Moreover, the presence of the troops stimulated economic growth, and with growth came a greater interest in the arts. As the Toronto *Daily Telegraph* of 26 July 1867 noted: 'It is estimated that a regiment is worth at least 50,000 [pounds] per annum to any place in which it may be quartered.' Little wonder then that the garrison communities saw themselves as quite different from other Ontario towns.[5]

In the social hierarchy of Ontario the officers of the British regiments were placed automatically at the highest level,[6] and their arrival was viewed by any local élite as an exciting addition to the existing social life of the community.[7] How the colonials were viewed by the officers was not always so positive. Lord Minto remarked that the Toronto upper classes fell short of English standards of gentility, but he considered them 'a good set of people.'[8] Senior officers warned their younger comrades to beware of intermarriage with colonials. Colonel Garnet Wolseley in his autobiography, *The Story of a Soldier's Life*, comments on the pitfalls of the extensive hospitality shown the young officers by the charming ladies of Montreal: 'We had very successful garrison theatricals in the winter, and many were the sledge expeditions we made into the neighbouring country. Altogether, it was an elysium of bliss for young officers, the only trouble being to keep single. Several impressionable young captains and subalterns had to be sent home hurriedly to save them from imprudent marriages. Although these Canadian ladies were very charming, they were not richly endowed with worldly goods.'[9]

Given their superior social position, the actions of the British officers had great influence on the inhabitants of garrison cities. 'In society,' an 1851 manual on *The British Officer* reminds us, 'the British Officer should be remarked for unobtrusive courtesy and easy elegance of manners; he should be distinguished in ballrooms as well as in battle fields, and be as familiar with polite accomplishments as with professional attainments.'[10]

Traditions of Garrison Theatricals

Amateur theatricals were an integral part of the social calendars of the British military garrisons around the world:

In its formal parades and other elaborate ceremonials, not to mention its predilection for distinctive uniforms for occasions both professional and social, the army has always displayed an affinity with theatre as a spectacle. Moreover, in the 18th and 19th centuries its officers were drawn from social classes which delighted in country-house charades and theatricals. It was natural, therefore, for officers stationed in garrisons scattered across the face of a world-wide empire to turn to amateur theatre as one means of allaying the tedium of, for example, a monsoon season or a long Canadian winter.[11]

Regiments transported their theatrical traditions to each new posting, and so the performances that were given in Ontario communities can be seen as part of a much larger and well-established custom. Some of the greatest military leaders were associated with amateur theatre. Nelson encouraged theatricals to keep the seamen contented and to avoid mutiny on his ships.[12] And what was good enough for the greatest sailor of them all was certainly good enough for British naval personnel stationed in Kingston, as well as for the sailors under Admiral Perry exploring the far north.[13]

Another famous patron of military theatricals was the Duke of Welling-ton. Antony Brett-James, in *Life in Wellington's Army*, describes the frequent amateur productions presented during the inactive winter months of the Peninsular War. These were usually private theatricals for the entertainment of the officers and men of the various regiments stationed in the area, and on several occasions Wellington and his staff attended, sometimes after a twelve-mile ride in frozen darkness.[14] In Ontario certain garrison amateurs also attracted prestigious patrons. The officers of the 60th, for example, were able to include in their advertisements the statement: 'Under the Patronage of His Excellency Lt.-Gen. Sir Charles Windham, K.C.B., Commander of the Forces in British North America, His Excellency, Major-General Stisted, C.B., Lieut.-Governor of Ontario, Commanding the District, and Colonel Radcliffe, R.A., Commandant' (Toronto *Globe*, 29 December 1867). The patronage of the commanding officer of the garrison was noted in every advertisement for military theatricals, and such public acknowledgment doubtless was one reason for its regular inclusion.

The theatrical tradition can also be attributed to the concern of the officers for the intolerable hardship of their men. Through performances for the local community, the officers raised money to assist the wives and dependants of their men in an effort to atone for the neglect of the Treasury.[15] Indeed, the vast majority of the garrison performances recorded in Ontario were given for the purpose of raising money for charitable causes, though the recipients were not always associated with the military. Many productions raised money for the poor of the city in which the regiment was stationed. Advance notices made frequent reference to the benevolence of the garrison amateurs as a means of encouraging attendance: 'We anticipate a crowded house, as the programme is an attractive one, and the object for which the entertain-ment is being given is very praiseworthy' (Toronto *Globe*, 30 March 1864). 'As the amateurs play for the benefit of the poor, they will doubtless be very liberally supported' (London *Free Press*, 7 April 1864).

Sometimes the charitable purpose was not always clear: following a production of three farces by the 30th Regiment in Toronto, the Toronto *Globe* announced, 'As there seems to be some misunderstanding as to the disposal of the proceeds arising from the two performances of the Garrison Amateurs, we have been requested to state that the balance, after defraying the necessary expenses, such as hire of Theatre, costumes, printing, &c., will be devoted to the following charities in this city, in equal proportions, viz: The Boys' Home, The Orphans' Home, The Deaf, Dumb and Blind Institution' (25 March 1862).

Charitable motives affirmed the morality of such activities, a necessary step for social acceptance; but some would always frown upon the theatre. In Kingston during the winter of 1829–30, for example, there arose a violent controversy concerning the moral aspects of the theatre. This began when W.R. Payne, a clergyman of the Church of England, refused to accept charitable donations from the proceeds from the Naval and Military Amateurs. His letter to the editor of the Kingston *Chronicle* of 23 January 1830 began: 'Sir: I have had the honour of receiving from you as Secretary and Treasurer to the Naval and Military Amateurs, the sum of One Pound for charitable distribution. Whilst I feel flattered by this mark of their confidence in my anxiety to promote the welfare of those around me, I am constrained to observe that cherishing, as I do, a decided conviction of the evil tendency and effects of theatrical performances, it would appear to me an inconsistency on my own part to become the almoner of money raised by such performances.'

Money raised through box-office receipts went first to offset production costs, and the remaining funds were donated to charity. In 1864 the amateurs of the 47th Regiment found themselves in the unfortunate position of having spent more than they had raised, and so they announced, 'In consequence of the proceeds from the Series having been found insufficient to meet the current expenses, the Management have determined to give an extra performance, in aid of the Garrison Amateur Dramatic Fund' (Kingston *Daily News*, 26 January 1864). The following set of accounts for the first military season, 1815–16, which appeared in the Kingston *Chronicle* four years later, on 22 December 1820 (after the books were discovered), provides some interesting details about the methods of fund raising and the specific expenses incurred by garrison productions. This particular company, the Kingston Amateur Theatre, was made up of officers of the army and navy, with a sprinkling of some gentlemen of Kingston.

CREDITS

By original subscription from the Army and Navy	£74.0.0
By original subscription from inhabitants of Kingston	£27.0.0

Receipts from the above-mentioned plays. i.e. the
    28 plays and 29 farces already referred to   £1323.1.2
                                                  £1424.1.2

DEBITS

To pay (as per receipts) for timber and carpenters' work   £266.1.1
To pay (as per receipts) for insurance on theatre,
    merchants' and Tradesmen's accounts, light, fuel,
    furniture, canvas and paints for scenes, printing,
    musicians, artificers, labourers, doorkeepers,
    servants, etc.   £1038.10.1
To remittance, 'Waterloo Sufferers,' as per receipt   £118.10.0

                                                £1423.1.2

Leisure Activities and Private Theatricals

Garrison theatre was designed also to fill the leisure time of the officers and men of which there was a great deal; for the military life was one best described as aeons of peace interspersed with flurries of war. The resulting boredom contributed significantly to the desertion rate.[16] Clearly, anything that the officers could do to provide pleasurable pastime for the men would alleviate this problem. Of course something had to be done as well to counteract the effects of the demon rum. Left to themselves, the men would gladly spend their free time and money on alcohol, with predictable results.[17]

It was not only the men who were in desperate need of structured activities to fill their leisure time. The officers had few responsibilities for the peacetime management of the regiment and so were also susceptible to the peril of extreme boredom.[18] The officer corps was dominated by men with high cultural expectations: 'Urbane, sophisticated, and desperate for entertainment in provincial America, they tried to reproduce the cultural life their social peers enjoyed in Europe's urban centres.'[19] Any skills or interests an officer might demonstrate in any of the arts were particularly advantageous while the garrison was stationed in out-of-the-way communities such as those in Ontario. For it must be remembered that, much as the local residents of Toronto, Kingston, and London liked to bask in the glories of their towns, to the officers of the British regiments the postings could be viewed in the same manner as Francis Duncan described Kingston: 'I shudder when I think of the suffering there of Her Majesty's troops. No wonder my old friends of the Wiltshire

Regiment could stand it no more than a year; the wonder was that suicide had not become a daily occurrence among them after the first week. It speaks well for the internal heartiness and cheerful souls of the sixty-second that they stood it as they did.'[20] The 'internal heartiness' that a regiment brought with them to a posting such as Kingston was, in many cases, the tradition of amateur theatricals.

The life of an officer of a British regiment stationed in Ontario was not as gloomy as Duncan suggests. Many were the occasions of hospitality extended by civilians to these officers, and the result was 'a full amount of the social intercourse which is necessary to the well-being of a man, and to his happiness.'[21] J.E. Middleton gives us some idea of what these social activities might have been: 'The subalterns, with senior approval, followed the usual custom of entertaining themselves: formed friendships with the gentlefolk of the town, danced, fell in love, sometimes fell out again, organized horse races, did a little in the way of amateur theatricals, hunted ducks and deer, shot passenger pigeons, and in general conducted themselves as garrison officers in all parts of the world were wont to do.'[22]

As one officer remarked, 'Dancing and dinner parties, besides invitations to rides, drives and canoeing jaunts put us under many obligations to our kind entertainers, which later on we endeavoured to make some return for in the shape of a series of theatricals.'[23] Many of the garrison productions would have been private affairs attended by invitation only, another occasion on which officers could join the local gentry in a pleasurable social activity. Mrs Gilbert Porte, in her memoirs of London, recalled a Dr O'Flarity (83rd Regiment) with whom she was acquainted, as a result of which 'we saw a good deal of what was going on, and were once allowed to attend an amateur performance at a theatre on Wellington Street.'[24]

Such private theatricals were not customarily recorded by the local press, and so it is difficult to ascertain their frequency; indeed, there is little evidence of their existence. An exception is the following report, which appeared in the Kingston *Chronicle* of 18 March 1835: 'Private Theatricals. – Last evening, at the Old Marine Hospital, Point Frederick, a great number of the fashionables of the town were highly gratified with the performance of "The Rivals" by the Officers of the Garrison, assisted by one or two gentlemen civilians ... A splendid supper followed, and the gay dance closed the delightfully entertaining evening.' Unfortunately, there is at least one instance of a private entertainment's being misunderstood by the press. In Kingston in 1836 the officers of the 24th performed at the Kingston Hotel and then treated the guests to supper and a ball. They had neglected, however, to invite the editor of the *British Whig*, who retaliated by suggesting first, that their performance was not worthy of 'impartial criticism,' and later, elaborating:

If the officers of this garrison ... choose to give private theatrical entertainments to their friends, either at an hotel or in their barracks, we know of no right the public has to interfere; but when they offer tickets for sale, permitting only a privileged class to purchase, they deliberately wound the feelings of the great majority of the persons among whom they dwell. They may wantonly practice these things, but they shall not do so with impunity, for while the British Whig continues in existence, any insult shall be passed upon the inhabitants with just and severe retribution. (*British Whig*, 26 January 1836)

Such unabashed criticism of officers is notable in its isolation.

The inner workings of military amateur theatricals are apparent, to a certain extent, from the coverage these events received in the newspapers of London, Toronto, and Kingston. Indeed, any record of theatrical events must be assembled primarily from contemporary newspapers and therefore is filled with all the vagaries of its source. Newspapers for the first two decades of this study are scarce. More papers from the 1840s have survived, when clearly the military was of such importance to the social life of the communities that their theatrical activities received a fair amount of coverage in the local press. By 1861, moreover, there were daily papers in Kingston, London, and Toronto. These contain many local news items, but by this time the cities were of sufficient size to have generated professional and local amateur theatrical events. The activities of the garrison were still of immense importance to the socially prominent, but the average newspaper reader was neither interested nor involved. Consequently, although the papers recorded the occurrence of garrison theatricals, detailed reviews were infrequent. Even in the early years lengthy commentaries are rare. A review that appeared in the London *Free Press* of 23 February 1863 is an example of the generalized, brief, and equivocating notices that most frequently appeared: 'Garrison Theatricals. – The Amateurs of the Military Train performed to a crowded house last night, and were well received though the acting, as a general thing, was not of a high order. However, the players so quitted themselves in quite as successful a manner as could have been expected, and it is to be hoped that they will soon appear again.'

It is clear, from the absence of military theatricals in communities that lacked theatrical entertainment of any sort and from the presence of military theatricals in communities that also supported a full-time resident stock company, that egalitarian entertainment of civilians was not the primary motivation for these ventures. Rather, the impetus towards theatre was tied to the military tradition of amateur productions and the specific tastes and energies of the members of the garrison. If there was a sufficient number of charismatic, interested participants, plays would be performed. Otherwise, leisure time could and likely would be spent hunting, playing sports, gambling, or generally socializing in the guise of picnics, balls, and soirées. On the other hand, any inclination towards amateur theatricals would doubtless be encouraged by the existence of a receptive civilian population.

Regimental Players

It must not be assumed, however, that theatre was the sole province of the officers. Some regiments supported the creation of a *corps dramatique* made up entirely of NCOs and enlisted men. As with the members of the regimental bands, a few talented soldiers might be singled out for special treatment in order to make possible an ongoing presentation of theatre performances and accompanying music.[25] The regiment would maintain the amateur troupe through a subscription deducted from the officers' pay, plus a system of voluntary contributions from officers and local civilians.[26] Some regiments became well known among civilians as a result of the success of their *corps dramatique*, for example, the 24th in Montreal in the 1830s.

In some regiments the troops undertook to organize themselves. 'The non-commissioned officers and privates of the 4th Battalion, 60th Rifles, at present quartered in London, have formed amongst themselves a theatrical club' (London *Free Press*, 10 January 1866). This may have been a loosely formed group of garrison amateurs who would have had no clear-cut status within the military structure. In those cases where the NCOs and men were maintained by the officers, the latter would presumably control many aspects of the organization. In all cases, regardless of the amount of direct control, all activities of the NCOs and men, but particularly public performances, would have had to receive the permission of the commanding officer and the officers of the regiment.

In their theatrical ventures the officers were able to call upon their troops to perform the menial tasks involved in production as well as to fill minor roles. John Spurr notes, 'The majority of these regimental theatres regularly cast privates as servants, train bearers and spear carriers, as it was understood that a gentleman could not possibly portray such inferior beings.'[27] These participants were seldom mentioned, the following being an exception: 'We cannot close this article without mentioning the Amateur soldiers of the Royal Artillery, who performed in these entertainments, and to praise them duly for the zeal, ability, and taste with which they assisted the officers' (Kingston *Chronicle*, 27 February 1830). The soldiers who were assisting the Naval and Military Amateurs of Kingston received this rare praise for the smooth running of the scene changes, which the reviewer also noted: 'We discovered a very favourable change in the management of the scenery. Every thing connected with the scenes and properties were [sic] done as though a good steam engine was the motive power, so regular and faultless did it appear.' The soldiers of the 63rd in London received similar praise for 'the order and precision which characterized their performances' (London *Free Press*, 27 March 1863). Indeed, military performances were frequently praised for their punctuality, smooth running, and efficient management, all probably a result of the participation of well-drilled soldiers.

Interregimental theatrical ventures occurred in garrisons that housed not only the regiment on duty, but also detachments or wings of other regiments posted in Ontario, as well as troops and officers of the Royal Artillery, who were stationed throughout Canada. Other theatrical groups were more completely the property of a single regiment, though 'guest artists' from neighbouring regiments might put in an appearance. The groups of NCOs and men were almost entirely identified as being from a single regiment, and co-operative ventures were rare, but not unknown. For example, the Amateur Club performing in London in March 1863 was composed of 'the most choice talent of the 63rd Royal Artillery and Military Train Corps. Each division has its "star"' (London *Free Press*, 27 March 1863). An even rarer example of collaboration occurred in London on 27 and 28 May 1863, when three separate organizations, the officers of the garrison, the NCOs and men of the Royal Artillery, and the NCOs and men of the Military Train, each presented one farce.

It is impossible to know which performing group, the officers or the NCOs and men, exhibited the higher level of artistic success, or if rivalry existed between the military theatre organizations. When the 17th was stationed at Toronto in 1868, the regiment boasted two theatre groups, one of officers and the other of NCOs and men. The local press was vehement in its praise of one Sergeant George Smith, who played the leading roles. The Toronto *Globe* of 16 October 1866 lauded his performance as Bailie Nicol Jarvie in *Rob Roy*, an adaptation of Sir Walter Scott's novel, and as Dick in the afterpiece *The Turned Head*, by Gilbert Abbot A'Beckett. The article concluded: 'This gentleman is possessed of a versatility of dramatic talent and expression rarely to be found in an amateur, and if he gives up the profession of arms he may rely there is another one in which he can equally distinguish himself.' None of the officers who performed in their separate productions received similar commendation. Traditionally, officers do not appear to have performed in the productions of the *corps dramatique*, although the 17th again provides an exception. A review of Sheridan's *The Critic*, performed by the NCOs and men, contains the name of Major Fielding, but the leading role was played by the same George Smith, whom the writer again singled out for favourable comparison with professional performers (Toronto *Daily Telegraph*, 20 July 1867).

Woman's Mysterious Art

The female roles in garrison productions were most often played by male performers, that being half the fun of such ventures.[28] Ontario communities witnessed some successful female impersonators. The London *Free Press* of 29 May 1862 remarked of Sergeant Phillips, in his role as Ceralia Fitgig in *The Irish Lion*, a farce by John Baldwin Buckstone, 'Every movement was perfectly natural; every toss of the head feminine; every shrug of the shoulders indicative of women's mysterious art.' Of Mr Portal (83rd) in his role as Mary Copp in *Charles the Second*, a comedy by John Howard Payne, the Toronto *Examiner* of 1 February 1843 commented, '<u>Mr</u>. Portal's "Mary," with her pretty face, seemed to excite no small share of envy among the fair portion of the audience.' And the London *Herald* of 18 February 1843 complimented Daniel Lysons as Emma Leslie in John Poole's farce *A Nabob for an Hour*: '[Lysons] wore the petticoats with an ease and grace well becoming the character. Every emotion, every gesture, and movement, indicated a familiarity with the peculiarities of womankind, that does not fall to the lot of most men. Had we not known that <u>he</u> was a <u>man</u>, it would have been almost impossible to have convinced us to the contrary.' In his memoirs, Sir Daniel makes no reference to his success as a female impersonator. His comments are limited to: 'At London we had some very good theatricals. I had charge of the theatre and painted the scenes.'[29]

Not everyone appreciated female impersonators, and not every performer was as adept as Daniel Lysons in capturing the allure of a woman, as the following review indicates:

We shall not make any other special remark on the performers, except that nothing can render attractive men-women. Their hoarse voices, their clumsy figures, and their large extremities deprive the audience of every particle of romantic feeling and sympathy with their imaginary distresses or heroic sacrifices, or, their subsequent successes. One pities the poor hero, compelled to accept the affections of such Ratcliffe Highway-looking heroines, more like Portsmouth Jacks than any other specimen of the sex. The audience want real women, for real women only can excite those warm sympathies absolutely essential to the success of any play, appealing as all plays do so much to the imagination. We could not help thinking that if we were requested to describe the charms of Bridget, we should have been unable to reply as a certain poet once did: –

Some asked me where the rubies grew,
  And nothing did I say,
But with my finger pointed to
  The lips of Julia.
Some asked how the pearls did grow and where;
  Then spoke I to my girl,
To part her lips, and show them there
  The quarrelets of pearl.

Bridget would not have answered to this description. (London *Free Press*, 10 July 1862)

Although men continued to play the female roles throughout this period, there were also an increasing number of productions in which the military performers were joined by actresses, both amateur and professional. In the first months of 1830 the population of Kingston was treated virtually every week to a production from the military actors. The most notable of the performances in this season, however, was the staging of *The Merchant of Venice* on 9 March 1830, when the garrison was invited to use the local theatre. The Kingston *Chronicle* of 13 March reports, 'two ladies of the highest respectability made their first appearance [as] Portia and Jessica ... Notwithstanding the visible timidity of both Ladies, they continued to the last to exhibit, with most excellent taste and judgement, the true spirit of the author. We congratulate these ladies on their complete success, for a more favorable appearance, we hesitate not to say, was never witnessed.' Clearly, the existence of female performers willing to go before the public was the deciding factor in the appearance of women in any garrison production.

Some productions featured both actors and actresses in female roles. Vieth reported upon 'some theatrical performances in which Mrs. Sutherland, the wife of our new Commissariat officer, ably assisted us. Mr. Sutherland himself was a capital comedian. The other two "ladies" of our dramatic company were young "Jemmy" Carter, the son of Chief Justice Sir James Carter, and Sergeant Boyes. But they did admirably.'[30] Various other garrison theatre groups made use of the female performers of the resident professional company. This was the case in both London and Toronto in the 1860s.

Casting, Rank, and Privilege

Casting was a delicate matter, for as many senior officers as possible had to be satisfied. Vieth's diary again provides insight into the inner workings of the military theatrical tradition: 'I was cast for Falkland, but after reading it over I took a great dislike to the part and declined it. Lieut. Duncan of the Artillery was then pressed into accepting it in my place, and Fag was offered me which I played.'[31]

Occasionally the local press commented upon the assignment of roles within the play. The London *Herald*, in describing the 14 February 1843 performance of *A Nabob for an Hour* and *Fish Out of Water*, an afterpiece by Joseph Lunn, noted that the parts 'were cast with a discrimination as to the idiosyncrasy of the performers which was attended by the most happy results.' But there were times when adherence to rank in casting resulted in certain unfortunate effects. The London *Free Press* of 29 May 1862 remarked, 'We are convinced that to make an entertainment of this kind successful, in casting the characters, there must be no exclusiveness; very few, accustomed to a higher position, can readily assume a menial one, and give satisfaction ... it seemed rather out of place to hear servants addressing their masters with an air of perfect equality.' There were other occasions, however, when an officer was clearly capable and eager to play the role of a menial, if it was the leading role of the farce being performed: 'A genteelly humorous part is one really difficult to sustain with credit; to be a gentleman and a buffoon is a task which, desirous as some might be of accomplishing, has foiled many a clever actor. Thus it is that Capt. Cleather, as an amateur, proved himself equal to the demand made upon his powers and helped to carry off Betsy Baker [by J.M. Morton] amid enthusiastic applause' (London *Free Press*, 30 July 1864).

The Animateurs

Although public performances by garrison amateurs enhanced the social calendars of Kingston, London, and Toronto, the theatrical tradition was in fact not equally strong in all the regiments stationed in Ontario. Some regiments performed no theatre, some performed a great deal, and some performed only occasionally. Moreover, regiments that were active in one city sometimes contributed no theatre during a subsequent posting. As in all amateur theatre, these variations would be due to the presence or absence of an individual, or perhaps individuals, with a strong interest in theatre and no little determination to entice fellow officers to participate. Their role would be even more significant in ventures that united officers from several regiments stationed together in one garrison.

As might be imagined, the individuals who provided leadership for these amateur ventures played, for the most part, the starring roles. At times plays were chosen with certain 'specialities' in mind. In Toronto during the first four months of 1843 a group of officers of the 83rd Regiment provided the city with a series of seven performances in the Theatre Royal, located in the North American Hotel. Captain D'Alton of the 83rd had applied for the licence to perform.[32] Fellow officers from the 83rd and from the Royal Artillery played secondary roles, and they were joined by civilian performers, including Mr Deering, who owned the hotel and managed the theatre. But Captain D'Alton was the star of the productions, playing comic roles such as Artaxaminous in *Bombastes Furioso*, a burlesque by William Barnes Rhodes, Karl in Isaac Pocock's melodrama *The Miller and His Men*, Mack Meddle in Boucicault's *London Assurance*, and Rumfustian in *Rumfustian Inamorato*, a comic extravaganza by C.E. Walker. He was listed as the stage manager of the productions, and reviews were uniformly complimentary about his acting. When he played Tommy Dobbs in Pocock's farce *The Omnibus*, the Toronto *Examiner* of 22 February concluded that the 'crowning merit of the evening' fairly belonged to him. Of his role in *Charles the Second*, the Toronto *Examiner* of 1 February comments, 'Captain D'Alton's "Copp" elicited frequent bursts of laughter. There is genius in every thing he does & his good humoured buoyant ease even critics find contagious. He is a more pleasant person to see than many a professional and greater man.'

The combination of stage management and stellar performance was not limited to the officers. This was also the case for the NCOs and men of the 63rd: 'Sergt. Nolan, who has acted as stage manager, deserves much credit for the manner in which he placed the pieces upon the boards, and carried through various arrangements, while as an actor he possesses histrionic ability' (London *Free Press*, 5 May 1864).

Theatrical Repertoire

With a few exceptions, British regiments in Ontario followed the traditional repertoire of garrison performers, those comedies and farces that had enjoyed recent popularity in England.[33] In the first three months of 1830 in Kingston the Naval and Military Amateurs produced a series of Shakespeare's tragedies, an ambitious undertaking which met with an ambivalent response from the Kingston public:

Comedy would produce more profitable results than Tragedy, and we beg leave, to offer as a hint, to the Amateurs, that, we think, there would be a much greater opportunity, for displaying the full strength of the talent of the company by selecting for performance some of our plain English Comedies. (Kingston *Chronicle*, 13 February 1830)

We wish for our own parts, the Gentlemen Amateurs would now give us a Comedy or two. Tragedy when too often repeated, tires, and not all the fine acting of even a principal character, can prevent us from sometimes taking a little nap in the long speeches, which, in Shakespeare's plays, should always be judiciously curtailed, as they suit the closet better than the green cloth. (Kingston *Chronicle*, 27 February 1830)

Musical productions appear to have been a rare event for the garrison performers, and only two occasions are recorded. On Monday, 17 December 1866 the officers of the 17th featured the musical burlesque *Patient Penelope, or the Return of Ulysses* by Francis Cowley and M. Williams. In 1863 the 30th was stationed in Toronto and gave a final ambitious production on 8 July, presenting, along with two farces, the fourth act of *Il Trovatore*, mounted with the assistance of professional musicians and a chorus of thirty amateurs.

A particularly popular type of play for Highland regiments, such as the 79th Queen's Own Cameron Highlanders, was, not surprisingly, one set in Scotland. When on 16 November 1829 the amateurs of the 79th opened the new theatre they had created in a Kingston stable, they chose a performance of *Rob Roy; or Auld Lang Syne*, complete with a piper. The scene is emotionally described by the Kingston *Chronicle* of 21 November 1829: 'Piper D. Stuart played a pibroch on the prize pipes presented to him a few years since, by the Highland Society, of Edinburgh, which made us almost fancy ourselves again in our native glens, and seemed to afford much delight even to those who had not, like us, the accompaniment of early associations to enjoy it fully.'

Melodramas were not unknown in the military repertoire and often provided an opportunity for a special effort on the technical side of production. Elaborate scenery and costumes were a standard accoutrement of garrison theatricals, and the announcement of new scenes and costumes was prominently placed in many of the advertisements. The reviews often praise these aspects of the military productions: 'In the course of the evening several new and beautiful scenes were exhibited and obtained the most decided approbation' (Kingston *Chronicle*, 29 May 1830). This performance of *The Spectre Bridegroom*, a short comedy by William Thomas Moncrieff, *The Lancers*, a comic interlude by John Howard Payne, and *Mrs. Wiggans*, a farce by John Till Allingham, was presented by the Naval and Military Amateurs, who next undertook their most ambitious production, a full-scale scenic extravaganza entitled *The Inchcape Bell* by Edward Fitzball. An advertisement in the Kingston *Chronicle* of 10 July describes the 'entirely new Scenery, Properties and Decorations' to be exhibited: 'In Act Second – Destruction of the Bell by the Smugglers. In Act Third – Storm and Shipwreck. In Scene Last – The vessel is seen to founder as the piece terminates with the Death of the Smuggler and the rescue of the Dumb Boy, from the wreck, by Guy Ruthven.' As exciting as this must have sounded to Kingstonians, it proved beyond the capabilities of the amateurs. The same issue contains the following notice: 'In consequence of the unforeseen difficulty of constructing the moveable machinery and new scenery for the INCH CAPE BELL, particularly the construction of a full rigged QUARTER DECK; to do justice to themselves, the Gentlemen Amateurs are again obliged to announce to their friends, that the performance must be delayed until Wednesday, the 21st of July, when they hope to produce to the public a piece worthy of their patronage.'

But this was not to be. The review of the production, which appeared in the *Chronicle* on 24 July, records that the play was produced with 'some strikingly beautiful new scenery; but in justice to the Amateurs we feel ourselves compelled to state upon our own knowledge, that [an]other two scenes, which had been for three weeks in preparation, were accidentally so much injured during the performance, that they could not be displayed.'

Having acquired such elaborate stage dressings, as well as costumes and a variety of properties, regiments that received an overseas posting had to dispose of their theatre stock. In 1820 the Garrison Amateurs of Kingston did so by public auction. The proceeds, plus a small wardrobe stock, were donated to Kingston's Female Benevolent Society for the benefit of indigent sick.[34]

Kingston was the last Canadian city to provide a home for the 24th Regiment, which was well known to Montreal audiences also for its *corps dramatique*. In September 1836 the regiment was posted overseas and, as a result of transportation limitations, generously made over its entire theatre stock to Dyke's Theatre Company, a small touring troupe that enjoyed considerable popularity in Kingston. The Kingston *Chronicle* of 7 September 1836 reports: 'The Theatrical Amateurs of the 24th Reg., in transferring over to Mr. S. Dyke's Company, the whole of their property, Scenery, Wardrobe, &c &c, have been induced, with the sanction of their C.O., to appear before the public of Kingston one night, being positively their LAST and only appearance during the stay of the Regiment in North America. On the occasion, part of their Scenery, Dresses, &c, will be displayed, and they will be assisted by the Ladies of

Mr. Dyke's Co. and Mr. Bowes.' Sad to say, this close co-operation between the military and the professional performers had unfortunate repercussions: 'On Thursday one of the actors belonging to Mr. Dyke's Company, by the name of Robinson, a man who ought to have known better, enticed two of the band of the 24th regiment to accompany him in his flight to the States ... The two musicians were made drunk by Robinson, and while in that state absconded' (Toronto *Constitution*, 12 October 1836).

There is scattered evidence that British officers stationed in Canada also attempted some writing in association with their theatrical endeavours, limited mostly to original prologues spoken before the productions. In Kingston in 1830 this was the custom, and several examples of rhymed prologues are reproduced at length in the Kingston *Chronicle*. Similarly, the London *Times* of 10 July 1846 announced that 'An original Prologue, written by a gentleman of this place, will be spoken.' The only other piece that might have been written by an officer was reported in the Niagara *Gleaner* of 3 June 1818; a farce entitled *The Convention* contains among the characters certain military figures, for example, Colonel Wentworth in the role of 'Dramatis Personae.'

Culture and Class

The importance of military theatricals for the cultural life of a city in Ontario during this period is reflected in many a newspaper report. The London *Herald* of 18 February 1843 was enthusiastic about the performance of two farces on 31 January: 'The Officers of this Garrison, with a condescension and liberality which does them great credit, again entertained the lovers of the drama in this town, on Tuesday evening last, with another exhibition of their powers to ease the troubled mind, and drive dull cares away.' Similarly, the Kingston *Chronicle* of 5 December 1820 welcomed the news 'that the officers of the garrison have formed an Amateur company with a view, in some measure, to relieve the tedium of our winter evenings.' On the whole, the press recognized the importance of such entertainments in the social interaction of the military with civilians, and the *Chronicle*'s comment about a band concert given by the 83rd could well have been said concerning any of the public theatre performances by British officers and men: 'These and other acts of courtesy on the part of the officers and our Army contribute to strengthen those feelings of good will and friendship which happily exist, and which should always exist, between our gallant soldiers and their fellow citizens in civil life' (Kingston *Chronicle*, 19 June 1839). Support came also in the form of advance notices which encouraged attendance. This was particularly the case when a popular regiment was nearing the end of its stay in the community. 'As the 63rd Regiment is announced to leave the city shortly, and as the performance will be for the benefit of the poor, the citizens of London should willingly come forward and generously sustain the amateurs. It is to be hoped that all classes will make it a special duty to be present, tomorrow (Tuesday) evening' (London *Free Press*, 2 May 1864).

Ontario cities proudly adopted the military amateurs residing in their communities despite the short duration of the posting, which was usually two years.[35] In 1862 the 62nd Regiment, which boasted a theatrical group of NCOs and men, was posted to Kingston for only one year, but during that period the regiment participated fully in the cultural life of the city. When the citizens of Kingston learned that the 62nd was to be reposted in 1863, immediately following the exciting season of performances in October and December of 1862, the mayor sent a letter to the commander of the British forces in North America, which the Kingston *Daily News* reprinted on 28 February 1863, requesting that this popular regiment remain in Kingston until its scheduled departure for England in twelve months; for 'the utmost cordiality and good feeling has existed between the officers and men and citizens.'

The Civilian Audience

If a regiment offered a series of public entertainments, it became the community's equivalent of a resident stock company and thus could count on the eager anticipation of theatre-goers for each subsequent event:

Garrison Theatricals. – The amateur theatricals announced for next week are looked forward to with even more than the usual interest. These entertainments of the regulars have always been popular, and invariably draw the largest and most fashionable houses. Nothing, indeed, less than military histrionics seems powerful enough to draw some of our citizens to the theatre. Of course, to the efforts of the amateurs there is added the undoubted charm of the regimental band – a treat sufficient in itself to attract a large audience. As a large number of tickets have already been sold, and a few choice seats are only to be had, those wishing to be present should secure them without delay. (Toronto *Daily Telegraph*, 28 November 1866)

Attendance is impossible to gauge precisely. Most reports mention large audiences and enthusiastic response: 'Every seat in the dress circle was occupied by the *élite* of the city, while the parquette and family circle were well filled' (Toronto *Globe*, 12 July 1862). 'Her Majesty's servants have every cause to congratulate themselves on the happy termination of last night's entertainment, if a house crowded from pit to gallery, and this too, in the opening of Lent, bears any evidence of success' (Toronto *Globe*, 20 March 1862). Terms such as *large* and *crowded* were used regularly by the press as generalized indications of the relative success of the evening, and so must not be taken as precise descriptions of size. 'Fashionable' is another adjective commonly used to describe audiences at these events: 'A most fashionable audience attended the Royal Lyceum last night. The beauty and fashion of the city mustered in large numbers; opera-glasses were in great request, and were freely used, especially by the gentlemen' (Toronto *Globe*, 16 February 1865). 'And when one reads in the local press that a particular house was crowded with the "beauty, élite and fashion of Kingston," it can be safely assumed that official patronage was the order-of-the-day, for the presence of a commanding officer not only made the attendance of his officers and their ladies mandatory, but also assured a generous representation of the local civilian establishment.'[36]

These performances were attended by members of all social classes. In Kingston, for example, the efforts of the 47th Regiment in 1863–4 were witnessed not only by the gentry of the city, attracted to the social occasion created by the presence of the officers of the garrison, but also by lovers of theatrical entertainment in any form, who were starved for such events. The Kingston *Daily News* of 10 December 1863 described the audience attending one such production:

The second of the series of dramatic entertainments by the amateur theatrical company of the garrison was given on Tuesday night last, in the temporary theatre fitted up in City Hall. The attendance was quite good, the hall being filled. The reserved seats were occupied by a goodly array of ladies and gentlemen, officers and civilians, and the back seats were taken up by the mixed characters which constitute a theatre-going audience. The entertainment in fact was a public one in the fullest sense, offered for the enjoyment of all classes of society in the city, and accepted by all as a relief from the monotony of dull town life.

Similarly the Toronto *Globe* of 8 February 1862 evokes the atmosphere of a military theatrical evening: 'The announcement that a number of the officers of the 30th Regiment would give a grand theatrical performance last evening in the Royal Lyceum, filled the house to overflowing with the élite of the city. The dress circle and parquette presented a very brilliant appearance, the ladies and gentlemen being all in evening costume, while the officers of the Garrison, who were among the spectators, all appeared in full regimentals.' And the Hamilton *Spectator* of 24 February 1864 grew lyrical: 'The Mechanics' Hall presented a very gay and animated appearance, the scarlet jackets blending agreeably with the dresses of the ladies, and the showy uniforms of the Band forming a good background to the scene.' For certain ventures, like the 24 May concert given in Toronto in 1866 under the patronage of Colonel Lowery and the officers of the 47th Regiment, an extra effort was made to fill the house with as many uniformed personnel as possible. The advertisement in the Toronto *Daily Telegraph* of 22 May reads: 'N.B. – Officers (in uniform) and non-commissioned Officers of the Regular Force, and all Volunteers and Cadets (in uniform) will be admitted without Ticket.'

Such commentaries published in the local newspapers are our best indication of the community response to the garrison theatrical ventures. The artistic merit of the performances is more difficult to evaluate, since critical analysis tended to be based on standards of performance that are unclear, inconsistent, and unverifiable. This is particularly true of performances by local amateurs. On such occasions the accepted purpose of the evening was the enjoyment of familiar faces in familiar plays regardless of the relative artistic merit of the event. The majority of notices are correspondingly complimentary in tone, a bias on behalf of the performers being only natural: 'We find it a difficult matter to analyze the performance critically, first because the uniform which the actors wear insures ... our friendship and respect, and thus prejudices us favourably towards them, and secondly from the fact that it is at all times an ungracious task to play the part of critic to the efforts of amateurs' (Hamilton *Daily Spectator*, 24 February 1864). 'Many would be inclined to criticize the acting with the same severity and precision as that bestowed upon professionals. We do not participate in these feelings – but think that every allowance should be made for amateurs – and every encouragement given their entertainments. Our citizens are evidently well pleased with the Garrison performances' (London *Free Press*, 31 May 1862).

It comes as a surprise, therefore, to read strongly critical accounts of the performances of certain amateur military gentlemen. One such report appeared in the London *Free Press* on 10 July 1862, in a description of the performance of two of J.M. Morton's farces, *The Two Bonnycastles* and *Box and Cox*, and John Oxenford's farce *Only a Halfpenny* given by the Garrison Amateurs under the leadership of Lieutenant Keogh and Ensign Lockyear. The article is also an example of the critical perspective of the press of the period:

The Garrison Theatricals

Actors in Canada are scarce, but they would not have been scarce had they been much esteemed, and they would have been esteemed had they professed talents great enough to command esteem. We cannot say that the amateur performers we have lately seen in this city, have exhibited qualities sufficiently great to inspire the population with any deep love for theatrical performance. When we pay our money to see amateur performers, we buy the privilege of criticism, and if it pleases us to express our disapprobation of any particular actor, we have a perfect right, to do so in the ordinary manner, by means of the usual sibilations. If we did not exercise this privilege at the last performances of this Garrison, we abstained, from kind motives and not from an high estimate of the merits of the actors. We conceive that we have a right to expect that amateurs shall be somewhat perfect in their parts, and that the prompters shall not be heard throughout the house quite as frequently and very nearly as loud as the actor. Instead of sneaking towards the wings and leaning on the prompter for support, an actor should be

'Like strength, resounding on his own right arm'

He should have confidence in his memory, and know the words of his part, or else he never can sustain the character. Our amateurs were sadly deficient – in this first of all necessaries and having to think too much about what sentences came next, they had no leisure to give to the grace and finesse of the actor. They were mere recitors [sic] with much assistance from the prompter, and not by any means actors. We do not wish to particularise where all was bad, but the pre-eminence of badness ought certainly to be mentioned; and we can have no hesitation in assigning it to 'Box,' a more wooden Box was never seen on any stage, not even an imitation of any previous Box. Without the vaguest apprehension of a point in the character – without life or energy, or bustle, (if the sham women had possessed more of the latter it would have added to the effect of their make up) – a tamer representative of a part requiring great energy was never seen … it is quite inexcusable not to rehearse frequently before appearing in public. Frequent rehearsals would have disguised other inefficiencies, and would have made the best of the meagre talent the company possessed.

'This is no world in which to pity men,' but we did pity the men who must have felt their performance to be a sorry one, and we did also pity the audience who patiently bore as deep an infliction on their sense and temper. We hope the next amateurs who charge us for admission will think that they have a duty to perform to the paying public, and that they are, at the very least, bound to become as perfect as time and trouble can make them. With these remarks we close our friendly criticism.

'Cornichon,' in a letter to the editor of the *Globe*, felt much the same about amateur performances in Toronto:

A 'critique' on theatricals of this description, when the proceeds are to be dispensed in charitable purposes, or when the brunt of expense falls upon a small body of enthusiastic, enterprising caterers to public amusement, or when they are purely private theatricals – is decidedly invidious, and as much wanting in good taste as are fulsome praises bestowed upon undeserving actors; but upon an occasion of this kind, when amateurs become public property, by opening the doors to all musterers of the 'almighty dollar,' an impartial criticism cannot be regarded in any other light than just.

The well known talents and abilities which find their abode in the ranks of this popular regiment, it is to be regretted, did not gush forth. (Toronto *Globe*, 17 February 1862)

This is the same production that the reviewer for the *Globe* of 8 February had described as 'certainly the most successful amateur theatrical performance that has been given in Toronto for a series of years, and every one left the house highly delighted.'

The majority of reviews of military theatricals did not treat these public performances, regardless of ticket prices, as being suitable topics for impartial criticism. Nor was the tenor of most reviews fulsome praise. In most cases there was a mixture of praise for the most experienced performers coupled with delicate observations as to the relative lack of stage presence of the less successful. The Toronto *Globe*'s 8 February 1862 review of the 30th Regiment's production of *Used Up*, a short comedy by Dion Boucicault and C. Mathews, contained just such carefully worded evaluations of the actors. Captain Lamert as Sir Charles Coldstream 'gave ample evidence that he is possessed of high histrionic talent as a light comedian.' Lieutenants Brownlow and Lindsay performed 'in good style; but it was not surprising that both appeared to be a little nervous when so many bright eyes were watching their every movement.' And of the two captains who played supporting roles the reviewer commented: 'They had little to do or say, but taking everything into consideration that little was done well.'

Insufficient voice projection appears to have been a relatively common fault. The Toronto *Globe* of 16 February 1865 noted that Mr Lang, in his role as King Artaxaminous in *Bombastes Furioso*, 'articulated so indistinctly that it was with difficulty he could be heard by the audience, and half, at least, of what he said never left the region of the stage.' The reviewer for the London *Free Press* of 31 May 1862 was more imaginative, observing, 'The intonation of most of the characters in this piece was very imperfect, the performers speaking as if they had plums in their mouths.' Occasionally the amateurs received some useful advice: 'The actors should take positions as near to the footlights as possible, and address themselves more to [sic] audience than to each other, as without this it is very difficult for those in the middle of the hall to hear what is said; a little more speaking from the lungs would add to the success of the performers' (London *Free Press*, 30 April 1864).

A more serious problem was the inability of some performers to remember their lines. A comment that appeared in the Toronto *Globe* of 4 January 1868 would seem to indicate that the absence of the prompter's voice was more rare than otherwise: 'A most uncommon circumstance in amateur theatricals was that only one of the actors showed that he had forgot his part, and he only for a few minutes.' Such mental blocks were generally the result of either insufficient rehearsal or excessive consumption of alcohol taken to counteract performance anxiety (or both), though this second reason was never directly stated by the press. Jonathan Leach, a military thespian during the Peninsular War, recorded, however, that the performers forgot lines mainly because of the amount of wine and grog that had found its way backstage.[37] The London *Inquirer* of 3 March 1843 gently commented that the farce *Is She a Woman*, by William Collier, 'was tolerably sustained by the characters, taking into consideration the short period allowed them to get up the piece previous to the performance.'

Some of these gaffes resulted in amusing anecdotes for newspapers to report:

But it was an amateur performance, and towards the close it became evident that the stretch of memory was becoming too much for some of the company. The gentlemen concealed the defect by retiring from the stage, and though the soubrette and stage-manager did their best to afford an opportunity for renewing the interrupted scene, the curtain dropped upon a dénouement very different from what the author intended. The audience in front were too well bred to be hilarious over the unexpected turn given to affairs; but the 'gods in the gallery,' that is to say, a few of the youthful gentlemen on the back seats, made loud manifestations of their perception of the 'breakdown.' Then there was subdued merriment throughout the whole house, enlivened by laughable excuses from the stage, which only the rapidly following music silenced ... But for the ludicrous termination of the leading piece, which a little better prompting and a bolder courage would have prevented, the whole entertainment would have been capital. As it was, we think the audience appreciated the efforts of the gentlemen to amuse, and went home well pleased with their taste of amateur theatricals. (Kingston *Daily News*, 10 December 1863)

Although generally supportive, on occasion the local press were predisposed against the military performers. This appears to have been the case during the first months of 1863 in London, when the Garrison Amateurs under the leadership of Keogh and Lockyear received a series of negative reviews, such as the lengthy one reproduced above, and the following short scorcher, an advance notice that appeared in the London *Free Press* on 7 March. The writer began with praise for the generous conduct of the Garrison Amateurs in performing in order to raise money for the widow and five children of a soldier of the Royal Canadian Rifles but then continued:

In some parts of the plays which the amateurs appeared in during their first performance, they were very deficient, both in the management of the voice and also in acting, the majority of them conducting themselves as though they had no real conception of the parts allotted to them, and rendering their pieces in that cold, lifeless manner which is the peculiar and decisive sign that an actor has not really studied his part. However, saying all with the most kindly desire to see the Military Train corps distinguish themselves, giving patrons every satisfaction, we proceed, as intimated, to furnish the programme.

It is impossible to know how, if at all, these amateurs had offended the writer for the London *Free Press*, but it is doubtful that their performances were much worse than those of other military actors about whom the London papers were exceedingly complimentary. The only clue is in the oblique and repeated references to entertainment 'free from objectionable sentiments and low stage expressions' (London *Free Press*, 21 June 1862). Clearly, on one occasion offence was given; for in the review of the first of this series of performances, the comic song 'Guy Fawkes' was declared to be unsuited to a mixed audience (London *Free Press*, 31 May 1862).

'Though the garrison amateurs will help enliven the winter ... it must be confessed that amateur theatricals are a great bore,'[38] the correspondent of the New York *Albion* commented somewhat grumpily of the officers performing in Montreal. We shall never know if this opinion was widely shared or was even an accurate gauge of the quality of the military amateurs, whose productions probably ranged from tedious to entertaining. It is also possible that some performers were as talented as the leading professionals concurrently visiting Ontario. Several soldiers who appeared in the *corps dramatique* received their discharge in Canada and did in fact become professional performers. John Nickinson, later a leading actor and manager of a touring company, was a prominent member of the enlisted performers of the 24th and received excellent notices until he purchased his discharge in 1836.[39]

Practice does not always make perfect, but it helps. The London *Free Press* of 29 May 1862 gently criticized the officers of the 63rd and then commented, 'However, having time before them, we are sure our military

John Nickinson as Havresac in *The Old Guard*

friends will not be slow to take advantage, and improvement, as a matter of course, must follow.' Improvement being the natural result of repeated stage experience, it may be assumed that the praise received by the theatrical officers of the 47th after they had performed regularly in Kingston, London, and Toronto from 1863 to 1865 was not exaggerated or fulsome. When *Still Waters Run Deep*, a comedy by Tom Taylor, and *Timothy to the Rescue*, a farce by Henry James Byron, were staged in Toronto, the *Globe* concluded that they had been 'performed in a style which we have never seen excelled on the boards of the Toronto Theatre' (*Globe*, 13 October 1865).

The Military Patronage

Regimental patronage of professional theatre was as much a part of military traditions as amateur theatricals were. The regimental band was made available to select touring companies and, after the establishment of resident stock companies, for benefits for popular performers or special charities, as when the band of the 13th Hussars joined professional and amateur civilian performers in an event for the relief of the starving widows and orphans of the south (Toronto *Globe*, 3 August 1867). As the military musicians were highly proficient, the announcement of the presence of the regimental band could be counted on to increase box office sales.

At other times officers attended a particular performance en masse. 'Among the residents of Toronto at this period [1852–7] were Lord Elgin, the Hon. Colonel Bruce, the brother of Lord Elgin, and Sir Hue [sic] Dalrymple, the colonel of the 71st Highlanders, then stationed here. It was their custom to bespeak a favourite play in advance, and then engage all the boxes for themselves and their friends.'[40] Such an evening would be an important social occasion for the gentry of the city.[41] Similarly, it was reported that 'Sir Francis Head has come out as the patron of a play-house here, which is therefore called the "theatre royal," and on the evening of last Wednesday week, the play was "three weeks after marriage," and the opera "Bombastes Furioso"' (Toronto *Constitution*, 2 August 1836).

On 15 July 1846 in London the role of military patron of the arts was taken over by the officers of the local militia, joined by those of the 82nd, who supplied their regimental band. The London *Times* of 17 July described the audience that gathered: 'The House was a bumper, graced by the beauty and fashion of the Town and neighbourhood – a full muster of the officers of the 82nd were present, with the officers in command of our Town Volunteer Companies, the Artillery and the

Rifles, under whose immediate patronage the performances were got up.'

Those professional companies that, as a result of winning the patronage of senior officers of the garrison, could include such an announcement in advertisements rose in the estimation of the local civilians. Not only did this bring more of the theatre-going public to the performance, but also, given the condemnation of the theatre by many religious people,[42] regular public support from the British officers contributed to the acceptance of theatre by the community.

Indigenous Canadian Theatre

All these military theatrical activities hastened the development of indigenous Canadian theatre but were not the sole determining factor. Kingston, London, and Toronto follow similar patterns in the emergence of civilian theatrical entertainments: an early period when the indigenous population was of insufficient numbers to generate local activity, a middle period in which the local community generated some amateur activity but of a limited sort, and a mature period when the cities could support resident professional theatre companies. Social historians have suggested that cultural activities such as theatre emerge habitually when a city reaches a certain population, and so these three phases can be attributed to the changing size of the city rather than to a process of cultural or social maturation.[43] Moreover, the lively theatrical activities of centres such as Belleville indicate that a garrison was not necessary for the emergence of theatre, either amateur or professional. What, then, was the unique function of garrison theatricals in the emergence of indigenous theatre in Ontario?

The most important contribution was the development of a taste for drama and the confirmation of its moral and social acceptability. An advance notice for the final performance of the 47th in Kingston included the following observation:

Through the good efforts of the Garrison Theatrical Club, Kingston has had during the past season more than the usual share of dramatic performances. It is not improbable that the excellent rendering of comedies and light plays with which the military amateurs have favored us during the winter may have revived the local taste for theatrical representations. It is to be hoped, at all events, that they have done so, for it is undeniable that the drama, when in good hands and well-directed, is an effective means of instruction and amusement. Another opportunity of gratifying the awakening taste is about to be afforded to the play-going portion of the people of Kingston. (Kingston *Daily News*, 23 May 1864)

By the 1860s amateur theatricals for the local gentry appeared to serve many of the same functions as the military ventures. These events could bind together the members of the élite in a social struggle to maintain standards imported from their English forbears.[44]

In 1862, following a successful series of productions by the officers of the 63rd, there emerged in London a local amateur group. The London *Free Press* of 3 June 1862 published the following exhortation:

Theatrical. – A Suggestion. – As the Garrison Amateurs have expressed their intention of not appearing again upon the stage for some time (and we are very sorry to hear it), why do not some enterprising civilians take the matter in hand, and give a public entertainment? We are sure the gentlemen of the Garrison club would kindly allow the civilians to use the stage and its properties, so far as available, and the proceeds no doubt would be acceptable if devoted to some benevolent fund. What says young Canada?

Apparently young Canada responded in the affirmative:

'Civilian Theatricals'

We learn that our suggestion relative to the formation of a Civilian Dramatic Society has been acted upon, and a club is in course of organization. The Garrison Co. has signified its willingness to allow the stage, with appurtenances, for use, and several gentlemen possessing more than an ordinary share of histrionic talent, have volunteered to superintend the matter in hand, and will, we doubt not, bring it to a speedy and successful issue. The first item is to call a meeting, which will shortly be done, and it is very desirable that those who favour this movement attend and join in the proceedings. Our military friends having taken initiatory steps, the least that can now be done is to reciprocate their efforts to fill up the *role* of amusement for the season. Relative to public encouragement, we feel assured that this will not by any means be withheld, particularly as the proceeds derived from each entertainment will be distributed amongst the charitable institutions of the city. In conclusion, we would advise those interested to work at once, and not delay proceedings. 'No time like the present,' is an adage for consideration. Meanwhile, we wish the undertaking every success. (London *Free Press*, 17 June 1862)

There are several examples of civilian amateurs following the lead of the military, as in London. In repertoire, stated aims, and associated problems and successes, these productions differed little from those of the military. The officers offered support for the fledgling civilian theatre groups in many ways. An advertisement that appeared in the Kingston *Chronicle* on 12 April 1837 described the aspirations of one such group:

The Kingston Dramatic Amateurs, in conjunction with Mr. A. Ashley, respectfully inform the public, that having, by the kind permission of Lieut. Col. Hughes, obtained the assistance of Quarter Master Sergeant Turnbull and Sergeant Greer, 24th Regiment, they propose devoting Four Evenings' Performances during the present Month, to CHARITABLE PURPOSES. The proceeds of the first Evening to be placed at the disposal of the Rt. Rev'd Bishop McDonnel [sic], and the Venerable Archdeacon Stuart, to distribute among the suffering POOR OF KINGSTON.

Mr and Mrs Ashley, one-time Kingston amateurs and later members of several small touring companies which had visited Kingston in 1830–6, played the leading roles along with the two military stars, while inexperienced amateurs played supporting roles. Lack of discipline among the amateurs, however, led to the ultimate disaster that brought their efforts to a close. One 2 May 1837 the lady who was to play Anne in *The Tragedy of Douglas* by John Home refused to go on, and the play was performed without her, leaving Mrs Ashley, in the role of Lady Randolph, entirely unsupported.[45] This was the unfortunate end to the Ashleys' efforts to form a semi-professional, resident theatre troupe in Kingston.

In Toronto, three years after the successful season presented by Captain D'Alton and the officers of the 83rd, a local civilian amateur used the military model when forming another ambitious theatrical organization. In 1846 the Amateur Theatrical Society gave a series of productions which received the support of the local military: the regimental band was present at every performance given in 1844 and in the following years on special occasions such as benefit performances. T.P. Besnard, the leading actor, manager, and clearly the driving force of this venture, continued his activities until 1852, by which time the group could well be considered professional. Besnard himself went on to act in Toronto's first resident stock company. Thus one can see in Toronto a pattern similar to that found in Kingston: military amateurs provided the model for civilian amateur ventures, which merged with the professional aspirations of leading participants.

Collaborative Theatricals

A variety of forms of theatrical co-operation occurred in garrison communities. In Kingston in 1830 efforts to raise money for a proper theatre in the city drew together everyone with a commitment to the cultural life of the city. The committee included Colonel Roberts and Lieutenant Ward of the Royal Artillery, Lieutenant Crombie of the 79th,

John Glover and John Marks of the Royal Navy, and three gentlemen from the city: John Macaulay, James W. Armstrong, and Dr James Sampson (Kingston *Chronicle*, 2 January 1830), all important residents of Kingston who shared an interest in the theatre with their military friends.[46] In London Captain Joseph Cowley, ex-officer of King George IV's personal guard, was involved in the creation of 'The Shakespeare Club' in 1845.[47]

In all three cities military performers joined civilians to present public entertainments. However, as complete cast lists were published irregularly, it is impossible to verify exactly how often this collaboration occurred. John Spurr contends that 'the amateur company of a regiment or garrison normally welcomed the participation of civilian gentlemen who, it goes without saying, were socially eligible for entrée to the officers' mess.'[48] This assumption is confirmed in the diary of William Mercer Wilson, a leading citizen of London who participated in amateur theatricals with the officers of the garrison in 1839 and 1840. Wilson recorded five separate performances, three of which went 'famously' and two of which were less than perfection. In an entry for 3 January 1840 he described the second as going 'pretty well – the actors were not very correct in their parts, but the audience were extremely good natured.' On 21 March of the same year he recorded the following: 'On Thursday 19th in the afternoon, I was requested by the theatrical managers to aid in the performance of that night. Rather short notice but to work I went and in the evening played Slang – Roger – Jeremy and Sir Charles Marlow in "She Stoops to Conquer." House good and everything went off well.'[49]

In Toronto in 1847, in the middle of an ambitious season produced by T.P. Besnard's group of civilian amateurs, now calling themselves the Gentlemen Amateurs of the city, Besnard recruited two officers from the garrison to replace two of his group who had resigned (Toronto *Examiner*, 4 May 1847). On 11 February 1868 the NCOs and men of the 17th joined forces with the Toronto Dramatic Club, a civilian organization, to produce a show in aid of the Nova Scotian fishermen. Meanwhile, the officers of the 47th carried their theatrical enthusiasms to the civilians in each of their Ontario postings. In Kingston they gave three performances, the final one being a benefit for Miss Florence Grosvenor, who had joined the officers in most of their ventures. For this occasion her father, John Townsend, a professional actor specializing in Shakespeare roles, returned to the stage after an absence of thirteen years. Civilian amateurs also participated, and they continued to support Townsend and Florence Grosvenor in a further series of Shakespeare productions given that year, joined on occasion by officers from the garrison even after the 47th had left the city. At London, their new posting, the amateurs of the 47th offered their first performance just weeks after their arrival. They were joined by Mrs Brunton, a popular local civilian amateur who was still remembered for her performance as Mrs Mildmay in *Still Waters Run Deep*, presented by the London Amateur Theatricals in 1862 (London *Free Press*, 30 July 1864).

These co-operative ventures were not only memorable social occasions but also significant landmarks in the emergence of local theatre organizations. Civilian amateurs gained invaluable experience from observations of the inner workings of the well-established military theatrical traditions. A few, such as John Nickinson, were inspired by the charismatic individuals who provided leadership for these groups and went on to become leaders of a civilian organization. The merging of amateur experience with professional ambition resulted in several attempts to establish professional theatre companies. And throughout these civilian activities, successful and otherwise, the military remained a source of patronage, encouragement, and co-operation.

Professional theatre organizations also recognized the mutual benefits of close co-operation with garrison amateurs. The infrequent garrison productions were guaranteed to attract those who otherwise did not attend the theatre on a regular basis, and so it was to the advantage of a local theatre manager to be the host of a public performance by the military performers. Often the female roles were taken by the actresses of the resident company, usually with pleasant results. Vieth writes of the 62nd officers' performing with actors from Edward Sothern's Halifax stock company. Such collaboration also occurred in Toronto in 1862, when the amateurs of the 30th made use of the professional actresses of Harry Lindley's company at the Royal Lyceum. The result was special praise for the performance of the company's ingenue in the 17th's performance of *The Barrack Room*, a comedy by Thomas Haynes Bayly: 'The amateurs were ably assisted by Miss Sallie Holman, who, as "Clarlase," gave expression to an amount of feeling we had hardly expected her capable of. In fact, her acting on the occasion, was one of the finest pieces of impassioned sentiment witnessed on the stage here for some time' (Toronto *Globe*, 29 January 1869). The benefits of such co-operation between officers and local professional troupes are obvious: patronage guaranteed attendance of the gentry, and this patronage would be more readily extended upon the occasion of actors' benefits if those same actors had aided the officers in one of their public entertainments.

Collaboration was not always painless, particularly when the personalities of the professionals clashed with the amateur stars. Reports of such contretemps would not normally reach the public, and our only indication that they existed is a letter from Mary Shaw, the professional

who played Arabella in *The First Night*, a short comedy translated from
the French by Alfred Wigan and produced by the 30th on 19 March 1862.
The play, according to the review which appeared in the Toronto *Globe*
of the next day, was 'in no way adapted to the performance of Amateurs'
as the entire burden fell to a single performer, 'for the exhibition of whose
"specialty" it was evidently selected.' This was Captain Lamert, one of
the leaders of the Garrison Amateurs. In response to an article in the
Toronto *Leader*, Mary Shaw firmly denied any mistreatment by the
officers: 'Everything at rehearsal and during the play passed off most
agreeably – with the exception of a little *fracas* which occurred between
"Achilla Talma Duford" [Lamert] and myself, which has since been
settled to our mutual satisfaction.' We can only speculate as to the clash
of temperament that occurred when the intrepid amateur performed beside
the experienced leading lady.

Theatrical Facilities

Another significant factor in the emergence of indigenous theatre in
Ontario was the involvement of British troops in the creation of performance spaces in all three cities. In most cases this activity consisted of
renovations of an empty warehouse or alterations to a room in a hotel.
These theatres were generally unpretentious facilities, as a description of
London's first Theatre Royal indicates. Orlo Miller has recorded the
recollections of Dick Butler, an old-time employee of the London *Free
Press*: 'It was an old, former frame barn that held an audience of about
two hundred, seated with benches in the pit and with an attempt of style
in the box departments ... Price of admission to the old "Royal" was
fifty cents for seats for the highbrows in the boxes, while the lowbrows
filled the pit at a quarter each.'[50]
   In May 1862 British troops again fitted up a performance space the
labour of which delayed their premier performance in London: 'The
construction of the stage and scenery has been a much more arduous
undertaking than was at first contemplated, and the work has been
executed in a very efficient and permanent manner. Mr. S. Smith has had
the charge of the painting, and has not only given satisfaction to the
officers, but the work now finished reflects the greatest credit upon him'
(London *Free Press*, 14 May 1862). It was this performance space that
the garrison loaned to the London Amateurs later in the year.
   In Kingston the naval presence proved instrumental in the creation of
the city's first theatres. An association of naval and military performers,
calling themselves the Garrison Amateurs, created Kingston's first theatre

late in 1815. The association took over a building owned by the Royal Navy, a former brewery purchased during the war to be used as a naval hospital. Between January 1816 and July 1817 the Garrison Amateurs functioned as a form of resident theatre company, mounting and producing a series of plays and farces.[51]

Military theatricals did not return to Kingston until the last months of 1829, when the amateurs of the 79th (Queen's Own Cameron Highlanders) fitted up an old stable opposite the Court House with stage, pit, boxes, and gallery. As already mentioned, military and civilian representatives joined forces in 1830 to raise money to renovate the old Brewery Theatre, which remained a theatre until the dismantling of the Navy Dockyards in 1833, when the brewery building was probably sold.[52]

Patronage and Precedent

The three periods created by the movement of British imperial troops in Ontario provide an interesting chronological measure against which to place the pattern of theatrical development, which also falls into discernible phases. During the first phase the military provided virtually the only theatrical entertainment for the community, and their contribution often included the actual building of performance spaces. The second phase was marked by the emergence of civilian amateur groups. These were often formed around a nucleus of military performers, sometimes retired officers who had settled in the community, and at other times members of the resident regiment who combined forces with civilian thespians. Out of these ventures emerged civilian amateur groups who modelled themselves on the example set by the military amateurs. During this phase the military often provided invaluable support in the way of costumes, scenery, use of performance space, and patronage. The final phase of development involved the emergence of indigenous professional theatre companies. In each city a series of productions was given by a group that combined professionals with civilian amateurs, or by an organization that began as amateur but developed professional status through ongoing productions and the aspirations of the leading individuals. However, civilian and military amateur theatricals continued unabated even after the establishment of fully professional resident stock companies; so it is apparent that each consecutive phase by no means superseded the previous activities. Rather, the older traditions continued only slightly altered alongside more recent theatrical forms.

NOTES

1 Stow Persons in *The Decline of American Gentility* (New York: Columbia University Press 1973) defines 'gentry élite' as 'those who articulated the code of gentility most effectively, and ... those in positions of prominence who were looked to by the rank and file as exemplifying the ideals of the gentleman' (61); the officers of the British Army were drawn exclusively from the landed gentry and professional military families; cf C.B. Otley, 'Social Origins of British Army Officers,' *Sociological Review* 18 (July 1970), 223.

2 Richard D. Brown, 'The Emergence of Urban Society in Rural Massachusetts, 1760–1820,' *Journal of American History* 61:1 (June 1974), 45

3 John Philip, 'The Economic and Social Effects of the British Garrison on the Development of Western Upper Canada,' *Ontario Historical Society Papers and Records* 41 (1949), 48; Desmond Morton, *Canada and War: A Military and Political History* (Toronto: Butterworth 1981), 21. Canadian military theatricals in Kingston are recorded in Leslie O'Dell's 'Theatrical Events in Kingston, Ontario 1879–1897,' PH D dissertation, University of Toronto 1982.

4 John W. Spurr, 'The Kingston Garrison, 1815–1870,' *Historic Kingston* 20 (February 1972), 15

5 Hector J. Massey, *The Canadian Military: A Profile* (Toronto: Copp Clark 1972), 58–62; Frederick H. Armstrong and Daniele J. Brock, 'The Rise of London: A Study of Urban Evolution in Nineteenth Century Southwestern Ontario,' in F.H. Armstrong, H.A. Stevenson, J.D. Wilson, eds, *Aspects of Nineteenth-Century Ontario* (Toronto: University of Toronto Press 1974), 90; Charles Perry Stacey, in *Canada and the British Army 1846–1871* (Toronto: University of Toronto Press 1963), notes that 'each British regiment had been a little section of the mother country set down on a distant shore' (261).

6 R.J. Burns, 'God's Chosen People: The Origins of Toronto Society,' in J.M. Bumsted, ed., *Canadian History before Confederation* (Georgetown: Irwin-Dorsey 1979), 267. J.M.S. Careless in 'Some Aspects of Urbanization in Nineteenth-Century Ontario,' in Armstrong et al. eds, *Aspects of Nineteenth-Century Ontario*, 75, suggests that the officers contributed to the polarization of garrison communities along class lines. Massey confirms this, adding that the presence of the British garrisons helped to 'perpetuate a distinction between Canadian society and American society' (*Canadian Military*, 67).

7 Elinor Kyte Senior, *British Regulars in Montreal: An Imperial Garrison, 1832–1854* (Montreal: McGill-Queen's University Press 1981), 170. There is no reason to think that Montreal was remarkably different from Toronto, London, or Kingston: 'Unlike modern army establishments that tend to be so hidden away that the civilian population is hardly aware of their existence, the British garrison in Montreal was so involved in a multitude of social activities,

sports, religious functions, and fraternal and cultural relationships with townsmen that the townspeople seldom went a day without encountering the military at some level.'

8 Fred Dreyer, 'Three Years in the Toronto Garrison ... 1847–1850,' *Ontario Historical Society Papers and Records* 57: 1 (1965), 34; cf Spurr, 'Kingston Garrison': 'The garrison officer was not only the darling of society, but one of its natural leaders. Unfortunately his appeal to Kingston's numerous and influential small merchants and tradesfolk was strictly limited because of a characteristic they described as "arrogance" '(22); this view must be balanced with the assertions made by Dennis Carter-Edwards in *Garrison Life: The 89th Regiment at Fort Malden, 1841–1842* (Ottawa: Parks Canada, n.d.): 'Officers were popular guests at local outings, balls and other social events, adding a touch of class and elegance with their dress and polished manners' (16).

9 Viscount Wolseley, *The Story of a Soldier's Life*, vol. II (Westminster: Archibald Constable 1903), 116; Massey notes that when the Civil War brought large numbers of impressionable young officers to Canada, the number of marriages contracted with Canadian ladies increased (*Canadian Military*, 60).

10 Carter-Edwards quotes from J.H. Stocqueler, *The British Officer: His Position, Duties, Emoluments and Privileges* (London: Smith, Elder & Co. 1851), 5.

11 John W. Spurr, 'Theatre in Kingston, 1816–1870,' *Historic Kingston* 22 (March 1974), 37

12 E.S. Turner, *Gallant Gentlemen, a Portrait of the British Officer 1600–1956* (London: Michael Joseph 1956), 98

13 Moira Dunbar, 'The Royal Arctic Theatre,' *Canadian Art* 15 (Spring 1958), 110–13

14 Antony Brett-James, *Life in Washington's Army* (London: George Allen and Unwin 1972), 159–64; also Turner, *Gallant Gentlemen*, 144

15 Turner, *Gallant Gentlemen*, 73

16 Spurr, 'Kingston Garrison,' 27

17 Ibid., 19. A detailed account and analysis of the life of the British soldier in Canada can be found in Carol M. Whitfield, *Tommy Atkins: The British Soldier in Canada, 1759–1870* (Ottawa: Parks Canada 1981).

18 Brian Farwell, *For Queen and Country* (London: Penguin Books 1981), 67

19 Sylvia R. Frey, *The British Soldier in America* (Austin: University of Texas Press 1981), 66

20 Francis Duncan, *Our Garrisons in the West; or, Sketches in British North America* (London: Chapman and Hall 1864), 193

21 Ibid., 22

22 Jesse Edgar Middleton, *Toronto's 100 Years* (Toronto: Toronto Centennial Committee 1934), 19

23 Frederick Harris D. Vieth, *Recollections of the Crimean Campaign and the Expedition to Kinburn in 1855* (Montreal: John Lovell and Son 1907), 274

24 Harriet Priddis, 'Reminiscences of Mrs. Gilbert Porte,' London and Middlesex Historical Society *Transactions* 4 (1913), 68

25 Frey, *British Soldier*, 68

26 Spurr, 'Kingston Garrison,' 18. Spurr's description of the regimental band could be applied to any regimental *corps dramatique*: 'The regimental band belonged, in fact, to the officers, each of whom was obliged to subscribe 20 days' pay on joining the Mess and eight days' pay per year toward its support. In practice, however, it was exclusively at the disposition of the Commanding Officer.' The traditions associated with the enlisted performers of music or drama continue to the present, as E.S. Turner notes in his comments on the British Army during the Second World War: 'Men with useful social accomplishments, like skill in amateur theatricals, or ability to play a trumpet, would not have to exert themselves quite as hard as others' (*Gallant Gentlemen*, 306).

27 Spurr, 'Kingston Garrison,' 22; also Frey, *British Soldier*, 66

28 Frey, *British Soldier*, 28

29 General Sir Daniel Lysons, GCB, *Early Reminiscences* (London: John Murray 1896), 161. Lysons does refer to his performances in Quebec, noting: 'I was a smooth-faced boy then, so I was enlisted for the ladies' parts, and got great applause for my "Caroline Dorma" in *The Heir at Law* [by George Colman the younger], and for my "Ravina" in *The Miller and His Men* [by Isaac Pocock]' (62).

30 Vieth, *Recollections*, 286

31 Ibid., 130

32 Patrick Bernard Anthony O'Neill, 'A History of Theatrical Activity in Toronto, Canada: From Its Beginning to 1858,' PH D dissertation, Louisiana State University 1973, 82

33 Frey, *British Soldier*, 68; also Spurr, 'Theatre in Kingston,' 53; Claudette Lacelle, in *The British Garrison in Quebec City as Described in Newspapers from 1764 to 1840* (Ottawa: Parks Canada 1979), provides a list of the plays performed in that city by garrison theatre groups.

34 Spurr, 'Theatre in Kingston,' 39

35 Charles H. Stewart, *The Service of British Regiments in Canada and North America* (Ottawa: Department of National Defence Library 1962). In 1864 the theatrical officers of the 47th, then stationed in Kingston, went to Toronto to give dramatic performances to raise money for the Military Orphan Asylum at Quebec. The Kingston *Daily News* of 8 March proudly boasted, 'The Toronto people will then have a chance of seeing how admirably our Garrison amateurs acquit themselves on the stage.' That the warm feelings of civilians towards their resident British regiments were reciprocated is affirmed by the comments of the officers posted to the city. Walter Henry, in his autobiography, *Events of a Military Life* (London 1843), vol. II, 228, describes the return of the 66th to Kingston in 1834: 'Our numerous friends ... received us with a warm welcome.

Our former stay of two years in their kind hearted town had produced an almost affectionate intimacy.' Departures and arrivals of regiments focused attention on the role of the regiments in the social life of the community. Mrs Amelia Harris recorded in her diary the departure of the 63rd from London on 14 September 1864: 'The regiments marched at 7, bidding a long adieu to London. It is very doubtful whether there will be any more British soldiers stationed in London as the home Government say they will not defend the colonies. We all feel dull and the town looks dull' (Amelia Harris Diaries, Regional Archives, University of Western Ontario).

36 Spurr, 'Theatre in Kingston,' 37
37 Brett-James, *Life*, 160
38 Senior, *British Regulars*, 170; Mary Shortt, in 'From *Douglas* to *The Black Crook*: A History of Toronto Theatre, 1809–1874,' MA thesis, University of Toronto 1977, 57, provides another example of a brutally honest and, perhaps, more objective opinion, in this case of the performances of D'Alton and friends in 1843. She quotes from Larratt Smith's diary of 30 January 1843: 'miserable acting – Charles II bombastic, none of the officers could act but D'Alton.'
39 Spurr, 'Theatre in Kingston,' 49–50; Shortt, 'From *Douglas*,' 108–10, describes Nickinson's military fervour and extensive activities with the Toronto militia.
40 John Ross Robertson, *Robertson's Landmarks of Toronto: A Collection of Historical Sketches*, First Series (Toronto: Robertson 1894), 487
41 Senior, *British Regulars*, 170
42 O'Neill, 'A History,' 89–90; also Shortt, 'From *Douglas*,' 15, 26–7
43 Brown, 'Emergence,' 47. Brown suggests that the population range necessary to generate and sustain cultural activities is 1,000–2,000, with at least 20 per cent of the men engaged in non-agricultural callings.
44 Persons, *Decline*, 153
45 Spurr, 'Theatre in Kingston,' 45–6
46 Spurr, 'Kingston Garrison,' 22
47 Orlo Miller, 'History of Theatre in London,' manuscript, Regional Archives, University of Western Ontario, 5; Elinor Senior documents the important contributions of part-civilian, part-military organizations to the cultural life of Montreal. Two such ventures were the Shakespeare Dramatic and Literary Club and the Garrick Club. What is of interest in the history of these groups is the merging of interested parties from both spheres of the community, and the importance of the guiding personalities, for the most part officers or ex-officers from British regiments. These groups also appealed directly to the military for their support in the form of patronage and participation. Senior, *British Regulars*, 170–1
48 Spurr, 'Theatre in Kingston,' 37

49 William Mercer Wilson's diary is held in the Regional Archives at the University of Western Ontario (John Arthur Bannister Papers).
50 Miller, 'History of Theatre,' 4
51 Spurr, 'Theatre in Kingston,' 37–8
52 Ibid., 43

4 *The Nineteenth-Century Repertoire*

ROBERTSON DAVIES

When we think of the Canadian theatre in the nineteenth century we are in danger of being deceived by an accident of history; the economic depression that began in 1929 and continued until the Second World War greatly curtailed the visits of those touring companies from the United States and Britain that had provided so much of our theatrical fare until then, creating a theatrical void which we slowly filled with producing companies and a body of plays of our own. But it would be a misunderstanding to suppose that our theatre before that time was meagre or backward. It was not indigenous: plays and most of the players came from beyond our shores, and about the theatre there was always the enchantment of what was brought from afar; but they came in great numbers, and they brought us the best that the stage of the two principal English-speaking theatres had to offer. Although many Canadian plays did get one production, very few remained within the professional repertoire and so will not be dealt with here.[1] Nevertheless our nineteenth-century forbears were by no means theatrically naïve or ill served.

Consideration of the calendars that tell us what audiences patronized in the nineteenth century reveals a heavy concentration of trivial pieces and catchpenny shows, and here again we must not be deceived. At the present time theatrical entertainment in the broadest sense is offered not only in the playhouse, but in the film theatres and by television. A calendar of what is offered to the public in a single month by all three sources would show an immense quantity of entertainment that has little content of imagination, taste, wit, insight, or artistic seriousness and is meant only to pass the time for people who imagine that their wealth of time has no bounds. To judge the theatre of the last century in the light of the theatre today is seriously to misunderstand it. A vast amount of mere pastime has retreated from the playhouse to the film theatre or the TV set, and in spite of the efforts put forward to improve the quality of film and TV entertainment, it will always be so. Why? Because a majority of people do not want imagination, taste, wit, insight, or artistic seriousness in any form, and they have a right to be given what they like, just as people with a finer sense of what the theatre is have a right to be served. But the lovers of intellectually and emotionally demanding theatre now have the playhouse almost to themselves, and the lovers of simpler entertainment need never go near it. In the nineteenth century the theatre had to provide for every taste, and it did so with enthusiasm, if not always with success.

As we look at the nineteenth-century repertoire, therefore, we shall be well advised to separate the offerings into categories, and certainly we must not fall into the error of supposing that because trash predominated, the theatre as a whole was trashy. Nor must we suppose that the same audience went to the local 'opera house' every time it opened its doors.

Most important, we must look at the nineteenth-century repertoire with imaginative sympathy. If some plays that won great audiences seem to us to be preposterous, we may be sure that many popular pieces of our own time will seem equally absurd to audiences a century hence. Drama may profitably be looked at as one aspect of the history of society, as a reflection of what is popularly believed outside the playhouse, of what the age desires, and of what it fears. Many of the plays that were widely accepted during the nineteenth century tell us what the spirit of that time was and what its predominating attitude towards the great concerns of life was. The more we look at their theatre the more we find that what appears to be casual inspection is deceptive, and that the hopes and the fears and the unfocused terrors of our forbears show through the lace curtains of their plays as they do not always show through their novels or their poetry. Reading is a private approach to art, and what the reader will understand and accept is nobody's affair but his own. Theatre and also painting and sculpture are public arts; as we enjoy them we are aware of others about us, and our acceptance and condemnation are affected by public attitudes. Let us not forget that in nineteenth-century theatres, well into the 1870s the auditorium lights were full on all through the performance. Although enjoyment of a play has many aspects of the enjoyment of a dream, it is a dream we experience with our neighbours all around us, and unless we are keenly critical, our attitude towards what we see is a community attitude. What were the community attitudes of Canadian audiences in those playhouses of the past?

The Moral Climate

There was a substantial body of opinion that was utterly opposed to the theatre in any form, for complex reasons that are not simply to be explained as puritanism. The hatred of pretence, of assuming a personality not one's own, of bodying forth actions that had no precise correlative in 'real life' is a complex study, and those who wish to pursue it may do so in Jonas Barish's admirable *The Anti-Theatrical Prejudice* (1981). The theatre was suspect, as a home of what was not wholly serious. Even a sophisticated playgoer like the Rev. Charles Lutwidge Dodgson (Lewis Carroll) can say in the preface to *Sylvie and Bruno* (1889):

Let me pause for a moment to say that I believe this thought of the possibility of death – if calmly and steadily faced – would be one of the best possible tests as to our going to any scene of amusement being right or wrong. If the thought of sudden death acquires, for *you*, a special horror when imagined as happening in a *theatre*, then be very sure the theatre is harmful for *you*, however harmless it may be for others; and that *you* are incurring a deadly peril in going. Be sure the safest rule is that we should not dare to *live* in any scene in which we dare not die.[2]

This a comparatively calm and reasoned expression of a widespread nineteenth-century attitude. But – the farther from Rome, the stupider the priest – many clergymen in Canada West roared against the theatre because they thought that it provoked a frivolous and potentially evil attitude towards life, and in it scenes of immorality were made attractive, sometimes by women, such as Sarah Bernhardt and Lillie Langtry, who were of notoriously unchaste life. Many people who went to the theatre regularly were aware that, in the eyes of their neighbours, they were risking their salvation, and such disapprobation cannot have been without its effect.

Inevitably the theatrical companies felt this disapproval, and their protestations of blamelessness sometimes become distasteful. As will be seen over and over again in the chapter on vaudeville, entertainment of all kinds was advertised as 'suitable for the family,' or as teaching a moral lesson. When Jimmy Brown, in his *Adventures* (1891), tells us that his Pa permitted him to go to the circus (with Pa) because 'the elephant is a Scriptural animal, James, and it cannot help but improve your mind to see him,' the caricature of a prevailing attitude is not extreme. When the leading man and leading woman of a theatrical company were married, it was made known as a guarantee of respect-ability. Even players so high above commonplace criticism as Henry Irving and Ellen Terry, when they travelled on this continent stayed at separate hotels, so that there could be no suspicion that they were associated other than as artists. Nineteenth-century morality was profound in profound people, but there is plenty of evidence that among the masses it was fusty and prurient, and the theatre – which has never been rich in stoics or deep philosophers – had to draw its audiences from the masses. In consequence the theatre sometimes took on a disagreeable smarminess of tone in its public relations. The catchword about *The Black Crook* (1866; performed at Toronto's Royal Opera House in 1876 and again two years later) was '50 ballet girls, damning to the soul to see' – an extraordinary attitude, surely?

This prevalence of a morality primarily concerned with saving the individual soul was at least in part an outcome of the deeply romantic spirit of the century. The teaching of the Wesleys, which created nothing short of a revolution in the way in which the working and middle classes of society regarded themselves, was romantic in spirit, because of its insistence on individual spiritual responsibility, as opposed to the ministrations of a church. The romanticism of the poets, who insisted on their individual response to experience as the ground of their writings, was only a part of an exaltation of the individual that affected the whole of life and culminated, at the end of the century, in the teachings of Sigmund Freud, which carried human-kind into deeper realms of its soul than had been achieved in the past by any but the saints and seers. Romanticism, the cult of the individual, expressed itself in the theatre in the form of melodrama, which concentrates on individual suffering, individual redemption, and the belief in an ultimate righting of individual wrongs best described as poetic justice. Melodrama is more 'moral' in the popular sense of the word than either comedy or tragedy.

Melodrama was not merely a genre of theatrical writing: it was a prevailing spirit that influenced the way in which the nineteenth century looked at life and desired to see life presented in art. The nineteenth-century novel is predominantly melodramatic in its attitudes, and nowhere more so than in the writing of George Eliot. It is the literary art of the novelists that blinds some critics to the melodramatic quality of what they offer, and when they praise the psychological subtlety of the novelists, they forget that it is the melodramatic attitude that makes such insight possible in ways that classically comic or tragic attitudes do not. Comedy may be more adroit, witty, and downright funny, and tragedy may carry its hero higher and into nobler realms of expression, but melodrama can provide both the comic and the tragic aspects of life, side by side, in terms that reflect the ordinary life of ordinary mortals.

That writing for the English-speaking stage in the nineteenth century never achieved the greatness of the contemporary novel is explicable on many grounds, most of which are economic; the wretched pay, and the contempt of the players for writers, kept the geniuses of the novel safely in their writing-rooms and left the theatre to people who rarely rose above the level of hacks.

Nevertheless, the stage thrived, carried to unprecedented heights of popularity by the genius of a succession of splendid players, men and women who performed in the virtuoso mode so popular during the era. Paganini and Liszt had their stage counterparts and it was not so much *Hamlet*, as Booth or Irving as Hamlet, that the public thronged to see. And if *Hamlet* was set aside, and it was *The Fool's Revenge* (1869) or *The Bells* (1871) that occupied the stage, Booth and Irving, splendid as ever, were at the centre, bathed in eerie limelight.

What did they see in their theatres (many in Toronto, but in most towns a single opera house) in Ontario in the nineteenth century? Everything, must be the answer. Plays from New York and London were performed either by travelling troupes or by local stock companies within months of their original appearance. *Our Boys* (1875), H.J. Byron's popular comedy, ran nine performances between 25 November and 4 December 1875 in Toronto's Grand Opera House while it was still in its first run in London. *Carmen*, with the first American singer of that role, Minnie Hauk, was played in Toronto, also at the Grand Opera House, in November 1882, within seven years of its première in Paris (1875) – faster than new operas travel now, as a usual thing. Before 1850, a Toronto playgoer could have seen all the dramas of Lord Byron that ever reached the stage, and nothing in contemporary reports suggests that they were not at least adequately presented. We must rid ourselves of any notion that Ontario was a theatrical backwater in the time of our great-grandparents; the theatres were here, and the audiences were here, and the players came gladly and regularly.

In what follows, the dates appended to plays of the nineteenth century are those of their first productions: readers seeking the first Ontario appearances of a play will find it, customarily, in one of the calendars of Toronto theatre.[3] It has proved impossible to mention plays in chronological order without sacrificing other and more important considerations.

Shakespeare

Shakespeare's plays were offered frequently, in the melodramatic mode the nineteenth century liked. That mode required a concentration on a single character – or at most two – which involved substantial reshaping of the original text. Such cutting raised no compunction among either players or spectators; Shakespeare, if he had been writing for contemporary audiences, would certainly have sharpened up his plays and put the emphasis where it obviously ought to be – right on the star actor. He would also have shortened them and arranged the scenes to allow for plenty of fine scenery, so much to be preferred to descriptive poetry – and so these improvements were made for him. In *The Merchant of Venice* there was no point in playing the final act, in which Shylock does not appear at all, and where Portia is simply allowed some fine poetry, which she has no need of, having knocked 'em with her Mercy Speech in act IV. Get rid of the rubbish, and, when Lorenzo runs off with Jessica, there is room for a Venetian Masque, with plenty of pretty girls in tights; it is also possible to put in a telling scene, which Shakespeare inexplicably forgot, where Shylock returns after that abduction and can knock unawares at the door of his empty house. Robert B. Mantell, to name but one, included non-Shakespeare lines to fatten the roles of his wife and leading lady, Genevieve Hamper.

Hamlet, *Macbeth*, and *Othello* were likewise trimmed here, expanded there, and given the melodramatic emphasis audiences expected and that the virtuoso actors felt to be their due. A Christmas offering of *A Midsummer Night's Dream* promises a 'grand production,' with singing and dancing fairies and splendid Amazons; we can be sure that these would have been fairies in the popular style of the time, which is to say dancing-girls in what we should now recognize as classic ballet dress, and that they sang 'glees' and 'concerted numbers' written by Henry Rowley Bishop, to words from other Shakespeare plays. *Henry V*, with George Rignold, whose role it especially was, offered archaeological splendour as well as Rignold's contemporary waxed moustache. (It is extraordinary that however hard the players and designers laboured to produce an authentic effect of 'olden times,' some contemporary feature always crept in, such as Rignold's moustache, or Salvini's huge walrus moustache, which he displayed as Othello, or the crinolines Ellen Tree wore as Lady Macbeth, when she appeared with her husband Charles Kean.)

Shakespeare, then, was offered in the nineteenth-century mode. And who are we to criticize, who have seen in our own time in Ontario a

Midsummer Night's Dream which seemed chiefly determined to demonstrate that all aristocrats are degenerates and that Oberon is a nasty sexual trickster, not to speak of a *Merry Wives of Windsor* in which Falstaff was a shabby-genteel crook, stealing from an infatuated bourgeoisie? Every age gets the Shakespeare it wants, or that its determined theatre artists think it ought to want.

Not all of Shakespeare was presented, by any means. No plays appeared in full versions. *The Taming of the Shrew* was seen in Garrick's two-act form called *Katherine and Petruchio*, and *Richard III* was always played in the rewritten and melodramatized version of Colley Cibber. The popular plays numbered not more than ten, and in addition another four – *King John, Measure for Measure, Richard II,* and *Antony and Cleopatra* – made occasional appearances. The plays most often presented were those that could most effectively be accommodated to a star actor. This fact doubtless accounts for the fact that *Twelfth Night* was rarely seen.

For the serious playgoer there was, as well as Shakespeare, a large body of plays which may be defined as Drama but within that compendious description fall into at least three well-defined categories.

Costume Drama

The first of these categories was Costume Drama, and, as its name implies, its scenes were laid in periods of history of picturesque appeal, like the reign of Louis XIII in Bulwer-Lytton's *Richelieu* (1839), or the early Napoleonic period in the same author's ever-blooming *The Lady of Lyons* (1838), or Renaissance Italy in Tom Taylor's *The Fool's Revenge* (1869), which was a reworking of Hugo's *Le Roi s'amuse* (1832). The Reign of Terror was popular and was the scene of Watts Philip's *The Dead Heart* (1859), *The Two Orphans* (1874) by d'Ennery and Cormon (1874), and – somewhat later in historical period – *Plot and Passion* (1853), by Tom Taylor. In Sheridan Knowles's *Virginius* (1820) the scene is defined as 'chiefly Rome,' and from contemporary portraits we see that the characters are dressed in what the nineteenth century thought appropriate to Romans, with the costumes of the ladies inclining towards Victorian taste. So also in Maria Lovell's popular *Ingomar the Barbarian* (1851) we see that the costumes of the barbarians consist of short shifts, skins wolfish or possibly doggish, and the pink 'fleshings' with which the nineteenth century simulated, without actually displaying, bare legs. There was no limit to the pillaging of history that went on in order to provide backgrounds for Costume Drama, or to the assiduity of actors and managers in seeking verisimilitude of dress, in so far as popular taste would permit it.

Actors prided themselves on the skill with which they could assume the dress and deportment of past ages. They learned the art of wearing costume, and they learned fine manners; the management of a cloak, or a feathered hat, or a train gave keen satisfaction to their audiences and was a substantial part of the pleasure of going to the play. When Richelieu gathered his scarlet robes about him, or the miserly Louis XI mumbled over the lead images of saints on his disgracefully shabby hat, or the evil Fouché in *Plot and Passion* showed how a villain – as opposed to a gentleman – took snuff, it was a significant detail of the show and did much to plump up the meagreness of the dialogue. Thoughtful rehearsal went into such 'business,' as in the moment in the first act of *The Corsican Brothers* when Fabien Dei Franchi, without appearing to give the matter any attention, rolls himself a cigarette with one hand, and lights it with a flint and steel. Elegance was greatly appreciated in a player; it was called 'polish,' and to be a polished actor was to shine indeed. It is not for us to laugh, though we may smile nostalgically; polish is not much in evidence in our theatre.

Drama these costume pieces certainly were, and many of them were superior melodrama, such as *The Corsican Brothers* (1852) mentioned above. Its action hangs upon the resemblance of twin brothers, both of whom love the same French lady, though only one of them goes to Paris to seek her; when he is killed in a duel by a man who attempts to compromise her, the brother who has remained at home is aware of it in a vision, goes at once to Paris, finds the murderer, and kills him. This piece, with its famous Corsican Trap, by means of which the dead brother was enabled to appear mysteriously to his twin, its eerie musical score, its evocation of psychic sympathy, and its theme of renunciation and chivalry, was played by many of the best romantic actors of the nineteenth century. To play both the Dei Franchi brothers – it was that popular dramatic device, a 'dual role' – it was necessary to be a fine swordsman and to have the quality of implacable vengeance which made the final dagger fight terrible to the onlookers. The best players of the nineteenth century could dance, duel in several fashions, and make love with style; the training was arduous and the effect was of careless masculine superiority. For the actresses the fan, the handkerchief, and the art of weeping real tears had the same sort of importance. Style and polish partnered emotional evocation.

For the actresses also there were many plays in which their male supporters were little more than lay figures. Consider *Ingomar* (1851), in which a Greek girl, Parthenia, subdues Ingomar, a noble barbarian, by her pretty feminine arts of making garlands, which prove to be unbreakable chains, and by the iteration of the motto of the play:

What love is, if thou wouldst be taught,
Thy heart must teach alone –
Two souls with but a single thought,
Two hearts that beat as one.[4]

But although Parthenia teaches this to Ingomar, in practice as well as
in words, it is he who speaks it at the end of the play, so that we may
suppose that honours are even. Or, alternatively, that the noble savage,
having been reduced to a Greek city-dweller, had simply learned his
lesson.

Not all Costume Drama offered pictures of fashionable life. *The
Corsican Brothers* in its first act showed the simple dignity of a
Corsican manor, later contrasted with the Balzacian atmosphere of
fashionable Paris. Irving's very popular drama *The Bells* (1871), which
he would never allow to be spoken of as melodrama, took place in the
bourgeois surroundings of an Alsatian inn, where the atmosphere of
Alsace was emphasized by the use of folk tunes in the strongly
atmospheric music written by Etienne Singla.

In all such dramas, although the period and costume might be of a
past age, the morality and the language in which it is expressed are
very much of the nineteenth century. A feature of these plays is a kind
of 'period' language, which suggests the speech of an earlier time,
without actually going to great pains to reproduce it. This is a fustian
prose, such as is found, for instance, in Moncrieff's *Rochester; or King
Charles the Second's Merry Days* (1818), in which something like the
speech of Restoration drama is attempted, without any of the Restoration freedom of expression or breadth of wit. Such stage language was
sometimes contemptuously referred to as 'tushery,' because it made
frequent use of words such as 'tush,' and 'faugh,' and 'hoity-toity.'
Noel Coward particularly cherished a line from *The Scarlet Pimpernel*:
'Hoity-toity, Citizen Alice, what in the world are ye doing in Calais?'
But in the main it was just high-flown speech of no particular period,
though certainly not contemporary. Here is a scrap of tushery that
concludes the popular drama *Lady Clancarty* (1874) by Tom Taylor,
which was seen at Toronto's Grand Opera House in November 1884
with Mrs Morrison in the title role:

Clancarty: What say'st thou, sweetheart, canst thou sacrifice court and
country for thy husband?

Lady Clancarty: My court is where thou art. My country is in thine arms.

(Embrace)

This admirable sentiment is Victorian, rather than of the time of William of Orange, which it is supposed to reflect. We may presume that such dialogue gave the spectators a reassuring sensation that as things were in their day, so things had always been.

An interesting subspecies of Costume Drama is that which concerned itself with famous players of the past, who were always represented as superior beings, artists in feeling, and greatly to be preferred to either the aristocracy or the plutocracy. A favourite was Tom Robertson's *David Garrick* (1860), in which, without any historical warrant whatever, the great actor is represented as attempting to disgust a beautiful girl who loves him by an assumption of drunkenness, in which he shows himself vastly more elegant than the bourgeois company before whom he makes it; but in the end love conquers, and the girl's vulgar merchant father acknowledges that the player whom he has patronized is the better man. In Tom Taylor's *Masks and Faces* (1852) the heroine is Peg Woffington, who is scorned by the aristocracy for being an actress and loving somewhat indiscriminately, but she has a great heart and a distinguished mind, and at the end of the play she appeals to the audience to understand that these are the attributes of the artist and must be given their due. Another popular play of this sort was *Adrienne Lecouvreur* (1849), adapted from the French of Scribe and Legouvé, in which Helena Modjeska enjoyed one of her triumphs. She performed it in Toronto's Grand Opera House in March 1878. In the play the French tragedienne, having displayed her superiority as an actress by humiliating her rival, at whom she recites an apposite fable of Lafontaine and, having won the love of the spirited Count de Saxe, dies of the rival's poison. But before doing so she has shown that a fine actress can beat the aristocrats at their own game, whether it be love, intrigue, or wit. These plays, which make such extravagant assertions for the players, reflect the uneasiness that was felt all through the century about the claim of theatre people to be considered artists and acceptable members of society.

Drama of Modern Life

The second aspect of drama includes plays that were intended as representations of contemporary life, even though some of them might have been several decades on the stage. One of this sort was *The Stranger*, written in German by Kotzebue in 1789 and first presented in English in 1798. Its theme, which is that the breakdown of a marriage may be due to faults on both sides, was considered modern and somewhat daring until the coming of Ibsen, and the principal female role of Mrs Haller was popular with many actresses, the last and greatest of whom was Sarah Bernhardt. The problems of women in a restrictive society provided themes for many plays of lasting success; a favourite was *Frou-Frou*, translated from the French of Meilhac and Halévy (1869) by Augustin Daly and advertised as 'A Comedy of Powerful Human Interest.' But a comedy it is not; for poor Frou-Frou (so called because of the enchanting rustle of her silken skirts) is made a fool of by the men in her life, discovers it, suffers for it, and finally dies because of it. It is a precursor of *A Doll's House* (1878), handled by a dramatist with his eye on the popular theatre; Frou-Frou is a lovable, misguided child, rather than a woman, stunted by uncomprehending love.

Many of these plays had as heroines women who were, for some reason, at odds with popular morality. Many were what society called 'fallen women' and thus were of particular interest; for although in the nineteenth century plenty of women fell and subsequently picked themselves up again, they could not do so on the stage. Wilkie Collins's two successes, *The Woman in White* (1871) and *The New Magdalen* (1873), both performed in Toronto in 1874, offered sensational versions of this theme. Most popular of all was *Camille*, as the English version of Dumas *fils*' play *La Dame aux camélias* (1852) was called. It is a rare combination of an archetypal theme, deep feeling, and literary skill, and it strikes into the hearts of playgoers of all kinds. Women weep at it because they feel that they, too, might have sinned beautifully and paid their debt with distinguished grace; men weep at it because every man nourishes in his heart some whisper of a romantic, ill-fated *affaire*, even if it is no more than an aspiration never to be fulfilled; the morality of the piece is of that never-failing literary kind that permits the spectators to eat their cake (by delighting in the heroine's charm and fated beauty) and have it too (when she dies of tuberculosis, remorse, and quite simply from being too good for this world). As *La Traviata* ('The Erring One,' 1853) the play is still a perennial favourite on the opera stage. The version usually seen in Canada was that of Matilda Heron, and it betrays the original, partly from Victorian American prudery, and partly from a want of understanding of the Parisian scene.

Melodrama

The third category of drama that was offered in Ontario theatres is melodrama, the fast-moving, highstrained exhibitions of adventure, conflict with fate, and poetic justice. Favourites still known by name to people who have never seen them on stage are *Uncle Tom's Cabin* (in many versions after 1852), *East Lynne* (1865), and *Lady Audley's Secret* (1863). All are coarsely adapted from popular novels. All have a primal appeal because they present in bold colours characters of never-failing interest; Uncle Tom is the Suffering Servant and Little Eva is the Miraculous Child who brings blessing on the household; Lady Isobel Carlyle is the Erring but Great-Hearted Woman who pays for her sin with her life and the life of another Miraculous Child, Little Willy; Lady Audley is the Unrepentant and Resourceful Villainess – womanhood on the rampage. These plays go for the jugular; there is no attempt at well-rounded character or carefully motivated incident. Their prolonged and widespread success has, perhaps, some message for theorists of the drama who spin a gossamer thread instead of a sturdy cable of hemp.

Here, perhaps, is the place to make mention of a small but popular group of Temperance Plays, of which the most successful and long-lived was *Ten Nights In A Bar Room*, adapted in 1858 by William W. Pratt from the novel by T.S. Arthur. Pratt, who knew his business as a melodramatist, contrasted the pitiful drunkard Joe Morgan, whose little daughter Mary dies in a tavern brawl, with a Yankee comic man, Sample Switchell, whose drunkenness is a source of amusement. This device permits the spectators to deplore vice, while laughing at that perennial butt, the funny drunk. In the last act both Morgan and Switchell reform and have the puritan reward – material prosperity. The play is coarsely but powerfully contrived.

By no means all melodrama is of such rough workmanship. Douglas Jerrold's *Black-Eyed Susan* was popular in Canada, as it was everywhere else in the English-speaking world after its appearance in 1829; the tale of the true-blue sailor who risks death rather than see his wife dishonoured is very good drama. So also is *The Silver King* (1882), so warmly commended by Matthew Arnold, and *The Ticket-of-Leave Man* (1863) because it makes a fine plea, in terms of its time, for a man who has taken a false step and wants to re-establish himself in society. Nor can we look down on the work of that genius of melodrama, Dion Boucicault, whose skilled contrivances of plot are cloaked under picturesque scenes and characters that first-rate actors were glad to sink their teeth into and make their own.

Boucicault appears in many guises. In *Jessie Brown, or the Siege of Lucknow* (1858) he touches the patriotic string, in the tale of the humble Scottish girl who keeps up the spirits of a beleaguered fortress by her insistence (aided by a power of hearing nothing less than magical) that the Highlanders are coming to lift the siege. In *The Octoroon* (1859) he does an extraordinary feat of tightrope walking in a play, which pleased both North and South, on the touchy subject of slavery and miscegenation. In *The Colleen Bawn* (1860), *Arrah-na-Pogue* (1864), and *The Shaughraun* (1875) he produced three romances of Irish life which gave pleasure in many professional presentations and could not be wholly extinguished by the most heavy-handed amateur presentation on uncounted St Patrick's Day celebrations. It was Boucicault who said that good plays are not written, but rewritten, and although this cannot be taken as a general truth, he proved its applicability to the sort of sure-fire, well-contrived melodrama he himself put on the stage and in which he played leading roles.

There were innumerable melodramas which we can read now only as curiosities, and one such was *The Dog of Montargis*, which first appeared in 1814 and lasted as long as a trained dog could be found to play the leading part. This sagacious, morally alert animal discovers and brings down the murderer of his master, springing at the throat of the villain who falls, screaming, 'Call off the dog! Call off the dog!' in his agony. (Cynics who said that the dog was leaping at a bundle of chopped meat concealed in the villain's cravat were beneath the notice of decent playgoers.) The drama in which picturesque affliction is exploited may be represented by T.E. Wilks's *The Maniac Lover* (1839) and *The Dumb Girl of Genoa* (1840) by J. Farrell. *Monte Cristo* must be mentioned, if only to assure Ontario readers that Eugene O'Neill's father, James, did not neglect us in his innumerable tours in that indestructible but crudely made romance, carved out of Dumas' novel by Charles Fechter in 1868. It is of interest that Fechter, when he visited Toronto in July and again in October of 1875, played in classical drama, yielding towards melodrama only in a favourite play of his, *The Duke's Motto* (1863) by John Brougham, and *Don César de Bazan* (1844), a curious offshoot of Hugo's *Ruy Blas*.

All the above melodramas come from Europe or Britain, but the United States was not behindhand with a type of melodrama particularly its own, the prevailing theme of which was that country dwellers were of unassailable virtue (except for the girls, who were frail, because of an excess of trusting heart), and that life in the city tended to corrupt. One that was much admired was *Hazel Kirke* by Steele Mackaye (1880) which reads oddly now, because the harsh and unforgiving morality exhibited by Miller Kirke is no longer accepted as assurance of a strong character. Nor can we quite swallow the notion that humble, rustic parents produce daughters who are paragons of high breeding and without whom an aristocratic suitor cannot consent to live.

Other examples were *The Old Homestead* (1887) by Denman

Thompson, in which the erring child is not a daughter but a son, who has gone to New York and become a drunkard. In the 1870s Thompson ran a saloon and dance hall in Toronto where he created the one-act rural sketch *Joshua Whitcomb*, which he later developed into *The Old Homestead*.[5] Later came *Way Down East* (1898), which is wholly conventional, with a city seducer, a staunch rural lover, a father in whom morality assumes the proportions of a disease, and a strong assertion that however frail girls may be, they are better off on the land than in the city. This sort of melodrama made a strong appeal to audiences who had some association with country life, having very probably abandoned it without losing their conviction that the farm was the abiding place of all true worth. Ontario was full of such people, and their descendants are still to be found, often in politics.

Old Comedy

Turning to comedy, let us look first at that category of the genre which was, in the nineteenth century, called Old Comedy. The term referred to a small group of plays that gave a special sort of pleasure; for they were not Costume Drama but genuine plays from the eighteenth century that had not lost their lustre. Had, indeed, gained in attraction, because they answered the call for nostalgia (by no means always a reprehensible emotion) and took their audiences back to an eighteenth century that had been idealized, and that they beheld in the mode of the pretty pictures of Kate Greenaway and Randolph Caldecott's delightful illustrations of popular classics such as *John Gilpin*. The yearning towards the eighteenth century was part of the yearning for England – England as Home, as the Great Good Place – which was a part of the psychology of many Ontarians during the whole of their lives. Old Comedy presented an England that probably never was, but that was none the less real to the imagination.

The repertoire of Old Comedy was not large. Sheridan's two comedies, *The Rivals* (1774) and *The School for Scandal* (1777), headed the list of favourites, along with Goldsmith's *She Stoops to Conquer* (1773). Add to these *The Heir at Law* (1797) by George Colman the younger, and *Wild Oats* (1794) by John O'Keefe (called 'the British Molière' by no less a judge than Hazlitt, and of whom it was said that he sent 'the audience laughing to their beds'), and the list is pretty well exhausted. But the appeal of these plays was strong all through the century, and it is not hard to see why, quite apart from their appeal to nostalgia; they are written with literary skill, in language that is as fresh as the language of comedy can be. The sentimentality never gets out of hand, and humour can bear frequent repetition, whether it be the acute verbal wit of Sheridan, or the humour that expresses itself in keenly but indulgently observed character, as in Goldsmith and O'Keefe. Humour of this golden sort was uncommon in the plays of the nineteenth century, save in rare instances. There was a quality of sheer delight to be derived from Old Comedy, which the actors emphasized (for many of them were specialists in this genre) by a purity of speech and an elegance and distinction of address that had its counterpart in the acting of Costume Drama. An actor of the nineteenth century who wished to equip himself thoroughly in his art sought experience in Old Comedy; for it taught him much that was useful in anything he chose to play afterward.

Not only the pleasant England of Old Comedy, but the high-coloured, melodramatic, grotesque England of Dickens had its place in the theatre, and there were countless adaptations of the more popular novels of the great genius of the age. To read these plays is puzzling and disappointing, for they are hacked out of long works, and the quality of the original writing has not been – probably could not be – transferred to the stage. Merely to speak Dickens's dialogue is not the way to make Dickens stageworthy, for so much of his power is conveyed in descriptive writing and interjected comment on character. We know, however, that it was the actors who made these poor adaptations attractive, because they enabled their spectators to *see* what they had read with so much pleasure; George Fawcett Rowe in his own adaptation of *David Copperfield*, called *Little Em'ly*, enabled his audiences to see and hear Micawber as presented by an actor who could make manifest in appearance and deportment what was missing in the lines. The only play written by Dickens (in which he collaborated with Wilkie Collins) to achieve success on the stage was *No Thoroughfare* (1867), in which none of his remarkable characters appears, but which provided a vehicle for the fine actor Charles Fechter. Who, in our time, thinks of that play when they think of Dickens?

Nineteenth-Century Comedy

Because theatre was an imported pleasure in Ontario, the social attitudes it reflected were imported also; nor can we imagine that this gave any disquiet to the playgoers, who regarded themselves as part of the English-speaking world and followers of a widespread moral and social code. In what follows we shall discuss, necessarily in somewhat general terms, the nineteenth-century comedy they enjoyed, which was in no respect different from what was acceptable to their contemporaries in the United States or in England. The comment was attributed to Henry Irving, by the late Hector Charlesworth, that a Toronto audience greatly resembled an Edinburgh audience – which meant that it was not a London audience, but a somewhat soberer, educated, and, in the best sense, provincial audience. What was the comedy such an audience would receive with satisfaction?

Comedy comes as close as it dares to forbidden subjects, and in the nineteenth century sex was the forbidden theme that nevertheless demanded discussion. As a usual thing nineteenth-century comedies contain one love story that ends happily; a young couple, charming in every way, are brought together in the end, and it is assumed that they are going to live happily ever after. The truly comic content of such pieces suggests that this hope is a triumph of optimism over experience, for quarrelling and disaffected couples are found everywhere. Husbands yearn for sexual freedom, sometimes find it, and are brought to heel by clever or tearful wives. Wives flirt, husbands are outraged, and in the end it proves that all is well and the matrimonial boat has not sprung a serious leak. Real adultery, in comedy, is not to be admitted as a possibility. The suggestion that a hero might, before his marriage, have had an association with another girl – usually of a lower class – is not to be endured, and though a nice girl may flirt innocently with other men before her marriage, she loves but once and then forever – or until she reaches the age of the ladies who are having trouble with their husbands elsewhere in the comedy.

These beliefs are simply conventions, and are neither more absurd nor more seriously considered in real life than the notion that people in comedy never work, and that their money is generated by magic – unless, of course, they are comically impecunious, which is thought to be a great joke.

Money as a source of social disruption is a permissible theme, however, and is finely handled in Bulwer-Lytton's comedy *Money* (1840); it was a favourite in Canada throughout the nineteenth century, though the theme cannot have had much local application, because rich inheritances were rare in colonial society. A refreshing breath of harsh common sense about money appears later in the century, with *The Mighty Dollar* (1875) by Benjamin E. Woolf. This comedy, which enjoyed in all more than 2,500 performances, concerned a venal American congressman, the Hon. Bardwell Slote, whose perpetual crooked scheming is what gives movement to the play; his naked greed is refreshing after so much pretension of scorn for money in other comedies. The play was influential, too, in providing North American slang with some new expressions: PDQ (pretty damn quick) and OK (orl kerrect) (which was popularized by the play, if it did not originate with it) and DDS (damn dirty shake) which was what Slote was always receiving from his fellow conspirators against the public good. Slote was played by W.J. Florence, a fine comedian, and his wife played a social-climbing widow, Mrs Gilflory, whose frequent request, 'Excuse my French,' has also passed into the vernacular. The Florences twice performed *The Mighty Dollar* in Ontario, in 1878 and again in 1883.

Another play which must be mentioned because it was often seen is *Our American Cousin* (1858), which was famous not only because it was the play Abraham Lincoln was watching (and apparently enjoying) when he was assassinated, but because E.A. Sothern built up the small role of Lord Dundreary, a silly-ass Englishman, into a creation that eventually made him the star of the piece and led to later spin-offs, as they would now be called, such as *Dundreary Married and Done For* (1876). Sothern toured Ontario with both plays in 1875 and returned with *Our American Cousin* in 1880. But *Our American Cousin* was an English play, by Tom Taylor, and on the whole Ontario received its comedy from England, and lighter entertainment from the United States. The popular comedy in British North America was what was popular 'at home,' which is to say the work of industrious professional playwrights such as H.J. Byron, T.W. Robertson, and W.S. Gilbert.

Byron's work has not endured and is of interest here because it is so intensely characteristic of its time. He was a thorough professional, achieving success after initial failure by insistence on what the critic Joseph Knight calls 'homeliness and healthiness,' combined with 'pun and verbal pleasantry,' although 'character and probability were continually sacrificed to the strain after a laugh.'[6] He wrote an enormous body of work, some of which was seen here. *Our Boys* (1875) was the greatest success; it ran for four years in London and was presented in Toronto while a production was still on the London stage. Mrs Morrison's Grand Opera House company gave nine performances in 1875. It is homely and healthy in that it concerns two young men, both sons of wealthy fathers, who give up family assistance in order to make their own way in life and win the respect of the homely and healthy girls they love. The two fathers are contrasted roles for two comedians; one is a starchy aristocrat, the other a butterman who has made his pile and is crammed with homely wisdom and nobility of soul, though his manners and grammar are of the low-comedy order. Of course the young men triumph; for they exist for a year by their own efforts, though they seem to come close to poverty, and the fathers are delighted with their boys. The girls, after being reassured that, appearances to the contrary, their beaux have not been associated with any loose women during their year of trial, are satisfied as well. The comedy now makes somewhat curious reading, since the social attitudes are of a time long gone. But that is precisely why we must show them understanding indulgence.

What made *Our Boys* so popular? Exactly what made plays like *Peg O' My Heart* (1912) and *Abie's Irish Rose* (1922) popular in their day: it struck a note that was resonantly and entirely of its time. It offered on the stage not what was observable fact, but a dream of what the audiences wished were true, spiced with enough contemporary fun to give it a spurious air of reality.

Another of Byron's plays enjoyed popularity in Ontario. This was *Uncle Dick's Darling* (1869), which Mrs Morrison offered in Toronto in 1875 with a visiting star, no less than the great J.L. Toole, who was praised in the local press for his 'irresistible drollery' (*Mail*, 4 May 1875). It has as its theme a young woman who seems to scorn her humble lover and her benefactor – another character made comic by his vulgar manners and want of grammar – but this lapse from desirable behaviour is shown later to be nothing but Uncle Dick's horrible dream, from which he wakes to find his darling as true as ever. Something is striving to be said here about contemporary social attitudes, but the stage convention that low-comedians may bring up models of delicacy and propriety silences the criticism. The snobbery in both plays appears to have been greatly to the liking of audiences that cannot have been wholly composed of the leisure class.

The plays of T.W. Robertson are of finer workmanship than those of Byron, and they are too well known to students of the theatre to call for extended comment. *Ours* (1866) and *Caste* (1867) were popular here, the former doubtless because of its high-hearted celebration of Britain's military glory and the daring appearance of several English girls in the midst of the Crimean War, and the latter because it was an excellent play, and remains so still, and questions social convention far more bravely than Byron was to do nearly ten years later. The theme of *Caste* is that kind hearts may very well be more than coronets and simple faith than Norman blood, but perhaps it is as well to watch your step and make sure you marry the right sister.

Robertson's *School* (1869) was also popular in Canada, and this appeal should puzzle no one, for it is a charming treatment of the Cinderella theme.

W.S. Gilbert must be mentioned, since at least four of his plays were popular in Ontario in their day, before his reputation as a librettist had obscured his by no means trivial achievement as a dramatist.

Pygmalion and Galatea (1871) was successful everywhere, though to a modern reader it seems to bring a suburban Victorian morality into a classical setting; Pygmalion's wife discovers that her husband apparently has Another Woman in his studio, and she nags about it, rather like Mrs Caudle. But Gilbert was not at ease with commonplace morality, and he gives greater pleasure in fantasies such as *The Palace of Truth* (1870), the whimsically charming *Sweethearts* (1874), and the truly comic *Tom Cobb* (1875), which contains one of the best grotesque families in all drama. Popular also was the still fresh and funny *Engaged* (1877), though how the satire of Scottish duplicity and cupidity in that comedy sat with Canadian audiences, to many of whom Scotland was the Great Good Place, we can only guess.

Further consideration of comedy would be repetitious, for popular comedy rarely explores new themes. Perhaps it should be mentioned that in 1877 Grand Opera House audiences in Toronto saw the typical and forgettable *Tears, Idle Tears*, by the theatre critic Clement Scott, in which the great attraction was the British matinee idol H.J. Montagu; when we look at photographs of Montagu now, we may be at a loss to understand his extraordinary attraction for women, for ideals of masculine beauty are even more fashionable than those that define the beauty of women. His ringlets and curled moustache are no longer *à la mode*. But at his benefit in Toronto, 23 March 1877, where he appeared in Scott's play attired in a 'velvet jacket and puce-coloured trousers,' every lady was presented with an autographed copy of his photograph, and the place was mobbed. That has a very modern sound; in comedy, as well as in drama, the star was frequently more of an attraction than the play.

Farce

A curious instance of time lag presents itself when we consider the farce popular in Ontario during our century, but it is observable that farce, like wine, can improve with age. It was a particularly popular mode of theatre among amateurs, and a particularly enthusiastic group of amateurs in the nineteenth century were the military. As Leslie O'Dell describes in more detail, they seem always to have been 'getting up some theatricals,' which was the phrase of the time. The spirit in which they did so is brilliantly reflected in the novels of Charles Lever, *Harry Lorrequer* (1839) and *Charles O'Malley* (1841) offering examples. Rehearsals and performances seem to have been more high spirited than professional, but the audiences at the performance (at which the regimental band invariably played, by kind permission of the officer commanding) were delighted, because they knew, entertained, and frequently were in love with, the actors.

English farce during much of the century bore the imprint of C.J. Mathews (1803–78), the most distinguished light comedian of the time. He tinkered with the pieces in which he appeared until it might almost be said that he wrote them, and most of them contained at least one long monologue in which he addressed the audience directly, sitting astraddle a chair, raising laugh after laugh with jokes that arose from his charm of personality and his brilliant timing, rather than from any inherent humour. He had many imitators, professional and amateur, and apparently a great many young officers saw themselves in the Mathews pattern. *Used Up* (1844) was a perennial favourite; for in it the Mathews character, imagining himself guilty of a murder, is compelled to disguise himself as a farm labourer, with effects, in the term of the time, 'inexpressibly droll.'

Officers stationed in Canada imitated Mathews, in this play, and in *Little Toddlekins* (1852) in which a young man wishes to marry a girl of suitable age but is embarrassed by the presence of his ward, a fat woman much older than himself and of uncertain temper who is the Little Toddlekins of the title. *My Wife's Mother* (1833) is another farce whose nature may be inferred from its title. Such farces were innumerable, skilfully contrived, and just the thing for amateur performances of a strong society flavour and for young officers who fancied themselves as possessing that 'genteel comedy in your walk and manner' combined with 'touch-and-go farce in your laugh' that Mr Vincent Crummles immediately detected in Nicholas Nickleby. Just the thing for *Raising the Wind* (1802), in which Irving made an early success, and for *Ici On Parle Français* (1859), for *Old Gooseberry* (1869), and for *The Private Secretary* (1885), which was adapted, unusual for farce, from the German, and, of course, for *Charley's Aunt* (1892). The dates do not matter; for farce exists in a world less linked with time than is the world of comedy. All these, and dozens of others, were the farce offerings of our nineteenth-century theatre, and very rarely do they seem to have failed to rouse enthusiasm. But of sex, the principal farce theme in Europe, they spoke in guarded terms.

Opera, Light Opera, and Opéra Bouffe

Such a survey as this is not, perhaps, the best place for a consideration of opera as it appeared in Ontario during the nineteenth century, since the subject properly belongs to a history of music. But as opera had a special place in nineteenth-century estimation because of the social

Picton, *Grand Mogul* presented by the Picton Amateur Operatic Company, 1908

cachet attaching to it, and as it was not so definitely cut off from other theatrical entertainment as is now the case, something should be said, if only to indicate the direction taken by the taste of the time. The type of opera that was seen most frequently was French opera, Gounod's *Faust* (1859) being the undoubted favourite, surpassing even Auber's *Fra Diavolo* (1830). The latter was an *opéra comique*, and in considering the operatic taste of the century, it is not always easy to understand the distinction between this piece and Donizetti's *Don Pasquale* (1810), which was billed as an opera, unless one accepts the rule, which is not invariable, that *opéra comique* or 'light opera' usually included some spoken dialogue. Donizetti's *Daughter of the Regiment* (1840) is classed as opera, but the very popular *La Fille de Madame Angot* (1796), which was equally high spirited and performed in an English translation (like *The Daughter of the Regiment*), was unquestionably 'light.' Verdi's *Ernani* (1830) and *Il Trovatore* (1853) were operas by reason of the seriousness of their melodramatic themes, but Auber's *King for a Day* (1852), which was played in an English translation by the industrious Boucicault, was not taken so seriously. Thomas's *Mignon* (1866), sung in French, was opera, as were *Lucia di Lammermoor* (1835), Boito's *Mefistofele* (1868), and Rossini's *Guillaume Tell* (1829), but we may be surprised to find the same description applied to Michael Balfe's *The Rose of Castile* (1857).

Mention of Balfe reminds us that unquestionably the most popular operas in Ontario during the nineteenth century were the three

Hamilton, *The Mikado*, Grand Opera House, c.1900

described satirically by Sir Thomas Beecham as 'the English Ring' –
The Bohemian Girl (1843) by Balfe, *Maritana* (1845) by Vincent
Wallace, founded on the melodrama *Don César de Bazan* by d'Ennery
and Dumanoir but popular in English in a version by A'Beckett and
Mark Lemon, and *The Lily of Killarney* (1860) by Julius Benedict,
founded on Boucicault's *The Colleen Bawn*. They were offered again
and again, and their most popular arias – 'When Other Lips,' 'Yes,
Let Me Like A Soldier Fall,' and 'The Moon Hath Raised Her Lamp
Above' – were favourites in the concert hall and the drawing-room
alike. They were opera for a public with a taste for melodrama and a
sweet tooth for music.

As a period curiosity of drama and music it should be recorded that
on 12 April 1882 University College in the University of Toronto
presented Sophocles' tragedy *Antigone* in Greek, with music which had
been adapted from the works of Mendelssohn, a combination of genres
unquestionably novel and seemingly impressive to its audience.

In the realm of undoubted 'light' opera the favourite during the latter
part of our century was *Les Cloches de Corneville* (1877) by Planquette, which was also known as *The Chimes of Normandy*. It was
performed many times by professional companies and also by
amateurs, doubtless because its innocently romantic plot could not
possibly offend anyone, or bring a blush to the cheek of any Ontario
girl who was asked to assist in 'getting it up' in aid of a local charity.

Such innocence was vitally necessary to distinguish a light musical show from the dreaded *opéra bouffe*, which had a very bad name. The monarch in the realm of *opéra bouffe* was Jacques Offenbach, and his works were known everywhere in the world, with delight by some and with horror by many who had not actually heard them but had heard about them. Even so advanced a woman as Louisa May Alcott warned young men against *opéra bouffe*; attendance at the theatre when it was offered could, it appeared, dangerously weaken the moral fibre. Their success only made them more dangerous, because more enticing. In Ontario the youth of the period were exposed to the dangers of *Orphée aux Enfers* (1858), *La Belle Hélène* (1864), *Barbe-Bleu* (1866), *La Grande Duchesse de Gérolstein* (1867), *La Princesse de Trébizonde* (1869), and *La Périchole* (1874). It was not simply that they involved a generous display of leg – though we all know where legs lead to – but the underlying spirit of the operettas was hedonistic and cynical and the music was irresistible, whereas *The Chimes of Normandy* was insipid. François Mauriac declared, 'The laughter I hear in Offenbach's music is that of the Empress Charlotte, gone mad.' But if Offenbach was wicked, he shared with other wicked geniuses a powerful attraction, and was a refreshing change from the prevailing spirit of Ontario during the era of his earliest popularity.

No such reproach was brought against the operettas of Gilbert and Sullivan; their popularity was unfailing. One may wonder how it was that the moralists who condemned the sexual implication of *opéra bouffe* missed the quality of the Gilbertian heroines, who are not all that they appear to be at first sight. Over and over again these girls, who seem to be so winsome, so wanting in worldly experience or guile, express at some point in the libretto the estimation of themselves that Yum-Yum puts forward in *The Mikado*:

Ah, pray make no mistake,
  We are not shy
We're very wide awake,
  The Moon and I.

Gilbert's heroines, and his sometimes brutally drawn portraits of man-hungry, middle-aged women, suggest an attitude towards femininity that Victorians might have found startling, if they had understood what was being said to them. But it was the most extraordinary of Gilbert's gifts that he could gild the bitterest pill and make his hearers swallow it as a bonbon.

Hamilton's Kate Gunn in *The Mikado*, c. 1896

Minstrels and Burlesque

Our forbears had no squeamishness about what is now called racism. Every nation had its genially derogatory description: Scots were stingy, Irish wrong-headed, Dutch stupid, Jews crafty, French women-chasers, Yankees boastful, and even the English had their caricature figure in Lord Dundreary. Negroes were unfailingly funny because of their supposed ignorant simplicity, which tumbled into a kind of wit. Minstrel shows were to be seen right through the century, and their form changed little: after an initial scene where the whole company sat in a half-circle around the Interlocutor – a white man of supposedly superior understanding and culture – and answered his questions or sang and danced at his behest, the show consisted of a succession of individual acts, or brief sketches, and culminated in a Grand Finale in which old minstrel favourites and the hit tunes of the day were combined. Sometimes the actors were real blacks, sometimes white men in a special kind of ridiculous black-face, in which a huge white mouth shone forth from a face as black as a stove, surmounted by a black wool wig.

There were a few black companies of a superior order, such as the Great Slave Troupe of Jubilee Singers – '20 Genuine Coloured Artists' – who sang slave songs and spirituals beautifully and affectingly. Readers of the once popular *Helen's Babies*, by John Habberton (1876), will recall the effect on the two little boys of hearing the Jubilee Singers:

> Mary and Martha's just gone 'long
>   To hear those charming bells

and they cannot have been alone in their response. But, upon the whole, minstrel shows were simple entertainments in a vaudeville style, ranging from those that were advertised for family attendance to those that offered rougher fare.

In addition to the many professional tours described by Gerald Lenton-Young, amateurs frequently got up minstrel shows, usually to raise money for worthy causes, but perhaps more honestly to give pleasure, and feel pleasure, in high-jinks and self-display. Such 'home talent' shows were too much a feature of the entertainment world of the nineteenth century to be neglected here, and although their atmosphere is not easily recaptured, we know that they contained a great many jokes of local reference and brought in the names of people who were well known to the audience and might actually be present in the theatre. But such jokes had to be strung together on some sort of cord, and happily many books have survived that tell us what this connective material was like. A brief example will suffice:

Mister Interlocutor is interviewing Rastus, a potential cook:

- I want a chef. Give me your idea of a menu for lunch.
- With the greatest of meningitis. Now first, I'll give them Gold Soup.
- Gold Soup! How on earth do you make Gold Soup?
- With fourteen carrots.
- I see. And what to follow?
- Herring *à la Maître d'Hôtel*.
- How's that?
- Soused.
- What sort of pudding?
- I'd give 'em Hop-It Pudding.
- What on earth's Hop-It Pudding?
- Sometimes called Buzz-Off Pudding.
- I don't understand.
- Say – GO!
- Anything else?
- Oh, sure, boss. My special Quality of Mercy Coffee.
- What's that?
- Not strained.
- Of course, some of my guests might want a quick lunch.
- Dat's fine. I'd give 'em a lighted candle.
- A lighted candle? Why?
- So they can have a quick blow-out.

And so on. While demonstrably not from the pen of Oscar Wilde, nobody can deny that this is 'wholesome.' The catalogues of Ethiopian and Comic Dramas are many, and the sketches offered have names such as *One Night In A Bar Room*, *Zacharias' Funeral* (with comic sermon), and *Gambrinus, King of Lager Beer*. Shows containing these elements might be called *Darktown Swells*, or *A Trip To Coontown*. Even after Lincoln had freed the slaves, the black population remained in these toils for many, many years.

Burlesque offered 'sketches' as well as a chorus of more or less pleasing and agile dancing girls. The cohesiveness of the theatre as a whole, and the manner in which a burlesque audience might be expected to have knowledge of the more serious drama, is reflected in shows such as *Dick Mit Dree I's*, which was a Dutch Comedian version of *Richard III*; similarly, *Two Off-Uns* made game of *The Two Orphans*, and when a comedian spouted –

Love is a nightmare with one foot,
  Two children with one bun;
Two turnips with a single root,
  Two cabbage-heads in one.

– his hearers were expected to make the association with the well-known motto verse of *Ingomar*.

Elaborate musical shows that were neither Comic Opera, minstrel show, nor burlesque emerged in the latter part of the century, and the undoubted favourite was *The Black Crook* (1866) which was in character somewhat like the later *revue*. What distinguished such shows from ordinary burlesque was taste in presentation and matter.

Burlesque was rowdy and irreverent, and sometimes it was dirty, as well. As dirty sketches did not achieve the dignity of print they are almost irrecoverable, but the late George Jean Nathan recalled a characteristic example:

The drop curtain shows an expanse of desert with on it the Sphinx and the Pyramids. Enter red-nosed comedian in ragged brown suit three sizes too large for him and derby three times too small.

Comedian: Say, look what's coming! A juicy piece!

Enter girl in revealing black gauze. She shakes her middle.

Comedian: Um. A piece proposal. (*He moves to put his hands on her.*) Um. A piece doo resistance. Say, what's your name, Baby Doll?
Girl: I am Cleopatra.
Comedian: If you're Cleopatra, I'm Mark Anthony. Looka (*pointing*) that's the mark.
Girl: You're too cocky.
Comedian: You said it, Cleo! But what are you doing here, kiddo?
Girl: I was lonely. My tomb was cold and gloomy.
Comedian: I'll whitewash it for you like new. Come along, show it to me babe.

Exit. Comedian reappears instantly.

Comedian: Me Mark Anthony, I saw, I came, I conquered. Oboyoboyoboy![7]

Exact definition of entertainment in this realm is difficult, and not particularly helpful when attempted. The money spent could raise a girl-show such as *The Black Crook*, in any of its many revivals, or *The Twelve Temptations* (1877), which promised an 'Army of beautiful coryphees, Amazons, etc.' in costumes that had cost $5,000, to a level far above a simple, possibly dirty, show with a company, chorus included, that might not exceed sixteen inferior players. Some of the more elaborate shows may be considered forbears of what was later called Musical Comedy, an early and popular example of which was Victor Herbert's first success, *The Wizard of the Nile* (1895), with its rowdy chorus of –

Bang! Bang! The most harmonious song

and its catchy song for the chief comedian –

There's one thing a Wizard can do
  It's a trick of the trade that is new:
I can make politicians
Resign their positions,
  And be just as honest as you!

Miscellaneous Entertainment

At the beginning of this essay it was said that the theatre in the nineteenth century was the scene of every kind of entertainment that was not positively circus. People who might find themselves in the theatre this week to see *Faust* had sat in the same seat last week to see Blind Tom, the famous negro pianist who could play any piece of music that he had heard once – or so it was asserted by his white manager. (Unquestionably he had a curious facility to pick up tunes, but spectators who were not impressionable said that he played badly, had a primitive sense of harmony, and from time to time whined and pleaded with his employer to be allowed to stop. He was, in fact, an *idiot savant*.) The same stage that displayed one of the many productions of *Mazeppa* (1831) – in which the sensation scene was that where the hero (sometimes played by a personable young woman) was strapped on the back of a supposedly untamed horse and dispatched to roam the steppes (portrayed on a moving panorama behind the treadmill upon which the horse placidly galloped) – might shortly afterward see Charles Fechter as Hamlet, or possibly Miss Julia Seaman, clearly an early proponent of women's liberation, who also played the Prince of Denmark at the Grand Opera House, Toronto, in 1875. The Davenport Brothers, although they had been exposed many times as frauds (once, in his early career, by Henry Irving) travelled very profitably, offering demonstrations of the unseen spirit world, which manifested itself with floating trumpets, mysteriously agitated chairs, and other oddities, which seem curious occupations for spectres from a desirable afterlife. From time to time an Ontario community might receive a visit from 'the four smallest people in the world,' General Tom Thumb, Commodore Nutt, Lavinia Warren (Mrs Thumb) and Elfin Minnie Warren. The troupe toured Ontario in 1876 and again in 1882. The writer records with pride that his mother, when a small child, shook hands with the eminent Thumb, who, at thirty-one inches, was roughly her own size, though a man in years. And there were the mesmerists, the magicians (the Great Herrmann, who appeared at the Grand Opera House on two separate occasions in 1880 and returned to Toronto in 1882, was a special favourite; apparently he was an illusionist of unusual quality), the Swiss Bell Ringers – prodigies of agility – and people who exhibited skill in sharp-shooting and feats of strength. There was only one theatre, and they, however humble, were a part of it.

There were also lecturers. Nineteenth-century Canadians, like their neighbours to the south, were inordinate in their zest for information and the spoken word. Some of the lecturers approximated to what are now called 'one-man' shows; some, like Oscar Wilde and Matthew Arnold, who toured Ontario in 1882, were exponents of culture; some were providers of sensation, like Edith O'Gorman, the Escaped Nun, who was a convert to Protestantism and who toured in 1878; or the Rev. Henry Ward Beecher, lecturing the following year on The Reign of the Common People. The great phrenologist of the era, Professor Orson Squire Fowler, lectured 'to men only' (a great drawing card) on Manhood, Its Decline and Restoration at Toronto's Royal Opera House in 1882. There were many comic lecturers, among whom Josh Billings and Artemus Ward were the acknowledged favourites. And there was Mrs Buchanan Hall, the Irish poet, who announced herself as a lecturer and reciter.

Reciters, or, as they were more often called, elocutionists, were popular, and they were frequently willing to perform on behalf of a charity for a percentage of the receipts, the organizers being expected to fill the house by selling tickets. A full study of this vanished breed is still to be undertaken. They fell into disrepute early in the twentieth century, when a number of poets, of whom John Drinkwater was a leader, attempted to raise verse speaking to a higher level and called for the abandonment of what Drinkwater denounced as 'jingling and usually insignificant rhymes.'

Elocution was an art that could be practised with a gentility not invariably attainable by actors, and there were many women in the profession who might be, like Harley Granville-Barker's mother, both an elocutionist and a *siffleuse* (one who whistled the simpler classics to piano accompaniment) and who performed in drawing-rooms. A great Ontario favourite during the late 1870s and early 1880s was Mrs Scott-Siddons, a distant relative of the great Sarah Siddons, who seems to have stuck to classical selections, unlike Mrs Esther Owen-Flint, 'The Young Canadian Elocutionist,' who, during a tour of Ontario in 1882, declared herself to be unrivalled in dramatic and dialect recitations. Richard Cooke confined himself to a one-man presentation of *Hamlet*, but J.H. Siddons, 'the lecturer-humorist,' might, as the evening wore on, imitate a Red Indian reciting *The Charge of the Light Brigade* –

Half a leg, Half a leg,
  Half a leg onward

– this being sure-fire comedy, yet acceptable even in church halls.

There were innumerable amateur and semi-amateur elocutionists, and because collections of verse were published for their use, we can recover some notion of what their performances were like. The temptation to dwell on them is great, but as they are not of foremost importance in a study such as this, mention of them must be confined to essentials. Some offered excerptible passages from Shakespeare and Browning and occasional portions of Shelley and Tennyson, but in the main elocutionists' verse was drawn from the work of writers who specialized in providing them with the 'telling' material they wanted. Of these George R. Sims should be mentioned in the melodramatic class and J.K. Jerome among the funny writers. Male practitioners of the art recited such sure-fire dramatic verses as Sims's *Billy's Rose* or the ever-popular *In The Workhouse – Christmas Day* –

It is Christmas Day in the Workhouse,
  And the cold bare walls are bright

– which was frequently parodied, often with shameful irreverence, by Burlesque comedians, who appealed to those who were untouched by the thrilling dénouement –

At yonder gate, last Christmas
  I craved for a human life,

> You, who would feast us paupers,
> What of my murdered wife!

J.K. Jerome, author of the immensely popular drama of spiritual import, *The Passing of the Third-Floor Back* (1908), had a strong comic vein, and *The Cheese*, about a man who attempts to transport some old cheese in a railway-carriage, was a famous rib-binder, though the squeamish might have taken exception to the remark of an undertaker who shared the carriage, that 'it put him in mind of dead baby.' No less a theatre star than Sir Frank Benson often performed *The Cheese* for charity.

Anyone anxious to explore the repertoire of elocutionists would do well to look through old files of *The Theatre*, a magazine published in London between 1878 and 1897, aimed at enthusiasts for the stage, and offering in most issues some new gem for performance by professional or amateur reciters. In 1883, for instance, it offered two poems, of which one 'The Women of Mumbles Head' makes a strong, and almost modern beginning –

> Bring novelists, your note-book! bring
>   dramatists, your pen!
> And I'll tell you a simple story of what
>   women do for men.

– and continues with the thrilling, and historically true, tale of a rescue from a sinking ship:

> 'Give one more knot to the shawls, Bess!
>   give one strong clutch of your hand!
> Just follow me, brave, to the shingle,
>   and we'll bring him safe to land!'

It was written by the editor of the magazine, Clement Scott, remembered now as a theatre critic of wide influence. But in his magazine, on 2 April of that year, we find another reciter's offering from his pen:

> Oh! promise me, that some day, you and I
> May take our love together to some sky
> Where we can be alone, and faith renew,

And find the hollow where those flowers grew –
The first sweet violets of early spring
That come in whispers, thrill us both, and sing
Of love unspeakable that is to be.
Oh, promise me!

In 1890 the American composer Reginald de Koven included a setting of these verses in his comic opera *Robin Hood*. It won immediate and vast popularity, was sung (during the signing of the register, as Social Notes never failed to record) at countless weddings, and is still not wholly forgotten.

Conclusion

The foregoing account of what was seen and what gave pleasure in our theatres during the nineteenth century is necessarily selective and is meant only to offer an impression of popular entertainment in its uttermost variety. Changes in taste came slowly, and it would be difficult to discover any strong move towards the newer drama, though in 1905 some version of Ibsen's *Ghosts* (possibly that with the happy ending the dramatist was compelled to write for the German theatre) was played, and in 1903 Canada saw *The Second Mrs. Tanqueray* by Pinero, which dealt with the question of the Woman With A Past more frankly than *Frou-Frou* or *Camille*. But *Only a Farmer's Daughter* (1902) suggests that rural melodrama had not lost its hold, and *The Prisoner of Zenda* and *Rupert of Hentzau*, seen here just after the turn of the century, show that romance was still very popular fare; in them the themes of chivalry and renunciation are as powerful as in *The Corsican Brothers*: only the language has changed. *When Knighthood Was in Flower* (1898) was as popular a piece in the Costume Drama realm as *Rochester, or King Charles the Second's Merry Days*, and *The Little Minister*, after 1897, was as sweet to the palate as anything that had gone before it in the nineteenth century. It was not until after the First World War that Canada made any perceptible move towards the newer sort of theatre, and even then the taste of an earlier day remained strong.

Whatever we may read about nineteenth-century riots in European theatres during plays of revolutionary tendency, the playhouse in Canada was a place of entertainment, little troubled by ideas but rich in feeling.

NOTES

1 See Ann Saddlemyer's 'Introduction,' 9–10.
2 Lewis Carroll, *Sylvie and Bruno* (London: Macmillan 1889), xix–xx
3 See, for example, James Russell Aikens, 'The Rival Operas: Toronto Theatre 1874–84,' PH D thesis, University of Toronto 1975; Mary M. Brown and Natalie Rewa, 'Ottawa Calendar of Performance in the 1870s,' *Theatre History in Canada / Histoire du théâtre au Canada* 4:2 (Fall 1983), 134–91; Leslie Anne O'Dell, 'Theatrical Events in Kingston, Ontario: 1879–1897,' PH D thesis, University of Toronto 1982.
4 Apart from those few plays that have found their way into popular anthologies, most nineteenth-century plays are no longer easily available outside specialist or university libraries. For an excellent selection see Michael Booth, ed., *English Plays of the Nineteenth Century*, 5 vols (Oxford: Clarendon 1969).
5 Thompson was formerly partner of the famous minstrel 'Cool' Burgess, of whom Gerald Lenton-Young writes in his essay on variety theatre.
6 'H.J. Byron,' *Dictionary of National Biography*, vol. III, 608
7 George Jean Nathan, *The Entertainment of a Nation, or Three-Sheets in the Wind* (New York: Alfred A. Knopf 1942), 225–6

5
Entertainers of the Road

MARY M. BROWN

Beginnings

The first theatrical performers came to Ontario in the summer and set up business on a street corner, in a market square, in an inn or tavern. Itinerant magicians, phrenologists, elocutionists, musicians, and temperance lecturers continued to tour on their own erratic circuits for the whole of the nineteenth century. Especially prevalent were trained animals and their keepers. Animals acts were, of course, the precursors of circuses and equestrian shows which travelled in their own wagons and did a roaring business in Ontario. The most famous of these, P.T. Barnum's Menagerie and Museum, featuring the famous midget, General Tom Thumb, was seen as early as 1852 in Guelph where it was reported to have grossed $1,300 (Guelph *Herald* 6 July 1852). These peripatetic shows, the garrison theatre tradition, and immigrants' memories of theatrical performances in their homelands were the backdrop for the development of touring theatre companies and the various forms of variety theatre that flourished in Ontario from the mid-nineteenth century to 1914.

In the first decades of the century, inns and taverns, which dotted the landscape and offered overnight accommodations to farmers on their way to market, to officers, and to other travellers, provided playing space and captive audiences for small, visiting theatre companies. Edward Ermatinger 'paid 12 1/2 [pence] or a York shilling' in 1830 to see Mr Long's company whose 'performance consisted of slack-wire dancing, balancing tobacco pipes ... etc.'[1] Similarly, Frank's Hotel in York was the locale for a variety of performers. *The Siege of Algiers* played there on 21 August 1825, and *The Taming of the Shrew* was seen in October 1826. These makeshift premises were inefficient, and, in addition, the patrons were not always civil.

Cobalt, Silverland Theatre: Theatre in the wilderness

Solomon Smith, an American, commented in 1825: 'Our first essay in his majesty's dominions was at Niagara, where our performance was interrupted by a dozen well-dressed fellows, who took a room immediately adjoining ours, and amused themselves and annoyed us by roaring out "God Save the King," "Rule Britannia" and other loyal tunes. All this was done because they could not obtain admission to our performance at *half price!*'[2]

These early performers who came to Ontario before the completion of the railway from Montreal to Detroit in 1856 depended upon ferries and steamers operating between American and Canadian ports on the Great Lakes and on stage coaches that travelled daily between most towns. Individual performers and companies worked out their own routes, which often followed the old highway called Dundas Street in so many towns and cities of southwestern Ontario. Companies advertised by posting bills and through the newspapers. The installation of the first telegraphs to connect Toronto, Hamilton, St Catharines, Niagara Falls, Montreal, and Quebec speeded communications. In the early days, moreover, travellers no doubt acted as unofficial advance agents, and reports of good and bad shows circulated informally. As dozens of small newspapers sprang up, theatrical news, both local and international, received good coverage.

Improved travel facilities and popular interest in theatre in the growing towns and cities of Ontario spurred the building of proper theatres. Toronto had its Royal Lyceum and London its Theatre Royal in the 1840s and by 1850 there was a second-floor theatre in Hamilton (at the corner of King William and Catherine streets) which was soon superseded by the Hamilton Royal Metropolitan.[3] Her Majesty's Theatre in Ottawa was built in 1854, and Brunton's Varieties opened in London a year later.

Real theatres provided better accommodation than the old hotels, mechanics' halls, and town halls and attracted American, British, and Irish actors, who had gained their initial experiences in Albany, New York, Philadelphia, or Boston. Moreover, some actor-managers such as John Nickinson, John Spackman, George Skerrett, George Holman, and Augustus Pitou found touring Canada sufficiently encouraging to establish themselves here on a semi-permanent basis.[4] Later, managing the Canadian circuit and the interaction between American and Canadian entrepreneurs would become significant elements in the development of professional theatre in Ontario.

Managers

Among the many actor-managers John Nickinson and George Holman became well known and influential. Both had Canadian connections; Nickinson, who had been stationed in Canada as an army officer, immigrated to Quebec and first acted there; Holman's father and family had settled in London, Ontario. Holman and Nickinson toured Canada in the 1850s with their companies, which included foreign actors, many of whom subsequently toured Ontario on their own or in other troupes.[5] Charles Walcot and his wife, who was Nickinson's daughter, and the Herons came from New York to join Nickinson in Toronto. W.H. Crane, Denman Thompson, and Johnny Chatterton (who became 'Seigneur Perugini') were, at various times, members of the Holman Company.

At first, Nickinson's company played Toronto and Hamilton only in the summers, but eventually he adopted Toronto as his base of operation. In the late 1860s George Holman managed a theatre in Toronto before opening the Holman Opera House in London in 1873. Similarly, William Marshall brought his London Comedy Company to Hamilton in 1868, and John Townsend's family acted in Kingston in 1864–8

London, two performers from Holman Opera Company's production of *H.M.S. Pinafore*, 1878

before they settled in Hamilton.[6] Marshall's company was well known in Ottawa, Kingston, and Hamilton during this decade. The Townsend family also toured, presenting Shakespeare; later, he became Julia Arthur's first drama teacher. Other early actor-managers, such as W.Y. Brunton in London and John Spackman in Hamilton, made a substantial contribution to the establishment of the touring routes which were heavily travelled between 1880 and 1914.

Touring companies frequently crossed the American-Canadian border from Detroit or Buffalo, or, like William Marshall's company in 1870, arrived via the Rome and Watertown Railway which connected with a ferry from Cape St Vincent to Kingston. Many other companies came from Montreal on the Grand Trunk Railway and played towns along the north shore of the St Lawrence River and Lakes Ontario and Erie. The northern route from Montreal passed through Ottawa, Arnprior, and Renfrew and then doubled back through other small towns. To the west and south of Toronto, theatrical stops were very close together indeed as theatres became available in Brantford, Hamilton, Guelph, London, Chatham, Woodstock, and St Thomas. The Canadian Pacific Railway connected Toronto and the towns around Georgian Bay (Barrie, Collingwood, Orillia, Midland) and to the north of Lake Huron (North Bay, Sudbury, Blind River, and Sault Ste Marie). The Michigan Central also serviced southwestern Ontario.

Although touring companies from the United States regularly visited Ontario, its theatre managers and audiences were not the unwilling victims of American entrepreneurs and syndicates who dictated theatrical taste. Aside from the fact that it has never been possible to force audiences to see a show they did not wish to see, most Ontario theatres in the nineteenth century were locally financed, owned, and operated. Certainly Holman, Nickinson, Pitou (Grand Opera House, Toronto), Martin (Martin's Opera House, Kingston), and Ambrose Small did their own bookings by going to New York and Chicago in the early summer and by keeping in touch with Canadian troupes on tour. Companies such as those of E.A. McDowell, 'Cool' Burgess, Albert Tavernier, the Marks Brothers, Denman Thompson, and James O'Neill appear to have made their own arrangements in Canada, as they did elsewhere, in Australia, the West Indies, or England. Moreover, although the cause of imperial federation had a significant measure of support in the latter part of the century, theatre-goers were more interested in the product than in its point of origin, and Canadians accepted British, Canadian, American, or European plays and companies on their merits.

It is true, on the other hand, that after 1875 towns and cities in

Ontario were *claimed* by various American circuits in their propaganda. These circuit managers' advertisements were, of course, calculated to attract the managers of companies intending to tour and must be read in that light. When Alfred Bernheim, in *The Business of the Theatre*, refers to C.R. Gardiner's claim in 1880 to represent the principal theatre in every city in the United States and Canada 'excepting two,' we need to remember that managers of theatres in Ottawa, Hamilton, Toronto, London, Brockville, and St Catharines were advertising in the New York *Dramatic Mirror* for companies for the coming year and Augustus Pitou was said to 'control' 'the entire Canadian circuit.' Mr Pitou's control of the entire Canadian circuit was at best tenuous; for the following spring John Ferguson, manager of the Grand Opera House in Ottawa, was quoted in the New York *Dramatic Mirror* of 28 May 1881: 'The Opera House will be thoroughly renovated and the scenery repainted this Summer. Managers intending to play Canada next season will do well to remember that Ottawa, the best show town in the Dominion, is not in any way connected with the so-called ''circuit'' and that terms will have to be arranged for personally or by letter with the manager of the house.' Nevertheless, if one remembers that a general indication of territory rather any proprietorship is involved, the claims can be seen in perspective. There was a Canadian circuit (1883) which included Brockville, Belleville, Kingston, Port Hope, St Catharines, Hamilton, and London, as well as Montreal. In 1886 a Mr Taylor of New York said his Managers' New Exchange 'represented' one hundred first-class theatres in the United States and Canada. H.R. Jacobs claimed Toronto as part of his New York, New Jersey, Ohio, Illinois, and Pennsylvania circuit in 1889.[7]

The establishment of various syndicates to control the booking of touring companies changed the picture considerably after 1896.[8] Theatres in many major American towns gave up their independence in exchange for reliable bookings. Canadian managers, apparently, were better able to remain independent without being shut down. It may be that the theatre managers with no theatrical experience accepted the convenience of syndicate bookings happily, while those whose training enabled them to make good contracts and wise choices survived as independents. In any case, Ontario was conveniently located between two large production centres, New York and Chicago, and was, for that reason, less vulnerable than parts of the United States, especially towns on the east and west coasts. In addition, there were many independent American and British companies based in Ontario, beyond the reach of the New York syndicates.

A classic example of an independent regional circuit was that started

London, Grand Opera House program decoration from 1894–5 season

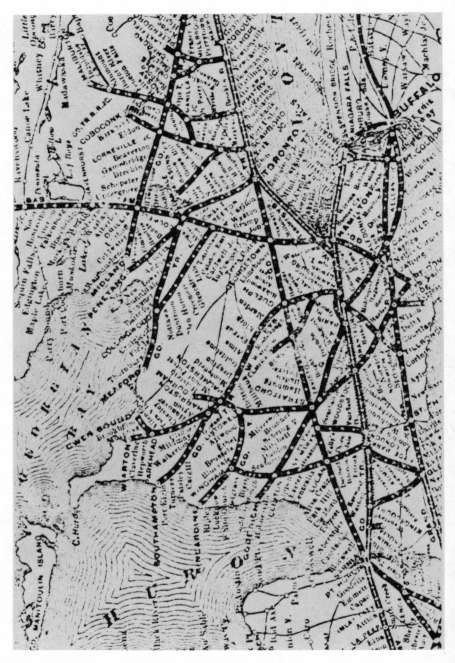

Map of touring routes from Julius Cahn's *Theatrical Guide, 1906–1907*

Rat Portage (Kenora), Hilliard's Opera House

by C.J. Whitney of Detroit. With capital earned in the lumber business he constructed his first theatre in Detroit in 1875 at a cost of $135,000. In the late 1870s he managed the Holman Opera House in London while the Holman Opera Company toured. In 1880 Whitney signed a lease for the new Grand Opera House, part of a masonic temple in London, and this theatre became the first Canadian link on Whitney's chain which then included Wheeler's Opera House in Toledo, Hill's Opera House in Ann Arbor, and the Battle Creek Opera House. By 1891, in partnership with E.D. Stair, Whitney controlled six Michigan theatres, three in Ohio, and four in Ontario (two in Toronto, one in London, and one in Hamilton). By 1893 Woodstock and St Thomas had joined the chain. By 1900 Whitney had another partner, Ambrose Small, and together they built London's second Grand Opera House after fire destroyed the original one. When Whitney died in 1903, his estate claimed various percentages of the profits from three Toronto houses (the Princess Theatre, the Grand Opera House, and the Toronto Opera House), the Grand Opera Houses in Hamilton, London, and Kingston, the Russell Theatre in Ottawa, and all the 'Canadian one-night stands

Harold Nelson as Hamlet

booked by Whitney and Small,' as well as theatres in Michigan and Ohio.[9]

Theatrical circuits such as Whitney's were constantly changing. Some theatres were owned, others leased, and still others connected in an informal booking arrangement. Even playbills that list manager, lessee, and circuit for each season often confuse more than they enlighten. One, for the 1900–1 season of the Toronto Opera House, stated that this house was under the 'direction' of A.J. Small and E.D. Stair and was 'operated in conjunction with the strongest chain of theatres extant.'[10] The list included no other Canadian theatres, even though Small was involved with several and, at the time, was building the Grand Opera House in London. Whitney's name is not mentioned, but his theatres in Detroit were named.

The frequent alterations in circuits reflected the independence of theatre managers in Ontario. In December 1892, for example, when the Town Hall in Fort William was receiving its finishing touches, the local paper reported that scenery had been ordered so that 'in future Fort William may offer inducements to good troupes visiting this part of the country' (*Times Journal*, 28 December 1892). Companies moved from Nipigon to Fort William / Port Arthur and on to Rat Portage (now Kenora) and sometimes played three weeks in each place.

Similarly, when Hilliard's Opera House opened in Rat Portage in 1898, the manager hired the Harold Nelson Company as the first attraction.[11] Nelson, a Canadian who had taught elocution and acting in Toronto, was to become well known from Toronto to British Columbia for his superior productions of good plays. Mr Hilliard subsequently offered to finance Nelson's stock company, if he would make Rat Portage his base. He opened there on 14 February 1899 before proceeding to the Fort William Town Hall and on to Port Arthur. His connection with Rat Portage remained strong, and he returned in 1901, 1902, and 1904–5.

The first decades of the twentieth century were a turbulent period in which vaudeville and film changed the economics of entertainment and added adjustment and adaptation to the already complex system of touring theatrical companies. In the process plans were made to offer vaudeville and movies in many buildings that had been devoted to dramatic presentations. It was in these years, too, that Ambrose Small consolidated his theatrical empire, after Whitney's death, by buying opera houses in Hamilton, Kingston, Toronto, St Thomas, and Peterborough. By 1912 he was advertising the A.J. Small Circuit as 'the most carefully booked territory in the world,' a claim supported by M.B. Leavitt, a manager with fifty years' experience in North America, who called Small's operation so successful that 'time is now eagerly sought by all leading producers and owners of prominent productions.'[12]

Ambrose Small was the right man in the right place at the right time. By carefully booking in the peak years around 1900 when there were more than 300 companies on tour, by taking advantage of English stars such as Lewis Waller and Martin Harvey, who wanted to tour Canada[13] without booking through New York, and by introducing some moving pictures as the number of road shows declined, Ambrose Small made a fortune and, at the same time, gave audiences in Ontario the best entertainment available. His wheeling and dealing progress from usher to theatrical magnate, his colourful connections at the race tracks of America and with the chorus girls of the 'ballet,' the sale of his theatres and leases for $1.75 million in 1919,[14] and his mysterious disappearance the same day make Small one of the most colourful impresarios in the theatrical history of this country. His career marked the high point of the age of the touring company and the transition to the new age of vaudeville and film.

Performers

Although skilful management had much to do with the successful growth of the touring stage in Ontario, stellar performances by great actors and actresses gave the Victorian theatre its special place in the history of Ontario and other parts of the North American world. James O'Neill in *The Count of Monte Cristo*, Henry Irving in *The Bells*, E.A. Sothern in *Our American Cousin*, Joseph Jefferson in *Rip Van Winkle*, Sarah Bernhardt in *Camille*[15] – audiences in Ontario saw all these artists and many more and used their hallmark performances as standards against which to judge a host of other players, many of whom were Canadians.

It is impossible to name all the actors and companies who came and went, bartering culture for cash. Five stars with roots in the province – Arthur McKee Rankin, Ida Van Cortland, Albert Tavernier, Julia Arthur, and Margaret Anglin – won international acclaim and greatly advanced the cause of theatre in Ontario.

Arthur McKee Rankin was born at Sandwich, Ontario, in 1841 and died in 1914. His father was a member of parliament and, among other things, was the author of *The Experiment: a Farce in One Act*. A brother, George Cameron Rankin, was a novelist and playwright. McKee Rankin was, in real life, the same handsome maverick he played so often on the stage. One contemporary account says that

Hamilton-born actress Roselle Knott, wife of film producer Ernest Shipman

Rankin ran away from Upper Canada College to become an actor and took the stage name of George Henley when he joined a company in Rochester in 1861. A year later he was a member of Mrs Drew's company in Philadelphia. The Drews and the Barrymores were important influences on his career, and his daughter Doris became the first wife of Lionel Barrymore, while Gladys Rankin, another daughter, became Mrs Sydney Drew.[16] With at least five New York shows to his credit, in 1869 Rankin set out to tour the United States and Canada with his own adaptation of *Rip Van Winkle*. In the same year he married Kitty Blanchard, who co-starred with him for over twenty years.

In 1870 McKee Rankin copyrighted his version of *Rip Van Winkle* and played it in the United States and Canada in theatres of all descriptions, including one in California where the orchestra was so inadequate that Rankin had to whistle the dance music, while his wife sang to accompany herself. In a press interview years later he recalled that the audience applauded the 'whistling orchestra' which they thought was an original stunt. These tours through the mining towns and west coast ports were a schooling in survival, but they yielded an adequate living and valuable experience. He played for gold-dust in mining towns, bartered tickets for produce in Salt Lake City and for salmon in Seattle and Vancouver. In Utah Rankin played *Rip Van Winkle* with the resident stock company in Brigham Young's well-run theatre, though he was not allowed to perform *Oliver Twist*, because Young thought the brutal killing of a woman dangerous for prospective Mormon mothers to see.[17]

McKee Rankin's experiences among the Mormons resulted in a play called *The Danites*. 'I wanted,' he said in an interview much later, 'to depict the broad-gauged people that I met in the West; the miners, the plainsmen, the Mormons, and the adventurers and promoters. All these people were people of personality and energy and men who did things.'[18] Rankin roughed out a scenario based on Joaquin Miller's *The First Families of the Sierras* and an anonymous short story called 'The Schoolmaster of Bottle Flat.' He commissioned an out-of-work actor friend, P.A. Fitzgerald, to write dialogue to fit the scenario he had devised, for a fee of $25 per act. Joaquin Miller sold the use of his story and his name to Rankin for $5,000. 'When the money was paid a few days later, *The Danites* became my sole property for all time, and poor old Fitzgerald, who really wrote most of the play and introduced the most beautiful thoughts into the whole work, only realized $125. out of it.' (Fitzgerald died about four months before the play was produced in August of 1877 at the Broadway Theatre in New York.) Rankin and his wife made a handsome profit from it over the years, both in England and in North America.

McKee Rankin himself was the author of several plays.[19] Most of them have disappeared, but one, written especially for his daughter Doris and his son-in-law Lionel Barrymore, still exists in typescript. Titled *Confusion*, this one-act sketch has parts for a beautiful girl, her absent-minded scientist uncle, and a crotchety old general, her father-in-law. The plot relies heavily on stereotyped characters and coincidence and the production on comic technique, timing, and a good set. Whether or not this play was seen in Ontario is unknown, but others were. *The Golden Giant*, his five-act drama written with Clay Greene, toured this province in 1888 following its New York première on 4 April 1887, as did his comedy-drama *The Runaway Wife* in 1890. His *True to Life* was also seen in Kingston in 1897.[20]

Of particular interest to Canadians is his production of *The Canuck, a Play of Anglo-American Life* (copyrighted in Washington, 1899), which was first performed in New York in July and in Montreal and Kingston in October 1890. Rankin played the Canuck, Jean Baptiste Cadeaux. The registered authors were Arthur McKee Rankin and Fred C. Maeder, an American actor. Though no copy has been found, the play probably was based on the novel *Border Canucks, Our Friendly Relations*, by George Cameron Rankin.[21] In any case, the reviews for *The Canuck* were not wildly enthusiastic, and Rankin seems to have dropped it from his repertoire.

McKee Rankin was always good copy, and stories about his latest escapades were usually carried in Canadian newspapers. In 1880, for example, *Grip* (24 January) reported that Rankin had refused to go on stage in a southern city until five 'dead-head' policemen (holders of free tickets) had left the theatre. In an announcement to the audience he said that he had paid the city for his licence and taxes and that he expected city officials to pay their way into his theatre. The audience applauded and the police left. Frequently, the press carried juicy tidbits about Rankin's domestic problems. Kitty Blanchard was a jealous wife, not without reason, and they finally separated. Rankin then discovered the talented Nance O'Neill and promoted her career; they appeared on several Canadian tours and played a summer season in Minneapolis.

An old-style entrepreneur, Rankin was never happier than when he was cobbling up a new version of an old play or negotiating to buy an island (he owned Fitzwilliam Island, near Manitoulin) or busy on some new mechanical invention.[22] In his versatility, stamina, and creative drive he was very much like E.A. McDowell. Both came into prominence as actor-managers in the 1870s, but while McDowell was an American who spent most of his professional life in Canada, Rankin

Ida Van Cortland as Billie Piper in *The Danites*

was a Canadian whose connections were primarily in New York, Philadelphia, and California.

In contrast Ida Van Cortland (or Courtland), came from England to Toronto as a child and chose to base her career in Ontario, although she was well known in the Maritimes[23] and in those American states that bordered on the Great Lakes. Born in 1855, she got her first professional experience in Toronto, where she watched and learned from Mrs Morrison's resident stock company at the Grand Opera House. It was there she carried Fanny Davenport's wraps and luggage on stage in *Pique* and spoke her first line in a professional company in 1877.[24] There she met Mme Modjeska, the elegant Polish actress she idolized. By 1878 Ida Van Cortland had progressed so well that she was given a lead in *The Two Orphans*, a tear-jerker about a poor blind orphan. A critic from the *Mail* (27 March 1878) had this to say about Van Cortland's performance: 'The sudden transition from despair to hope, the unobtrusive resignation with which she bears her troubles, and the quiet, unmistakable joy manifested at their happy close – all these marked the true artist, and indicate for this young lady a still more successful future.'

A year later, she was touring the Maritimes to good reviews as a leading lady in William Nannary's company. In the same company was a Boston-born actor who had grown up in Hamilton and Toronto. His name was Albert Taverner (later modified to Tavernier), and he and Ida were married in 1881. After a stint with the W.J. Florence Co., the young couple formed their own troupe and, with Horace and Portia Lewis, toured the Maritimes as the Tavernier-Lewis New York Comedy Company and later as the Tavernier Company. From that time until 1896, this husband and wife team toured Ontario, Quebec, and neighbouring states every season, gradually playing fewer towns for longer runs in plays guaranteed to please urban audiences.

They prepared each season at a summer cottage in Muskoka, where Ida rehearsed and made many of the beautiful costumes for which she was noted. Photographs of her reveal a small, dark-haired beauty who wore the beaded gowns and plumed hats of her day to perfection. She was also a dedicated artist: 'Miss Ida Van Courtland is probably the most conscientious actress of the day, and this is in a measure the secret of her success. I believe if there were only a dozen people in the theatre she would work just as hard and as conscientiously as if it were filled to the doors' (Grand Rapids *Star*, 30 March 1889). Each season's repertoire included 'new plays,' that is, Tavernier versions of current successes, chosen for the challenging roles they offered Ida. These included *The Danites, East Lynne*, and *The Colleen Bawn* in 1886;

Ida Van Cortland as Juliet

Pygmalion and Galatea, The New Magdalen, Fanchon the Cricket, and *Arrah-na-Pogue* in 1888; and in 1898 *Lucretia Borgia, Lady of Lyons*, and *Camille*. In 1895 she toured *The Two Orphans*, her Toronto success of 1878, and a London *Free Press* critic called it 'well played and richly costumed,' noting that 'the company is now better organized than ever before' (1 May 1895).

Typically, the Taverniers played two-week engagements, offering seven to fifteen plays, with performances every night except Sunday and matinees on Wednesday and Saturday. By 1896, however, constant touring, financial reverses in the management of theatres in Jackson, Michigan, and Guelph, Ontario, along with domestic tensions had taken such a toll that the company disbanded. Albert Tavernier left his wife and children to act in various companies. Ida retired from the stage and lived in Ottawa for many years until her death in 1924.

Readers in Hamilton may recognize the name of Julia Arthur, who was a native of that city. Born Ida Lewis in 1869, the future star showed musical and dramatic talent as a child and later recalled playing Portia to an audience of dolls when she was eleven. Her first appearance on stage, in 1881, was in that same role, at a benefit for John Townsend, her tutor. In 1884 she and her six-year-old sister, Ella, were featured in a production of *Mabel Heath, or The Farmer's Daughter* at the Grand Opera House in Hamilton.[25] In the same year, Sir Henry Irving first visited Toronto; possibly Julia Arthur saw him there and determined to become one of his company, as indeed she did ten years later. Those ten years prepared her for eventual stardom. In 1885 she was Maritana in Daniel Bandmann's production of *Don César de Bazan* in her home town. Bandmann took the young actress into his company 'on probation,' which meant without salary, and gave her a variety of small roles, primarily in Shakespeare plays. A couple of years later, good reviews in a Cincinnati paper for Tennyson's *Dora* turned her into a professional with a salary of $10 per week. She continued to act, under various stage names such as Nellie Hazlewood and Enos, but by 1890, when she was in E.A. McDowell's company, she was Julia Arthur.

As an apprentice she played many small parts in Shakespeare plays before graduating to the roles of Gertrude, Ophelia, Portia, Juliet, and Desdemona. In San Francisco, in A.R. Wilbur's Company, she was a featured actress in more than a dozen contemporary American and British plays and acquired the technique necessary for prose drama. From San Francisco she went to New York and, under the management of A.M. Palmer, played a number of parts, including Lady Windermere and Sister Mary (in Clement Scott and Wilson Barrett's play of that name).

Ida Van Cortland as Lucretia Borgia

Hamilton-born Julia Arthur (as Hamlet)

By 1894 she had her heart set on a London engagement and from several offers chose Sir Henry Irving's company. English audiences and critics loved her portrayals of Elaine in *King Arthur* and Rosamund in *Becket*. The role of Imogen, opposite Irving's Cymbeline, was her third British heroine in two years. To work is to play – was Julia Arthur's motto, and her relentless efforts made her the first Canadian to be acclaimed a star in England.

Subsequently, she commissioned Frances Hodgson Burnett and Stephen Townsend to dramatize Burnett's novel *A Lady of Quality*. The play opened in 1896 and was seen in Ontario in 1898. It was not a success, but the critics greatly admired Arthur's performance. Her acting was described as 'fervent, passionate, intense,' her voice as distinct and pure, her emotional reserves as prodigious. Fifteen years of experience, a wide variety of parts in good companies, beautiful costumes, and technical skills honed to perfection combined to make Julia Arthur a lady of quality both on and off stage. By 1896 she was the darling of the press and the toast of Anglo-American society.[26]

When she returned to Shakespeare in 1899, it was to triumph as Juliet and as Hamlet. Not content to be an Italian heroine and a Danish prince in one season, she added the Empress Josephine to her repertoire. The play was Emile Bergerat's *More Than Queen*, one of a number of plays centred around the charismatic Napoleon. 'Julia Arthur,' wrote an admirer, 'by her superb portrayal of the enchantress, who in fulfillment of the prediction of a carib prophetess, becomes "More Than Queen" ... nightly wins a distinct and most gratifying triumph. Her beauty, style, voice, magnetism ... all lend themselves to her fascinating portrayal of this marvellous Empress.' Offstage she enchanted Mr Cheyney, a Boston millionaire, and after their marriage retired from the stage for some time. She frequently returned to Ontario to visit family and in 1926 acted in *Saint Joan*.

Margaret Anglin, the last mentioned of this group of stars, was born in Ottawa in 1876. She came by her dramatic talent naturally; for her father, an MP from New Brunswick, stage-managed debates in parliament as speaker of the House, and her mother took part in Lady Dufferin's theatricals at Rideau Hall. Training in New York prepared Margaret Anglin for the part of Madeline West in *Shenandoah* in 1894 in Charles Frohman's Company; two years later she was touring Ontario as Mercedes, opposite James O'Neill, in *Monte Cristo*. When she was only twenty-two, she created the role of Roxanne in the American premiere of *Cyrano de Bergerac*. Richard Mansfield was Cyrano in this production at the Garden Theatre, New York, and on tour in Ontario in May 1898.[27]

Another Canadian, Henry Miller, was also acting at the Garden Theatre in 1898, and it may have been there that the two expatriates met. In any case, they toured together in Ontario on several occasions and became favourites on both sides of the border. In a double bill in 1903 Miss Anglin starred in *Cynthia* and Henry Miller in Clyde Fitch's *Frederic Lemaitre*. *Cynthia* was praised as 'a clean play' in this 'heyday of inane farce, hodge-podge musical comedy and rip-roaring melodrama' (London *Advertiser*, 8 December 1903). Nothing was said about the Fitch play.

Anglin was seen here again in the 1910–11 season (in *Green Stockings*) and in 1914 in *Twelfth Night*, *As You Like It*, and *Antony and Cleopatra*. She was at this time her own manager and commissioned splendid new scenery for the 1914 tour. Audiences found all three productions fresh and imaginative but preferred the comedies. She subsequently mounted spectacular open-air productions of *Electra, Medea*, and *Iphigenia* at the University of California in 1915 and a memorable version of the Clytemnestra myth in New York six years later.

Henry Miller was a star in his own right. Sixteen years older than Margaret Anglin, he grew up in Toronto. At fifteen, he took voice lessons from C.W. Couldock, a well-known English actor who was then a member of Mrs Morrison's Grand Opera House Company. Miller's first role was the bleeding sergeant in *Macbeth* in Toronto in 1878, and in the same year he was taken on by Mme Modjeska and shared the 'utility' parts with Robert Mantell. The young Miller gradually rose in the ranks in New York at Daly's and Palmer's Madison Square Theatre in the early 1880s, after which he played male leads for Minnie Maddern Fiske. At twenty-three he married the actress Bijou Heron, daughter of Matilda Heron, who was well known to Toronto audiences as early as the 1850s.

Henry Miller may have toured Ontario in companies starring his mentors C.W. Couldock, Mme Modjeska, Robert Mantell, and Mrs Fiske. He did play there as a featured actor in 1886 in *The Three Students*, in 1887 with Clara Morris in *Miss Multon*, in 1902 in *D'Arcy of the Guards*, and in his own adaptation of *The Lancers* in 1907, 1910, and 1913.

In 1908 Henry Miller and Margaret Anglin toured Ontario as co-stars in *The Great Divide*, a play by the American poet William Vaughan Moody. Miller played Stephen Ghent, a rough and tough frontiersman who eventually won the love of the woman forced to marry him. The proud, genteel, New England wife was played by Margaret Anglin, and she so managed the range of emotions from terror and shame to conjugal passion that the play was acclaimed 'a new American drama' rather than the sensational melodrama it might well have become.[28]

Rankin, Arthur, Anglin, and others achieved fame in Canada; many talented performers left the country, however, to seek a life in the theatre. One example will have to suffice. Like many actresses of her day, Canadian-born Clara Morris made her career in the United States.[29] She left Toronto six months after her birth on St Patrick's Day 1846; in *Life on the Stage* she describes her first appearance in the ballet *The Seven Sisters* in Cleveland during her teens. Schooled in western stock companies, Morris became leading lady of Wood's Theatre, Cincinnati, before venturing to New York, where she made her debut at Daly's first Fifth Avenue Theatre in 1870, scoring an unexpected though immediate success as Anne Sylvester in Wilkie Collins's *Man and Wife*. She reached the height of her achievements as an emotional actress two years later as Cora in *l'Article 47*. Her Cora was the sensation of the day, memorable for the impression that she produced in the mad scene. Other notable productions in which she displayed her emotional range included *Alixe*, *The New Magdalen* (Mercy Merrick), *Madeleine Morel*, *Camille*, and *Miss Multon*.

After an illustrious career, mostly under Daly's and Palmer's management, Clara Morris was compelled by ill health to retire from the stage in 1885. She spent her time writing short stories, novels, and three volumes describing her life as an actress. In 1904 she returned briefly to the stage in all-star revival of *The Two Orphans*. The veteran actress, who was once hailed by her critics as a great emotional performer and who had taken New York by storm in the 1870s, died in November 1925.

In addition to these stars whose roots were in Ontario, it must be said that there were many, many more, born in Europe, Britain, or the United States, whose contribution to our theatrical heritage was significant. Some, such as Thomas Keene, brought Shakespeare plays almost every year in the 1880s and 1890s. Others, such as Minnie Maddern Fiske, E.A. McDowell, and Robert Mantell, toured more contemporary fare through this province for many years.

The development of acting skills and the popularity of the theatre were fostered after 1870 by the construction of new theatres and the renovation of old ones, in which resident stock companies became established and shared the stage with touring actors and companies. The best of these was managed by Charlotte Morrison, daughter of John Nickinson, at the Grand Opera House in Toronto, but there were others: Daniel Bandmann in Hamilton; the Holmans in London, Toronto, Ottawa, and Montreal at various times in various theatres; and William Marshall, the Herndons, and Harry Lindley in Ottawa.

As actor-manager, Mrs Morrison gave her audiences well-balanced seasons and brought in important guest stars. In 1874 The *Canadian Monthly* noted:

Of Mrs. Morrison, known in former days of early triumph as Miss Charlotte Nickinson, there is no reminiscence which her best friends could desire to forget, and the same may be said of those who worked for her. As an actress, she would have made her mark on any stage. Intelligent, refined and well educated, she always threw her whole soul into the work for which she was so well qualified by gifts natural and acquired. There was a native grace and a hatred of inborn coarseness and impropriety ... between Ophelia and Meg, or Lady Teazle and Nan in *Good For Nothing*, there would seem to be no great gulf fixed; but Mrs. Morrison had so studied all these parts that they were true without being unfaithful to art without over-stepping the modesty of nature ... For these reasons her name is a tower of strength to the new Opera House.[30]

The Grand Opera House opened on 21 September 1874 with *School For Scandal*, in which Mrs Morrison played Lady Teazle. As actor-

Eugene A. McDowell as the Shaughraun: 'The Hounds are on your track,
Harvey Duff!'

Fanny Reeves (Mrs Eugene A. McDowell), leading lady of Eugene A. McDowell's Shaughraun Company

manager she supervised 275 performances in the 1874–5 season, took the roles of Jessie Brown in *The Siege of Lucknow* and Ophelia in *Hamlet* and directed a mammoth production of *A Midsummer Night's Dream*.[31] Mrs Morrison's sister, Virginia Marlowe, also played leads, as did two English-born actors of some note, C.W. Couldock and John L. Toole.

In November and March Mrs Morrison imported Adelaide Neilson, easily the most famous star to visit Toronto up to that time. Between 16 and 24 March Neilson drew an audience of over 13,000. Her Juliet was said to be an exquisite, original, and moving interpretation of that role. She was warmly applauded for her Isabella, Rosalind, and Beatrice, as well for her performance as Julia in *The Hunchback* and as Pauline in *The Lady of Lyons*. Isabella was 'acted by Miss Neilson with a tragic grandeur worth of a Rachel or Siddons.' Her Rosalind was considered almost perfect. 'As Julia in *The Hunchback* and as Pauline in *The Lady of Lyons*, Miss Neilson was also better than any of the numerous actresses we have seen in them; though in the latter she was at times too tragic for her character, which is not tragic, but melodramatic,' wrote the reviewer in the *Canadian Monthly*.

Agnes Booth, who, like Adelaide Neilson, played Juliet, Rosalind, and Beatrice, came to Mrs Morrison's Opera House in 1876 to be Lady Constance in a production of *King John*, said to be the first presentation of that play in Canada. The title role was taken by her husband, Julius Brutus Booth, Jr. The *Canadian Monthly* reported that *King John* 'was mounted with fidelity to historic reality and splendour, and attention to scenery, appointments and accessories, that would have done credit to a London or New York stage.' Of Agnes Booth the *Monthly* wrote:

the Lady Constance is a marvellous bit of portraiture, and exhibits the feminine character in one of the most touching and impressive features capable of presentation – that of maternal solicitude and affection. With quiet dignity and the finesse of true art Miss Booth unfolded the character of Constance in a series of representations which did full justice to the beauty of the creation. The rapid mental transitions that follow the development of the play were admirably brought out, and the passages that gave expression to the ever increasing anxiety and interest in the boy Arthur ... were powerfully and feelingly rendered. The effect of the representation is much enhanced by the interest attached to the child Arthur, who was personated by the youthful Miss Virginia Marlowe with an intelligence and artlessness that won the sympathy of the audience.[32]

Adelaide Secord (née Flint), leading actress in many companies, including
Harry Lindley's

Daniel Morrison, theatre critic and editor, and Charlotte Nickinson Morrison, noted performer and theatre manager

The Irish-American star Barry Sullivan received good reviews for his *Richard III* in the same year. Sullivan had been in Toronto before, but this was his first visit to the new Opera House. Of his Richard it was said, 'The impersonation was one of extraordinary fidelity and vigour: the deformity of the man, his cruelty, his cunning, his impetuosity and resolution ... were all vividly and powerfully realized.'[33]

Adelaide Neilson came back in 1877 and 1880 and gave audiences and critics a chance to compare her acting with their memories of her earlier visit. On her last visit, when as Juliet she asked 'Oh, thinkest thou we shall ever meet again?' a Toronto writer said, 'even the swoon, the partial swoon, into which the actress lapses at the close of the scene, is an innovation not found in the text but possibly an allowable one, in view of the fact that, to the modern society girl, fainting is not the unfamiliar thing it was to the robuster and less sensitively organized women of Shakespeare's time.'[34] Perhaps, too, Adelaide Neilson swooned more convincingly than the boys who had played the female roles in Shakespeare's theatre.

Her Rosalind, however, appeared 'to have lost some of its old charms by reason of having become something artificial and mechanical. Her Viola, on the other hand, is altogether stronger and deeper. There is far more of the feeling and loving woman, and far less of the perky page. In particular, the first scene with Olivia, where Viola urges the suit of the Duke with such moving eloquence, was very nobly acted. In Pauline also, there was improvement.' After her last performance as Juliet, she took her final curtain calls with tears in her eyes and in a choking voice said goodbye to the standing audience. It was, indeed, goodbye. She died later the same year in Paris, at the age of thirty-two.

In between visits by stars such as Sullivan and Booth, Mrs Morrison presented her own stock company in repertory. In the late 1870s she also toured to Ottawa and probably played in other cities as well. The physical and financial strain was enormous, and Toronto, like other North American cities, began to tire of the same faces and to favour the new 'combination' companies which toured the country with one show each winter. Touring companies, as opposed to touring stars imported by resident stock companies, soon became the norm and completely changed the theatrical life of Ontario towns and cities in the last two decades of the nineteenth century.

Seasons' Repertoire

Four seasons, suggestive only as a designer's sketch suggests the finished costume, will have to represent more than three decades of activity between 1880 and 1914. The theatrical seasons 1881–2, 1892–3, and 1912–13 each must stand for a decade.

There were many good theatres in Ontario to serve touring companies in the 1881–2 season, and even a small city like London saw well over a hundred professional troupes between August and May. Toronto audiences saw more and smaller towns attracted fewer companies. James O'Neill was the only star of the 1881–2 season in Ontario whose name most readers will recognize. Two years later he would begin a twenty-nine-year love-hate association with *The Count of Monte Cristo*, but during this season he appeared in a play called *Deacon Crankett* in Toronto, early in September. At about the same time the beautiful, temperamental American actress Rose Eytinge opened the new Grand Opera House in London with *Felicia, or Woman's Love*, described as a successor to *Camille*. Though one might think that a play about the passionate, vain, spendthrift mistress of a rich Parisian who brings up their child to call her 'aunt' would shock

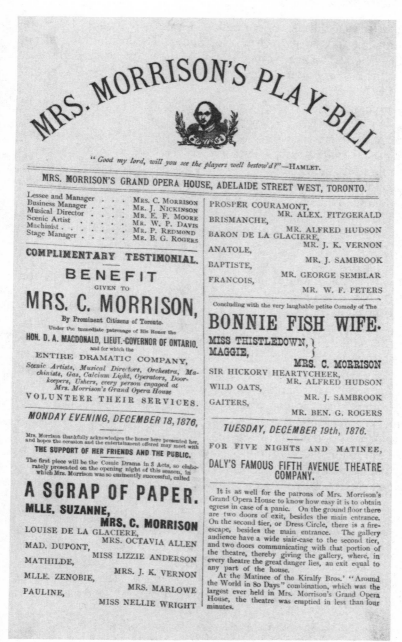

Toronto, Mrs Morrison's playbill, 18 December 1876

the Victorian sensibilities of a London, Ontario, audience, the show was a great hit and the star warmly applauded. The local critic was not as kind when Mlle Rhea, sometimes called the American Bernhardt, appeared in *Camille* later in the same season:

When the play *Camille* was written, why, being written, should it ever be played; and why being played, anyone should pay money to see it, are mysteries that the present writer does not pretend to solve. But it is certain that if it must be played, few, if any better representative of the character can be found than Mlle. Rhea. It has been the lot of the writer to witness the same play by Bernhardt, Clara Morris, Matilda Heron, and all the famous ones who have made a specialty of it. It is sufficient to say of Mlle. Rhea that she is as good as many of them, while her version of the play is decidedly less prurient than the same piece produced by Bernhardt ... Rhea was recalled again and again.[35]

The most exotic event of the season was, without doubt, the performance by the Italian star Ernesto Rossi, *in Italian* but supported by an English-speaking cast, of Hamlet and Romeo. Rossi was famous in Paris, where he supported Ristori, in Vienna in the plays of Goldoni, and in Madrid, Lisbon, Paris, and London in Shakespeare's works. Hamlet was his favourite role. Ontario audiences, while they wished he would speak English, were properly impressed. They found him handsome – a broad, impressive forehead, dark eyes, curly hair, and a fine figure. His voice was clear and powerful and his manner and movements graceful. 'Perhaps the most remarkable characteristic of his temperament is intensity,' wrote one reviewer of *Hamlet*, referring particularly to the play-within-a-play scene. Said another: 'His conception of the Danish prince varies on many points from the conventional Hamlet as presented by Irving and McCullough and other noted actors, and this variation rather increases than deteriorates from the effect of this rendition' (London *Free Press*, 17 January 1882). Of his Romeo it was said, 'The contrast [between his Hamlet and his Romeo] was most marked. In the one he gave full vent to the passions and emotions which stirred the Danish Prince and in the other he was all gentleness, full of poetry and sentiment' (ibid., 18 November 1881). No mention was made of the fact that Hamlet–Romeo–Rossi was fifty-two years old.

Of all the Shakespearian actors who toured this province, the most frequent visitor was Thomas W. Keene. In the spring of 1882 he brought *Richard III* in the Colley Cibber version of this play which, it was said, he performed 2,525 times in Canada and the United States during his long career. Although the crippled king was his best-known role, he toured Ontario in *Macbeth, The Merchant of Venice, Hamlet,* and *Julius Caesar.* Keene was also associated with the role of Cardinal Richelieu and, in fact, gave his last performance on any stage in the cardinal's robes in Hamilton, Ontario, on 23 May 1898.

Bulwer-Lytton's *Richelieu* was also a favourite role for Lawrence Barrett, whose production was seen in Ontario in June 1882, though not for the first time. Hamiltonians had seen it in 1874 and 1876.[36] Otis Skinner remembered Barrett as an attractive, mercurial man, self-educated, ambitious, and impatient.[37] Though critics disagreed about his stature as a tragic actor, all agreed that he had done much to encourage the production of good plays. Four of the many he produced were seen at various times in Ontario: *Dan'l Druce, Yorick's Love,* Boker's *Francesca da Rimini,* and Browning's *A Blot on the 'Scutcheon.*[38] Franklin Graham, in his history of the stage in Montreal, recalled, 'Lawrence Barrett moved among an army of critics, but he moved like a general among his recruits.'[39]

Many stars who visited in the 1880s returned in the 1890s. There was also a great deal of music. Light operas such as *Robin Hood, La Mascotte, The Chimes of Normandy,* and *The Bohemian Girl* were part of the 1892–3 season. Other touring concerts included the Chicago Symphony Orchestra, something called the African Native Choir, and the Toronto University Glee Club, which was assisted by the College Banjo and Guitar Club and the Mandolin Quintette.[40] Music was very much part of every season in the hundreds of halls and theatres of this province.

Dramatic stars followed one another around Ontario in quick succession: Ida Van Cortland, Mlle Rhea, E.S. Willard, Robert Mantell, Thomas Keene, Robert Downing and Eugenie Blair, Mme Janauschek, and James O'Neill were some of the favourites seen between September and May 1892–3 in Ontario. The only Canadians in this group were Ida Van Cortland and her husband Albert Tavernier; they toured *The Devil's Web* and Tobin's *The Honeymoon, or How to Rule a Wife,* among other plays.

The first British star of this season was E.S. Willard, who brought Henry Arthur Jones's *The Middleman,* the play he produced in England to free himself from a series of villain roles. Its successes there and in New York encouraged him to tour, and he returned to Ontario often in later years. Copious advance notices heralded his initial tour in Canada in 1892–3, and 'nearly every seat' in the Grand Opera House, London, was sold before he arrived. In his spacious suite at the Tecumseh House Hotel he received a reporter, who subsequently wrote that

Willard 'had a face classic in the serenity of its feature [sic], a magnificent head covered with a rich growth of iron grey hair, strong blue eyes, a slow yet emphatic delivery, a gentle manner and air of good breeding' (London *Free Press*, 19 October 1892). This 'man with a purpose' said that *The Middleman* was a play with a purpose; that night he held his audiences spellbound: 'At no time does he become strained or unnatural though he has scenes of such tremendous power that anyone of less reserve force and quiet intense strength would make them ridiculous' (ibid., 20 October 1892).

Another English play seen during this season was Knowles's *Virginius*, starring Robert Downing and Eugenie Blair, both favourites in Ontario. A critic said that 'Mr. Downing filled the title role with much dignity and vigour, and showed the ability of judicious restraint in some of the most pathetic parts where exaggeration would produce just the opposite of the intended effects' and that 'Miss Eugenie Blair as Virginia was a dream of white-robed innocence' (ibid., 3 November 1892).

Contemporary popular American theatre was represented by Lawrence Marston's *Lady Lil* which starred his wife, Lillian Lewis. The advance notices described Miss Lewis as the American Bernhardt and the play as a succession of panoramic stage pictures. 'There is the departure of the army ... the flaying of the faith curer, the ministering of the sisters of mercy on the battlefield, the trial, conviction, sentence and execution of the spy, the establishment of a field telegraph during action.' Lady Lil vividly describes the heroic death of the telegraph operator at his post: 'Then comes the circus amphitheatre, with its acrobats and clowns, its spangles and its tights' (ibid., 11 November 1892). Lillian Lewis was, in this act, a bareback rider who had to compete with a man-eating tiger for the audience's attention.

The local critic, however, was more restrained, perhaps in reaction to the elaborate publicity. 'The members of the company are first class and should have a better vehicle for the display of their several abilities than *Lady Lil* ... Miss Lewis is a handsome woman as well as talented actress ... Her many admirers hope to see her in the future in a play more adapted to her artistic capabilities' (ibid., 12 November 1892).

Mlle Rhea, who was even more frequently and appropriately described as 'the American Bernhardt,' appeared in November in *Josephine*, a role for which she was well suited because she was French speaking and had made a specialty of French plays (she toured *Camille*, *Adrienne Lacouvreur*, and *Frou-Frou* in Ontario between 1882 and 1884), and because her research into the Napoleonic era was exhaustive. Before she began her *Josephine* tour, she instructed her cast: 'Let us live together for this season at least, like a happy family, and try to imagine that we are in or near France at the time Napoleon was harassed by intriguers and diplomats and when Josephine was burdened with the sorrow that sprang from the inconquerable love she bore towards her royal husband' (ibid.). Her care and devotion were rewarded by warm applause and excellent reviews: 'Most American playgoers are aware that the Josephine of Mlle. Rhea is a touching and womanly address to the heart. She is in lively sympathy with the character, and her interpretation of it is fine in texture and persuasively sincere in tone. Moreover, she wears her imperial robes with the grand manner that warrants the observation that Rhea, more than any other player before the public, adorns her adornment' (ibid.).

A most interesting production of *Macbeth* arrived in the spring of 1893. Its star was Mme Francesca Romanana Magdalena Janauschek, a Bohemian by birth and sometime member of the Duke of Meiningen's theatrical company. She was, like Ernesto Rossi, a star in Europe before she came to North America in 1867. And, like Rossi, she originally played in a foreign tongue (German) with English-speaking casts. By the time she toured Ontario in 1867, however, she was speaking English, albeit with an accent, in productions of *Bleak House* and *Deborah*. She was also seen in *Mary Stuart, Mother and Son,* and *Deborah* in 1879 and in *Macbeth* and *Guy Mannering* in 1890.[41]

Robert Mantell and James O'Neill are two stars of the 1892-3 season whose names are still likely to be familiar, since both toured after 1900, Mantell in plays written for him by W.A. Tremayne of Montreal[42] and O'Neill in *The Count of Monte Cristo* and other romantic dramas. In 1892-3, Mantell appeared in *The Face in the Moonlight* by Osborne, and O'Neill in *Fontenelle* by Harrison Gray Fiske and Minnie Maddern Fiske.

As one century gave way to another, theatrical activity became diversified; lavish dramatic productions vied with early movies and vaudeville in small as well as large towns. A spectacular production of *Faust* ('four tons of magnificent scenery'), starring Porter J.White as Mephisto and Olga Verne as Marguerite, played Ottawa, Goderich, St Marys, and Chatham in 1899 and 1900. For 75 cents patrons could have the best seat in the house, and, if Goethe's story palled, marvel at the special effects: 'rain of fire, electric sword duel, electric fireflies, electric morning glories, electric stove, electric necklace, electric owls, snakes and many other weird and dramatic effects' (Goderich *Signal*, 17 May 1900). The cast of twenty-three made a full choir for the cathedral scene and sang Mendelssohn's celebrated quartette for good measure. *Quo Vadis* followed in September 1900, and the next year

May A. Bell in the Marks Brothers' production of *Little Starlight*

Goderich saw *The Holy City, or The Way of the Cross*, 'Reverently acted by actors of the Greatest Christian Abilities' (Goderich *Star*, 20 December 1901).

Fairly typical of the first decade of the twentieth century was the 1902–3 season. Musicals and historical pageant plays continued to be popular, as did Irish, English, and western frontier dramas. Visiting stars included Henrietta Crosman, an old trouper but a recent star, in *The Sword of the King*, Robert Mantell in Tremayne's *The Dagger and the Cross,* Herbert Kelcey as Sherlock Holmes, E.S. Willard in *The Cardinal* by Louis N. Parker, and Sir John Martin-Harvey in *The Only Way*, an adaptation of *A Tale of Two Cities*.

Elaborate historical romances found great favour. Two road companies of *Faust*, one starring Lewis Morrison and the other Alan Tabor, moved tons of equipment and costume from one 'opera house' to the next. A less sombre and quite beautiful production of *When Knighthood Was in Flower*, starring Effie Ellsler (Mary Tudor) and Walter Seymour (Duke of Suffolk), received much attention. The sets for this extravaganza were painted from sketches prepared 'especially' at Windsor Park and Greenwich Palace, and the stage furniture was

May A. Bell as Little Starlight

modelled on pieces at Hampton Court.[43] A surviving poster at Theatre London shows Mary Tudor on the edge of a huge four poster bed, surrounded by gentlemen of the court, all brocaded, ruffled, bewigged, and buckled in great style. It would be some years before the movies would equal this kind of spectacle.

Most of the shows touring Ontario immediately before the First World War were musicals, farce comedies, and standbys such as *East Lynne* and Denman Thompson's *The Old Homestead*. The frequent appearances of Thomas A. Edison's Genuine Talking Pictures were a constant reminder of how much cheaper it was to transport a film than a company of live actors. When Robert Mantell toured in *The Merchant of Venice* in 1913, he was competing with a 'two-reel' version filmed by the Tanhouser Co., for which the admission was 10 cents.

Still, the 'legitimate' stars persevered. On 1 December 1913 the Sault *Daily Star* advertised the appearance of Margaret Anglin with this comment: 'Miss Anglin's present tour brings to mind that there are a large number of prominent actors playing Shakespeare this year. Besides Miss Anglin, there is William Faversham, whose production of *Julius Caesar* last year will be remembered, Sothern and Marlowe, Sir Johnston Forbes-Roberston and his wife, Miss Gertrude Elliott, and the Stratford-on-Avon Players under the direction of Mr. F.R. Benson.' The 1912–13 season also brought to Ontario Mme Nazimova in *The Marionettes* and *Bella Donna*, Annie Russell in *She Stoops To Conquer*, Marie Dressler's Players in *Tillie's Nightmare*, Klaw and Erlanger's production of *Ben Hur*, and Shaw's *Man and Superman* (London *Free Press*, 9 September 1902).

The highlights of the last season before the war were undoubtedly *Peter Pan*, starring Maude Adams, and the tour of Sir John Martin-Harvey in three plays: *The Only Way, The Cigarette Maker's Romance*, and *The Breed of the Treshams*. Because the season included visits by other stars including Mrs Fiske, William Faversham, John Drew, Nat Goodwin, and Cyril Maude, it seems fairly rich to readers now, but contemporary critics bewailed the decline of the road and the preponderance of mindless comedies such as *Mutt and Jeff in Panama* and *Bunty Pulls the Strings*.[44] It is perhaps symbolic that the great Pavlova, billed simply as a 'dancer,' played one-night stands and in London followed the May A. Bell Marks Stock Company's production of *The Ranch Queen*, while the next show, *The Little Co-ed* by Perry's Peerless Players, waited its turn at a local hotel. The Golden Age of the road was over, and suddenly the trains that had carried actors and 'carloads of scenery' were needed to transport soldiers, supplies, and ammunition.

NOTES

1 Edwin C. Guillet, *Pioneer Inns and Taverns* (Toronto: Ontario Publishing 1956), 4, 139–40
2 Solomon Franklin Smith, *Theatrical Management in the West and South for Thirty Years* (New York: Harper and Bros 1868), 40–2
3 Advertisement dated March 1854 reproduced in 'Reminiscences of Early Days in the World of Thespis,' Hamilton *Herald*, 18 May 1901. The Hamilton Royal Metropolitan was a converted chair factory at the corner of Rebecca and John streets. It burned in 1866.
4 For Nickinson, see James Russell Aikens, 'The Rival Operas: Toronto Theatre 1874–84,' 2 vols, PH D dissertation, University of Toronto 1975; Murray Edwards, *A Stage in Our Past* (Toronto: University of Toronto Press 1968), 12, 25, 27, 87; and Franklin Graham, *Histrionic Montreal* (Montreal: Lovell 1902; reprint New York: Benjamin Blom 1969). For Holman, see these three titles and also Frances Ruth Hines, 'Concert Life in London, Ontario, 1870–1880,' M MUS thesis, University of Western Ontario 1977.
5 Aikens, 'Rival Operas,' gives a detailed account of John Nickinson and his family and information about the Holmans in Toronto. See also 'The Holman Family,' in Hines, 'Concert Life.'
6 'Reminiscences of Early Days in the World of Thespis,' Hamilton *Herald*, 8 June 1901
7 Alfred Bernheim, *The Business of Theatre* (1932; reprinted: New York: Benjamin Blom 1964), chaps 8–9
8 Accounts of the various syndicates may be found in ibid.; Travis Bogard, 'Actors in the Hand,' *The Revels History of Drama in English*, vol. 8, 19–23; Jack Poggi, *The Theatre in America: The Impact of Economic Forces, 1870–1967* (Ithaca, NY 1968), chaps 1–2; Gerald Lenton, 'The Development and Nature of Vaudeville in Toronto from 1899 to 1915,' PH D dissertation, University of Toronto 1983
9 For more detail on the Michigan, Ohio, and Canadian Circuit, see Mary Brown, 'Ambrose Small: A Ghost in Spite of Himself,' in L.W. Conolly, ed., *Theatrical Touring and Founding in North America* (Westport, Conn.: Greenwood Press 1982).
10 The theatres listed are

Detroit:	Lyceum, Whitney Grand, and Empire
Cleveland:	Lyceum and Cleveland
Chicago:	Great Northern, Alhambra, Academy, Bijou, and Criterion
St Louis:	Havlin's and Grand Opera House
Louisville;	Avenue
Toledo:	Lyceum and Burt's New
Grand Rapids:	Power's and Grand

Cincinnati: Heuck's and Lyceum
Milwaukee: Alhambra
Kansas City: Gillis
Washington: Academy of Music

11 Douglas Arrell, 'Harold Nelson: The Early Years (c. 1865–1905),' *Theatre History in Canada / Histoire du théâtre au Canada* 1:2 (Fall 1980), 83–110

12 Michael Bennett Leavitt, *Fifty Years of Theatrical Management* (New York: Broadway Publishing 1912), 567

13 New York *Dramatic Mirror*, 29 April 1914, 6, carried the following item, titled 'Canada for the British':

> The English invasion of Canada, as it has been termed in some quarters, is evidently bearing fruit. Moreover, it has 'undoubtedly' as the Toronto correspondent of the London *Stage* puts it, 'received only slight attention at the hands of the United States producers and booking powers.'
>
> According to all indications, 'Canada for the British' is becoming an issue which will merit the attention of the producing and booking powers of the United States. Mr. MARTIN HARVEY has been able to make a profitable tour of Canada, playing his repertory to approximately $12,000 a week.
>
> Declares the above correspondent: 'According to plans made known here, it is the intention to increase the number of British theatrical visitors here next year by one hundred percent, thereby reducing the extent of American bookings throughout Canada.'
>
> This sudden influx of British stars and their London companies is due largely to the British Canadian Theatrical Organization Society, which has as its object the linking up of theatrical bookings throughout the British Empire, so that London companies can cross Canada to Australia and New Zealand assured of thirty or forty weeks' booking. 'However, it was Mr LEWIS WALLER'S capture of Canadian money-bags during the two previous seasons,' declares the correspondent, 'that started the procession into the Dominion. The novelty of the scheme is that the companies begin and sometimes end their labour independent of United States management, a thing that has scarcely happened hitherto.'

In London, Ontario, Waller was in *A Marriage of Convenience* on 8 January 1913; Martin Harvey presented *The Only Man* on 20 February 1914 and *The Cigarette Maker's Romance* and *The Breed of the Treshams* on 21 February 1914. The plan to increase the number of British stars touring the empire died with the outbreak of the First World War.

14 Trans-Canada Theatres Ltd, a consortium of Montreal businessmen, bought from Ambrose Small the Grand Opera Houses in Toronto, Hamilton, London, St Thomas, Kingston, and Peterborough, and all booking contracts for all other theatres now existing (in Small's control). In 1919 Small had one-year contracts with theatres in North Bay, Sudbury, Orillia, Barrie, Trenton, Galt, Stratford,

Midland, Lindsay, and Sarnia, and five-year contracts with theatres in St Catharines and Renfrew as well as a contract of unspecified duration in Brantford. The agreements of sale are in the E.W.M. Flock Papers, in the Regional Collection, D.B. Weldon Library, University of Western Ontario. Flock was a London lawyer who acted for Small.

15 Unless otherwise specified, events are dated from the author's calendar of performances for London's two grand opera houses, published in *Theatre History in Canada / Histoire du théâtre au Canada* 9:2 (Fall 1988). Sarah Bernhardt toured Ontario in 1881, 1887, and 1891 (Toronto), 1896 (London and Toronto), 1905 (Ottawa, Kingston, and Hamilton), 1910 (London and Toronto), 1911 (Toronto), and 1917 (Hamilton, Kingston, and Ottawa). See John Hare and Ramon Hathorn, 'Sarah Bernhardt's Visits to Canada: Dates and Repertory,' *Theatre History in Canada / Histoire du théâtre au Canada* 2:2 (Fall 1981), 93–116. The many appearances of O'Neill, Irving, Sothern, and Jefferson have not yet been documented.

16 Vanderheyden Fyles, 'An Apollo of Long Ago,' *Green Room Book* (July 1914), 39–42. Quoted by William C. Young in *Famous Actors and Actresses of the American Stage* (New York and London: R.R. Bowker Co. 1975), 944–6

17 Interviews with Rankin resulted in three (undated) articles printed in the San Francisco *Examiner*, found in the Performing Arts Collection, Shields Library, UCLA, Davis: 'McKee Rankin Taps Fund of Memories,' 'McKee Rankin Tells of Plays before the Early Mormons,' and 'McKee Rankin Tells of Old Days of the Stage and Early Stars.'

18 'McKee Rankin Taps Fund of Memories,' San Francisco *Examiner*, n.d.

19 See Dorothy Sedgwick, *A Bibliography of English-Language Theatre and Drama in Canada 1800–1914*, Nineteenth Century Theatre Research Occasional Publications, 1 (Edmonton, Alberta, 1976), nos 212–25. The typescript of 'Confusion' is in the Performing Arts Collection, UCLA (Davis).

20 See calendar of performances in Martin's Opera House in Leslie Anne O'Dell, 'Theatrical Events in Kingston, Ontario: 1879–1897,' PH D dissertation, University of Toronto 1982.

21 This opinion was fortified by the discovery of a copyright dispute. In 1893 a lawsuit for $10,000 in personal damages was filed in London, Ontario, by George C. Rankin against Arthur McKee Rankin. The suit alleged unlawful use of the plaintiff's work without recompense. Since no judgment is recorded, it may be safe to assume that the brothers settled out of court. I owe the discovery of this document and the subsequent search for judgment to M.A. Jameson of the D.B. Weldon Library, University of Western Ontario. The papers are in the Regional Collection.

22 The Performing Arts Collection at UCLA (Davis) has personal correspondence to and from McKee Rankin, much of which relates to his non-theatrical enterprises.

23 For Ida Van Cortland's experiences in the Martimes, see Mary Elizabeth Smith, *Too Soon the Curtain Fell: A History of Theatre in Saint John, 1789–1900* (Fredericton: Brunswick Press 1981); Linda M. Peake, 'Establishing a Theatrical Tradition: Prince Edward Island, 1877–1896,' *Theatre History in Canada / Histoire du théâtre au Canada* 2:2 (Fall 1981), 117–32; and Kathleen D.J. Fraser, 'Theatrical Touring in Late Nineteenth-Century Canada: Ida Van Cortland and the Tavernier Company 1877–1896,' PH D dissertation, University of Western Ontario 1985.

24 The Taverner Collection in the Theatre Department, Metropolitan Toronto Library, includes scripts, correspondence, account books, photographs, etc., belonging to Ida Van Cortland and Albert Tavernier. See also chapter 2 in Edwards, *Stage in Our Past*, and Aikens, 'Rival Operas.'

25 In 1884 Julia Arthur was using the stage name Nellie Hazlewood.

26 Information about Julia Arthur's career may be found in T. Allston Brown, *History of the New York Stage*, 3 vols (1903; reprinted New York: Benjamin Blom 1964); *Canadian Magazine* 11 (1898), 31–4; Hamilton *Herald*, 3 February 1905 and 25 June 1910; Amy Leslie (pseud.), *Some Players: Personal Sketches* (Chicago: Stone 1899); Lewis C. Strang, *Famous Actors of the Day in America*, First Series (Boston: L.C. Page 1900); and Denis Salter, 'At Home and Abroad: the Acting Career of Julia Arthur (1869–1950),' *Theatre History in Canada / Histoire du théâtre au Canada* 5:1 (Spring 1984), 1–35.

27 Anglin's various New York engagements were traced in Brown, *History of the New York Stage*, vol II, 588; vol. III, 528, 544–5.

28 For further information on Miller's early career, see Strang, *Famous Actors*; Aikens, 'Rival Operas'; George C.D. O'Dell, *Annals of the New York Stage* (London, England: George Redway 1888). The plays given for the 1886 and 1902 tours are from Edwards, *Stage in Our Past*; the others were performed in London, Ontario. The production of *The Great Divide* is discussed in Frank P. Morse, *Backstage with Henry Miller* (New York: E.P. Dutton 1938).

29 Clara Morris, *Life on the Stage: My Experiences and Recollections* (New York: McClure, Phillips and Company 1901), 3

30 *Canadian Monthly* 6 (1874), 385

31 From Aikens's calendar of performances, compiled from the Toronto *Mail*

32 *Canadian Monthly* 9 (1876), 171

33 Ibid., 454–5

34 *Rose-Belford's Canadian Monthly* 4 (1879–80), 333

35 Ibid., 334

36 Graham, *Histrionic Montreal*, 261–2

37 Otis Skinner, *Footlights and Spotlights* (Indianapolis: Bobbs-Merrill Co. 1924), 109–12; quoted by Young, *Famous Actors and Actresses*

38 Young's list of roles checked against my calendar of performances in London, Ontario.

39 Graham, *Histrionic Montreal*, 261
40 Musical events seen and heard in London, Ontario
41 All seen in London, Ontario, in these years
42 Mantell toured Ontario with Tremayne's *A Secret Warrant* in 1899 and his *The Dagger and the Cross* in 1900 and 1902–3. Both playscripts are in the Robert Mantell Collection in the Player's Club in New York. See Murray D. Edwards, 'A Playwright from the Canadian Past: W.A. Tremayne (1864–1939),' *Theatre History in Canada / Histoire du théâtre au Canada* 3:1 (Spring 1982), 43–50.
43 Robert Toll, *On with the Show! The First Century of Show Business in America* (New York: Oxford University Press 1976), 347, 353
44 In the previous season audiences saw the Oscar Straus / Stanislaus Stange operetta, *The Chocolate Soldier*, and in the next season *Fanny's First Play*.

6 *Variety Theatre*

GERALD LENTON-YOUNG

In 1914 Toronto's four large vaudeville theatres had a combined weekly capacity of 150,000, approximately one-third of the city's population. Toronto's three legitimate theatres held less than 35,000, only 2,000 more than the city's burlesque houses.[1] The available seats for the two principal forms of variety theatre therefore outnumbered the legitimate's capacity by more than five to one. Although their frequency throughout the century was not as great as the culminating forms of vaudeville and burlesque, it is safe to say that in all its forms variety theatre presentations outnumbered dramatic presentations in nineteenth-century Ontario. Some of the types seen – puppetry, acrobatics, and magic, for example – descended directly from ancient times, but others, such as the minstrel show, dime museums, and panoramas, developed to satisfy the demands of different segments and new classes of a rapidly evolving society.

Development of the various forms followed a predictable pattern of growth. Because there were no formal circuits or permanent playing spaces for early performers, wandering players and travelling exhibits were first on the scene. They were followed by menageries and circuses, the circuit pioneers everywhere in nineteenth-century North America. Then the minstrel performers who travelled with circuses broke away and established variety in theatre buildings. This innovation spawned a mushrooming of other forms that created permanent homes for variety. It then became fully institutionalized in concert saloons and dime museums, the two nineteenth-century forms that were transformed into the twentieth-century big-business forms of burlesque and vaudeville.

None of the nineteenth-century forms was unique to Canada. They were often special to North America but were developed primarily in the eastern United States as soon as large population bases began to form. Throughout the century the vast majority of all professional entertainers seen in these fields were American or European, as was the case with the legitimate theatre. In this sense the entertainment was not indigenous. However, our forbears chose to import the product because it filled a need, and in that sense it is as indigenous to the cities and towns of Ontario as to anywhere in North America.

Wandering Players and Travelling Exhibits

On 30 March 1801, to service a population of 336, six persons in the town of York were 'granted licenses for selling wines and spirituous Liquors, and for Keeping Tavern.'[2] By mid-century, with a population of 25,000, there were 152 taverns and 206 beer shops.[3] Given the density of these institutions, it is not surprising that early variety entertainments in Toronto centred around them. Until mid-century theatrical activity of every kind, including dramatic presentations, was most often associated with taverns and connected hotels, which served as centres of political, social, economic, and cultural activities: 'By necessity and often also by choice, an innkeeper arranged for his guests a variety of amusements and kept an assembly room for dances, local debates, political and religious meetings, exhibitions of various kinds, and dramatic presentations.'[4]

The earliest recorded performance of this type in York (Toronto) was a puppet show on 3 October 1800. Unfortunately the diarist Joseph Willcocks offers no details about the place or the nature of the show. But the town was soon visited by itinerant performers who did so. Messrs Potter and Thompson from London, for example, presented an exhibition of 'Philosophical, Mathematical and Curious Experiments,' and a 'Theatrical performance consisting of Songs, Recitations, and Ventriloquisms' (*York Gazette*, 5 May 1810). Another foreign artist, a Master Dixon from New York's Park Theatre, visited York with a concert of comic songs, recitations, and dancing at Snyder's Ballroom (*Upper Canada Gazette*, 12 November 1821). Four years later the puppetry, acrobatics, and songs of Glause were seen in York (*Colonial Advocate*, 19 February 1825). Not long after, the town received a lecture and demonstration on electricity (*Colonial Advocate*, 22 April 1830). In 1834 another ventriloquist, Mr Kenworthy, offered details of his program in order to assure Toronto's citizens there was 'nothing which could offend the nicest delicacy' (*Canadian Correspondent*, 11 October 1834). Moreover, he pointed out for religious persons that his entertainment presented 'the unusual attraction of being an amusement which possesses not the slightest demoralizing tendency.' The inverse implication, of course, was that such amusements were immoral, an argument presented throughout the century by the puritan elements of Ontario's society.

During the early part of the century the idea of presenting these entertainments probably came from the itinerant players wandering through Upper Canada's towns and villages as often as it came from their employers. Patrick O'Neill points out that strolling companies on the American frontier continually changed personnel, 'and while making their way from one company to another, actors stopped at various towns along the way to give an evening's amusement to help finance the trip.'[5] They needed no equipment other than the few items they dragged along, and they would perform wherever paying customers could be assembled. As the century progressed, most were absorbed by other forms. The major exceptions were reciters, particularly elocutionists, and lecturers, particularly on scientific subjects. Numbers of both multiplied furiously throughout the century as the puritan base of the expanding population looked for edifying pastimes.

Another early variety theatre entertainment that satisfied those with the strictest codes of 'life as enlightenment' were panoramas, for example, *The Vision of the Heavens*, seen in Toronto in 1845, *Adam and Eve in Paradise* (1852), and *The Panorama of Jerusalem* (1856). The early exhibits were simply very long paintings put on a roll and slowly revealed to the audience by a lecturer who singled out the important people and landmarks with his pointer, letting the viewers use their imaginations to create the resemblance.[6] One of these simple panoramas presented in York in 1831 featured a 'Grand Panoramic View of Bytown,' eighty-two feet long and eight and a half feet high, painted by W.S. Hunter (*Colonial Advocate*, 29 September 1831).

By the 1860s numerous travelling panoramas were visiting Ontario's towns illustrating fictional, historical, and even current events. Kingston, for example, saw Milton's *Paradise Lost, The Napoleonic Wars, The River Thames and The City of London, A Moving Panorama of England, Ireland and Scotland*, and *The American Civil War*. By this time, too, the exhibitions had become much more elaborate. *La Rue's Great War Show*, which visited Kingston in 1863, included 90,000 moving figures of soldiers, horses, animals, and ships (Kingston *Daily News*, 23 June 1863). In addition to moving miniature figures, the shows started making greater use of lighting, including back lighting and translucent sections that created spectacular changes in colour, and of special effects such as sound, smoke, and gunpowder explosions. The ultimate achievements in this art form were created in large buildings especially designed for panorama displays. Toronto's

Cyclorama Building, built at the corner of Front and York streets in 1887, was Ontario's landmark in this field. Unfortunately it had a short history; for all such shows were quietly replaced after the turn of the century by movies. In fact, during the first decade of the twentieth century most of the films shown in theatres and town halls, when live attractions were unavailable, were travelogues like the early panoramas, complete with narrator. The great attraction of both types of exhibits was undoubtedly the opportunity to enjoy the spectacle of places and things most had only heard of. Perhaps too, for many mid-nineteenth-century Ontarians an element of homesickness prompted attendance at the large number of panoramic visions of Edinburgh, Ireland, the Thames, London, and the Highlands.

Panoramic splendour played a part in another variety entertainment that became popular in mid-nineteenth-century Ontario. In this case, however, the panorama was natural and helped focus the eyes of the world on Ontario. On 30 June 1859 a thirty-six-year-old Frenchman known as Blondin, born Jean François Gravelet, crossed the Niagara Falls gorge on a tightrope. As one of North America's greatest natural wonders, the falls already enjoyed some fame, but after Blondin's feats the 'Golden Age' of Niagara Falls truly began.[7] Blondin performed five separate crossings during the first summer, adding more difficult stunts each time. He saved the best for last: walking above the torrent on a tightrope carrying a man on his back! Blondin's instant fame prompted a host of imitators. Funambulists cropped up everywhere, crossing rivers, canyons, and city streets, but only one directly challenged Blondin. During one of Blondin's first crossings a young man in the crowd told his girlfriend he could duplicate the great man's feats. The following summer Blondin moved his rope downstream to the whirlpool rapids and found his original site, about three-quarters of a kilometre below Horseshoe Falls, occupied by a Signor Giullermo Antonio Farini.[8] The head-to-head competition produced the greatest daredevil feats of their kind ever seen. Blondin crossed blindfolded, on three-foot stilts, at night by the light of fireworks, and carrying a man on his back again. Farini duplicated all but the stilt crossing and added his own novelties: 'He shrouded himself in a sack; he staggered across in his role of "Mickey Free, the Irish Pedestrian," he wore a crinoline like a pantomime horse. He walked by night, but his fireworks went off prematurely in a burst of flame along the rope, singeing his costume and leaving him to make his way home by dark. As "Biddy O'Flaherty, the Irish washerwoman," he carried out a large washing machine – wooden tub with two-meter levers attached – and washed ladies' handkerchiefs in water hauled up in buckets from the river. He left them out to dry overnight on the rope and his poster challenged, ''If anyone doubts their being washed, they can go out and examine them.'''[9] Finally Farini faced the greatest challenge, crossing with a man on his back. He offered the doubtful honour of being passenger to the Prince of Wales, but Albert Edward wisely declined, and Farini looked elsewhere for a volunteer. A Port Hope tailor's son named Rowland McMullen appeared from nowhere, successfully performed his part as relaxed deadweight, and vanished immediately afterward.[10] Signor Farini was, in fact, a local boy. Born in 1838 as William Hunt, his family moved from Orangeville to Port Hope when William was just an infant. He studied medicine at Victoria College but rejected the then poorly paid profession to become a lecturer on physical culture, a performance that always included demonstrations of feats of strength. His show business career took him around the world for the next twenty-five years, and he caused a sensation in the late 1870s when it was revealed that the beautiful young daughter he fired from a cannon was actually a boy, his adopted son, El Nino Farini, who years before had been featured in the family trapeze act. Farini's more important legacy, however, was the cannon out of which he shot 'Lulu.' He invented and patented the mechanism that is still used in circuses today. In the late 1880s Farini remarried, to the daughter of the kaiser's aide Count von Mueller. For the next forty years the couple moved between Germany, England, and Canada, while Farini dabbled with inventions, painting, sculpture, and writing books. In 1919 they settled in Port Hope, where Farini died in 1929 at the age of ninety-three.

Following Blondin's and Farini's successes, daredevils of every type risked their lives for money. Most appeared in the circus, where high tents and wide-open space left the spectator's mouth suitably agape. Some toured on their own, performing outside in summer and squeezing indoors in winter. Whenever possible, daredevil acts made it into the theatre, walking on wires over the audience, balancing on tall poles, and even looping the loop on small stages. But none of these performances offered the same thrill as the crossing of the Niagara Gorge on a tightrope with a human payload.

Before we leave the famous falls, a few words might be said about the infamous mile-long front, a collection of souvenir stands, curio shops, museums, taverns, tepees, and medicine shows which Duncan McLeod describes as 'the playground and workshop of some of the continent's worst scoundrels.'[11] Some might label these early hucksters performers, but they were salesmen more than anything else and deserve no further consideration or comparison to the wandering players of the nineteenth century who collected their wages for general entertainment skills. The front was expropriated by the Ontario government in 1888 and made into a public park.[12]

Menageries and Circuses

A sharp contrast to the lone wandering player was provided by the large menageries and circuses that visited Upper Canada in the early 1800s. The menagerie was the older of the two forms. The first circus did not appear in North America until 1793, but as early as 1716 a lion was exhibited in the colonial settlement along the Atlantic coast that was to become the United States.[13] At first the displays were isolated incidents, the product of enterprising tavern owners or hotel keepers trying to increase business. Because there were no zoological gardens or other permanently located collections of animals in Ontario at that time, and indeed until a long time after, exotic animals attracted considerable interest. Gradually the simple exhibit expanded into collections.

York was first visited by a menagerie in 1826. The 'Grand Exhibition of Living Animals' was presented at Mr Snyder's Inn and included a zebra, a camel, a Mediterranean pony, and two African emus.[14] Two years later lions, tigers, jaguars, leopards, baboons, and monkeys were seen with 'The Grand Caravan of Living Animals' at the Steamboat Hotel.[15] And in 1833, at the Court House Green, York residents saw their first pachyderm, Columbus, probably the most famous elephant in North America during the first half of the century.[16] By the mid-1830s visiting menageries had grown to include rhinoceroses, kangaroos, ostriches, llamas, boa constrictors, etc. Occasionally the exotic nature of the animals was enhanced to attract patrons. In 1836, for example, Toronto was visited by a menagerie featuring a 'unicorn':

This animal has been a subject of much speculation among naturalists. It has been considered, by Theological Commentators, as the Unicorn of Holy Writ, as mentioned and described in the book of Job. This animal certainly ranks next to the Elephant in size, and many writers consider him equal in bulk. He is usually found about 12 feet long, and the circumference of the body about equal to the length, and his height about 8 feet. He is a native of Asia and Africa, and is usually found in those extensive forests that are frequented by the Elephant, Lion and Royal Tiger, and subsists entirely on vegetable food. The one here offered for inspection is the first Living Rhinoceros ever brought to this country; he is 8 years old, his weight is Four Thousand Two Hundred

Pounds; he was taken at the foot of one of the Himalayan mountains. (*Canadian Correspondent*, 13 July 1836)

The early local appearances of such exotic collections occurred because Ontario fell into the territory controlled by the Zoological Institute, which monopolized the business after 1835. The only major exhibitor to remain outside the combine was Issac Van Amburgh, a lion-tamer who gained such fame that his name was still used as a show title almost a hundred years after his death. His menagerie was more than just an exhibit, it included tricks by the animals, clowns, and equestrians, similar to the circuses of the time. In fact, by 1835 the distinction between menagerie and circus was starting to cloud. The exhibit featuring the rhinoceros-unicorn, for example, included three minstrels and a twelve-member orchestra. Before beginning the story of the merger, however, the separate beginnings of the circus should be considered.

Most historians agree that the circus as it is known today is less than 200 years old. The credit for founding the first circus is generally conceded to Philip Astley, an English war hero. In the 1770s, on the outskirts of London near Westminster Bridge, he presented his equestrian entertainment, with acrobats, clowns and rope-walkers as subordinate performers.[17] The first complete performance in North America was presented in Philadelphia on 3 April 1793 by John Bill Ricketts, a pupil of one of Astley's major British rivals. Ricketts's show did so well he took it on tour, making appearances in New York, Boston, and Albany, slowly moving northward along the eastern seaboard until he found his way into Canada and presented seasons in Montreal and Quebec City.[18]

Ontario's first visitor was the Royal Circus, owned and operated by a George Blanchard, who used Montreal as his base between 1824 and 1830. In August 1826 the Royal Circus visited Brockville, Kingston, and York. The troupe included two equestrians, one clown, and an actor. Little is known about the exact nature of this first entertainment. Does the presence of an actor suggest drama? By mid-century the few equestrian shows that survived presented full dramas with great spectacle, daring rescues on horseback, jousting, etc. It is more likely, however, that Blanchard's troupe followed the common pattern of performing pantomimes and playlets between equestrian tricks. Shortly after Blanchard's visit Ontario got its own resident circus, also called the Royal Circus, described by Edwin Guillet:

As early as 1827 York had a resident circus under the management of Besnard and Black. This was held in the barn of De Forest's Hotel on King Street, east of Sherbourne. There was no menagerie connected with it, the entertainment consisted of 'riding and feats of horsemanship, trapeze and horizontal bar performances, and tricks of juggling.' Mrs. Besnard was the favourite of the circus-goers of that period, and her 'tossing of balls and knives was one of the principal features of the show.' From De Forest's the Besnard circus ring was moved to George Garside's Hotel on the west side of New (Jarvis) Street, near Duke; thence it was removed to Barney Roddy's Tavern on the west side of Church, just below King; and it finally was located on the south side of Wellington Street, a short distance west of Church. Here, enclosed by a high board fence, the circus was long operated by Besnard and was a well-patronized place of amusement.[19]

The circus was in fact run by a Mr Bernard, not Besnard, and generally included six performers and an orchestra. Contemporary references focused on the equestrian feats, the slack-rope work, clowning, and acrobatics. In 1831 a Mr McCleary was added to present recitations and songs, but there is no evidence that York's first resident circus presented Equestrian Drama (*Canadian Freeman*, 13 October 1831). McCleary and a slack-rope artist by the name of Jackson remained with the company when it was taken over by A. J. Parker and renamed the York circus in 1832 or 1833. No record of performances by the circus in 1834 has yet been found.

By the 1830s these small circuses started to feel the pressure of larger organizations that were amalgamating under the more acceptable 'menagerie' label. J.M.S. Careless describes the negative attitude towards amusements in early nineteenth-century Ontario. Of all the travelling shows in the early years, however, the menageries, because of their educational value, managed to avoid much of the harshest condemnation. It therefore became common practice to place the words 'menagerie' or 'museum' in the most prominent position of the title, often excluding the word 'circus' altogether. In the first half of the century, when there were still some differences between the menagerie and circus, the former often found it advisable or even necessary to include in their publicity a reference to the accuracy of the 'menagerie' title. One such organization, visiting Cobourg in 1840, included the assurance in their advertisement that the exhibition was 'so entirely foreign in its nature from all circuses or Mountebank shows, that it meets with the most cordial communities' (Cobourg *Star*, 20 August 1840).

In 1856 the Toronto City Council refused to grant a licence to the second circus visiting that summer, prompting a great debate about such entertainments. The public rallied to their support, however, and the reopening of Toronto's toll gates to circuses that same summer testified to their popularity.[20] A large part of the objection to visiting circuses was related to the gamblers and flimflam men who followed them. Circus owners usually had no association with these hangers-on but could do nothing to stop their activities. Later in the century even the large Barnum and Bailey and Ringling Brothers circuses, known as the Sunday School Circuit because they were supposedly free of gambling and crime, were constantly plagued by ever-present pickpockets, bogus ticket sellers, and other charlatans.

Attempts to avoid the circus label continued for the first three-quarters of the century. G.F. Bailey's advertisement in Toronto's *Globe* of 1 July 1867 displays another reason for the avoidance. Calling his show 'G.F. Bailey's & Cos. Metropolitan Quadruple Combination,' he avowed: 'For the gratification of Teachers, Schools & Children and for those who, from religious or other scruples, do not desire to witness the Equestrian and Gymnastic Exercises, there will be a Grand Morning Exhibition, on Wednesday, July 3, of all the attractions and specialities of the large and comprehensive Menagerie, including the comical Performing Elephants and the Lilliputian Baby Elephant From Africa, without the Circus Performances.' When familiar labels weren't enough, new terms were invented. J.B. Lent, for example, who toured his show throughout Ontario in the 1860s and 1870s used, titles such as 'People's Hipposoonamadon,' 'The Equescurriculum,' and 'J.B. Lent's World Fair Leviathan Universal Living Exhibition.' And the company that bought Van Amburgh's name in 1872 advertised itself in the Belleville *Intelligencer*, on 2 August that year as 'Van Amburgh and Co.'s Great Golden Menagerie Combined with Wombwell's Royal English Menagerie, Together with the Siegrist and Zanfretta French and Spanish Troupe and the Wonderful Russian Athletes from St. Petersburg.' Two other large circuses visited Belleville that same summer. W.W. Cole's Museum, Hippodrome and Menagerie promised 300 men and horses and 200 living animals and a grand procession of twenty cages and forty vehicles (Belleville *Intelligencer*, 24 May 1872). 'O'Brien's 4 Great Shows Consolidated: Museum, Menagerie, Circus and Caravan,' promised a thousand wild beasts and a mile of horses, cages and dens in their parade (ibid., 9 August 1872). Reviews reveal that there was some hyperbole involved, but all were large shows that pleased the audiences. The increasing number and size of these shows mark the beginning of what is commonly referred to as the 'Golden Age' of the American circus, a period that lasted until the start of the First World War.

By 1880 there were more than forty circus organizations travelling each season; in 1890 there were approximately seventy circuses operating in North America; and by 1903 there were at least ninety-eight.[21] As the number of organizations grew, so did the size of the show. By 1910 the Barnum and Bailey Greatest Show on Earth required eighty-four railway cars to move from city to city.[22] With so many organizations travelling the continent, all Ontario towns enjoyed frequent visits. In June 1867, for example, Bailey's circus was followed around Ontario by Lent's, visiting many of the same towns only a few days apart. Bailey's more extensive route included thirty-six Ontario towns: Brockville, Prescott, Ottawa, Aylmer, Perth, Kingston, Napanee, Belleville, Trenton, Percy, Cobourg, Port Hope, Bowmanville, Port Perry, Whitby, and Markham in June; and Brampton, Guelph, Berlin, Stratford, St Marys, Woodstock, Paris, Galt, Dundas, Hamilton, Caledonia, St Catharines, Brantford, Simcoe, St Thomas, London, and Chatham in July. J.B. Lent's route in June included Cornwall, Williamsburg, Ottawa, Brockville, Kingston, Belleville, Port Hope, Toronto, Guelph, London, and St Marys (Toronto Globe, 18 June 1867). By this time circuses included numerous side shows and carnival elements. Freaks were displayed, often featured in the most prominent place of the advertisements, as were scientific discoveries and lecturers. Competition at the start of the new century, not only with each other but with new forms of popular entertainment, forced amalgamations. Even the big three, Barnum and Bailey, Ringling Brothers, and Forepaugh-Sells circuses, agreed to divide territory. Before the First World War all three were controlled by the Ringling Brothers, who ran them as separate entities until 1919 when they merged the two largest into Ringling Brothers' and Barnum and Bailey's Greatest Show on Earth. The Golden Age of the American circus was past. The large number of visiting organizations that had saturated every city in the United States and Canada a few decades earlier had dwindled to a few large ones that visited only occasionally, a pattern that exists to this day.

Animals continued to play an important role in the circus, but primarily as performers. The menagerie aspect was taken over in the last quarter of the century by museums and permanent resident collections or zoos. One of the best of these early institutions was established in Toronto by Harry Piper, a native son who later distinguished himself as an alderman:

Always the showman, Harry decided to open a small zoo and a couple of years later, 1874, moved the enterprise to the northeast corner of Front and

York Streets. Included among 'zoological garden' specimens were two elephants, Sir John and Laurier by name, each costing their owner $1,000.

As the gardens expanded in both size and popularity, Piper acquired two lion cubs from the Central Park zoo in New York City. Named Romeo and Juliet, these additions cost the entrepreneur $500 each.

The most prominent feature of the Front Street menagerie was a large long-dead whale which Harry had purchased in 1881, from some Northumberland Straits fishermen where the unfortunate beast had run ashore. As long as the weather remained cool, the 60' attraction was quite a hit with visitors lining up inside the mammal's propped-open jaw to have their portrait taken. As the temperature began to increase, the whale began to decompose and Piper was forced to exhibit his 'star' in less inhabited surroundings in High Park and the Exhibition Grounds where souvenir hunters made off with bits and pieces until Piper's whale was no more. The rest of Piper's zoo eventually made its way to High Park where they formed the nucleus of the small collection still visited by thousands year round. (*Sunday Sun*, 26 February 1984)

The Minstrel Show

The next and perhaps historically most important variety organization to develop in nineteenth-century North America was the minstrel show. It popularized variety entertainment, moved it into theatre buildings, and fostered most of the specialty acts seen later in vaudeville and burlesque. The first famous black-faced white performer was Thomas D. Rice, who introduced his famous 'Jim Crow' song and dance in 1828. Over the next decade and a half these 'Ethiopian Delineators,' as they were then known, popped up all over the continent between acts on the legitimate stage, in circus side shows, saloons, fairs, and hotels. Ontarians got an early look at the entertainment in 1831, when a touring menagerie carried three American performers 'to sing several comic Negro Songs, among others the celebrated JIM CROW' (*Canadian Correspondent*, 13 July 1836). Two other minstrel performers were able by themselves to attract Ontario crowds in 1840: they were albino negro children, aged six and eight, who sang and danced 'à la Jim Crow' (*British Colonist*, 10 June 1840).

During this early period, and unique to the history of Toronto, opposition developed. The black population petitioned Toronto's mayors in 1840, 1841, 1842, and 1843 to forbid licences to circuses and menageries that allowed 'certain acts, and songs, such as Jim Crow and what they call other Negro Characters.'[23] O'Neill claims that the failure of City Council to act on the petitions was more likely due to the limited influence of the small negro population than to the

Patrick Redmond, banjo player and theatre manager

popularity of such acts. However, their immense popularity would have been the deciding factor shortly after 1843.

In February 1843 Billy Whitlock, Frank Pelham, Dan Emmett, and Frank Bower, all unemployed black-face entertainers, joined together to form the Virginia Minstrels. Their instant success prompted a host of competitors, and 'Ethiopian Delineators' everywhere joined forces to become 'Minstrel Troupes.' Inadequate records, amateur troupes, and frequently changed names make it impossible to determine how many troupes were spawned during the first decade following the formation of the Virginia Minstrels, but it is quite clear that minstrels became extremely popular throughout the country.

Ignoring the petitions of their own black population, Ontarians embraced the new entertainment as soon as it began to appear. As early as 1849 the Ethiopian Harmonists proved the new form's popularity by drawing large audiences at Toronto's Royal Lyceum, a phenomenon that prompted some stranded actors in the city to enlist their services to run the theatre on a professional basis.[24] In 1851 more than half a dozen prominent troupes visited Toronto, including the Nightingale Ethiopian Serenaders and White's Serenaders. Then in 1855 T. 'daddy' Rice, the original Jim Crow, played Toronto's Lyceum for a week. The popularity of the form mushroomed throughout the province in the 1860s. In 1868, for example, Ottawa and Hamilton each were visited by nine different minstrel troupes. The city of Kingston was also on the itinerary of dozens of the most renowned companies, including those of 'Cool' Burgess, Sam Sharpley, Duprez and Green, J.H. Haverly, and the Georgia Minstrels, the first all-black troupe.

'Cool' Burgess is of particular interest to Ontarians because he was a native son. Born in Toronto in 1840, he began as a performer specializing in negro characters with two other well-known local figures, Denman Thompson and Patrick Redmond. The original trio was together for only a short time before Burgess moved to the United States to join J.H. Haverly, forming the Haverly-Burgess Minstrels in 1862.[25] Haverly bought Burgess out in 1866, and Burgess toured the United States and Canada with his own company, occasionally forming alliances with others but always keeping his own name front and centre. Through the 1860s and 1870s he toured Ontario extensively, returning to most cities and towns every year. In the 1880s he settled in Toronto and became a wealthy land owner.

Denman Thompson was an American, but he spent the better part of twenty years in Toronto, where he married and raised his children. He often sought success with his Irish caricatures elsewhere, but he returned to Toronto several times and tried to establish a resident

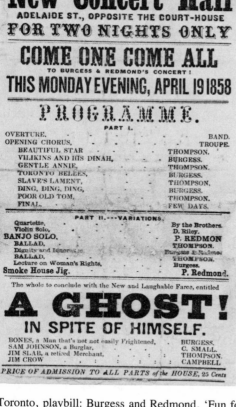

Toronto, playbill: Burgess and Redmond, 'Fun for the Million,' 19 April 1858

Colin 'Cool' Burgess, 'burnt cork' performer

minstrel troupe, his last attempt being at the Varieties Saloon on Bay Street in the early 1870s.[26] He finally got the break he had been looking for in the mid-1870s, when he discovered *The Old Homestead*, and he toured in the lead role of Joshua Whitcomb for more than twenty years. The third member of the original trio was Patrick Redmond, a theatre-machinist who sometimes performed as a banjo player. In the late 1870s he too opened his own variety theatre in Toronto, but it failed and he returned backstage.

Toronto's original trio, like most early minstrels, performed a simple collection of individual songs and dances, comic monologues, and perhaps the occasional comic interaction or sketch. But soon the minstrel show grew larger, performers became more specialized, and feature roles emerged. It therefore became necessary to organize the show in such a way as to ensure a well-mixed, rapidly paced, varied performance. By the mid-1850s, after a great deal of audience-performer interaction and experimentation, the minstrel show had evolved a standard format:

To open the three-part show, all the performers entered singing an up-beat song, took their places in a semi-circle, and waited for the command:

'Gentlemen Be Seated!' The order came from the interlocutor, the master of ceremonies and on-stage director – the ringmaster of the minstrel show – who sat in the center of the semi-circle. On the ends sat the company's leading comedians, Brudder Tambo and Brudder Bones, who were named for their instruments, the tamborine and the rhythm-clacker bones. In addition to comic repartee between end men and interlocutor, the first part of the show offered individual and group songs and dances, ranging from sentimental tear-jerkers to foolish nonsense songs, from ballroom dances to high-stepping Irish Jigs. The first part closed with an upbeat, group musical number. After an intermission, the second part, the variety section or olio, offered a wide range of individual acts, including song and dance teams, acrobats, comedians, and novelties, like people playing combs, porcupine quills, or water glasses. This part of the program, which ultimately evolved into the variety show, took place in front of a drop curtain with only the performing act on stage, so the stage crew could set up the scenery for the one-act skit that concluded the evening's performance. In early minstrel shows these finales were almost invariably set on plantations. But by the mid-1850s many minstrel troupes closed with take-offs on current events or popular fads.[27]

In summarizing the attraction of the minstrel show, Daily Paskman claims that it was the spontaneity of the olio, sharing with all folk music and folk literature the spirit of improvisation, that contributed most to its success.[28] Paskman also points out that topical humour, exchanges with the audience, and sing-alongs were important features. Entertainers were very aware of their audience's desires, which helps explain the popularity of the specialty acts developed during the olio portion of the show, where each performer worked to please the audience with a solo.

First among the specialty forms were comic stereotypes. The negro stereotype was developed in every possible form, but so was the Dutch Act or German dialect comedian, performed as early as 1858 in a minstrel show, the Comic Hebrew, developed by 1868, and the Comic Irishman, all performed in black-face! Other important specialities were the comic monologue or 'stump speech,' as it was referred to in its original form of bombastic political nonsense; dances: the cake walk, the buck and wing, the clog, and tap dancing; and female impersonation, an inevitable development, considering that someone in the all-male troupe had to play the female role in the afterpieces.

The basic format and specialties of the minstrel show remained unaltered to the end, but in the last quarter of the century other factors did change. Competition from new forms forced the minstrel show to broaden its appeal. The entertainment had to be refined to guarantee

Minstrel entertainments, 1872: 'The Apple of My Eye' and 'Washing Up'

that no one would be offended. And reflecting the general public's shift in concern, the shows began to focus on urban problems and on new immigrants, thus developing a new set of stereotypes. In addition, as other forms became increasingly lavish, the minstrel show was forced to compete.

One of the leaders in the expansion and 'refinement' of minstrelsy was George Primrose, born in St Catharines in 1852. When only sixteen he was already touring Ontario as a singer and dancer. On one of these tours, when passing through Chatham, he was hired by Murphy's Minstrels. Shortly afterward he joined Haverly's Minstrels, where he met Billy West. Both quit over a salary dispute and formed their own company in 1877. They eliminated virtually all negro material, shifting to less offensive subjects, light songs, dances, and still more lavish productions. Instead of the tattered old clothes of a Jim Crow, their performers wore satin coats, vests, breeches, silk stockings, low-cut, white satin shoes with diamond buckles, lace collars, and white wigs. The show's broader appeal soon made Primrose and West the 'Millionaires of Minstrelsy.' But they had brought the minstrel show to the point where it was indistinguishable from other forms of legitimate light musical comedy and variety, and it was only a matter of time before what was left of the minstrel show, the black-face act, was absorbed by the other forms. The pair split in 1896 to form separate companies. Primrose operated on his own for a couple of years but then joined forces with Lew Dockstader, the most famous of the late minstrel-managers. Five years later Primrose left the minstrel show to play vaudeville, where he enjoyed success for many years. He died in San Diego on 23 July 1919.

Large companies such as Primrose and West's soon drove the smaller ones out of business. By the turn of the century only one important minstrel troupe of the original form had survived, that of Lew Dockstader. Most of the companies still using the minstrel label were in fact combination troupes which presented part of a minstrel show with a legitimate play. A popular combination in Ontario in the 1890s was a minstrel show plus *Uncle Tom's Cabin*. Johnson's Minstrels went a step further, touring Ontario in 1895 with *The Underground Railroad Company*, 'a sequel to *Uncle Tom's Cabin*,' plus minstrel show (Port Hope *Daily Journal*, 15 August 1895).

The only other factor preserving minstrel entertainment was the continued popularity of amateur companies. An ideal outlet for fledgling talent, the format allowed for every type of performer. There were resident amateur minstrel troupes in every Ontario town of any size during the last quarter of the century. Some even toured, a risky business considering the likely partisan attitude of the competitor's home crowd. When the Stratford Minstrel Troupe visited St Marys in 1896, for example, the local paper noted that the company failed because 'It is believed that the local St Marys Troupe is far superior' (St Marys *Argus*, 21 May 1896).

Early Variety Theatres

Once minstrel troupes had pioneered the acceptance of a variety show on its own, other enterprising showmen joined them in supplying entertainments for the expanding urban populations which needed ways to pass their leisure time. The demand was reflected in the boom of buildings that could be used for public presentations, particularly in what Careless describes as High Victorian Ontario. In addition to the theatres, town halls, and opera house complexes described by Robert Fairfield, there were a vast number of other public buildings, or non-theatres: concert halls, lecture halls, horticultural pavilions, etc. As the mushrooming of spaces took place in the 1870s, so did variety entertainment. The stock system was doomed to extinction, and managers of legitimate houses needed touring shows to fill their theatres; during the early years of this transition the supply of legitimate productions could not keep up with the demand. In addition, the public was not nearly as supportive of a production without a star.[29] Consequently, variety shows were used to fill the demand; they were cheaper to produce and appealed to a broader cross-section of people. But there was still a great deal of suspicion about their nature and quality. One troupe, visiting Belleville's Masonic Music Hall in January 1872, echoed early menagerie claims by advertising that it did not want to be confused with 'the many itinerants that perambulate the country and gull the people' and that there would be 'nothing offensive to the most fastidious' (Belleville *Intelligencer*, 8 January 1872). The people of Belleville had particular reason to be suspicious: the troupe visiting during the previous week had given a poor entertainment and fled town without paying their hotel bill. In sharp contrast to the small fly-by-night companies were the large variety shows that grew out of the olio portion of the minstrel show. Most featured a star who would attract audiences and provide respectability. Billy Whitlock, for example, one of the original Virginia Minstrels, called the show he brought to Toronto in 1850 a 'Grand Olio Entertainment' (Toronto *Globe*, 4 June 1850).

Perhaps the most famous combination of names associated with these early touring variety shows was P.T. Barnum and General Tom

Thumb. Barnum created a phenomenal success with midget Charles S. Stratton, first in England and then in the 1850s and 1860s in North America. Thumb was a sensation when he first appeared in Toronto in 1848, and he enjoyed success throughout Ontario in the 1860s. His success prompted a host of imitators, but no one other than Commodore Nutt proved a worthy rival. Some managers stooped to disguising talented children as small adults, an indication that the variety troupes at mid-century still needed some gimmick or unusual element to attract patrons. The most common devices were declarations of foreign origin and use of exotic material. Even Barnum originally billed the American Stratton as a dwarf from England. Oriental acrobats and conjurers, Swiss bell ringers and foreign 'serenaders' became regular visitors in the 1860s. Most eschewed the variety label completely, preferring to use the names of their performers and the word 'troupe' or 'company.' These were the first vaudeville-variety shows, however, and as early as 1871 that label appeared in Ontario, when 'Cool' Burgess called his company the Gaiete Vaudeville Company. Tony Pastor, generally considered the father of modern vaudeville, toured Ontario regularly through the 1870s using 'Variety Combination.' Other big name shows, Sam and Kitty Morton or Riley and Woods, for example, started using the 'variety' or 'vaudeville' label. In the 1880s and 1890s dozens of these shows were seen every year in Ontario's legitimate theatres and town and concert halls.

In addition to those that made no pretence of being anything other than variety, there were a large number of shows that save for the thinnest of plots were much the same. Newspapers published complaints about companies that deceived the public by calling themselves legitimate, when in fact they were specialty shows. The practice thrived, however, and continued into the next century, although as at least one Toronto critic noted, the crudity of the device started to wear off as the century progressed: ' "While my mother-in-law is kicking the bucket, I guess I will sing a little song." That is about the way the old-fashioned comedian used to introduce his specialty into the play. If he were to do that kind of thing now, he would have to dodge bricks. Now when a specialty is introduced, it is done naturally, so that the actor of the play could hardly go on without it ... When their songs or dances or acrobatic diversions come in they fit the place at which they make their appearance and the whole is done in an artistic and pleasing manner' (Toronto *World*, 7 November 1898). These shows developed into musical comedies and revues, reaching the height of their popularity with *The Ziegfeld Follies*, *The Passing Shows*, and other spectacular vehicles for stars such as Al Jolson in the 1920s.

Concert Saloons

Part of the reason for eschewing the 'variety' label in the last quarter of the nineteenth century was the term's common association with the type of 'girlie' show that became burlesque in the twentieth century. Its roots rested in the first permanent homes of variety theatre: concert saloons. By mid-century the nature of the taverns and the entertainments offered in them had changed considerably from country-style inns featuring wandering players. The rapid expansion of the urban working class produced a corresponding growth in the number of taverns and beer shops which were the main diversion for the working man.[30] This was also the period when class distinctions began to develop in entertainments. Richard Plant notes, for example, that Torontonians attending local amateur theatre in the 1840s were the fashionable set, the aristocracy and upper class of Toronto, not the working class: 'for many reasons – lack of time and money, a Puritan anti-theatre bias, and distrust of those things apparently "intellectual" – the lower classes chose not to go to the theatre.'[31] The large number of drinking establishments, however, clearly indicates they were regularly frequented and that some sort of metamorphosis in the institutions themselves took place. One historian suggests that the changes were all for the worse: 'the saloons of the city in the 1850s were in general little more than miserable dens of dissipation, vulgarity and fighting.'[32] He does admit, however, that there were at least two exceptions in Toronto: the Apollo Saloon and Concert Room, and the Terrapin. They must indeed have been respectable, for they received special mention in the *Descriptive Catalogue of the Provincial Exhibition* in 1858, a guide for visitors to the exhibition and Toronto.

The Apollo Saloon and Concert Room and the Terrapin were two examples of the concert saloons that began to appear throughout North America in the 1850s. The name of the first adequately reflects the nature of the institutions in their original form, drinking establishments that presented concerts in order to attract clientele and encourage their longer stay. Prior to the 1850s most offered their entertainments only as temporary promotions. In the 1850s, however, saloon keepers began to experiment with installing small stages for variety entertainment, although it was not commonly referred to as 'variety' until the 1860s, when such establishments were becoming known as 'variety resorts' and were spreading the idea of live entertainment throughout North America.[33] Many proprietors tried to escape the 'saloon' label by classifying their establishments as 'concert rooms,' 'concert gardens,' or 'music halls,' and by giving them fancy names such as Toronto's

Terrapin and the Shakespearean Saloon. Regardless of the nomenclature they remained essentially saloons; most were makeshift efforts built in disused churches, barns, warehouses, dye works, livery stables, markets, and other abandoned buildings. The only requirement was a large open space, at one end of which a small crude platform propped up against an unadorned wall could become a 'stage.' Filled with smoke and overflowing tankards in every corner of the hall, the atmosphere was always boisterous and coarse.

The Apollo Saloon and Concert Room represented the more respectable of these 'for men only' institutions:

The Saloon is comfortably fitted up, and provided with private rooms, &c. In connection with the saloon there is an excellent CONCERT ROOM, which is open every night for the performance of NEGRO MINSTRELSY, comic and sentimental singing &c. The performances are on the whole excellent. Mr. Burgess and Mr. Den Thompson – the one a negro performer, and the other as a 'broth of a boy' from the Emerald Isle, – are inimitable in their way. The price of admission is 12 1/2 cents, which entitles the visitor to a refreshment ticket which procures him a smoke or a drink. The place is worthy of a visit.[34]

The performers described at the Apollo were typical of the pot-pourri of acts presented on the first concert saloon stages, drawn almost entirely from the specialty skits of black-face minstrelsy and the circus.

In the 1870s many of the larger establishments began calling themselves 'variety theatres' rather than concert saloons. Den Thompson, in Toronto, for example, dropped the fancy nomenclature Athenaeum for 'the Varieties.' According to Hector Charlesworth, however, it remained 'a not very reputable saloon and dance hall.'[35] What the new labels indicated was a change in the relative importance of amusement. 'Variety theatres' presented more stage entertainment, a full variety program that often concluded with an afterpiece assimilating the talents of all performers. The afterpiece usually took the form of a risqué burlesque or pantomime. By this time, in fact, the familiar format of the twentieth-century burlesque show, borrowed from the minstrel show, was in place: opening banter and song by the whole company, followed by the olio of specialty acts, and closing with the extravaganza or burlesque. And although no theatres in Ontario called themselves burlesque houses until the end of the century, that is exactly what most 'variety theatres' were. The following colourful description of a show presented at Toronto's leading variety theatre in 1879 gives the reader a clear indication of the nature of these entertainments and the contemporary critic's attitude towards them:

Toronto has its variety theatre, but, under the present management, it is unquestionably one too many. The Lyceum Theatre – its aristocratic name – is situated on the north side of King Street, midway between Bay and York Streets. Over the entrance leading to the place is nightly stationed what is supposed to be a band of musicians who, so to speak, 'make Rome howl' with the unearthly music blown from their trumpets. The visitor makes his way along an arched alleyway to the place of amusement (!) where an admission ticket is purchased from a masculine looking female stationed at a wicket. The building, a very small one, is well filled with spectators, foul air and tobacco smoke. In the rear of the 'pit' rises a gallery, its principal occupants being boot-blacks and street arabs.

Following the example set by their elders seated in front, the lads sit with head uncovered, blowing clouds of smoke from cigar 'stubbs' or clay pipes, and ever and anon vigorously expectorating tobacco juice. The music of the orchestra, consisting of a piano, violin, and coronet, is drowned amid the noise of the boisterous youths, who clamor for the 'rag' to be hoisted. In due time the rag is rung up, and the 'beautiful minstrels' are presented to view. The scene that follows is almost indescribable. Jokes – save the mark – of the vilest and most pernicious character are bandied between the end and middle men. These are received with loud shouts by the 'gods' who attempt to improve on them, 'just' as they say 'to help the thing along.' This encourages the performers and they redouble their efforts to make their filthy sayings, if possible, plainer. A female (one of the beautiful) attempts to sing but she is recognized by some of the lads, who cry out 'Bella McDonald, go home. Your mother wants you.' At the conclusion of the minstrel part of the program, the specialty performers are introduced. Bad singing and worse dancing appear to be the leading features of this portion of the entertainment. When the Sparring Exhibition between a man and a woman is introduced, it is thought by the uninitiated that the performance had got as low in the scale of morality as is possible to descend. This is a mistake: the choice morceau remains to be witnessed. While the 'only male and female exponents of artistic boxing in the world' knock each other around the dirty-looking stage, the excitement runs high, especially among the 'unwashed' in the gallery. The woman appears to be the favourite and she is encouraged by such remarks as 'You're a brick,' 'Now give it him with your left,' 'that's a daisy, old woman,' etc., etc. Three rounds are fought, lasting probably twelve or fifteen minutes, in all of which the female comes off the best. On retiring they are greeted with loud applause, and a demand is made for a further sample of their skill. The man, on behalf of the woman, pleads the heat of the room as an excuse for not continuing the contest. The woman, however, speaks for herself, and says that 'if her opponent wishes it, she will give him another round.' Her opponent has no wish in that direction, and the woman is looked upon as a heroine, and leaves the stage amid cries of 'She's gritty, you bet.' The performance is brought to a close with as scandalous an afterpiece as was ever produced in the lowest 'free and easy' of London or New York. 'Paris by Moonlight,' in which 'living statuary' is introduced, is an appropriate finale to the night's performance, and to which the earlier part of he entertainment appears tame and innocent. The 'can-can' dance, with all the improvements and flourishes is gone through. So utterly low and debasing was it, that frequent cries of 'shame' were heard from different parts of the house during the progress of the dance. Amid the hooting, yells and cheers of the spectators, the curtain descends – it could be hoped forever – on one of the vilest performances ever witnessed in this city. (Toronto *Mail*, 13 October 1879)

This attitude often made it difficult for variety theatres to operate in nineteenth-century Ontario. Toronto had several that opened and closed with different management for twenty years following the Lyceum's failure. Other Ontario cities, such as Hamilton and Ottawa, saw such establishments come and go, facing the same type of vitriolic attack by the press. But there was a demand, evidenced by their persistence and eventual transformation into permanent burlesque houses.

The losers in the nineteenth-century censorship battles were managers who attempted to operate 'respectable' variety theatres. Even individuals with previously established respectability had trouble with the variety label. The earliest attempt in Ontario was made at Toronto's Queen's Theatre in 1874 by T.J. Herndon. His 18 July 1874 advertisement in the New York *Clipper* for stars and combinations for the 'vaudeville and novelty season' marked a very early application of the term vaudeville to a theatre. At the same site four years later Patrick Redmond also tried to run a clean variety theatre. Initially, he enjoyed some success: 'There is a certain prejudice against variety entertainments – a prejudice that arises from the many lower class dens classed as variety theatres – which Messrs. Redmond and Bailey are striving hard to combat: and in conducting this new enterprise they promise to present nothing of an objectionable nature. Since the opening the house has been well attended each night, many ladies being present' (Toronto *Mail*, 9 May 1878). Even Redmond's reputation in Toronto was not enough to combat the negative attitude towards variety, however, and before long, like all the managers before and after him who tried to establish a permanent variety theatre in Ontario during the nineteenth century, he had to give up his theatre. As soon as he closed it, the theatre was taken over by the burlesque form of variety. It was left to another institution, the dime museum, to develop family or 'clean,' variety.

The Dime Museum

Dime museums have a shorter history in Ontario than most other forms of nineteenth-century variety theatre. They existed only in the larger cities and tourist sites and were relatively few in number. But they are historically important because they cracked the puritan bias that still affected most variety entertainment late in the century. The dime museum was the institution that attracted families to variety theatre in large numbers and established permanent homes for what was to become vaudeville.

Small commercial museums were a fixture in Ontario throughout the nineteenth century. Most were accepted immediately because they were considered educational, generally exhibiting some combination of paintings, stuffed animals, live birds, historical artifacts, scientific inventions, and wax figures. All these elements could be found in York during the late 1820s and early 1830s at Mr Wood's British Museum. Surprisingly enough, the exhibits and collections themselves never attracted sufficient clientele; Wood was forced to follow the lead of other North American museum proprietors and offer live entertainment of some kind. In keeping with the educational credo, Wood hired lecturers and demonstrators. One of his most successful was a 'fancy glass blower' by the name of Mr Smith, who spent the entire 1830–1 season with Wood.

When Phineas T. Barnum, considered by most to be the father of American show business, purchased John Scudder's New York Museum in 1841, the museum business changed. In order to attract a broader range of patrons Barnum added collections and novelties from around the world, eventually boasting 600,000 items on display. He also expanded the narrow, uncomfortable lecture room into a modern, 3,000-seat theatre; but he continued billing his presentations as 'chaste, scenic entertainments' properly presented for 'all those who disapprove of the dissipation, debaucheries, profanity, vulgarity and other abominations, which characterize our modern theatres.'[36] Barnum apparently delighted in telling the story of the spinster who constantly reminded him she had never set foot in a theatre in her life and never would, yet she so much enjoyed his 'educational exhibitions.' On her way to the lecture room to see a lurid melodrama based on a popular sentimental novel she asked Barnum 'are the services about to commence?' 'Yes,' he sanctimoniously replied, 'the congregation is now going up.'[37] Barnum's congregation grew very quickly, tripling the earnings of the museum during the first year of his proprietorship. His success naturally prompted a host of imitators, who used the same formula on a smaller scale. By the third quarter of the century the dime museum was considered an American institution.

Early attempts to establish dime museums in Toronto included H.R. Jacob's Royal Museum and Novelty Company (1883); Drew, Pride and Sackett's Museum (1884); Mountford's Museum (1884); and the People's Dime Museum (1885). None of these lasted for more than a year. They were small operations and did not in fact follow the successful American formula. But Toronto's Musee Theatre, which opened at 91–93 Yonge Street in 1890, used the key ingredients and enjoyed success. A detailed description of the building's opening reveals what the elements were:

Entering from the street is a large lobby lighted with 50 incandescent lights and laid with tiles, and the foyer, with ticket office on the one side and the check room on the other, leading to a bright and comfortable little theatre capable of accommodating 700 ... On the left of the entrance is an excellent exhibition of waxwork figures, including Christ on Calvary and King Solomon and his court. From this room is a spacious stairway leading to the second floor, where stands a magnificent life-size representation of Queen Victoria and the Prince of Wales, with elegant and costly costumes. On this floor is a large lecture parlor, 125 feet long and 50 feet wide, for the exhibition and explanation of curiosities, freaks, etc. There is also a miniature Japanese village and an exhibition of glass blowing. At the side there is an art gallery, 50 feet long by 25, lighted by an ingenious arrangement of electric lights, which are draped from view ... On the third floor is a large and well-appointed menagerie, containing live civet cats, armadillos, a mongoose, chinese rats and anteaters, monkeys, a large baboon, a vampire or flying fox and a large aviary with 400 beautiful birds, in the centre of which plays a fountain. There are also wax representations of Birchall in his cell, a family made wretched through drink with its counterpart a sober and happy family, a group of Chicago Anarchists, and Columbus with some of his followers planting a flag in the new world ... To-day among other wonders will be Barney Baldwin, a living man with a broken neck, constituting a puzzle for the scientific world. In the theatre Knoll and McNeil, the celebrated cornetists, engaged at a large figure, will give a number of selections. There will also be a first class variety performance. The Hungarian band of a dozen first-class musicians will play in the lecture room. (Toronto *World*, 9 December 1890)

In addition, advertisements promised 'Aztec mummies 3000 years old,' 'London's greatest Punch and Judy show,' and 'A Wild Prairie Dog Village,' in total more than '1000 Other New Novel and Interesting Curiosities' (ibid., 1 December 1890). The magic formula for a successful dime museum at the time included three ingredients: first and foremost the 'educational content' – thus the museum and menagerie elements, not to mention the wax display contrasting the horrors of alcoholism with the joys of abstinence; then a show that would give the clientele their money's worth – thus the variety show; and finally something to draw audiences to this new institution – thus the freaks.

Freaks held a continued fascination for North Americans everywhere throughout the nineteenth century. Itinerant showmen, such as those with the albino negro boys travelling in Ontario in 1840, made small fortunes with lengthy tours. Circus advertisements, particularly during the third quarter of the century, always featured human freaks in the most prominent position. As the exotic nature of menagerie animals wore off, poster pictures of human freaks such as Jo-Jo the Dog Faced Boy replaced those of the rhinoceros-unicorn. Freaks drew crowds and dime museums needed star attractions to get established. So the advertisements and publicity surrounding the Musee during the first five years of its existence (it changed owners and altered names a few times during the period but operated continuously) featured this element:

Despite the downpour of rain, immense crowds packed the lecture hall and theatre of the Musee all day yesterday. The leading attraction, of course, was Jonathan Bass, the living ossified man. Nearly everyone is familiar with the history of this wonderful freak of nature. When a boy he was strong and active as other boys. At the age of 17 he was seized with pains all over his body, and after several years the pain ceased and left him as he is today, a mass of solid bone. He has been blind for many years, and not being able to move his limbs, he is perfectly helpless. Several years ago he was seized with lock-jaw, and since then he has received nourishment through an aperture made by the knocking out of several teeth. For 25 years he has lain helpless, and his limbs have become flattened by his having been confined to a bed for such a long period. He is the most marvellous of nature's many freaks and should be seen by everyone. (Ibid., 17 November 1891)

In addition to the Ossified Man, Musee patrons were greeted by the Two-Bodied India Boy; Rose, 'The Raving Wild Girl – Half Woman – Half Monkey, Untamed and Uncivilized'; the Giant from Missouri,

'An 8' eighteen year old girl still growing'; Con Cameron, 'at twenty-three inches and thirteen pounds the smallest human being in existence'; Jo-Jo the Dog Faced Boy, The Human Scotch Terrier; the Disjointed Man; the Bearded Lady; an albino family; Siamese Twins; the Phantom Lady and Skeleton Dude, the 'two thinnest people in the world soon to be married'; the Two-Headed Boy; and the list goes on. These were unquestionably the stars that made Toronto's dime museum a popular amusement centre in the early 1890s.

Ontario contributed a major figure to this world: Charles Tripp. Born without arms in Woodstock in 1855, Tripp began using his feet to write, shave, and comb his hair, and then he mastered woodworking tools and became a carver and cabinet-maker.[38] When he was seventeen he asked his parents to take him to P.T. Barnum in New York. As soon as Barnum saw what Tripp could do with his feet, he hired him, and for the rest of his life Tripp was known as the 'Armless Wonder.' He toured around the world three times and lived to be eighty-four years old.

Dime museums continued to flourish in North America until the turn of the century, but in the 1890s the competition of family variety started to cut into the box office returns. As variety increased in popularity the clever museum managers emphasized that aspect of the entertainment and gradually phased out the freaks and curio hall. Many others resisted the change, however, and lost their business to the new form. Finally, when motion pictures became widely available to the working classes prior to the First World War, dime museums became a thing of the past, a curiosity in their own right.

Burlesque

Like all forms of variety theatre, the burlesque show developed over a number of years and was a combination of several elements. The most important aspect was always the exhibition of the female form. The first displays began at mid-century in the legitimate theatres with tableaux vivants or living statuary, where women wearing only revealing body stockings began posing in portrayals of classical subjects. As long as there was a classical association and total stillness, these portrayals were accepted as art. The first seen in Toronto, for example, took place under the direction of high society's 'first lady of the theatre,' Charlotte Morrison, in February 1875. Shortly after this initial presentation, living statuary became a regular feature of shows in concert saloons and variety theatres in Toronto, in spite of constant virulent remarks in the press: 'The ''Art Pictures'' presented by living models ... was a repulsive feature of the performance' (Toronto *Mail*, 25 February 1879).

The other 'respectable' method found to reveal the female form was the presentation of legitimate plays with women in traditionally male parts, complete with revealing male costume. Short classical tunics were the favourite. Thus Adah Isaacs Menken caused a sensation in 1861 when she became the first woman to star in *Mazeppa*. Menken appeared in the famous scene strapped on a horse's back wearing tights, shorts, and a sash covering her breasts. The horse galloped up a spiral ramp, giving the audience plenty of opportunities and angles to admire the many segments of her body that appeared bare, earning her instant fame and fortune as 'The Naked Lady.' Five years later the incorporation of a troupe of ballet dancers, stranded in New York, into an extravaganza titled *The Black Crook* marked the next stage in burlesque's development. The resulting combination of spectacular scenery, scantily clad female forms, music, dance, and song was so popular that it ran for fifteen months and spawned a host of imitators. Then in 1868 Lydia Thompson and her British Blondes invaded North America. Although the Blondes performed burlesque as parody in the classic sense of the word, their main attraction was the amount of figure revealed by their 'classical,' and hence respectable, costumes. Their first American show, and the first the troupe presented in Ontario, was *Ixion*. Critics were not taken in by the disguise: 'The whole success of the piece depends upon dressing up all of the above named good-looking ladies as immortals lavish in display of person ... to represent Minerva with a fan and whisky flask, Jupiter as a jig dancer, Venus with a taste for the cancan, is all done we suppose, in a laudable spirit of burlesque ... It resembles an Irish stew, as one minute they are dancing a cancan and the next minute singing a psalm tune. It is a bewilderment of limbs, belladonna and grease paint.'[39] The success of the British Blondes guaranteed the rapid development of 'girlie' burlesque.

It did not take long for enterprising showmen to realize that the pretension of staging classical plays was unnecessary. Leader in the field was M.B. Leavitt, who is generally conceded to be the founder of 'burlesque troupes,' as he labelled them. Leavitt combined the elements of the minstrel show with those of the new girlie shows; the result was the premiere of Mme Rentz's Female Minstrels in 1870. Within a year there were eleven female minstrel companies on the road. By the end of the century there were dozens of companies openly selling female sexuality. The shows featured most of the types of acts developed in the old minstrel show and gaining popularity in vaudeville but always included some aspect of sexual titillation or off-colour humour.

Most of the early troupes included Ontario's cities on their early North American tours. The British Blondes were seen in Ottawa, Toronto, and Hamilton within two years of their first appearance in New York. Dozens of female minstrel troupes, including the original Rentz company, toured Ontario from 1870 on. Their appearances were surrounded by controversy, particularly in the 1880s when some managers were trying to establish permanent homes. The attitude expressed by one Toronto critic was probably shared by a great segment of the general public: 'Nothing is announced as yet for next week but I hear we are to have a Red Stocking Female Minstrel Company. I hope for the sake of the new manager of this house [Toronto's Royal] that the statement is false, for it has suffered enough this season with such entertainments, no less than four blonde troupes having appeared already, one of them so bad that the newspapers called upon the police to suppress such performances ... the house is better closed, than open with such people' (New York *Dramatic Mirror*, 13 May 1879).

The call for closure of theatres presenting burlesque performances continued throughout the history of burlesque into the 1930s. The pattern was always the same: just when it appeared the critics and the general public had resigned themselves to the existence of the undesirable, some new flare-up occurred. In 1893, for example, Little Egypt introduced the 'Cootch Dance' at the Chicago World's Fair. The sensational belly dance was immediately introduced into burlesque, prompting a whole new wave of criticism. The movement from tableau vivant had gone full turn; the female form was seen gyrating and undulating in the most suggestive manner. Fifteen years later with the Cootch dance an accepted part of burlesque shows seen everywhere, including Ontario, the Salomé dance appeared.

The dance of the seven veils was introduced to North America by Gertrude Hoffman in 1908. Within a year there were hundreds of Salomés in burlesque. The controversy was on again, only this time the events that transpired shed considerable light on the double standard that had been operating in the province for decades. Salomé dances were being allowed on the stages of Toronto's legitimate theatres but not on those of burlesque houses. Words like 'hell' and 'damn' were frequently heard on the legitimate stage but were strictly forbidden at burlesque houses (Toronto *Star*, 9 January 1909). As the controversy grew, it was revealed that the morality department of the police force had cut out parts of twenty of the first twenty-two burlesque shows seen in Toronto that season but had not investigated any of the legitimate shows (ibid., 29 January 1909). Expressing surprise, the mayor promised a full investigation into the department's practices (ibid., 27 February 1909). City Council soon ordered the supervision of all theatres, regardless of the type of show presented. But when Gertrude Hoffman presented her Salomé dance at the Royal Alexandra Theatre, the head of the morality department admitted that he had no real power to stop her. The police let Hoffman's performance continue, wisely deciding not to test their power against an international star in Toronto's most respected theatre. They chose to challenge, instead, the owner-manager of the Star Burlesque House; Fred W. Stair was convicted and fined and the double standard continued. Legitimate theatres were constantly given permission to use children under the age of sixteen, but the special permit required by Ontario law was always denied burlesque companies, even when the application was for a pre-school child of one of the performers (ibid., 11 November 1911). At the Gayety Theatre in 1912 the morality department declared a female acrobat standing on her head indecent, in spite of her full clown suit (ibid., 9 March 1912). An order was issued forbidding any female performer to stand on her head. That same year a female patron was caught smoking in a private box at the Gayety. Smoking was permitted in burlesque houses but was thought strictly the privilege of men, and the effects that burlesque had on women were duly noted in the newspapers. The double standard evident in the theatre was not always confined to the burlesque houses. In 1911 the morality department ordered all theatres to pay men to go over all posters and cover up cards, drink, and cigarettes if there was a woman in the picture. When theatre managers argued that plenty of billboard advertisements by liquor companies featured women, the response was 'Ah, that's different. Those are advertisements of a legitimate business, licensed by the state' (ibid. 9 December 1911). Ultimately this duality was simply a reality that theatre managers, particularly those of burlesque houses, had to live with.

By 1910 burlesque was highly organized throughout North America, a process that had begun at the turn of the century. Throughout the 1890s, because there were not enough touring shows to supply a theatre for an entire season, most owner-managers of burlesque variety theatres tried to maintain a stock company; when a good road show was available, the manager could send his company out on the road. There were usually two of these operations competing with one another in Toronto throughout the 1890s, although the constant change of management, locations, and policies often makes it difficult to keep track. By the turn of the century there was a sufficient number of these shows for managers to band together and supply each other. They formed circuits, or 'wheels' as they were known in burlesque, guaranteeing a full season for performers and association managers.

As soon as they were organized, burlesque managers looked for ways to attract larger audiences. They issued strict edicts about what was acceptable on their stages. The olio portion of the show was broadened with a variety of specialty acts; many of the skits were 'whitewashed'; and closer attention was paid to each theatre manager's instructions regarding what was acceptable in his town. Most of the 'wheel' shows now contained less suggestive material than burlesque had featured in the 1890s. The resulting entertainment was a mixture somewhere between musical comedy and vaudeville. The primary difference, of course, was the display of the female form. And as long as this was still the primary attraction, burlesque remained an entertainment for men only. The managers of Toronto's two burlesque houses in 1908 admitted that less than one-hundredth of box office receipts came from women, in spite of six afternoon matinées a week.

Given the nature and reputation of the entertainment, it is no surprise that burlesque houses were not abundant outside Toronto before the First World War. Ottawa had one for a brief time in 1912, Hamilton encouraged different managers several times during the first decade, but operations were restricted to large cities and the major circuits established themselves firmly only in Toronto. Just before the war the two major circuits merged under the name of the more powerful Columbia Burlesque Circuit and agreed to put only one burlesque house in most cities. Toronto had representatives from both of the old circuits, but it was decided that only the Columbia's Gayety Theatre would be included in the amalgamation. The owner-manager of the other, the Star, was Fred W. Stair, a pioneer of burlesque in Toronto. He had given up his position as press agent and business manager at Hamilton's Grand Opera House in 1901 to buy Toronto's old Royal Theatre. At that time it was operating as a burlesque house, but the continuous scandal associated with it was unquestionably causing some difficulty for its owners: the Policeman's Benefit Fund. Stair turned the marginal operation into one of the most profitable theatres in Toronto. He endured dozens of censorship court battles during the first fifteen years of the century, and it was his success that prompted the Columbia Circuit to invade Toronto in 1907. He retaliated for being left out of the merger by forming the Progressive Burlesque Circuit with thirty other independent owner-managers. Stair was elected president of the new organization, and finally, in 1922, the Gayety was dropped from the Columbia Circuit and the Star, renamed the Empire, became the Toronto stop on the major burlesque wheel.

After the First World War, burlesque, like most other high-spirited entertainments, enjoyed a growing popularity. During the roaring twenties, with the strictest Victorian suppressions long gone, dance halls, revues, night clubs, and cabarets burgeoned everywhere. They combined with legitimate stage reviews and musical comedies to put added pressure on burlesque. The great *Ziegfeld Follies* and *Winter Garden Passing Shows*, for example, featured increasingly risqué elements. At first burlesque managers tried to move in the direction of vaudeville, keeping their shows family oriented with only the chorus line to titillate. The vaudeville market was more controlled, however, and burlesque managers were forced in the other direction, joining big revues in featuring nude women in artistic poses. Soon, with the introduction of the strip-tease, new controversy surrounded burlesque.

During the 1930s, when most other forms of live entertainment were suffering, burlesque enjoyed its biggest resurgence. Robert Toll suggests why:

Movies, which hurt live vaudeville and revues and greatly narrowed the audiences for musicals and plays, did not offer the public, the male public, the titillation that burlesque provided. Burlesque stripteasers appeared in person, always offering the prospect, the hope that the patron might catch an intimate peek at forbidden 'territory.' Furthermore, burlesque was a special kind of escapism, one especially well suited to the 1930s. The strippers acted out basic male fantasies which could provide at least temporary boosts for the damaged egos of the many men who were thrown out of work and were unable to fulfill their normal roles as providers during the Great Depression.[40]

During the 1920s and 1930s burlesque appeared in most of the province's cities. Even Ottawa finally had the Casino Theatre during the 1920s. But as the strip-tease element became more and more dominant, objections increased, eventually producing censorship restrictions that forced its demise. The only vestiges of the entertainment in Ontario today are the saloons that feature strip-tease shows, male and female performers, any time of the day.

Vaudeville

The term 'vaudeville' found its way to North America from France in the late nineteenth century when variety-hall owners were looking for ways to enhance their reputations. There is still some question about the first North American usage of the word to refer to a variety show. The Gaiete Vaudeville Company's usage during their Ottawa visit in 1871 predates most references in vaudeville histories. The term did not become popular until the 1890s, however, and was not widely used until the turn of the century. Unlike the name, the entertainment was not new to audiences. They had seen the same performers in minstrel shows, circuses, dime museums, and variety theatres. But there were two important differences: beautiful theatres and big stars. These improvements were possible because vaudeville was organized on the principles of big business: widely developed in every city and town throughout the United States and Canada, scientifically exploited, with control vested in the hands of a small, centralized, and concentrated group of entrepreneurs and capitalists.

The way in which circuit owners monopolized vaudeville was simple: they controlled the theatres in the biggest cities and gave work only to performers who promised not to play rival circuits. Theatre owners who wished to book the best talent therefore also had to join one of the syndicates. Anyone who broke the rules was immediately blacklisted from the circuit. This scheme was devised and developed by B.F. Keith and E.F. Albee, who must be considered the founders of vaudeville.[41] They were the first dime museum managers to turn their operation into a straight family theatre, they presented the first continuous variety show, built the first vaudeville palace, and organized the first major vaudeville circuits. Less than twenty years after they organized the B.F. Keith and the Orpheum Exchanges they had a complete monopoly on first-class vaudeville and controlled more than 50 per cent of all other types. The next two largest syndicates were Loew's and Pantages, although they did not begin to exert control until after the First World War and had many of their holdings in motion picture houses.

The explosive success of vaudeville is all the evidence one needs to prove that it provided audiences with the entertainment they wanted and probably needed. Rapidly expanding cities at the turn of the century were filled with citizens who faced a completely new life style. Those who moved from the country found cramped working and living conditions. Immigrants from Europe had a new culture and often language to learn as well. Even those born and raised in the city had to adjust to the rapid growth and changing mix of their home towns. All turn-of-the-century, urban Ontario workers, therefore, to some extent shared the problem of adapting to a changing society, one with new buildings, industries, transportation methods, and technologies. Major benefits of the new life were more leisure time and freedom from the most limiting of Victorian attitudes. The new society was therefore hungry for leisure activity to fill its hours, preferably one that entertained, 'spoke their language,' and got them out of their cramped city dwellings. Vaudeville did all those things and more.

First came the beautiful new buildings, the key part in separating the new 'family' entertainment from the old variety. Some of the finest theatres built in Ontario during the first two decades of the twentieth century were built as vaudeville houses. The best known in Ontario today is the Winter Garden complex in Toronto. Its modern fame rests on its survival as much as on its unique double-decker style. When Marcus Loew opened it in 1914, it was by no means the biggest or most beautiful vaudeville theatre in Toronto. The auditoriums in the two Shea theatres were larger and the Hippodrome, which opened in the same year as the Winter Garden, was far more sumptuous. The Pantages and The Loew's Uptown, which opened six years later, also surpassed the size and splendour of the Winter Garden, as did the Pantages in Hamilton and Loew's other theatres in Ontario. One must realize, moreover, that many of these theatres seated 3,000 people or more and were often filled twice a day. Ontarians went because they were able to sit in the best seat of a theatre that outclassed most of the legitimate theatres and see many of the same stars for only 25 cents. The same privilege at the legitimate theatres cost $2 and $3.

The list of stars who appeared on Ontario's vaudeville stages is endless. Many who are remembered today are familiar to us only because, like the Winter Garden, they survived vaudeville. Most of them later made their reputations in radio, film, or television. Bob Hope, George Burns, Jack Benny, Charlie Chaplin, Sophie Tucker, Stan Laurel, the Marx Brothers, and Buster Keaton all appeared on the vaudeville stages in Ontario during the first two decades of the century. But none was a headliner in his/her early vaudeville appearances. The first stars were those who had made reputations in other fields, particularly in opera and drama. Like the new buildings, they created instant prestige for the entertainment. Few performers could resist the exorbitant salaries offered, even though they were warned about the perils of such action:

A very large community of amusement seekers take pleasure in variety shows, but there is an appreciable line of demarcation between them and the patrons of the regular theatre. Of late years there has been a disposition on the part of dramatic and operatic artists of repute to accept engagements with variety combinations, the persuasive inducement being the exceptional salaries offered. It seems to me that those who yield to the temptation are exposed to a double danger. A name of dramatic or operatic fame will at first attract increased attendance to the variety theatre, but the special audiences of these houses find that the art of the legitimate singer or actor is not sufficiently broad to suit their taste, and in a few seasons they become thoroughly wearied of it. When the actor returns to the regular theatre he finds that he has lost caste to a great extent with the constituency to which he once specifically appealed. In addition there is a suspicion in the minds of the public that an actor or singer who goes over to the vaudeville stage has begun to realize that his powers have commenced to decline. (Toronto *Globe,* 18 June 1904)

The reviewer's comments indicate that there was considerable reluctance to recognize the merits of vaudeville among some sections of the theatre-going public. In any case, legitimate stage stars, such as Edna Wallace Hopper, Jessie Millward, Grace Van Studdiford, Robert Hilliard, Trixi Friganza, Lillie Langtry, Julius Steger, and James K. Hackett, were not in a position to worry when they were being offered as much as $3,000 per week. Other stars made their names in vaudeville. Harry Lauder, Elsie Janis, Vesta Victoria, Vesta Tilly, Alice Lloyd, Houdini, May Irwin, Cissie Loftus, George Fuller Golden, McIntyre and Heath, Digby Bell, Marie Dressler, Eva Tanguay, Al Jolson, Irene Franklin and Jack Norworth, Julian Eltinge, and Gertrude Hoffman watched their pay envelopes swell from a few hundred dollars to several thousand during the first decade of the century. By 1907 a $1,000 weekly salary for the headliner was the rule rather than the exception in good vaudeville theatres (Toronto *Star,* 28 September 1907).

It was this second group of stars who were always most popular in vaudeville. Their rags-to-riches stories were not just something that the theatre-goers read about, but something they watched happen to their favourite performers. Nora Bayes, for example, appeared well down on the bill in 1899 at Shea's Toronto Theatre. But she returned season after season, gradually improving her position. When Shea's Victoria Street Theatre opened in 1910, she was one of the highest-paid performers of the season. After she became a star, she described her relationship with the audience:

It is not my intention to tell you how I hold my audience, because the situation is quite the reverse – they hold me. They represent the most valuable and comfortable relationship. They are my friends. It is therefore with the intimate safety of friendship, that I go out upon the stage and shake hands with them. My performances are exactly like an intimate chat with one or two close friends, who sit around the table and enjoy themselves ...

The vaudeville audience is the most sensitive, because it is there to meet old friends, to spend an hour or two in pleasant company, and it has no objection to tears if they start from the hearts of their friends on the stage. They are just as ready to cry with you in the theatre as they would be in their own homes, but they must be real tears, not stage tears.

As to laughter, I have felt the greatest delight when I can laugh with them. I do not want an audience to laugh at me, I want them to laugh with me, just as I want my friends to do when we are together.

As children play at being someone quite different from what they really are, so in vaudeville we try to pretend that we are playing a game of some sort, having a frolic all to ourselves.[42]

This relationship was fundamental, and performers of every kind looked for ways to involve their audience. Jugglers had audience members throw objects to them, acrobats on the bounding bed (trampoline) had audiences count successive somersaults aloud, magicians made audience members disappear or help tie someone up, commands were shouted from the auditorium for animal acts, and mind-readers worked directly with the audience. The practice was epitomized by Al Jolson's use of the ramp through the audience, although he was not the first to use the device. Other devices included singing plants in the audience, something Jolson himself had been in his early years, shining mirrors on bald-headed men in the audience, singing to and touching a patron in a stage box. One singer at Toronto's Majestic Music Hall in 1910 floated over the audience in a balloon, lowering herself every once in a while to shake hands with astonished patrons. But the most common device was the sing-along. Every top singer was noted for a favourite song, and the audience was always invited to sing along during the chorus. Thus whenever Maggie Cline returned to Ontario she had to perform 'Throw Him Down, McClusky,' or, as one local writer warned, 'she will not be able to get off the stage' (Toronto World, 31 October 1908). Similarly, 'Waiting at the Church' was compulsory for Vesta Victoria, 'I Don't Care' for Eva Tanguay, and 'Red Head' for Irene Franklin. In addition, vaudeville performers, in keeping with making the show more personal, often asked the audience for requests. The practice was becoming common enough in 1912 to be commented on in Toronto's newspapers: 'To Your Order Vaudeville ... These "sing any song you want almost" acts are getting to be quite the thing at Shea's. We have one every week or so now. Next thing we know they'll have vaudevillians who will dish up any old kind of entertainment from contortionism to grand opera, with all those old favourite middle courses on the variegated bill of fare, such as instrumentals and barrel juggling. Just yell up your order' (ibid., 21 May 1912).

Singers were not the only group faced with giving the audiences the material they wanted. John E. DiMeglio points out: 'Vaudeville audiences were not attracted by curiosity. Audiences came to see the acts they knew. Audiences tolerated no deviations.'[43] Hartley Davis noted this attitude as early as 1905, citing several performers who had changed their act in order to keep it fresh, only to find that the audience demanded a return to the old routines.[44] Bernard Sobel explains that much of the enjoyment of vaudeville stemmed from the 'pride in the recognition of wheezy jokes, the satisfaction of beating the comedian to the tag-line and joining in the familiar choruses. It was a comfortable belt-loosening familiarity. Of course the fans had their favourites.They could rattle off catch lines and bits of stage business, and many could almost repeat the entire act themselves.'[45]

The familiarity that was critical if the audience was to identify with the entertainment often translated into being contemporary. Election returns and sports scores were read from the stage. The latest fashions were always an attraction for matinée audiences, the majority of whom were women. Some stars shared their beauty secrets at special performances for women only. The newest dances were presented, including after-performance lessons to a lucky ticket holder. Efforts were also made to use local references. Successful comics relied on the theatre manager to fill them in on the latest gossip, politicians' names, and local news stories. Even special films were made for Ontario theatres. Shortly after the turn of the century films were used regularly as chasers, thus signalling the end of the show without forcing on live entertainers the indignity of the last place on the bill. In 1904, only one week after the King's Plate had been run at Woodbine, the race was on the screens of Ontario's vaudeville theatres. Newsreels were also very popular in the pre-radio era, as were scientific inventions. In 1911 an airplane was rolled out onto a Toronto vaudeville stage and started up. The lecturer was supported by films showing the airplane in flight.

The family nature of the entertainment was also a critical factor in vaudeville's success. Ontario's first vaudeville theatres regularly advertised special children's shows, and Christmas was always billed as 'children's week.' One of the most popular animal acts in Ontario was 'Little Hip the Elephant,' who handed out programs in the lobby and let children pet him on stage. Because vaudeville was a family-oriented entertainment, censorship was always strictly enforced by local managers. During its first twenty years in Toronto there was not one incident of police censorship of the vaudeville stage. The circuits had strict rules, and performers risked being blacklisted if they disobeyed any additional rules the local manager laid down about the particular taste of his community. The manager filed a weekly report on all the performers who appeared at his theatre.

The variety of entertainment, spectacle, fun, stars, and beautiful surroundings in Ontario's vaudeville theatres during the first two decades of this century in most cases outstripped all offerings on the legitimate stages. And if there was anything particularly outstanding or popular in the latter it was only a matter of time before it found its way into vaudeville. The sole adjustment generally necessary was in length, since the maximum time for a vaudeville act was thirty minutes; the ideal was twenty. During the 1904–5 season two hit musicals seen at Toronto's first-class legitimate theatre, the Princess, were *The Prince of Pilsen* and *The Maid and the Money*. During the following season vaudeville patrons in the city saw the *City Girls* and *The Dainty Dashing Polly Girls*, amalgamations of the best song and dance numbers from the musicals. They were given full elaborate productions and in one case featured the same star performer. There can be no question that vaudeville's success in this area contributed to the depression that legitimate theatre experienced during the first twenty years of the century.

The ability of vaudeville to present elaborate productions was the result of the size of its organizations. All Ontario's large theatres were supplied by major circuits and enjoyed the benefits. This did not mean, however, that there was no local control. Theatres were most often owned by local shareholders and were run by managers who knew their community. They often had considerable influence over the acts presented in their theatres, particularly in 'big time.' All big time in Ontario was controlled by the B.F. Keith Exchange, so all acts had to be booked in New York. But managers were free to choose them. The shows seen each week in Toronto or Ottawa were not necessarily the same as those playing Detroit or Buffalo that week. Each theatre put together its own bills; of the eight acts that might appear in Hamilton during one week, for example, one or two might go on to Ottawa, others to Toronto or back to New York.

There is a long tradition of vaudeville theatre managers serving for decades at their respective establishments in Ontario. Several deserve special mention. Most important is expatriate Mike Shea, who controlled all big time vaudeville in Toronto and Buffalo. Born on 1 April 1859 in St Catharines, he was still an infant when his family moved to Buffalo. In his early twenties, after working on the docks and with steel companies, where he earned the name 'Iron Mike,' he opened a saloon and bowling alley in Buffalo. After operating a couple of these establishments over the next fifteen years he opened his first vaudeville theatre, the Garden, in 1898. A year later he expanded into Toronto, giving Ontario its first big time vaudeville theatre. With the two best theatres in two good show cities, Shea was invited to New York in 1900 when Keith and Albee were organizing the Vaudeville Managers' Protection Association. From that point on Mike Shea was an influential member in the association. In 1912, for example, he contributed $100,000 to the Keith-Albee purchase of theatres that finally gave the organization their monopoly of big time vaudeville.

Mike was interested only in big time, the very best vaudeville, where performers gave only two shows per day but received the highest salaries. He could have used his connection with the B.F. Keith Exchange to set up and control all vaudeville in Toronto and Buffalo, but he was content to build the biggest and best theatres both cities had ever seen and fill them with the best popular entertainment. The first big project of the Shea Amusement Company was Toronto's Victoria Street Theatre, built in 1910. This was followed by the Majestic Theatre, built in Buffalo in 1913, and the two big Hippodromes, one in Buffalo and one in Toronto, both built in 1914.

After completing the Hippodrome, the Shea Amusement Company did not expand its Toronto operations. But in Buffalo Mike acquired more than a dozen community theatres through lease or purchase and built two new theatres, the Seneca and Shea's Buffalo. The beauty of the last became and remains a monument to the man and his work. Mike Shea died on 16 May 1934 at the age of seventy-five. The Buffalo *Times* devoted the front page and headline story for six consecutive days to his life story, concluding with an appropriate tribute from George M. Cohan: 'You know, it would be safe to say that he was the greatest single figure, in some respects, in the theatrical history of the country' (22 May 1934).

After Mike's death the Shea legacy was carried on by his younger brother Jerry, for forty-four years the man directly responsible for the Shea Amusement Company's success in Toronto. Born a twin in Buffalo on 15 August 1864, Jerry had no work history other than his association with Mike's theatres and was obviously the only choice for manager when the Toronto theatre opened in 1899. Jerry moved to the Victoria Street Theatre in 1910, the year he was elected president of the Theatre Managers' Club in Toronto. The appearance of twenty-five American managers from the B.F. Keith Exchange at the Victoria's opening indicated that Jerry had influence in larger circles as well.

Both brothers always hand picked the performers they wanted in New York and often auditioned and discovered new talent. They also insisted on personally handling the Monday morning censorship sessions, thus upholding the maxim of family entertainment. When the Hippodrome opened in 1914, Edward A. McArdle was manager, but Jerry had the final say. Jerry moved to the Hippodrome in 1926, when Famous Players rented the Victoria, and he remained there for almost seventeen years. When he died on 13 December 1943, the general manager of RKO-Radio Pictures of Canada noted that Toronto had lost not only one of its premier showmen of the first half of the twentieth century, but one of its most prominent citizens: 'Jerry Shea enjoyed the widest acquaintance in Canadian political, civic and entertainment circles of anyone from coast to coast. Michael Shea's reputation in the United States was equalled by his brother's on the other side of the border.'[46]

On the other end of the spectrum of Ontario's vaudeville entrepreneurs, in 'small time,' was John J. Griffin. A native of Toronto (*Globe*, 14 August 1931), Griffin worked his way up until he was manager of the huge Sells Brothers Circus. He always returned to Toronto in the off-season, and during one of these breaks he opened the first permanent movie house in Ontario, on Yonge Street. The Theatorium, later called the Red Mill Theatre, opened in March 1906 and started Griffin on a lucrative new career. Griffin did not believe at the time that movies alone would continue to attract audiences. He wasn't the only one. By 1909 nickelodeons, movie theatres that charged only 5 cents admission, had proved their popularity everywhere. Toronto had eighteen theatres with a seating capacity of 3,000 and an estimated overall daily attendance of 15,000! Yet one of the aldermen considering licensing applications declared in the newspapers: 'Let them multiply like rabbits, and they will soon sign their own death-warrant. They are almost overdoing it already, and if we get a few more of them the moving picture fad will soon fall flat' (*Star*, 22 May 1909).

Griffin found difficulty getting the ready supply of performers he needed, so he opened his own booking office. By 1914 he had added offices in Montreal, Buffalo, and Detroit and was providing attractions for more than 300 theatres in the United States and Canada. Most were 'little small time,' movie theatres with only a few acts of vaudeville, but they constituted an empire for Griffin, who always believed that vaudeville was necessary to make his ventures work if they were to be open from ten in the morning until eleven at night.[47] Griffin retired in the 1920s and died in 1931 at the age of seventy-seven at 217 Niagara Street in Toronto, his address for thirty-one years.

From 1900 to 1914, in between the Shea big time and the Griffin little small time, scores of theatres featuring vaudeville opened in Ontario. In the early years most found some way to align themselves with the two local vaudeville powers. C.W. Bennett, for example, who built beautiful theatres in London, Hamilton, Ottawa, and Montreal, could not get into Toronto. In 1906, from his theatre in London, Ontario, he formed a corporation with some of Ontario's richest businessmen in order to build a vaudeville circuit. Because he wanted to play big time, he had to join the B.F. Keith Exchange, which meant that he could not interfere with the territorial rights of the Shea brothers. He ran the circuit until 1909, when he had to resign because of illness.

The only other significant theatre chain operating in Ontario before 1914 was that of Ambrose Small, who controlled as many as thirty legitimate theatres in Ontario. Small's theatres did not always play regular drama; many of the stops on his circuit were one-theatre towns where the attraction changed in the middle of the week. Given the continued shortage of legitimate productions and the popularity of vaudeville, he often presented vaudeville for half of the week. The partner he most often chose in his vaudeville arrangements was Griffin, who, in turn, used Small's legitimate attractions in the towns where he controlled theatres.

While native sons played a large part behind the scenes in vaudeville, they played a much smaller role in front of the curtain. Of the 800 performers who headlined in Toronto's vaudeville theatres between the years 1899 and 1915 less than a dozen were Ontarians. But two of them, Marie Dressler and May Irwin, achieved international stardom. Today Marie Dressler is remembered for her screen roles, but she gained her fame in vaudeville long before films became a popular form of entertainment.[48] She was born Leila Koerber on 9 November 1869 in Cobourg, Ontario. Since her father was a highly respected church organist and music teacher in the community, she changed her name when she went to the United States in her early teens to pursue a stage career. She started her career in light opera, but in 1892, when a New York show she was in failed, she turned to vaudeville and propelled herself to the headline position with songs and imitations. For the next twenty years she was one of the highest-paid performers in both vaudeville and the legitimate theatre. Her most successful vehicle was the role of Tillie Blobbs, a boarding-house drudge in *Tillie's Nightmare* (1909), in which she sang 'Heaven Will Protect the Working Girl,' a song ever after associated with her. Her career took a downward turn during the 1920s until 1927, when she was offered a small part in a

Marie Dressler 'As she appears today,' c.1914

film, *The Joy Girl*. This led to other screen roles in *Anna Christie, Min and Bill, Dinner at Eight*, and *Tugboat Annie*, which established her as the screen's foremost comedienne.[49] She died at the height of her new career, in Los Angeles, on 28 July 1934.

May Irwin was born in Whitby, Ontario, on 27 June 1862 and began her career in Buffalo in 1876 in a straight show.[50] A year later she teamed with her sister Flora in a song and dance act which was seen by Tony Pastor. He signed them and enlarged their act to include comedy skits. But in 1883 Augustin Daly broke up the act by signing May to star in his musical comedies.[51] She then went over to Charles Frohman and continued in the legitimate theatre until 1907, when she headlined a vaudeville show at the Orpheum Theatre in New York. Throughout the 1910s May Irwin alternated vaudeville appearances with stage roles and in 1920 retired to farm in New York. She died on 26 October 1938.[52]

After Marie Dressler and May Irwin the most successful native headliners were Toronto-born Victor Stone and actress Mabel Barrison, who were leading players in vaudeville sketches for twenty years. Others, such as acrobat and trick cyclist Buckner and dancer Stewart Jackson, reached the headline position in big time only temporarily. There is one other interesting local story however, that of the O'Connor sisters from Mimico, the only natural six-sister act ever in vaudeville. It was unusual for amateurs to receive try-outs on a big-time vaudeville stage, but Jerry Shea gave the original O'Connor Trio a chance during a matinée show on 15 November 1906. Ada, Annie, and Mary were a big hit, so Jerry sent them to Buffalo where Mike recommended them for the big time circuit. They were joined by their sister Nellie but were just another quartet until they joined Clarence Wilbur and his school act. In Chicago, during the 1908–9 season, Wilbur became unhappy with two girls in his act and, upon learning there were more O'Connor sisters, invited Kathleen and Vera to join. The sisters stayed with Wilbur for two years, but their talent and the six-sister novelty enabled them to secure bookings on their own. They remained together until the First World War, when patriotic duty, marriage, and family responsibilities broke up the act. Nellie joined her husband in a successful song and dance act, and Mary, Kathleen, Vera, and a seventh sister, Madeline, played in different combinations as the O'Connor sisters until the end of vaudeville.

Ontario was also the home of one of the few natural six-brother acts in vaudeville. The Brown brothers, Tom, Alex, Fred, Harry, Will, and Nelson, were born on Simcoe Street in Toronto. They studied music with their father, Albert, a well-known musician, and their uncle, who became the director of the governor-general's band in Ottawa in 1914. All the brothers played wind instruments: their publicity photo showed them playing saxophones. They began with the Barnum and Bailey Circus, worked their way into minstrelsy, eventually playing with Primrose and Dockstader, and made a considerable name for themselves in vaudeville.

The gradual demise of vaudeville during the 1920s and 1930s is familiar to most readers. Most assume the movies were the cause, because during that period a performance was frequently headlined by a film. By the early 1920s vaudeville needed movie stars to attract audiences. The biggest events in Toronto's vaudeville theatres during the 1922–3 season, for example, were the live appearances of movie stars Francis X. Bushman and George Beban. Both performed live on stage in scenes that completed the movies audiences had been enjoying. This is not to say that vaudeville was already dead. In 1921 the Shubert Brothers felt there was still enough money to be made in big time vaudeville to challenge the B.F. Keith Exchange, a move that resulted in transforming Toronto's two best legitimate theatres into vaudeville houses: the Royal Alexandra in 1921, and the Princess in 1922. Large vaudeville theatres were also still being built. But all the big chains, the Loew's theatres throughout Ontario, the Pantages in Toronto and Hamilton, and the Shea's Hippodrome in Toronto were already featuring movies. By the mid-1920s there were no straight vaudeville theatres left in Ontario, and a decade later there was no vaudeville at all. But movies did not kill vaudeville.

Movies competed for the 5- and 10-cent patrons of vaudeville, but this had little to do with big time. Big time was variety theatre at its best, whereas movies concentrated on comedy and drama. Movies therefore did much more direct harm to the legitimate theatre, which had been struggling since the arrival of vaudeville at the turn of the century. The powerful owners of the legitimate syndicates turned the tables on vaudeville after the First World War. They filled their theatres with musical comedies and revues to save their industry, thus causing the next step in the evolution of variety theatre. Big time vaudeville was hurt most by movies through the loss of its stars, and when the legitimate joined in the raid by using performers such as Norworth and Al Jolson for musical revues, the end was near. 'Big time' vaudeville was nothing without its stars. As vaudeville declined, movies moved into the theatres to fill the void.

The other factor in vaudeville's demise was the development of radio. A *Billboard* story on 4 March 1922 warned actors not to mix their media, the same type of warning performers had received years earlier about trying to play both the legitimate and vaudeville stages. The result was the same: more performers moved to the lucrative new form and further strained the supply of top talent available to vaudeville. During the Great Depression free radio boomed and variety theatre had a new and permanent location: the living room. The final evolution occurred with television, the direct descendant of all variety theatre.

NOTES

1 Vaudeville and burlesque figures are based on twelve performances per week, legitimate figures on eight performances per week, their respective norms.
2 Y.S. Bains, 'Theatre and Society in Early Nineteenth-Century Toronto,' *Nineteenth Century Theatre Research* 3: 2 (Autumn 1975), 83
3 Edwin C. Guillet, *Toronto from Trading Post to Great City* (Toronto: Ontario Publishing 1934), 456
4 Bains, 'Theatre and Society,' 83
5 Patrick O'Neill, 'A History of Theatrical Activity in Toronto, Canada: From Its Beginnings to 1858,' PHD dissertation, Louisiana State University 1973, 19
6 Joseph Csida and June Bundy Csida, *American Entertainment: A Unique History of Popular Show Business* (New York: Watson-Guptill 1978), 47
7 For a full account of Blondin's feats at the Falls see Pierre Berton, *My Country: The Remarkable Past* (Toronto: McClelland and Stewart 1976), 272–85.
8 Gordon Donaldson, 'Farini at the Falls,' *Review* (Imperial Oil) 3: 2 (1979) 18. This work gives the life story of Farini.
9 Ibid., 19
10 Ibid.
11 Duncan McLeod 'Nineteenth-Century Niagara,' in Leslie Hannon, ed., *Maclean's Canada: Portrait of a Country* (Toronto: McClelland and Stewart 1960), 141
12 Ibid., 142
13 George L. Chindahl, *A History of the Circus in America* (Caldwell, Idaho: Caxton Printers 1959), 2
14 O'Neill, 'History,' 218
15 Ibid., 223–4
16 Ibid., 40
17 Robert C. Toll, *On with the Show! The First Century of Show Business in America* (New York: Oxford University Press 1976), 51
18 James S. Moy, 'The First Circus in Eastern Canada,' *Theatre History in Canada* 1:1 (Spring 1980), 12–23
19 Guillet, *Toronto*, 425. The 1827 date has not yet been confirmed by newspa-

pers, but the circus is regularly referred to in newspapers of 1830 and 1831. See, for example, *Colonial Advocate*, 5 August 1830, and the *Canadian Freeman*, 27 October 1831 or 3 November 1831.

20 O'Neill, 'History,' 182

21 Michael Bennett Leavitt, *Fifty Years of Theatrical Management* (New York: Broadway Publishing 1912), 137

22 Chindahl, *History of the Circus*, 93

23 O'Neill, 'History,' 50

24 Mary Shortt, 'From *Douglas* to *The Black Crook*: A History of Toronto Theatre, 1809–1874,' MA thesis, University of Toronto 1977, 69

25 Leavitt, *Fifty Years*, 416

26 Hector Charlesworth, *Candid Chronicles* (Toronto: Macmillan 1925), 341

27 Toll, *On with the Show!* 89

28 Dailey Paskman, '*Gentlemen Be Seated!*: A Parade of the American Minstrels*, revised edition (New York: Clarkson N. Potter 1976), 13

29 Donald Campbell Masters, *The Rise of Toronto, 1850–1890* (Toronto: University of Toronto Press 1947), 204–5

30 Guillet, *Toronto*, 362

31 Richard Plant, 'The Toronto Lyceum: A Study of Early Canadian Theatre in Miniature,' *Nineteenth Century Theatre Research* 4:2 (Autumn 1976), 75

32 Guillet, *Toronto*, 457

33 Parker Zellers, *Tony Pastor: Dean of the Vaudeville Stage* (Ypsilanti, Mich: Eastern Michigan University Press 1971), xiv

34 *Descriptive Catalogue of the Provincial Exhibition*, 1858, 79

35 Charlesworth, *Candid Chronicles*, 341

36 Toll, *On with the Show!* 30

37 Ibid.

38 *Saturday Night*, April 1980, 13

39 Toll, *On with the Show!* 217–18

40 Ibid., 232–3

41 Tony Pastor is most often referred to as the 'father' of modern vaudeville. He presented the first straight family variety show on 24 October 1881 at his 14th Street Theatre in New York, and made a success of the policy. He never attended the negotiations that established the big circuits, however, and never controlled more than the one theatre in which he himself performed in New York.

42 Nora Bayes, 'Holding My Audience,' *Theatre* 26 (September 1917), 128

43 John E. DiMeglio, *Vaudeville U.S.A.* (Bowling Green, Ohio: Bowling Green University Popular Press 1973), 78

44 Hartley Davis, 'In Vaudeville,' *Everybody's* 11 (August 1905), 231–4

45 Bernard Sobel, *A Pictorial History of Vaudeville* (New York: Citadel Press 1961), 49

46 *Saturday Night*, 14 December 1943

47 *Canadian Film Weekly*, 23 December 1943

48 Anthony Slide, *The Vaudevillians: A Dictionary of Vaudeville Performers* (Westport, Conn.: Arlington House 1981), 39

49 Ibid., 40

50 Douglas Gilbert, *American Vaudeville: Its Life and Times* (New York: Whittlesey House 1940), 97

51 Ibid., 98

52 Slide, *Vaudevillians*, 77

7 Theatres and Performance Halls

ROBERT FAIRFIELD

The study of theatre architecture goes hand in hand with the study of theatre history, since the design of theatre buildings was, in varying degrees, influenced by what was to happen in them. A dictum attributed to Winston Churchill has it that 'we make our houses and our houses make us.' The architecture of our early theatres doubtless influenced, for better or worse, the stage presentations of the day, as well as the manners and social customs of contemporary theatre patrons.

Instead of providing an annotated chronology of all theatres of record in the province, this chapter will concentrate on a selection of theatre buildings that can be deemed notable and representative. Because primary sources are few and, in many instances, not entirely reliable, the greater part of the descriptive information about early buildings, particularly those originating in the nineteenth century, has been gleaned from contemporary newspaper reports. The remaining data come from the odd photograph or hearsay accounts of old-timers and, in a few rare instances, from original drawings held in public archival collections.

Before we can proceed to the selection of buildings that contained theatres, it is necessary to settle on a definition of 'theatre.' In this chapter the term 'theatre' will refer to any enclosed public seating and a stage on which live theatrical performances can be presented, with or without musical accompaniment. On that basis, halls such as Shaftsbury Hall and Massey Hall in Toronto do not qualify, nor do halls designed primarily for events other than theatrical entertainments, such as the original Victoria Hall in Cobourg and Toronto's St Lawrence Hall.

Those theatres that originated before 1850 are examined first. Theatres existing in Ontario over the succeeding sixty-four years have been grouped as theatres in cities, the town hall and opera house, theatres of note outside the cities, and vaudeville houses.

None of the pre-1914 purpose-built theatres in Ontario displayed that elusive quality we choose to call indigenous Canadian architecture. Rather, they were largely the product of engineering innovation, new staging techniques, and changing fashions in architecture and interior decoration, all originating elsewhere, principally in Britain and the United States.[1] As it is, with one or two exceptions, they are now gone without a trace, burned or razed, leaving little visible evidence of their place in our cultural past.

The nineteenth-century theatres, or opera houses as they were called, outside the larger centres of Ontario, were for the most part incorporated in town halls and market buildings. Regrettably, many of those venerable and unique buildings have also been swept away, the victims of urban change. A considerable number remain standing, however, most of them in southwestern Ontario.

Outside the major cities of the province, a number of theatres were erected that were larger and better appointed than all but a few in the town hall / opera house group. A selection of those more substantial houses has been included here under the heading 'Theatres of Note outside the Cities.'

The last live performance theatres constructed before 1915 were vaudeville houses. Catering to a popular taste for the lighter forms of theatrical entertainment and designed to seat the mass audience, vaudeville houses were a short step away from the later movie theatres, into which many were ultimately transformed.

Early Theatres

In the first half of the nineteenth century in Ontario, halls for theatrical performance were for the most part makeshift affairs, contained in or attached to buildings having prime uses other than as theatres. With the exception of the newly restored Memorial Hall at Kingston, none of these early performance spaces survives to this day.

Among meagre references to the architecture of theatres before the 1850s we have a delightful description, attributed to Mrs Gilbert Porte, of the Gentlemen Amateurs' first theatre in London in the late 1830s: 'Standing trees supported the board roof and stumps sawed off pretty evenly supported the rough board seats.'[2] Better things were not long in coming to London, however, where the London Theatrical Company arrived on the scene in 1844, and another group appeared in 1846 calling itself the Shakespeare Club. These amateur groups

Hamilton, Town Hall, used for mid-nineteenth-century performances

presented theatrical entertainments at a converted Methodist church at the southwest corner of Queen's Avenue and Wellington Road and at the Mechanics' Institute at the southeast corner of Court House Square.[3]

In Hamilton the first theatre space of record (1828) is described 'only as a small room on Lovers Lane [later Wellington Street]. In 1835 the police building in King William Street had a room which was used by travelling players and lecturers. In 1840 the new Town Hall on James Street North provided accommodation for concerts, amateur drama and other theatrical events.'[4]

At Kingston, according to the *Whig Standard* of 3 August 1946, Imperial Army officers first presented amateur performances in a small theatre at the Freemasons' Tavern near the Tête du Pont barracks in the 1790s and until the building of Walker's Hotel in 1807, when the latter presumably offered better facilities for concerts and private theatricals. In 1815 a former brewery on what is now Rideau Street became the makeshift home of the Gentlemen Amateurs. So began the first properly constituted theatre in Kingston[5] and apparently the first public 'tut-tutting' over how and how not to behave while attending theatrical events, as evidenced by one local satirist, whose letter to the Gazette of 24 August 1816 is reproduced in part as follows:

On Monday evening last I attended the theatre, when I could not but observe the impertinence of a few gentlemen who seemed to take a peculiar pleasure in staring the ladies out of countenance. It would not be amiss that the managers of this edifice should adopt some plan, or throw out such hints as would preserve order and decorum within its walls. The indecorous custom of staring should be checked by branding the offender, or offenders, with the words Public Nuisance on the forehead for the first offence, and for the second they should be forthwith transported for life to prevent a third offence. Gentlemen wearing spectacles should not be allowed to enter the theatre without giving security for their good behaviour.

By the time the Atheneum Theatre, established in a new room next door to the *British Whig* on Bagot Street, opened its doors in 1841, we may assume the earlier novelty of theatre had given way to the orderly and easy decorum of a well-mannered theatre-going citizenry at Kingston. Two years later a two-storey frame building was erected at the corner of Montreal and Queen streets which was known as the Theatre Royal until it burned to ashes on 8 January 1851, after which its productions moved to Kingston's splendid new Town Hall. Butler's Theatre was another popular performance hall at the Montreal and Queen intersection from 1847 until 1854 when it, too, was destroyed by fire (*Whig Standard*, 3 August 1946).

With the completion of Kingston's Town Hall in 1844, a large and impressive second-floor room in the new building's north wing became available for civic meetings. Known first as Town Hall[6] then as City Hall, this imposing space was later dedicated as Memorial Hall on 14 December 1921, the name it bears today. From the outset the hall served Kingston as a cultural centre and locus for community gatherings and events of all kinds, including recitals, lectures, political gatherings, balls, band concerts, and theatrical presentations. So enthusiastically patronized was the hall that in 1870 it became necessary to replace the floor. Since it was an imperfect chamber for plays or musical recitals, its hall acoustics must have been vexing from early times, principally, it would seem, because both the stage back wall and the auditorium ceiling have hard-surfaced radius curvatures. Memorial Hall as it exists today was originally designed in the Tuscan manner by the talented young George Browne, who was awarded the Town Hall commission by the Council of the Town of Kingston over eleven other competitors in 1842.

Kingston, Memorial Hall after restoration, 1974

Most accounts have it that the first theatre in York was the ballroom of Frank's Hotel 'subsequent to the year 1820 and continued to 1830 or thereabouts.'[7] Situated at the northwest corner of Market Street and Market Lane (later Colborne Street) the ballroom apparently consisted of a wood-framed attachment to a frame hotel, approached by an outside stair and seating 100 or so patrons. An illustration of Frank's Hotel by Frederick V. Poole, produced ca 1912, shows us what the building possibly looked like.[8]

The publisher John Ross Robertson, looking back a half-century with questionable accuracy, tells us of a succession of early theatres materializing in Toronto, many of which were envisaged in pen-and-ink drawings reproduced in the *Evening Telegram*'s 'Landmarks of Toronto' of 16 May 1889. For the most part, all were frame buildings of no apparent distinction with the sole exception of the Royal Lyceum Theatre, erected by John Ritchie in 1848 on a site off the south side of King Street, a third of the way along the block between Bay and York streets. The Royal Lyceum was approached through an arched passageway then known as Theatre Lane.

The Royal Lyceum was the first building in Toronto to be erected for exclusive theatre use, the first proper theatre in town, and, from all

Toronto, pencil sketch of Royal Lyceum interior, dated 1849

accounts, the first proper theatre in Ontario. Histories differ on the matter of an opening date, although according to the Toronto *Globe* at the time, the theatre opened on 28 December 1848. The main façade of the building presented a two-storey masonry front with four pilasters carrying a pediment into which was inserted a half-round attic window. Below were three entrance doorways. Two precarious-looking wood stoops are indicated, with steps to grade.[9]

A sketch plan and interior perspective by F.H. Granger, dated 24 September 1849, gives a general picture of the likely arrangement of the house and backstage. The auditorium evidently had the usual pit seating, with a balcony and gallery on two levels above. Supported on posts and encircling the house in horseshoe fashion, the balcony and circle terminated at boxes on each side of the proscenium.[10] A *British Colonist* article on 21 December 1848 notes that the theatre accommodated an audience of 600 to 700 comfortably, although likely all the seating consisted of benches.

Granger's sketch of the stage indicates a depth of twenty-nine feet from curtain line to back wall and a width of twenty-six feet, giving a playing area eighteen feet wide inside the wings. A height shown of twenty feet possibly referred to the clear distance between stage floor

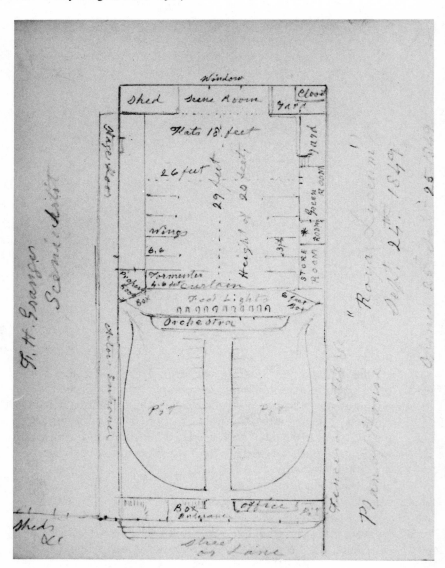

Toronto, ground plan of Royal Lyceum, dated 24 September 1849

and timber roof trusses above. Eleven footlight lanterns are indicated in the Granger floor plan, as well as an orchestra pit which did not appear to be depressed below auditorium floor level.

John Nickinson[11] leased the Royal Lyceum in 1852 and, after completing renovations of the premises, reopened the theatre on 28 March 1853. Nickinson possibly reconstructed the boxes, the occupants of which previously faced the audience instead of the stage. Later complaints concerning the Lyceum's uncharitable benches, dim gas lighting, and tarnished gilt suggest, however, that he had not improved conditions quite enough in matters of public comfort.[12]

Theatres in the Cities

TORONTO

Between 1850 and 1915 several theatres were erected in Toronto, none of which survives to this day except the Royal Alexandra, which opened in 1907.

Royal Theatre or Royal Opera House
Following a fire in 1874, the Lyceum was reconstructed by the new proprietor, James French, to the designs of his architect, Wallace Hume of Chicago. The building then became known as the Royal Theatre or the Royal Opera House. The best description of the Royal is likely that appearing in the *Mail* of 9 September 1874, which states that it was 'one of the most tastefully arranged interior theatres it has ever been the lot of our reporter to examine.'

The seating in the new playhouse totalled 1,450, the parquette, circle, and balcony having 850 and the gallery 600 seats. Four proscenium boxes were 'marvels of beauty,' the sides being framed by 'Abyssinian columns richly carved and gilded.' Seating on the main level consisted of iron folding opera chairs upholstered in crimson silk plush, with sofa seating in the balcony covered in gold terry. Two curving stairs at the rear of the parquette or orchestra level led to the balcony, to the distress of fire prevention authorities. Separate stairs, 'brilliantly lighted with gas jets,' gave access to the gallery.

The auditorium was lighted from a ceiling dome, the centre of which was 'frescoed in Egyptian design,' around which were 100 gas jets backed by twelve corrugated metal reflectors. Elsewhere were prominently displayed the busts of Byron, Burns, Moore, and Mozart, while over the proscenium arch appeared the bust of Shakespeare, together with the quotation, 'Nothing extenuate, nor aught set down in malice.'

As to the stage, we have only the *Mail*'s obscure reference to it as 'provided with every modern improvement and stocked with useful scenery which it is unfair to attempt to describe to the uninitiated.' However, for those less uninitiated than most, the *Mail* review goes on to note the width of the stage between side walls as fifty-seven feet with a depth of fifty feet, although it is not stated if the latter dimension was taken from the footlights, the house curtain, or elsewhere.

The orchestra pit in its full-fledged form, providing an adequate chamber for musicians between stage and audience, made its debut in Toronto at the new Royal Theatre.

On 8 February 1883 fire gutted the Royal Theatre interior, although it appears that enough of the building remained to provide the bulk of a warehouse on the site, which in turn went up in flames in 1922. The last remains of the Royal were removed in 1940 to make way for a parking lot.

Queen's Theatre

An early theatre existed on the north side of King Street West, ambiguously known as the Lyceum Theatre, until another theatre replaced it at that location, opening on 11 May 1874 under the name of the Queen's Theatre. By opening with *Lady Audley's Secret* plus a variety program, the Queen's sponsors clearly intended the new house to be a variety theatre.[13] According to the Toronto *Mail* of 29 April 1874, the theatre was 'constructed entirely without stairs, the whole occupying a spacious ground floor.' Audience capacity was reported to be 1,000, arranged in a parquette, dress circle, and amphitheatre, addressing a stage of sixty by forty feet. Destroyed by fire on 23 April 1883, the Queen's had catered to an abundant taste for the more popular forms of theatrical entertainment, which could have accounted in some measure for its more egalitarian floor plan.

Grand Opera House

Toronto's Grand Opera House, located on Adelaide Street, west of Yonge Street in Toronto, opened to the public on 21 September 1874 and was managed by the remarkable and popular Charlotte Morrison. The building was erected by the Grand Opera House Company, with Lalor and Martin of Toronto as architects and T.D. Jackson of New York the consulting architect.

The new Grand Opera House measured ninety-one feet by 208 feet, presenting a four-storey entrance front on Adelaide Street, described by one reviewer as a 'handsome rendering of florid Parisian renaissance.'[14] A more flattering description attributed to the architects before the opening, in the *Mail* of 30 March 1874, stated there would be an inclined passage fifteen feet wide leading from the street to a glass-roofed vestibule, which in turn was to connect directly to the main seating level of the house. On either side of the vestibule space, stairs would lead to two upper galleries. According to the *Canadian Illustrated News* of 29 August 1874, the Grand had 'a seating capacity of 1323 and campstool and standing room for 500 more.' Although accounts of seating distribution differ, there were 620 folding opera chairs upholstered in crimson rep in the orchestra stalls, with the remaining seats in the dress circle, family circle, and eight private boxes, each of the latter having four loose chairs.

The superb drawings of F.M. Bell Smith[15] in contemporary issues of *Canadian Illustrated News* are consistent with other accounts of the Grand's auditorium which could perhaps be described as a mixture of styles and pseudo-styles, from mildly Baroque to vaguely Moorish, with almost everything in between. Bell Smith's illustrations also show us an impressive elliptic proscenium arch rising to a height of some fifty feet above the parquette and the elaborately frescoed auditorium ceiling above, 'executed by some Italians from New York' as noted in the *Mail* of 9 September 1874. It is a pity that the identity of those gallant itinerant craftsmen may be forever lost to us. Perhaps the first convertible house of its time in Canada, the Grand had a temporary floor by which, on removal of the orchestra chairs, the entire main floor space could be turned into a ballroom ninety-six feet long and fifty-five feet wide.

Although the house lights were gas fuelled, they could be turned on and off 'by means of electric agency' from the prompt box. Ventilation, woefully inadequate in almost all performance halls of the time, must have been very inadequate in the Grand, since it consisted of a sheet-metal pipe three feet in diameter above the auditorium sunlight, into which had been confidently fitted 'a powerful exhauster.' The sunlight in the centre of the auditorium ceiling was said to be ten feet in diameter, with thirty-two gas burners in ground glass globes around its rim, backed by a reflecting cone of inverted prisms.

In the 30 March 1874 issue of the *Mail*, the stage is described as being thirty-five feet wide by fifty feet deep. Little evidence, so far, has been found to indicate what sort of fly loft existed over the stage, or how the scenery was moved about, except perhaps for the Bell Smith sketches, which show a stage of ample proportions having a loft

Toronto, Grand Opera House, c. 1875

Toronto, auditorium of Grand Opera House with seats removed for first annual ball, February 1875

height approaching forty-five feet. Backstage elements were placed along the west side of the building on three floor levels, including cast dressing-rooms, green room, property room, manager's office, and other facilities. A lane flanking the building on the east gave direct access to the stage.

The Grand Opera House burned on 29 November 1879, although apparently not to the ground, since it was reconstructed in fifty-one working days, reopening on 9 February 1880. Few changes were made in the house, it seems, although Julius Cahn's *Official Theatrical Guide* of 1900 gives a total seating capacity of 1,707, a figure hard to accept when it is compared with the original house capacity of 1,323. After the turn of the century, the Grand lost its place as Toronto's leading theatre, eclipsed first by the Princess and later by the Royal Alexandra. It had been empty for many years when in June 1928 it was pulled down.

Toronto Opera House

Early in the 1880s a prominent theatrical manager in New York, H.R. Jacob, and his Montreal partner, J.R. Sparrow, bought a roller-skating rink on the south side of Adelaide Street between Bay and Yonge streets and converted it into a theatre they named the Toronto Opera

Toronto, Princess Theatre ruins after the fire, May 1915, showing underside of balcony

House. The place was also known as Jacob and Sparrow's Opera House and it catered to patrons of lurid melodrama until it was purchased in 1889 by Ambrose Small and his partner E.D. Stair of Detroit, who redid the interior and continued to offer lurid melodrama. In March 1903 a fire gutted the building's interior, but the place was reconstructed in a bare seven months and christened the 'Majestic Theatre' on 2 November 1903 by Mrs Fiske, who played the lead in *Mary of Magdalen.* According to seating plans[16] of the Majestic published in 1904, the theatre at that time had 732 seats at orchestra level and 455 in the balcony. The gallery likely did not have space for more than 500 and fewer than that if safety and comfort became the governing criteria. Renamed the 'Regent' in 1920, the house became the 'flagship' of the newly formed Famous Players circuit, where the first film shown on 23 January 1920 was *Pollyanna,* starring Mary Pickford. The Regent was demolished in the 1930s.

Princess Theatre
Toronto's second academy of Music opened on 6 November 1889 on King Street near York Street. After being remodelled in 1895, the Academy became known as the Princess Theatre.

Beginning as a popular-priced playhouse, the Princess functioned later as a stock house under the management of O.B. Sheppard. By 1901 it had been decided to run the Princess as a high-priced theatre, and after extensive alterations the house was reopened as such in September of that year.

A seating plan published in 1904[17] shows the orchestra and balcony levels of the Princess Theatre as having 698 and 375 seats, respectively, and in addition eight boxes are indicated, providing seating for fifty or more. Together with gallery seating of some 500 patrons, the total seating capacity could have been in the order of 1,625. Less reliable perhaps is the Julius Cahn *Theatrical Guide* figure of 1,815 seats.

Photographs dated 10 May 1915,[18] taken by the city architect after a disastrous fire at the theatre, furnish the only illustration of the auditorium so far found. The roof having burned away, what was left of the auditorium and stage was seen bathed in natural light, affording a rare photographic opportunity and giving us a reasonably accurate record of the first Princess Theatre interior.

The main floor appeared to have a gentle rake, without seating risers. The balcony had been framed in timber and supported on wrought-iron posts, the latter extending upward to carry the gallery framing above. Both balcony and gallery plans suggest a radius curvature in the centre section, with seating in calipers on each side of the house, terminating at the boxes. The balcony front was of plaster, embellished with swags cast in the same material and likely picked out in gilt. The gallery balustrade was also plaster finished, although more modestly decorated, presumably in keeping with the cheaper seats.

The boxes, of which there were eight, seemed surprisingly untouched in the 1915 fire, even to the heavy velour draperies still elegantly framing each arched opening of the upper boxes. Richly detailed plaster work in the Edwardian mode framed the boxes and surrounds of the proscenium arch, displaying a stilted use of rosettes, swags, medallions, and other Baroque devices, all cast in plaster forms, which at that time could be purchased by the foot from mail-order houses.

From the 1915 photographs it would appear that the proscenium had a structural opening about thirty-five feet high and fifty feet wide. The stage appeared to be forty feet or so deep from curtain line to the upstage wall and about eighty feet wide. The height of the rigging loft above the stage could have been close to sixty-five feet.

Recent studies[19] suggest that the first Princess Theatre building accommodated an art gallery, a banqueting-room, and a drawing-room; also that stage and scene-handling equipment were, in some respects, unique in Toronto. The Princess, one can see, was a substantial and well-appointed theatre in its time, eclipsing the Grand in attracting discriminating audiences until the Royal Alexandra opened its doors in 1907.

Judging from the photographs, the fire of 1915 scarcely left the Princess a charred ruin. In any case a New Princess Theatre rose from the site of the old one in 1917, designed by architects C. Howard Crane and his associate Charles J. Read, on behalf of their client C.J. Whitney. Their building had a short life, however; for it was demolished in 1930 to make way for the extension of University Avenue.

Horticultural Gardens and Pavilion

A glass and iron pavilion put up in 1879 once occupied a site in what is now Allan Gardens in downtown Toronto. The *Mail* of 17 March 1879 described the structure as having the shape of a parallelogram seventy-five feet by 120 feet, with its long axis east and west and having side walls forty-three feet high, rising to a height of fifty-five feet at the end gables of the building. Dimensions of the stage were given as twenty-one feet by forty-six feet. The *Mail* of 5 February 1880 reported the Pavilion's seating capacity to be 2,500, from which we may deduce there must have been two or more snugly arranged audience seating levels. Whether or not the building served well as a drama theatre, it must have been, in any case, a dramatic spectacle in itself, inspired as it no doubt was by London's Crystal Palace, Joseph Paxton's masterpiece constructed in England in 1851.

Royal Alexandra Theatre

In 1905 a Toronto syndicate headed by Cawthra Mulock 'dreamed of a theatre that would be Toronto's centre for the performing arts,'[20] to present high-class entertainment from abroad, booked mainly from New York and London. Although the cultural fare was to be imported, John MacIntosh Lyle, a Toronto architect, was engaged for the project, in association with the New York firm of Carrere & Hastings and with William Fry Scott as the structural engineer. Born in Belfast in 1872, Lyle studied in Paris and subsequently gained his professional training in both Paris and New York, before practising in Toronto from 14 Leader Lane. When John Lyle executed the Royal Alexandra and later collaborated on the design of Toronto's Union Station (1913–18) he was an unwavering disciple of the École des Beaux-Arts. In the 1920s, however, he moved towards the new 'modernism,' in which decoration in architecture was no longer rooted entirely in classical forms, becoming instead an expression of the present through use of commonly recognized symbols and motifs. An example of Lyle's modernist work is the Runnymede Public Library in Toronto, where he dignified

Toronto, Royal Alexandra Theatre interior, showing royal boxes, 1907

Toronto, Royal Alexandra Theatre exterior, 1913

the building with replicated Canadian totem poles in place of the then customary classical columns.

Accounts have it that Mulock commissioned Lyle to build the most modern theatre in the world, giving him two years to do it and a budget of $375,000. The site was on the north side of King Street, between John and Simcoe streets on the recently vacated playing fields of Upper Canada College. By 1906 a royal patent was granted to the owners, giving the sovereign's permission to name the new theatre after the Danish princess and consort of King Edward VII. And so, as Haynes put it, Toronto's newest theatre, the Royal Alexandra, 'began its history in the glittering company of theatres royal in Montreal and London and became, not merely a cultural centre, but an object of civic pride.' Clearly this project had distinguished patrons.

The Alex, as it was and still is affectionately called by many Torontonians, opened on 26 August 1907 with a New York musical, establishing itself 'as a popular theatre right from the beginning.'[21] Those who came on opening night entered no ordinary theatre, but one that, for the richness of its finishes and the splendour of its gold and ivory auditorium, eclipsed any other of its time in Canada. Of greater consequence was the fact that behind a late French Renaissance façade and under the Baroque interior decoration, Lyle and his colleagues had created a twentieth-century building. Of structural steel and reinforced concrete, it was the first properly fireproofed theatre in the dominion and the first with balconies spanning the house without the aid of intermediate columns.

When Mulock had declared that excellence by world standards must be the goal, Lyle worked to that end, but in doing so he exceeded the syndicate's initial budget by 100 per cent. No doubt this caused some despondency among the owners, who likely saw their prospects for a return on investment fading, and justly so; for, according to C.H. Blackhall,[22] 'few theatres outside New York ever pay if the cost runs over $600,000.'

Essentially unchanged since 1907, the building itself measures about eighty feet by 185 feet in plan, divided into three distinct sections: administration and entrance block; auditorium; stage and backstage spaces. The first of these included a vestibule, entrance hall, box office, foyer at orchestra level, waiting-room, owner's room, smoking-room, and manager's office, together with lavatories and cloak space. Stairs on each side gave to a first-balcony foyer and tea room, from which stairs ascended to the gallery hall and thence to the precipitous, stepped aisles of the gods.

The auditorium proportions at the Royal Alexandra approach those of a cube, measuring about seventy-five feet wide, seventy-one feet deep and sixty-five feet high. The gallery seated 433, the balcony 384, with 652 at orchestra level. Four boxes each could accommodate fourteen, giving a total house capacity of 1,525.[23] A good seating plan, an adequately raked main floor, and balconies without column supports gave excellent audience sight-lines to the stage. With house lights up, patrons could view a splendid crimson stage curtain emblazoned with the Royal Achievement of Arms and above it, in Rubenesque magnificence, Frederick Challener's ceiling fresco, 'Venus and Attendants Meeting Adonis and Eros,' the very symbol of expectation for those moments before curtain time.

The architect's 1906 drawings for the building indicate a stage depth of thirty-seven feet eight inches measured from the act curtain and a width of seventy-five feet inside the fly tower. The structural proscenium opening was forty-two feet wide and thirty-eight feet high with a height of seventy-four feet from stage to the gridiron deck. Essentially a touring house, the Royal Alexandra had few backstage

London, Holman Opera House

accommodations for resident companies but more than enough for travelling shows, at least for a decade or more.

Sound investment for its builders or not, the Mirvish family wisely saved the Royal Alex from demolition in 1963 and so brightened its prospects as a continuing cultural resource for the citizens of Toronto for years to come.

LONDON

Holman Opera House
Of London's several performance halls,[24] the first important one opened on 8 May 1866 at the corner of York and Richmond streets. The new flat-floored Music Hall, seating about 580, was housed on the second floor of a handsome Palladian-style building constructed in locally fired buff brick. The building's bold cornices and window pediments were of wood, as were the brackets supporting them.

The proprietor in 1868 was not backward in proclaiming his pecuniary interest in the place, since he put up a commercial message in large lettering on one end of the building reading 'Music Hall Saloon, J. McAuliffe, Livery Stable.' A year later however, the tone

London, Masonic Temple and Grand Opera House

of the place got a boost with the arrival of the industrious George and Sallie Holman, who took over the hall and are credited with having increased the seating to 620, at the same time extending the stage seven feet into the house. Even the Holmans couldn't keep the Opera House afloat, however, and the building was demolished in 1891, the year London's first Grand Opera House opened its doors.

Grand Opera House

On 5 May 1880 a decision was taken in London to erect a new masonic temple at a proposed cost of $100,000 with the accomplished young George F. Durand (1850–89) of the firm of Tracy and Durand of London as architect for the work. A 1,228-seat theatre on the second and third floors of the new building would be known as the Grand Opera House, eclipsing London's existing Mechanics' Institute Hall and providing the first proper theatre in town.

Located on the northwest corner of Richmond and King streets, this splendid three-storey French Renaissance-style building measured 143 feet by 100 feet, roofed by an elaborately dormered attic in the manner of François Mansart. The building exteriors were primarily of red pressed brick, embellished with illuminated tile belts and with band coursing and window labels of Ohio stone.[25] The roofs were finished off in a delightful froth of cresting, finials, statuary, and wrought-iron, although not quite with the dash initially proposed by Durand if we are to judge by comparing his drawings with later photographs of the complete work.[26]

Durand's impressive auditorium placed the audience on three levels in a flat-ceilinged space nominally sixty feet wide, sixty-five feet long, and forty feet high. Seating rows in the parquette were stepped on eight-inch risers and the remaining main-level dress circle seating was arranged on twelve-inch risers, divided from the parquette by what appeared to be cast-iron balustrades. Upper seating levels were carried on two gracefully contoured galleries, encircling the house in horseshoe fashion and supported on slender wrought-iron columns, each daintily topped by Byzantine-like capitals. The lower of the two galleries, or the balcony, held four seating risers at the sides and seven at the centre. The upper gallery was the same except that it had bench seating and each seating row was divided from the next by a solid bulkhead, open only at access aisles. Two boxes adorned the house on each side of the proscenium, and these were swagged with curtains and lambrequins, no doubt further obstructing an already inadequate view of the stage.

What appear to be architect's drawings prepared for the construction contract show gallery railings of ornamental iron, although drawings of the auditorium produced at a larger scale and perhaps issued later distinctly show the gallery balustrades faced in solid material, probably plaster. The auditorium was most certainly outfitted with 'the latest thing in folding opera chairs' according to Durand, who is quoted in the London *Advertiser* on 2 September 1881 as stating that 850 such chairs would be installed, together with not such costly seating on the upper levels which would none the less be 'extremely comfortable.' It is also likely that a lantern projected above the auditorium roof, concealing a means of exhaust ventilation for the audience space below and no doubt providing support for a splendid chandelier, referred to by the architect as 'one of the finest in America.'

The drawings indicate an apron five feet downstage of the house curtain designed to carry footlights and projected over an orchestra pit which extended the full width of the proscenium. The proscenium, embellished on the audience side by a plaster ornamental frame, had a finished opening twenty-eight feet wide and thirty feet high. The moderately raked stage had a depth of thirty feet and a clear width of sixty feet. Backstage accommodations were equal to the best in other major Canadian touring houses of the time, that is to say, indifferent in matters of safety, sanitary conveniences, and the like, but equipped none the less with a luggage and property elevator, eight cast dressing rooms, and an ample scene dock measuring forty by sixty feet. Although spring traps in the stage are mentioned, no data on the rigging system or other theatrical equipment have so far come to light, but probably there was a grid of timber beams over the stage supporting blocks for hemp line rigging. Full height for flying appeared to be no more than forty feet.

On the evening of 8 September 1881 the Grand opened its doors to the public for the first time. ' "Fine, aint it," could be heard on all sides,' reported the London *Advertiser* in its edition of the following day, from which we gather that theatre going and a taste for good public architecture were well-practised arts in the city of London of that day.

New Grand Opera House

A disastrous fire on the night of 23 February 1900 gutted London's Masonic Temple, reducing the old Grand Opera House to ashes. Almost on cue, C.J. Whitney of Detroit announced to the press the next day that he would build a new Grand for the people of London, in partnership with the wily Ambrose Joseph Small of Toronto. Whitney then hustled off to Detroit, stating he would have his architect, Colonel Wood, apparently a Detroit carpenter who called himself an architect, get on with the plans.

In any event, Wood obviously wasted little time in getting drawings out to bid and site work started, since the new Grand opened eighteen months later on 9 September 1901. The London *Free Press* of 4 September had grumbled that London's new playhouse was 'not very prepossessing' on the exterior, adding that 'it has the appearance of a car barn with a cold storage at the rear.' The same paper carried only a perfunctory notice of the Grand's opening on the 9th, devoting innumerable column inches, however, to the condition of President McKinley, who had just been felled by an assassin's bullet.

Despite these inauspicious beginnings, it was clear that Wood or his hirelings had produced a theatre of first rank, not only in Ontario but in all of North America. The 1,850-seat Edwardian-style auditorium placed the audience on three levels with the customary boxes at first-balcony level on each side of the proscenium. Frederick Challener's impressive proscenium mural[27] in glowing colours of gold, amber, and green gave the house a touch of majesty, and happily that artist's great gift to the Grand survives to this day.

The Grand's stage was perhaps the most remarkable feature of the

Kingston, Princess Street showing The Grand Theatre (c. 1936) in the right corner

new theatre, being one of 'truly magnificent proportions. The proscenium opening was 42 feet – a width exceeded only by a bare half
dozen theatres on the whole continent and those few, like the Hippodrome in New York and the Academy of Music in Philadelphia, were
located in the very largest centres. It dwarfed absolutely anything else
in Canada.'[28] From footlights to back wall of the stage the house
measured forty-five feet, with eighty feet between side walls, giving
a set area of some 1,900 square feet. The height of the proscenium
arch is given as thirty-four feet and grid height about seventy feet.
Although the Grand's rigging system was no doubt a wonder at the
time, the flys were still worked with hemp lines operating through
blocks secured to a timber grid in the fly loft. The steel gridiron was
yet to be used in Canada and, along with it, steel wire rope and the
great convenience of counter-weighted scenery.

Electric lighting was available, however, and the Grand was fully
equipped in this respect, the wiring having been done by the London
Electric Company. All in all, the New Grand at London was probably
the most adaptable and best-appointed touring theatre yet to be built in
Ontario, not excelled until 1907 by completion of Toronto's Royal
Alexandra.

Hamilton, Grand Opera House

KINGSTON

Martin's Opera House

The first proper theatre in Kingston came into existence through the
enterprise and vision of a local citizen, William Martin, who
announced on 6 March 1878 that he and his son would put up a new
opera house near the corner of Princess and Montreal streets. With
Power & Son of Kingston as their architects, the Martins acted
promptly; for by July of that year the walls were well above ground
and by 6 January 1879 the new Martin's Opera House had its 'Grand
Dramatic Opening.' Likely the best and certainly the most engaging
description we have of the completed Opera House comes from the
pages of Kingston's *Daily News* of 2 January 1879:

The building is 110 feet long by 64 feet wide and, judging from its appearance, no one would suspect that one of the most compact and capitally
arranged houses of entertainment was enclosed within its unpretending walls.

The height of the (auditorium) ceiling is 35 feet and in the centre there is
a dome eight feet higher, with a diameter of 26 feet.

The size of the stage is 60 feet by 33 feet and the width of the proscenium opening being 30 feet. This gives ample room for the production of the most elaborate plays and allows for the presence of a great many people on the stage at one time.

The drop curtain is 30 feet wide and is really a work of art, the admiration of all who have seen it. One gentleman who has visited nearly every theatre in the old country and the United States informs us that he has never seen a better drop curtain.

The *Daily News* goes on to inform us that there was an orchestra pit, accessible from below stage, and that the auditorium had seating for 1,100 on two levels plus four boxes, each fitted with damask curtains and upholstered in crimson velvet. The parquette immediately in front of the orchestra pit held 225 opera chairs on four-and-a-half inch risers and the dress circle behind it had the same number of seats. The gallery, supported on iron posts, carried two rows of seats in front for 102 persons, known as balcony seats, the remaining seats in the gallery being for 'the gods, which class of individuals are, or seem to be, a necessary adjunct to all theatrical establishments.'

From Erdmute Waldhauer's excellent history of Martin's and the Grand Theatre[29] we learn that the building was renovated in 1897, even to a new house curtain depicting 'The Castle of Chillon.' In the auditorium the gallery seating risers were rearranged to run back from the balcony seats in a constant slope. The stage was enlarged, the proscenium was 'graced with a portrait of Queen Victoria,' and the box fronts were embellished with wax composition flowers, all prettily painted and picked out in gilt. Cast dressing-rooms were rearranged and refurbished and the building was converted to electricity.

On 6 December 1898 Martin's Opera House burned to the ground. After a brief and frenzied interval, a group of Kingston investors formed a stock company and negotiated a deal with Ambrose J. Small, who undertook to rent a new building on the site of the old one. The new Grand would have two galleries and four boxes, and 'the house was to seat 1,400 with an interior of 64 feet by 62 feet and a stage 62 feet by 35 feet with eleven dressing rooms.'[30]

Although no other description of the 1902 interior has been found, the architects likely borrowed from past styles to impart a respectable Edwardian flavour to the place and so gave the Grand an air of dignity and detachment as it entered the era of motion pictures. In 1938 the Grand opened as a movie house, closed as one in 1961 and was saved from wreckers in that year by local citizens who rallied to its defence. After a succession of alterations and face-lifts, the Grand Theatre at

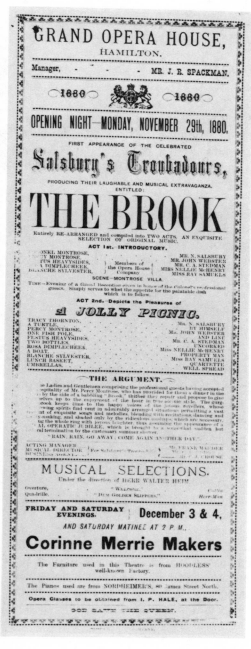

Hamilton, playbill from the opening of the Grand Opera House, 29 November 1880

Kingston functions today as one of the leading legitimate houses in the province.

HAMILTON

Grand Opera House
'The handsomest, most comfortable, beautiful, cosiest and most generally excellent opera house in the Dominion' declared the Hamilton *Spectator* of 30 November 1880, the day after Hamilton's new Grand Opera House opened. From an exuberant description of the Grand from the *Spectator* of that date, the following is borrowed and in places quoted verbatim.

The work of George H. Lalor, architect of Toronto, the new theatre was erected in conjunction with a hotel at the corner of James and Gore streets. A passage through the hotel from James Street gave access to public spaces which were 'liberally provided in the matters of ladies' and gentlemen's dressing rooms ... furnished and fitted up in a style that betokens liberality ... even to the place where the gentlemen go between acts to get a clove' (Hamilton *Spectator*, 27 August 1892).[31]

The auditorium held 1,169 seats, and the possibility existed of adding 100 or so more if need be. A parquette and dress circle occupied the main level, with a balcony and gallery on two levels above, each supported on iron posts. 'Proscenium boxes look out from between handsome carved and fluted pillars, in pure white picked out in gold.' The decorators lavished much attention on the auditorium with ceiling fresco work 'in a medieval pattern' exercising 'a perfect eye for the harmonization of colour by gaslight.'

A nicely painted dominion coat of arms cartouche dignified the proscenium arch, and on each side were frescoed borders in Queen Anne style, 'relieved by a little of the now fashionable Japanese style' of decoration. The stage of the Grand was twenty-five and a half feet deep and fifty-six feet wide, likely with grooves on each side for tracking on stock scenery. Leon Lempert of Rochester, known in the trade as the 'Lightning Scene Painter of the U.S.' did the frescoing and painted the house curtain in a romantic rendering of Constantinople and the Golden Horn. There was an orchestra box placed two feet or so below parquette floor level. The fly galleries were twenty-one feet and the rigging loft a bare thirty-seven feet above the stage.

After a decade or more of use, the theatre had become a 'shabby old barn' according to the Hamilton *Spectator* (27 August 1892) in announcing the Grand was about to reopen after extensive renovations, executed under the direction of architect Charles Mills. The following is taken in part from the *Spectator* of that date.

The Grand Opera House reopened on 6 September 1892 with a house of 1,256 seats: 420 on the main level, 336 in the balcony and the remainder in the gallery. Exits from the auditorium, considered almost excessive in 1880, were more than doubled, giving an aggregate exit width in front of the curtain of nearly seventy feet. Ventilation was installed 'even to the highest part of the gallery where gas jets will be kept constantly burning to provide a current.'

The proscenium arch got rather more attention than was good for it from Mills, who evidently scrapped the dominion coat of arms, replacing it with Francis Lathrop's 'Apollo Crowned by the Muses,' 'taken from a photograph of a similar picture in the Metropolitan Opera House of New York.' In what must have been a somewhat busy composition, there were marble panels on each side of the arch on which were mounted bas relief carvings depicting Shakespeare, Beethoven, Mozart, and Henry Irving, the whole being made even more distracting by the introduction of fifty electric lights 'with blended globes of delicate colours.' The new proscenium opening was surmounted by a metal sounding board, a device meant to reflect sound into the auditorium.

Improvements made in the stage in 1892 included its enlargement 'by more than one half.' New scene-handling equipment was installed, and evidently sufficient grid height was found to permit flying out the house curtain and act drop. The latest in speaking tubes and cue bells as well as an electric control board were installed.

The Hamilton *Spectator* reported on the last refurbishing of the Grand in its issue of 21 August 1900. The Opera House reopened on 14 September of that year with *The Evil Eye*. Apart from redecorating and electrification, the more significant changes occurred behind the curtain, notably replacement of the old grooved scene flats by the more up-to-date flown scene pieces.

The Grand eventually fell into disuse; today only a fragment of the hotel to which the building was once attached remains.

OTTAWA

Russell Theatre
Theatricals were staged in Ottawa's first Town Hall as early as 1850. In 1854 a professional company presented a series of plays on the premises and in the words of Lucien Brault 'enthusiasm was aroused,' fuelled, one would suppose, by the Town Hall's inadequacy for dramatic performance.

A local syndicate soon found the cash to put up a $7,500 playhouse on Wellington Street near O'Connor Street, calling it Her Majesty's and opening it to the public on 4 October 1856. Under this Metropolitan Dramatic Association classics such as *Richelieu* were presented there as well as amateur productions such as *To Prescott and Back for Five Shillings*.

In 1874 a new legitimate theatre was erected on Albert Street named the Grand Opera House and seating about 1,000, in what state of comfort we do not know. The Grand was later surpassed by the larger and more sumptuous Russell Theatre in 1897, but it lived out its life through the demeaning years of burlesque, vaudeville, and movie chasers, until it burned to the ground on the night of 5 July 1913, taking with it the adjoining Nickel Theatre. So frequent and so disastrous were the fires that plagued Ottawa in those early times that, fanciful or not, one wonders if Sparks Street had been named with conflagrations in mind.

It was not until the Russell Theatre opened on 15 October 1897 with the comic opera *Kismet or the Two Tangled Turks*, that Ottawa at last had a theatre of distinction. Adjoining the Russell Hotel at the corner of Queen and Elgin streets, the Russell had a seating capacity of 1,600, according to Cahn's *Theatrical Guide* of 1899–1900, although 1,500 may have been a more likely figure.

Patrons approached the Russell's arched main entrance from Queen Street. Moving through an environment of Italianate murals, tile mosaic floors, art glass, brass electroliers, and polished mahogany woodwork, they reached the entrance lobby where a gilded plaster bust of Queen Victoria looked down on all who gathered there. Two wide doors gave directly to an inner lobby from which stairs ascended each side to the balcony, family circle, and the gods. Two heavily draped portals opened to the orchestra seating, all upholstered in cardinal-red velour. A contemporary description of the auditorium tells us that 'the colour scheme on the walls is carmine, shading off to lighter tints. On the ceiling below the first balcony on entering the doors from the pit, one sees a beautiful figure design entitled "Psyche's Dream." On the sounding board are also three figures representing "Drama," "Music," and "Art." The remainder of the mural decoration consists of the chaste, simple and graceful borders of the style of the Italian Renaissance' (Ottawa *Citizen*, 16 October 1897). An early photograph[32] of the auditorium fails to show Frederick Challener's great mural on the sounding board, 'The Triumph of Drama,' but it does show the house drop on which a lesser artist had laboured over a gigantic scene of a CPR right of way in the Rocky Mountains.

Ottawa, Russell Theatre, *Yeomen of the Guard*, 28 February 1918

There were five boxes on each side of the house arranged in two tiers of two boxes each with a larger box on a level above, from which one could not likely see much of the stage. All the boxes were semicircular in plan, since they protruded into the auditorium, and all were heavily embellished in ornamental plaster designed to give visual impact but happily providing good sound reflection properties as well, to the benefit of those seated further from the stage.

The Russell's proscenium opening measured thirty-two feet square, and according to the contemporary Cahn *Theatrical Guide*, the liberally trapped stage was a respectable forty feet from foots to back wall and sixty-five feet between the side walls. The height of the rigging loft above the stage was sixty-four feet with a distance between fly girders of forty-eight feet. On the day it first opened, this substantial and well-appointed theatre had enough stock scenery to make up fifty scenes.

As happpened to so much of Ottawa's earlier architecture, fire destroyed the Russell in 1901; it was promptly rebuilt, surviving until the spring of 1928, when it was pulled down because it stood in the way of progress on the nation's largest roundabout, Confederation Square.

The Town Hall and Opera House

'The last half of the nineteenth century had few of the worries of the last fifty years. They were really comfortable years in which to live: no

St Marys, Town Hall

wars, no automobile or airplane deaths, no strikes, no singing commer-
cials, no communists, no "give me, give me," few government returns,
few robberies, but good music, fine hospitality, filled churches, real
amateur sport, an honest day's work, fewer needs, a happy people'
(R.N. Creech 1951). As Wooden observed in his delightful history of
Exeter,[33] Mr Creech may have gone too far in picturing an idyllic life
in rural Ontario during the second half of the nineteenth century. If not
quite idyllic, life outside the cities and larger towns was none the less a
good deal easier after the 1850s, and with better times came a growing
distaste for living on bread alone, a practice all but the well-off had
experienced off and on for a few generations. Also, our forbears in rural
Ontario eventually may have found wanting their renowned ability for
creating their own entertainment and so began longing for the cultural
stimuli open to them through the theatre.

As it happened, the growth of railroad transportation changed the
lives of most people in rural Ontario, just as the Model T Ford would
do for the inhabitants of western Canada early in the twentieth century.
The railroads brought an end to deep isolation for hundreds of commu-

Aylmer, Town Hall and Opera House with 1911 porch addition

nities across the southern regions of the province in which appeared theatrical touring companies of every imaginable stripe, all no doubt crying out for adequate performance halls in which they could present their wares. A popular call for new theatre space happily coincided with a burgeoning need for town halls, police lock-ups, market stalls, and fire engine sheds. Thus from the 1870s until well into the next century scores of Ontario communities put up public buildings to accommodate town offices, municipal facilities, and a theatre under one roof. Although many of those uniquely Ontario town hall / opera house buildings survive to this day in varying states of repair, this brief history will deal with only a few representative examples.

AYLMER

In April 1872 the townspeople of Aylmer voted sixty-three to thirty-seven to instruct Council to proceed with the building of a new town hall, not to exceed a cost of $7,000. The building, still standing today, was completed in 1874 to the design of architect George Watson &

Paisley, Town Hall and theatre, front, 1981

Son of London. Construction is credited to Thomas Wooster, a local contractor.[34] The St Thomas *Times* in December of that year declared the upstairs performance hall to be 'well adapted for oratorical displays or theatricals,' and so it was, although not well adapted enough to attract the better professional companies which toured the district later in the century. There were no performers' change rooms of any account, for example, nor did a rear stair exist for the cast, nor a hoist to bring a touring company's baggage up to stage level. Apart from those shortcomings, the building itself stood as a small masterpiece of Ontario Italianate architecture and a credit to its architect.

The original two-storey buff-brick building measured about forty by eighty feet, with a narrow façade on the street. Council chambers, a post office, and four large butcher stalls took up the ground floor, with a theatre seating 400 or so on a second level, reached by what must have been a cramped stair from a small front lobby. An entrance porch of classical proportions, topped with iron cresting, enlivened the building's street façade, as is shown by an early photograph dated 1874.[35] The first-storey windows are of domestic scale and modestly arched, whereas the upper-storey windows are much larger and are in pairs with half-round heads. The paired upper windows are set in raised-brick, arched surrounds, punctuated with keystones and divided one from the other by brick pilasters. Boldly detailed pediments of the building's gable ends receive support from elaborately shaped wood brackets. In the original work a handsomely proportioned octagonal lantern surmounted the building at the street end of the roof, and since the building was first heated by stoves, four brick chimneys added interest to the roof profile.

Upstairs the hall had a flat floor to which the seating was fixed in a conventional three-aisle arrangement. Wood stairs on each side of the auditorium gave access to a balcony. The orchestra level measured about thirty-nine feet by forty-eight feet and the balcony, distinguished by a particularly handsome cast-iron balustrade, was twenty feet deep and the width of the house. The flat auditorium ceiling was at one time embellished with an enormous Union Jack, painted on in full colour. The stage was shallow, having a depth of nineteen feet and a width of about thirty-nine feet. A frame wall divided the stage from the auditorium, with a proscenium opening of about twenty-three by fourteen feet.

With the passage of time the roof lantern weakened and was taken down, and the original chimneys were removed. In 1911 an awkward-looking office block was applied to the front of the building but, happily, was removed in the restorations of 1981.

PAISLEY

A gala concert on 20 March 1876 marked the opening of a new Town Hall at Paisley and its second-floor Opera House, as such auditoriums were popularly known. This handsome building still stands on Goldie Street and Queen Street South, at the meeting of the Saugeen and Teeswater rivers, managing to hold its own in spite of the visual atrocity of two highway bridges close by.

Built of red and grey brick, hand pressed on the site, the building shows a resemblance to the Aylmer Town Hall of 1874 but without the same richness of exterior detailing. The architect responsible for the

1976 building restorations at Paisley[36] reported that probably the original builder, William Anstead, constructed the building at a cost of $3,571 from stock plans. If so, one marvels at the happy results achieved in those days with such rudimentary documents, when today it seems we often achieve unpleasant results using fastidiously intricate ones.

Ascending an ornately classical oak and mahogany stair inside the Water Street entrance, one arrives at a second-floor landing giving directly to a flat-floored auditorium which with the stage takes up the entire second storey. The auditorium is an attractive room with its handsome windows and faceted ceiling into which has been inserted a centrepiece of intriguing design that serves not only as decoration but also as a room exhauster. The hall seats from 200 to 225 persons on fixed benches distributed between the orchestra level and a small balcony at the south end of the room. Although the stage is well proportioned to the hall, its size is somewhat limiting: a depth of only thirteen feet back of the proscenium and a width of thirty-three feet.

As to its history, evidently little happened to this charming building for a century except the loving care obviously brought to its upkeep by the good people of Paisley.

WHITBY

On 16 July 1877 Hopkins' Music Hall opened on Brock Street in Whitby, constructed by owner-builder George Hopkins to the design of his architect, a Mr Langley of Toronto. Following the death of Hopkins a year later, the ground floor of the building housed the Town of Whitby municipal offices and did so until the building was demolished in 1960.

This two-storey brick building, although scarcely a notable work of architecture, did exemplify a popular Ontario main-street style of its time with its barrel-arched window and door openings at street level and its stiffly ordered window labels and pediments with bracketed cornices above. According to the Whitby *Chronicle* of 5 July 1877, the hall had a capacity of 1,000, and, together with a gallery twenty-five feet deep, it took up most of the second floor, the balance being occupied by a stage of twenty-two feet by forty-two feet. No mention is made of scene-handling gear in newspaper accounts of the time, but much was made of the scenes themselves of which there were twelve sets.

CLINTON

According to newspaper accounts as early as 1874 and 1875, an active

Clinton, Opera House stage

performance space existed in a town hall at Clinton during those times, although evidence has not so far come to light identifying the size or site of that edifice. The minutes of Council in the first part of 1880 make reference, however, to a proposed new town hall, a building completed later that year to the design of George Proctor, architect.[37] Proctor's Town Hall at Clinton is among the finest examples of Victorian civic architecture in Ontario, expressing the confidence and pride of a southwestern Ontario town in times of growing prosperity. Still standing in the centre of town on Rattenbury Street, this imposing brick building originally housed the municipal and police offices, a fire engine house, and a large auditorium on the second floor.

A handsome wood stair leads from the street level lobby to a foyer space above, giving access directly to the auditorium, an impressive flat-floored room about fifty-two feet wide and forty-seven feet from back wall to the stage. Round-headed windows on each side of the room admit natural light and lend a sense of dignity and scale to the space. A surprising feature of the auditorium is the partly exposed, heavy-timber scissor trusses, which give the hall a curiously baronial air. Framing the stage is an equally surprising half-circle proscenium arch accented by a plaster surround resting on each side on elaborately detailed drops. The proscenium is twenty-eight feet wide at stage level and twenty feet high at the centre. The stage is a little more than three feet above auditorium floor and a bare fifteen feet deep. An apron with the usual curved front projects four feet into the auditorium.

It is likely the Clinton hall was used for balls and other social events as well as for theatrical presentations, and therefore the original seating may have been unattached to the floor. The size of the house indicates that the seating capacity might have been from 300 to 400, depending on the benches or chairs that were used and perhaps on the leniency of local fire authorities.

The more incontinent theatre-goers may have shunned the place in the 1880s, since it appears there were no public lavatories at the theatre; there are still none today, a century later. That omission was common to all public buildings of the day, but inconveniences aside, the hall at Clinton must be one of the more impressive nineteenth-century theatre spaces in all rural Ontario.

PETROLIA

In 1887 the town of Petrolia flourished as the oil capital of Canada; the price of crude was 80 cents per barrel, and local refineries were producing it at the rate of 5–6,000 barrels a week. No doubt the town fathers of Petrolia were riding a wave of prosperity in those days and therefore longed to erect an appropriate edifice to honour themselves, to be a tribute to Petrolia, and to serve the public weal. As early as 1881 Council had budgeted $13,000 for construction of a new town hall, but it was not until 1887 that members, concerned no doubt over lack of progress on the project, secured ratepayers' approval for spending $20,000 on a new town hall and opera house and hiring the brilliant George F. Durand of London as the architect.

Durand's Town Hall at Petrolia, with its handsome belfry and clock tower, is perhaps his finest work still standing today. The building is constructed of pale yellow brick on cut limestone foundations, all much in the manner of his Town Hall at Exeter. About 110 feet by seventy-two feet in plan, the Petrolia building displays a lively mix of styles and motifs from different periods, skilfully combined in a lively yet firmly ordered work, well illustrated by Durand's superbly drawn front elevation still on file in the Weldon Library Regional Collection, University of Western Ontario.

Theatre patrons entering the building from the front ascended stairs to a second level and emerged into the auditorium midway between the stage and back wall of the house. The front half of the auditorium floor

Petrolia, Victoria Hall after 1982 renovations. The building was destroyed by fire on 25 January 1989.

Gravenhurst, Opera House exterior at present

is flat and the back half is raked up about three feet. Seating capacity
of the hall was variously given as 800 to 1,000; today's standards
dictate a house capacity closer to 560. The audience was originally
distributed on orchestra and balcony levels and in two private boxes,
one on each side of the proscenium. The boxes are attractively framed
by pilasters and pediments and are ornately enclosed with cast-iron
railings, although those favoured to sit in them could have had only a
partial view of the set. The balcony railing, still existing in its original
form, matches those of the private boxes, lending a richness to the
interior that Durand no doubt had hoped to achieve in a similar manner
eight years before in his design of the first Grand Opera House at
London. Two splendidly ornate wrought-iron spiral fire escapes at the
rear of the building are connected to an iron balcony carried on elaborate brackets fixed to the wall, all done as though by the hand of Saul
Steinberg.

As in the hall at Clinton, the Petrolia auditorium ceiling is spanned
by partly exposed timber roof trusses. Arch braces at each end are
supported on corbels protruding from the wall, giving the room the
flavour of a parish hall. An orchestra enclosure interposes between the
stage and the auditorium and extends the full width of the proscenium.
The arched proscenium opening measures about twenty-two feet wide
and twenty-six feet high. The stage is twenty-two feet from proscenium
line to back wall and still relies on fixed sets or horizontally tracked
scenery.

Drayton, Town Hall and Opera House

Victoria Hall, as it is now called, officially opened on or about 3 January 1889 (Petrolia *Advertiser*, 11 January 1889), followed by a gala opening on the 14th featuring a stage performance of *Dr. Jekyll and Mr. Hyde*, by the well-known E.A. McDowell Company, with Percy Hunting in the lead role.

GRAVENHURST

In July 1897 the Gravenhurst Town Hall burned to the ground. Three years later Town Council passed a by-law 'to raise $10,000 for a new town hall and for the improvement of the streets.' Architect J. Francis Brown of Toronto was engaged to design the new building, which would house municipal offices as well as an opera house and be erected on Muskoka Street South near the centre of town.

Council evidently called for separate tenders rather than receive bulk bids for the work. Frank Hurlbut received the carpentry contract for $3,870 and William McKay the contract for masonry, brickwork, and plastering amounting to $1,600.[38] Both gentlemen discovered their bids were too low and on that account left the job to cut their losses. However, Hurlbut was apparently rehired and managed to complete his work with great distinction and at a daily rate negotiated with Council. The Opera House grand opening took place on 12 March 1901.

The building exterior is virtually unaltered to this day, except that later additions have partly obscured some original wall areas at the rear of the building. Constructed in red brick with steeply pitched, shingled roofs, the building rests on a coursed ashlar stone base measuring fifty-six by eighty-four feet. The entrance façade on Muskoka Street is the lesser of those dimensions and is flanked by two towers, one capped by a faceted conical roof and the other squared off below the main roof cornice line. Caught somewhat awkwardly between the staircase towers is an entrance porch of rustic design built of wood.

Two tall windows of tinted glass are protected from the weather by shingled roofs and rise above the main roof eaves on each side of the building, emphasizing the presence inside of a high-vaulted auditorium space. Stairs in each of the front towers give access to the handsome 345-seat theatre on the upper level. The auditorium floor is adequately raked down to the front, and the original tilt-up opera chairs are still in use. Overhead the arch-braced roof structure and ceiling planking, all in darkly mellowed pine, give the space an air of great warmth and dignity. From the superbly crafted timber ceiling hang the original brass chandeliers, each bearing a dozen or so electric lamps with tinted glass shades. A boldly arched proscenium opening in white plaster

Drayton, theatre chair, c. 1900

echoes the auditorium ceiling geometry, somehow making the stage seem larger than its seventeen by twenty-eight feet. The proscenium opening is twenty-five and a half feet wide and about eighteen feet high at the centre.

In the 1901 building, performers' dressing-rooms were little more than curtained alcoves off stage left; no good provisions apparently existed for the convenient storage and handling of properties, nor was there any plumbing on the premises as we now understand the term. Yet this charming Edwardian building, no doubt a colonial offspring of the English Vernacular Revival, has survived into the present, helped by a succession of devoted followers who saved it from demolition, supplied it with plumbing and other necessities, put plays on its stage and audiences in its theatre.[39]

DRAYTON

On the Conestoga River, some forty miles north of Kitchener, the village of Drayton once prospered after the Wellington Grey and Bruce Railway pushed through to Harriston in the early 1870s. At the turn of the century the Drayton Village Council confidently decided to seek ratepayers' approval for a by-law authorizing construction of a fine new town hall to contain an opera house, library, jail cells, council chamber, and fire engine house. On 4 March 1901 the ratepayers endorsed the enabling by-law by a vote of ninety-nine to forty-eight in favour of the project, and in due course George Gray of Harriston was retained as the architect with instructions to design the new building for a cost not exceeding $5,000. The taxpayers of our time may well marvel at the business-like way our forbears handled such matters and how in those days the citizens firmly held the purse strings. In spite of well-laid plans at Drayton, however, it was found that $3,500 more was needed to complete the project, which necessitated the passing of a second by-law before the building could be finished and opened to the public, which it eventually was on 3 September 1901.[40]

Dominated by its corner belfry tower, this modestly Romanesque, two-storey buff-brick building still stands on rising ground overlooking Drayton's main street. A maple staircase of generous proportions leads up to a second-floor lobby, handsomely panelled in black ash and giving directly to the auditorium. An attractive space fifty feet long and forty-five feet wide, the auditorium originally had 400 seats of which 372 were at orchestra level and the remainder in a small balcony. Seating capacity today is about 350. Elliptical in cross-section, an embossed sheet-metal ceiling in the hall is said to have excellent

Meaford, Opera House (former home of the Laughing Water Festival)

acoustical qualities. A ceiling height of thirty-five feet on the axis of the house gives the space a notably theatrical quality, enhanced by a proscenium arch twenty feet wide framed in fluted black ash.

A hardwood-surfaced stage eighteen feet in depth has fixed rigging above for lighting and curtains. A small control booth exists in the balcony as well as some low-level stage lighting, although those features were evidently not part of the original work. The Drayton theatre is certainly among the best turn-of-the-century houses of its type in Ontario.

MEAFORD

Completed in 1908, the existing Meaford Town Hall and Opera House at Sykes and Nelson streets replaced an earlier municipal building on the same site, constructed in 1864,[41] and destroyed by fire in 1907. The new Town Hall was an ambitious work of architecture in its time and still has an imposing presence in the centre of town, where it continues to be the seat of local government and a focal point for the community's cultural life.

Constructed at a cost of $26,500 by James Sparling to the plans of Ellis & Connery Architects, of Toronto, this Georgian-style brick building is fifty-four by ninety-five feet and some fifty feet from grade to the eaves. Originally the building housed the town offices, council chamber, library, police offices, and cells, with access stairs and a theatre taking up all the upper floor space.

Today the Opera House, its original pastel paint work still intact, seats 426 at orchestra level and 155 in a six-row balcony, a total of 583 seats. Originally the hall was said to have had a higher seat count, likely at the expense of adequate viewing of the stage. The main floor is sixty feet long by forty-seven feet wide with a rake of one to eighteen, an auditorium slope now considered insufficient for a house of this size. A flat auditorium ceiling spans the house twenty-five feet above the floor. A mildly Art Deco plaster surround frames a proscenium opening fourteen and a half feet high and twenty-nine feet wide over which is a frescoed replica of the town crest. The stage, slightly more than four feet above the auditorium floor, measures twenty feet from front to back wall and forty-one feet wide. The lack of a fly loft and scene dock space restricts productions to fixed sets.

Although primitive by today's standards, the backstage accommodations at the Opera House were likely superior to most similar theatres of the time in rural Ontario; for not only were there dressing-rooms and rooms for handling costumes and properties, but the early players at

Peterborough, Architect John Belcher's front elevation (1872) of Peterborough Town Hall containing Thomas Bradburn's Opera House

Meaford were endowed as well with a water closet and basin for their exclusive use.

Today the Meaford Town Hall and Opera House building is still ound, though much in need of repair and restoration if it is to survive efully into the next century.

ERBOROUGH

first substantial performance hall of record in Peterborough, known Hill's Music Hall, occupied the second floor of the old Market uilding on Water Street, constructed ca 1850. The lessee of the hall, locally known as Penny Hill, was evidently a man of some parts and considerable energy, since he combined managing the Music Hall with his other occupations, which included bill posting and organ building. A disastrous fire at the Market Building in 1861, caused very possibly by an overheated wood stove or by an ill-aimed cigar butt, destroyed Hill's Music Hall, leaving Peterborough without a theatre for more than a decade.

In 1872 a local philanthropist, Thomas Bradburn, offered to erect a new town hall in Peterborough, provided that he be named the licensee of an opera house to occupy the topmost story of the new building. In due course Bradburn retained John A. Belcher, a Peterborough architect, who prepared drawings for the building which were subsequently approved by Town Council. The building was to be erected on the east side of George Street between Charlotte and Simcoe streets, and, although it is not clear when construction began, it seems the new building was ready for use in the year 1875, giving it a life of one century before it was demolished by the City of Peterborough in 1975. Once more it was demonstrated that in Canada, as in the United States, decision makers so often fail to comprehend that many venerable buildings are vital symbols of our past, and, when they are demolished so that more money can be made on the lands they stand on, we become poorer and our children's children become poorer.

The 1875 Town Hall and Opera House building was indeed venerable by all accounts at the time of its demise. In its lifetime, however, it was an imposing three-storey brick masonry structure with a frontage on George Street of 107 feet and a depth of eighty-one feet extending back to a market square. At grade level there were four offices fronting on George Street, grouped in pairs with an arcade between on the building's centre line, providing through access to the market beyond. A grand staircase led up to town offices on the second floor and stairs at each end of the building ascended to a two-storey flat floored opera hall on the topmost floor. Paired with the performance hall was a second room of comparable size, likely used as a banquet hall. In its original state the building was adorned by a clock tower, executed in the late French Renaissance style. However it seems the clock was later taken away to equip the new and more ostentatious clock tower of an adjoining market building erected in 1889.

Little out of the ordinary deserves mention about the stage history of Thomas Bradburn's theatre until the advent of vaudeville, when it presented such memorable figures as Jimmy Wallbrook, billed as the World Champion Wooden Shoe Dancer, and Ned Hanlan, who in 1880 gave a demonstration on stage of his championship sculling prowess. In 1900 a youthful Winston Churchill lectured before a full house c the subject of South Africa and the Boer War.

Thomas Bradburn's handsome building almost certainly has one lasting distinction among all others of its genre in Ontario; for it left behind a tangible reminder of itself in the form of six original linen drawings prepared for its construction in 1872. These splendid drawings now in the collection of the Peterborough Centennial Museum make up by far the oldest complete set of such documents so far discovered in Ontario, and very possibly in the whole of Canada.

The remarkable Thomas Bradburn's son Rupert gave Peterborough another theatre in 1906. Predictably called the Grand Opera House, Rupert Bradburn's substantial theatre had three audience levels, and seating, it was said, for 1,500. With the decline of vaudeville and the growth of commercial cinema, the Grand went the way of so many of its namesakes and was demolished in the 1930s.

Theatres of Note outside the Cities

BROCKVILLE

A new town hall at Brockville on the corner of St Paul and Main streets opened on 20 December 1858. The Brockville *Recorder* of 23 December covered the event and supplied a cursory description of the project.

The building was constructed of brick and measured seventy feet by seventy-five feet in plan and fifty-three and a half feet in height. Rising from a cut-limestone base, it was described at the time as having been built in the Roman Italian style. That was probably true, since the door and window heads were arched in semi-circular fashion and topped with marble labels. Brick pilasters extended the full height of the building between windows. The building parapet incorporated a medallion cornice of brick, below which a frieze of uncertain design circumscribed the building.

Ground-floor space was largely occupied by a fire engine house, the remaining area being taken up by entrance lobbies, stairs and unspecified offices. A large hall measuring forty-two by sixty-eight feet took up the second level. The hall was said to have had a capacity of 450 persons with a gallery above seating 200. The *Recorder* made no mention of a stage, but, if there was one, we may assume it was scarcely more than a platform at the end of the hall.

Early in the twentieth century a decision was taken to reconstruct the old 1858 theatre and to add a stagehouse. According to the Brockville *Evening Recorder* of 16 September 1911, the New Theatre, as it was popularly called, reopened on 18 September 1911 with a stage

St Marys, Opera House interior, 1884

measuring forty by sixty-five feet and a flying height to the grid of sixty-five feet. The new auditorium had a total seating capacity of 1,400.

On 6 November 1937 fire destroyed the auditorium, although an asbestos curtain saved the stagehouse from serious damage. After a 1939 reconstruction, the premises reopened as a movie house. Renovations in 1960 and after have since given Brockville a fine, well-appointed theatre, now known as the Brockville Civic Auditorium.

ST MARYS

Constructed in 1879 for the then princely sum of $22,000 by Lodge 36 of the local Oddfellows, St Marys Opera House, as it has since been called, still stands on Water Street, a remarkable and imposing work in the Gothic Revival tradition by architects Weeks and Smyth of London.

Originally the building housed three shops at street level, an auditorium and stage on two levels above, with an Oddfellows meeting-hall and other rooms on the topmost floor. Materials of

St Marys, Opera House exterior, 1884

construction included local limestone laid in random ashlar fashion with dressings of Ohio sandstone. The latter apparently darkened with the passing years, lending a liveliness to the main façade not noticeable in early photographs, as though the building was quietly endeavouring to belie its years. At the front, tall lancet windows rising through two storeys express the interior opera house volume, and a central masonry gable with a rose window, now gone, once closed the west end of the Oddfellows high-ceilinged meeting hall. Stone corner turrets, castellated roof parapets, and other romantic devices, created an architectural ensemble of great power and dignity. Sad to say, however, nothing remains of the original interiors. The building was sold by the Oddfellows and converted into a flour mill in 1920 by St Marys Milling Co., and at that time the existing auditorium and stage were demolished to make way for new reinforced concrete interior construction. Therefore, what we can discover about the interior of the Opera House at St Marys comes to us from remembrance of the hall before the 1920s by old-timers and a few photographs collected by local historians.[42]

The auditorium, for an audience of 700 to 800, had a flat floor on orchestra level with a balcony above on three sides of the house supported on six posts, four of which were likely of wrought-iron as they extended up to carry the loads of the Oddfellows' meeting hall on the floor above. Seating on the main floor appeared to consist of loose opera chairs ganged together. Balcony seating consisted of six tiers of wood benches with tongue and groove wood backs constructed in yellow pine. Newel posts, lathe turned in cherrywood, marked the end of each seating row and gave a handhold to the patron negotiating the no doubt steep aisle steps of the balcony. A panelled and dentilled balcony front that curved gracefully to meet the proscenium on each side of the hall was fashioned from domestic cherry. From an early photograph it appears that a gas chandelier hanging centrally in the hall provided the principal house lighting. However, electric lighting was later installed, as evidenced by a 1914 photograph showing the hall decked out for the Bankers' Ball of that year.

Legend has it that the Opera House stage was vast, large enough it was boasted, for five horse-drawn chariots to dash across it abreast in a performance of *Ben Hur*. Hyperbole aside, the stage was no doubt commodious for its day, with a proscenium opening appropriate for a drop curtain at least forty feet wide and thirty feet high.[43] As to Opera House sanitary conveniences, little has come to light except from the recollections of the late L.W. (Curly) Wilson of St Marys, who remembered the absence of running water. What conveniences there were evidently existed only for the ladies.

St Marys, conversion of Opera House into apartments and ground floor shops, 1986–8

Also in St Marys is the imposing Town Hall in local stone, constructed in 1892 to the design of architect George W. Gouinlock. Located on Queen Street East, the building is a charming composition of towers, turrets, and stepped gables, topped by a belfry daintily perched askew on the roof of a massive corner tower that anchors the building to its corner site. Inside is a small but attractive hall seating 225 on a flat-floored orchestra level and a stepped balcony with bench seating.

ST THOMAS

At St Thomas the old Town Hall on Stanley Street was the scene of local theatricals before 1873, when the Grand Opera House was built on Talbot Street with George Claris its principal owner and manager. 'Claris House,' as it was popularly called, had a single-floor auditorium with a circular aisle separating the orchestra and section seats.

After a fire at Claris House in 1885 or thereabouts, the building was rebuilt and redecorated. Around that time George Claris withdrew from the scene, selling the building to Ambrose J. Small, who predictably changed the name of the establishment to the Grand Opera House. It

Seaforth, Cardno Hall 1985

is not clear if Small had a hand in reconstructing the auditorium, but it is likely he did in the course of negotiating his purchase of the place. In any case, two balconies and four private boxes were introduced 'with the front section of the auditorium becoming the orchestra seating.'[44] From an interior photograph of the Grand's auditorium from the Ian D. Cameron Collection we can see that the house was a respectable forty feet or so high at the front and that the proscenium was framed somewhat severely by a moulded plaster surround.

This interesting theatre was no doubt among the vanishing species of its kind, doomed to extinction by motion pictures early in the twentieth century.

SEAFORTH

On the main street of Seaforth stands Cardno Hall, opened on 15 December 1877 by owner John Alexander Cardno, who, it is said, could trace his ancestry to a castaway from the Spanish Armada who came ashore in the Hebrides. Old Cardno had apparently inherited an adventurous spirit from his Spanish ancestor, since he was known in Seaforth as a jack of all trades and is credited with both the design and

Seaforth, Cardno Hall interior showing stage with drop

the construction of Cardno Hall, on the good authority of his great-grandson, Kenneth Cardno, now owner of the property.

This fine Victorian building of the Cardnos, topped by an ornate clock tower, houses a performance hall and stage on the second floor, together with a banquet hall. Below at street level are retail shops. With a seating capacity of 600, the flat-floored auditorium measures about forty by sixty-five feet. Two columns carrying part of the clock tower structure intrude somewhat on the floor space at the west side of the auditorium. At the north end of the hall there is a narrow mezzanine reached by a precipitous stair from the public lobby and accommodating two rows of seats at most.

An elegant elliptical proscenium arch dominates the south wall of the hall, and under it protrudes a bow-fronted stage apron, not unlike the fantail of a schooner. The stage itself is forty feet wide and twenty feet deep, and there are two token performers' dressing rooms off it. A rolled house curtain in good working condition still exists. When lowered it depicts a lone fisherman slumped in a punt, evidently trying his luck in the moat of a particularly dolorous-looking castle. On each side of this scene are advertisements placed there by local merchants of bygone days.

Lindsay, Academy Theatre

Surprisingly, the original benches and gunstock chairs from the auditorium are still on the premises, giving the impression that Cardno Hall could spring to life again on a few hours' notice.

LINDSAY

In the 1860s a two-storey wing was added to the Town Hall at Lindsay by Thomas E. Bradburn, who leased it back to the town council. The second floor of Bradburn's wing housed a makeshift opera house that served as the only performance hall in town for the next twenty-five years.

In the spring of 1892 two citizens of the town, R.J. Matchett, agent of the Grand Trunk Railroad, and Fred Knowlton, town clerk, had plans and estimates prepared for a new theatre at Lindsay to be called 'The Academy of Music.' With the backing of a few spirited citizens known as 'the Push and Pluck,' a joint stock company was formed, and by July 1892 work had started at the southeast corner at Lindsay

Lindsay, Academy Theatre interior

Street and Kent Street East to the designs of the architect, W. Blackwell of Peterborough.

The Lindsay *Canadian Post* of 30 December 1892 gives an ample and effusive description of the new theatre; the following rhetoric is but a sample: 'Advancing into the auditorium the full beauty of the rich and chaste interior holds the visitor speechless for a time, its beautiful proportions, lofty ceiling and harmonized wealth of colouring creating a feeling in the soul averse to noisy admiration.' Be that as it may, the house capacity was given as 900, arranged on two levels, with 166 seats in the orchestra stalls and 218 in the parquette 'all arranged in crescent form.' A gallery enveloping the house in horseshoe fashion held 500 seats, and a private box looked out on the stage from each side of the proscenium. The auditorium fresco work and general detailing were said to have been 'executed in the richest style of French Empire art' and had been entrusted to R. Elliott & Son of Toronto.

The stage measured thirty-eight by fifty-four feet, and proscenium height was some twenty-eight feet. A fly gallery hung a full twenty-two feet above the stage with a rigging gallery up forty-eight feet. The original house had five drop curtains and twelve sets of scenery working in four grooves. The *Canadian Post*'s reviewer again waxed eloquent in describing the main drop as 'a beautiful specimen of artistic skill. It represents a portion of a street in a Moorish town situated upon the water's edge. The quaint old archways and the oddly tilted street half in shadow are delineated with startling accuracy, while in the distance is seen the lake upon which gondolas are lazily plying, freighted with youths and maidens.' That and other scene painting was executed by Albert Traito, reportedly from Chatham.

Four performers' dressing-rooms had been placed below stage. There were three furnaces in the building, and ventilation, which was likely abominable, was said to have been 'provided for upon the most approved scientific principles.' There were 160 incandescent lights in the original building, each of sixteen candle power and arranged in nine circuits.

It was in this theatre that Marie Dressler made her first stage appearance at the age of five in an amateur play, *Living Picture*, organized by her mother. Marie posed naked as Cupid with bow and arrow but tumbled off her pedestal and got the first belly-laugh of her long career in comedy. Apart from a few such anecdotes, almost nothing of significance remains to tell us of the Academy's early history, since apparently all the old records were thrown out a few years ago in a spate of housecleaning. But the Academy thrives today, to a large degree because it began as one of the more advanced theatre buildings in Ontario outside the larger centres.

ORILLIA

The Opera House at Orillia is possibly the finest surviving late nineteenth-century building of its kind in Ontario. Of all references to its style, the eminent historians Adamson and McRae[45] perhaps come closest by observing that the original building was 'dressed as a French Renaissance chateau.' Completed in 1895 at a cost of $26,500, the new Orillia Town Hall and Market Building, as it was first called, still stands at the corner of Mississaga and West streets on a two-acre site, part of which had been donated to the village in 1872 by Professor Goldwin Smith of Toronto. Credit for this splendid building rests not with Smith, however, but with the mayor and deputy reeve of the time, who fathered the project, and with the accomplished and able firm of Gordon & Helliwell, Architects, of Toronto, who won the commission to design the hall over eleven other competitors.[46]

Contractors for the work were Hammond & Robinson, who were given less than ten months to complete the job; not surprisingly they

Orillia, Opera House, 1906

failed to do so and were dismissed by Council. J.H. Tool & Sons, a firm of carpenter builders, was then appointed to complete the project, a task mainly involving rough and fine carpentry. Ironically, however, the superb masonry work of Hammond & Robinson has endured, while much of the wood construction of Tool & Sons was later reduced to ashes.

In its original form, before a fire in 1915 gutted the interior, the building is shown in a 1906 photograph[47] as seen looking northwest from the street corner. Faced in red pressed brick with Longford stone dressings, the main block of the building measured 100 feet long by fifty-nine feet wide. Projecting from the east front were two round staircase towers flanking the entrance, both handsomely topped with bellcast and slated roofs. A one-storey brick porch with three arched openings marked the West Street entrance. A brick and stone dormer perched jauntily over the main roof cornice, waiting, one must presume, for a clock that was never installed. On the south façade a well-proportioned brick tower, about fourteen feet square at the base, soared above the main roof, crowned by an eight-sided lantern.

The Orillia *Times* Christmas edition of 1895 gives a general account of the building's interior:

The front portion of the ground floor is allotted to the Council Chambers and Clerks offices and the rear portion to the market and stall uses. The upper flat is devoted to a large auditorium with stage, etc. to be known as the Orillia Opera House.

... There were four scenes; a forest scene, a parlor scene, a street scene, and a garden scene. These with the drop curtain, are all made on flat frames and do not roll up but ascend up into the space between the ceiling and roof by balance weights and pulleys. It is a very easy method of handling scenery and is a great preservative of its durability. Each scene has two 'wings' on each side and these also are flat frames mounted on rubber rollers and slide upward in grooves in a manner that is perfectly noiseless.

The auditorium had a seating capacity of 905, with 602 chairs at orchestra level and 303 in a gallery on three sides of the house. It had a semi-elliptical ceiling coved at the side walls. House lighting consisted of two twenty-amp electroliers suspended from the ceiling, together with bracket lights fixed to the walls and the gallery front. The stage measured thirty-two by twenty-five feet, and there were four dressing-rooms, two at each side of the stage.

The drop curtain by J.D. Fortier, 'our local decorator,' also won praise from the *Times*: 'It represents the voyage of "Lalla Rookh" and shows in the foreground the galley with its twenty oars projecting from the side and lateen sails on the quaint deck, while in the background is the picturesque city of Cashmere with its mosques and turrets, whither the heroine is going to her nuptials.'

The entire building almost went to oblivion in a disastrous fire on 15 July 1915, when the interiors were virtually destroyed. However, Town Council promptly asked for and received ratepayers' approval of a $35,000 debenture issue at 6 per cent which, with $18,000 collected from insurance, proved sufficient to restore the building more or less to its present form. Architects for the restoration were Burke, Horwood and White of Toronto, whose meticulous drawings of 1916 are still on file at the City of Orillia offices.

At a grand reopening of the Orillia Opera House on Thursday, 1 March 1917, the main attraction was the English pantomime, *Aladdin and His Wonderful Lamp*.

GALT (NOW CAMBRIDGE)

Galt's fine old 1857 Town Hall still stands today on Dickson Street. For two generations its second-floor ballroom had provided the town's only theatre space until Scott's Opera House on Queen's Square opened its doors on 5 January 1899, taking its name from John Scott, a local entrepreneur who assumed ownership of the Opera House when previous investors had failed to complete its construction. This 935-seat theatre was a notable and ambitious work in its time.

As the building was later demolished, what we know of it comes from a few photographs and a piece appearing in the Galt *Reporter* of 6 January 1899 which began by telling its readers that 'The opening of Scott's Opera House on Friday evening will be one of those experiences that individuals and communities meet with which evolve from uncouthness into refinement or mount upward with the charioteers of progress into fairer and more congenial realms of life.' We learn from the *Reporter* that Fred Mellish was the project architect and that the building cost about $28,000 to complete. A three-storey red-brick structure, rectangular in plan, the building was roofed in cottage style with boldly projecting cornices. Six retail stores occupied the ground floor and fourteen upper windows marched across the front in pairs, giving the building a spritely air in contrast to the sagging Gothic lines of Knox Church next door.

Entering a vestibule off North Square Street, patrons reached the auditorium at Scott's by ascending a winding stair to an upper landing giving directly to orchestra seating and from which another stair led to the balcony level above. There were '264 orchestra chairs, 309 in the parquette, 120 reserved seats in the two front rows of the balcony and 222 general admission seats behind these.' Four private boxes likely seated twenty or more for a total seated audience of 935. The *Reporter* informs us further that 'around the balcony entwine wreaths of olive leaves made of what is called "ornamental staff" and manufactured by Hymes of Toronto. The parts mentioned are covered with the "staff" and are finished in old gold and ivory, making an elegant effect ... The dome is architect Mellish's own conception and is extremely well designed. It acts as a ventilator as well as an ornament and has 36 incandescent lights in it, a veritable sun.'

The twenty-eight- by fifty-foot stage was apparently covered in reversible carpet, providing a green side for outdoor scenes and a red side for indoor ones. Scenes were shifted by windlasses worked from bridges above the stage, and the stage itself was trapped. There was an orchestra pit in front of the stage and below the projecting apron.

On 8 April 1910 a fire at the Opera House, attributed to faulty wiring, seriously damaged the interior. After its repair the theatre continued in use until 1928, when the building was demolished. Queen's Square was extended out to George Street and Knox Church was left by itself once more.

STRATFORD

Performance Halls
In 1857 the village of Stratford, then a community of 2,000 souls, put up a substantial town hall and market building at the convergence of Downie and Wellington streets where the present City Hall now stands. Constructed by Oliver and Sewell Contractors to the design of architect Peter Ferguson of Toronto,[48] this large, two-storey, buff-brick building was a formidable project for a small community. Bristling with chimneys and topped by a domed belfry, the new hall was among the earlier multi-purpose buildings of its kind in Ontario, containing town offices, a fire hall, a public library, a magistrate's office, and council chambers, together with a butcher shop and market stalls on the main level and an opera house space on the floor above, ample enough, it was said, to seat 500 – a quarter of the town's population. More is perhaps known of theatrical productions, music recitals, and other events that graced the Town Hall's busy stage than is evidently known about the building itself. Yet for two generations it stood at the centre of town, a symbol of the stubborn pride and faith in the future

Stratford, Theatre Albert, 1905 (now Avon Theatre)

possessed by the townspeople of Stratford, virtues sorely tested when on Wednesday, 24 November 1897, this fine building burned to the ground.

Construction of a new city hall was promptly put in hand in the following year, literally on the ashes of its predecessor, and as it transpired, to the great credit of its architects, George W. King and J.W. Siddall and of Young and Cawsey, contractors for the work.[49] Officially opened on 29 January 1900, when Stratford had a population of somewhat over 10,000, the new City Hall building contained a concert hall with a stage of modest dimensions and with seating on two levels intended for an audience of 500. Today, however, legal seating capacity in the house is 335. This splendid municipal building, renovated in 1974, has few if any rivals in the entire province for what it is, a boldly ordered work of architecture in the romantic spirit of the late Victorian period, beautifully executed, as though it was always intended as the centre-piece of a famous festival city, which happily it now is.

Theatre Albert

Albert Brandenberger,[50] a Stratford citizen and reputedly a theatre man of some considerable experience, had long wanted to establish a proper theatre in his home town, an ambition ignited, as it were, by the fire in 1897 that destroyed the old Town Hall and with it the only performance hall in Stratford worthy of the name. In due course Brandenberger acquired a building site at the corner of Downie and St George streets, purchased from Mary Patterson, grandmother of Tom Patterson, who a half-century later would be founder of the Stratford Festival.

The architect of Theatre Albert may have been Harry J. Powell of Stratford, according to the *Beacon Herald* of Friday, 7 July 1967. In any event, construction of the building began in 1900. Brandenberger named the building, designed to seat 1,250, Theatre Albert after himself and, some said, also after Queen Victoria's consort. The new theatre, although not completed, opened on 1 January 1901 with *The Female Drummer*, the first stage show in the city's first legitimate theatre.

By 1910 Brandenberger had enlarged and improved the building, giving most of his attention to the interiors as well as adding on a stagehouse of wall-bearing brick, the timber-framed ceiling of which hung forty-six feet above the stage. Stage dimensions were a respectable thirty-two feet back wall to proscenium line, by fifty-four feet wall-to-wall of the wings. The proscenium arch measured thirty-three feet wide and twenty-one feet high. There was an orchestra pit of modest size, part of it taken up by a storm water culvert that conducted Romeo Creek diagonally under the building, as it does today.

Audience seating for about 1,100 was arranged in aisle-access fashion on two levels, much as it is now except for the introduction of cross-aisles in the late 1960s. From a centre point five feet upstage of the proscenium line, the furthermost seats in this house were and are about ninety feet away, acceptable for lyric-stage productions but not so cozy for drama.

The auditorium decor, as it emerged from the 1910 refurbishings, was vaguely akin to Edwardian style, with bas relief touches reminiscent of the brothers Adam. The exterior façade of the building's commercial block fronting on Downie Street, mercifully replaced by a modern edifice in 1967, was of little architectural merit. In 1910 Brandenberger declared his theatre 'The House of Polite Vaudeville and Motion Pictures' and changed its name to the Griffin Theatre. He sold his interest in the place in 1924, when it was renamed the Majestic Theatre. Under yet another ownership in the 1940s the theatre was given the name it now has – the Avon Theatre. In 1956, some thirty years after Albert Brandenberger had gone to his rest, his building once more became the venue for legitimate theatre, opening in the summer of that year with Le Théâtre du Nouveau Monde in *Three Farces by Molière*[51] directed by the late Jean Gascon. With the founding of the Stratford Festival the renaissance of Theatre Albert had begun.

NIAGARA-ON-THE-LAKE

A Glimpse of Early History
In 1792 Newark was little more than a fortified site at the outfall of the Niagara River. As a result of what was soon acknowledged to be a bad decision, Newark, vulnerable location or not, became the first capital of Upper Canada. After an interval of four years, York supplanted Newark as the provincial capital, Lieutenant-Governor John Graves Simcoe went home to England, and Newark went on to an uncertain future. A statute passed in 1798 changed the town's name from Newark to Niagara and confirmed that it would continue as the county seat. The next great test of the town's precarious early life occurred during the war of 1812–14, when it was put to the torch by the Americans in 1813. In the reconstruction that followed, a new court house was erected in 1817, using a grant-in-aid of £2,000. The new building, since demolished, had been built at the western extremity of town, presumably to be out of range of Yankee guns at Fort Niagara on the far side of the river. After the completion of the first Welland Canal in 1829, the struggle for political primacy intensified between Niagara and the growing communities of Welland and St Catharines. After Niagara and St Catharines became incorporated towns in 1845, both put in hand the construction of impressive municipal buildings, each vying with the other to be invested as the seat of government for the united counties of Lincoln, Welland, and Haldimand.

As it transpired, St Catharines boomed while Niagara declined in commercial importance. Inevitably, in 1862 the courts were moved to St Catharines into the commodious Town Hall completed there in 1848 by the ubiquitous Kivas Tully of Toronto. Thus, old Niagara lost that long and bitter contest, but over the century to follow it was renamed Niagara-on-the-Lake and gained fame and a distinction that would prove to be unique.

Court House
The Niagara *Chronicle* of 10 July 1846 carried a notice declaring that

Niagara-on-the-Lake, amateur performance in the 1890s

the Board of Police (Town Council) had advertised for proposals from architects for the design of a new town hall and market house later to be known as the Niagara Court House. It was noted as well that the board had received three submissions, those of architects Henry Lane, William Thomas, and Kivas Tully, all of Toronto. Thomas, who won the commission, had practised in Britain before emigrating to Canada in 1842. Well known in Toronto circles, his work there eventually included buildings such as St Lawrence Hall and the Don Jail, both still in use today.

An imposing Classical Revival[52] building, solidly constructed in Queenston limestone, William Thomas's Court House at Niagara still stands on its Queen Street site in the centre of town. Recently restored, this venerable building, measuring about fifty-seven feet by 112 feet, now accommodates a library and rental offices on the lower two floors; a large hall and a banquet room are on the level above, the former occupying what was originally the courtroom for the three united counties. In the original the courtroom, or North Hall as it is now known, was an elegant high-ceilinged space, richly panelled and crowned by a coffered dome over which a glazed lantern or cupola soared above the ridge line of the building. The hall, ignominiously deprived of both dome and lantern after it no longer served as a court-room, was later to lose its furnishings as well and most if not all its fine wood panelling. However, the great North Hall survived those indignities, providing in time a splendid room in which the Shaw Festival presented its first season of plays in 1963, a full century after the courts had moved away to St Catharines.

One of the three theatres now used by the festival, the recently restored Court House is the setting for each year's open-stage productions, through the artful adaptation of the old former courtroom and adjoining spaces. Seating for as many as 364 was provided on demountable risers placed on three sides of a peninsula stage, not unlike the arrangement of the Third Stage theatre at Stratford. The coffered ceiling dome, a replica of the original one, and the courtroom windows were fitted with light-proof plugs. Floor-to-ceiling draperies were hung to reduce echo, absorb light, and visually neutralize the space. A stage-lighting bridge was installed. Miraculously a theatre was created where there was none before.

In the Shaw Festival's early years we have an admirable example of the way a fine old building can be brought back to life and can continue to be useful, while giving back to us a sense of dignity and benevolent old age that somehow enhances the artistic works presented under its roof.

Vaudeville Houses

The most casual glance at vaudeville theatre architecture makes one wonder what forces in American society of the 1890s gave rise to these extraordinary buildings. The most potent of those forces can perhaps be traced to the commercial ambitions of a few syndicates in the United States and Canada that brought mass-produced entertainment to the twentieth-century urban market, packaging it with the kind of theatre buildings they thought would lure a mass audience through the turnstiles. The result was a commercially inspired make-believe theatre architecture, aimed at creating an atmosphere into which one could pleasurably escape from the grinding realities of everyday life. In the years to come deluxe movie houses and motion picture palaces were to move those make-believe creations into new realms of extravagantly romantic fantasy.

Shea's Hippodrome was the last theatre constructed in a chain of vaudeville houses operated by the Shea Amusement Company of

Toronto, Winter Garden and auditorium as it appeared on opening night, 1914

Toronto between 1899 and 1914. The work of Leon J. Lempert & Son, Architects, this 112- by 164-foot building stood at Albert and Bay streets in Toronto until it was demolished in 1956 to make way for the new Civic Square. The Hippodrome's cavernous auditorium seated about 2,700 on two levels, including a five-aisle, twenty-eight-row orchestra flat, an enormous balcony, and twelve boxes. The balcony held nine rows of loge seats, and seventeen rows above extended to the back of the house. Called a 'Picture Cabinet' on the original drawings, a movie projection booth hung one flight above the topmost balcony seating.

A twenty-six- by forty-six-foot proscenium opened to an ample stage measuring thirty-three feet from foot to back wall, with a clear width of eighty-six feet at stage level. Above the stage were two fly galleries, each thirty feet wide, connected by a paint bridge and cross-over gallery along the back wall of the stagehouse. The gridiron deck hung fifty-six feet above the fully trapped stage. A spectacular feature of the Hippodrome was the great Wurlitzer organ that rose majestically into the house on its own lift, organist and all, before each show. The

Toronto, Elgin Theatre auditorium, 1915

theatre opened in 1914 with four performers' dressing-rooms and a chorus room below stage and six dressing-rooms stacked in pairs off stage right. A somewhat cramped (ten feet by ten feet) musicians' room located off the trap cellar gave directly to the orchestra pit from that level. The pit had a bowed front and extended ten feet nine inches into the house from the proscenium wall, providing ample space for a pit orchestra. However, the big bands that came to Shea's in the 1930s performed on stage so as to be seen as well as heard.

Although the Shea's Hippodrome interior decor did not, by some accounts, match that of its sister house, the Victoria, constructed in 1910, it was none the less a large and well-equipped theatre which attracted a host of devoted patrons over its active life time. It had the size and adaptability to accommodate vaudeville, orchestra concerts, motion pictures, and lyric theatre. Contemporary with the Royal Alexandra, perhaps it did for Toronto what the Alex did not do; it provided a theatre atmosphere in which even first-timers felt at ease. Thus its very plainness could have been a virtue.

Loew's Yonge Street and Winter Garden, a remarkable two-theatre complex completed in 1914, survives almost intact on the east side of Yonge Street near Queen Street in Toronto. Built by Marcus Loew to the design of his architect, Thomas W. Lamb, associated with Stanley

Toronto, the Elgin and Winter Garden complex: lobby, grand staircase, ticket booth

Makepeace, the lower theatre originally had 1,926 seats, later reduced to 1,624 when more comfortable seating was substituted throughout the house. The Winter Garden had seating for 1,422, although a capacity of 900 to 1,000 may be more reasonable by today's standards.

Lamb executed Loew's Yonge Street in a somewhat heavy-handed version of the brothers Adam style, but in the Winter Garden his near abandonment of classicisms hinted broadly at the coming 'atmospheric' mode of interior decoration which later came to full flower in John Eberson's movie palaces of the 1920s. Because it departed from contemporary fashion in its interior decoration and for other reasons, the Winter Garden is the more interesting of Loew's two theatres on lower Yonge Street.

Patrons entered the complex from Yonge Street and walked 150 feet through a tapestried lobby to the cage-style elevators that would convey them seven floors up to the Winter Garden. In lieu of the lifts, the young and the fit might have climbed seven flights of the grand staircase 'whose scagliola banister was swarming with chubby putti interspersed with hefty rinceaux and rosettes' as Hilary Russell so

Toronto, restoration work (1985) of the Elgin and Winter Garden complex

eloquently describes it in *All That Glitters*.[53] A small elevator foyer gave directly to the Winter Garden auditorium, which was and still is astonishingly decorated with real leaves and branches treated with fireproofing and festooned from the main ceiling, below the balcony, and under the arches on each side of the house. Additional inert vegetation clung to trellises bordering the upper boxes. Complementing Lamb's roof garden atmosphere were a hundred or more electrified frosted glass lanterns suspended in the leafy ceilings. Green carpeting on the auditorium floor added yet another sylvan touch. On the ceiling in front of the proscenium was a clumsy painting of a wood trellis with distant temple and mountain, all under a sky of azure blue, unnecessarily punctuated by an electric moon.

Though Lamb had likely gone far enough, if not too far, he none the less gave his attention as well to the exposed auditorium columns which were covered in cement plaster, then trowelled and painted to simulate rough tree trunks. Column points flanking the proscenium, the exit doors, and the sidewall arches were given similar treatment, creating tree trunk pilasters, all of which extended upward with plaster branches that grew, diorama-like, into surfaces painted to resemble branches and leaves.

Aside from mere decoration however, the Winter Garden as it is today exhibits many of the elements of a first-class legitimate theatre, with its well-proportioned auditorium and ample stage, now refurbished after sleeping in the dark for more than half a century.

Conclusion

Although a number of old Ontario theatres will almost certainly survive usefully into the twenty-first century, many more are either gone forever or will fall into disuse by the next millennium, abandoned by a television culture, just as so many legitimate houses went dark with the coming of motion pictures. Similarly, the attrition on all but a few old buildings of every kind came about through massive urban change, beginning earlier in this century and continuing today. As the cost of land grew out of proportion to the value of structures on it, older buildings in urban centres were progressively torn down and replaced with new ones. This process of redevelopment explains in part why so few older, non-residential buildings survive today in our larger cities and why relatively more such structures can be seen in smaller centres where the pressures of change are less compelling.

The Grand Theatre in London, Kingston's Grand Theatre, the Academy Theatre in Lindsay, the Opera Houses at Gravenhurst, Meaford, and Orillia, the Avon Theatre in Stratford, the Royal Alexandra, Elgin, Winter Garden, and Pantages theatres in Toronto: all are examples of enduring turn-of-the-century theatres in Ontario, still in active service and still attracting well-deserved public patronage.

As a last word, borrowing from vernacular of the day, one might hope for the unfolding of a best-case scenario, where theatre centres will eventually take root in Ontario and the teaching of theatre arts will flourish, all from the ageless desire to see the human condition revealed to us and revealed to us yet again.[54]

NOTES

1 As a comprehensive treatment of style evolution and related matters is beyond the scope of this chapter, those seeking a more detailed discussion of the

subject may wish to read Robert Hunter, 'Theatre Architecture in Canada: A Study of Pre-1920 Canadian Theatres' (Ottawa: Historic Sites and Monuments Board of Canada 1985).

2 Harriet Priddis, 'Reminiscences of Mrs. Gilbert Porte,' *London and Middlesex Historical Society, Transactions 1911–1912*, 68–9

3 Frances Ruth Hines, 'Concert Life in London, Ontario, 1870–1880,' M MUS thesis, University of Western Ontario 1977, appendix 1

4 Letter received from Katharine Greenfield, Special Collections, Hamilton Public Library, 18 March 1981

5 John W. Spurr, 'Theatre in Kingston, 1816–1870,' *Historic Kingston* 22 (March 1974), 37–55

6 Margaret S. Angus, 'City Hall and the Community,' *Kingston City Hall* (Corporation of the City of Kingston 1974)

7 John Ross Robertson, 'The Theatres of the Town: Theatrical Reminiscences from 1793 to 1893,' *Robertson's Landmarks of Toronto: A Collection of Historical Sketches*, First Series (Toronto: Robertson 1894)

8 Watercolour by Frederick V. Poole, ca 1812, Metropolitan Toronto Library Board (MTLB). Acc: JRB849, REPRO: T11013

9 Water colour by John W. Cotton, ca 1912, MTLB, Acc: JRR857, REPRO: T10018 (slide MTL1177)

10 MTLB REPRO: T12935 and T12936; Granger's two theatre sketches are the earliest such sketches so far discovered.

11 Spurr, 'Theatre in Kingston.' See Leslie O'Dell's chapter for additional information on Nickinson.

12 MTLB, Royal Lyceum fiche, undated newspaper article titled 'Crude Accommodation'

13 James Russell Aikens, 'The Rival Operas: Toronto Theatre 1874–84,' PH D dissertation, University of Toronto 1975, 1, 44

14 C. Pelham Mulvany, *Toronto: Past and Present; A Handbook of the City* (1884; reprint: Toronto: Reprint Press 1970), 119

15 *Canadian Illustrated News*, 30 January 1875, 76; 27 February 1875, 136; 12 June 1875, 380

16 *Toronto Theatres: Season 1904–1905* (Toronto: Murdoch Advertising and Publishing Company), 59. From a photocopy of the original which is in the New York Public Library. MTLB, Theatre Desk

17 *Toronto Theatres: Season 1904–1905*, 31

18 City of Toronto Archives

19 Joan Parkhill Baillie, *Look at the Record* (Oakville: Mosaic Press 1985), 150–6

20 Nancy Jane Haynes, 'A History of the Royal Alexandra Theatre, 1914–1918,' PH D dissertation, University of Colorado 1973 (Ann Arbor, Mich.: University Microfilms 1973), 13

21 Ibid.

22 Clarence H. Blackhall, 'The American Theatre ... I,' *The Brickbuilder* 16 (December 1907), 317

23 Mora Diane O'Neill, 'A Partial History of the Royal Alexandra Theatre, Toronto, Ontario 1907–1939,' PH D dissertation, Louisiana State University 1976, vol. I, 57

24 For an excellent account of other early London theatres see F. Beatrice Taylor, 'British Garrison Officers Staged Hamlet in Barn,' London *Free Press*, 15 June 1955, 32–5.

25 London *Advertiser*, 5 May 1880, 1, 2, 4

26 University of Western Ontario, Weldon Library, Regional Collection

27 M.D. O'Neill, 'Partial history,' 65

28 Orlo Miller, 'Old Opera Houses of Western Ontario,' OPERA CANADA (May 1964), 8

29 Erdmute Waldhauer, *Grand Theatre, 1879–1979* (Kingston: Grand Theatre 1979), 14–15

30 Waldhauer, *Grand Theatre*, 19

31 Facsimile reproduction by courtesy of Hamilton Public Library

32 National Archives, photograph C2147

33 Joseph L. Wooden, *Exeter* (Exeter: *Exeter Times Advocate*, 1973), 137

34 Aylmer and District Museum Collection, 14 East Street, Aylmer, Ontario

35 From a photograph supplied by Mrs Clair Barons of Aylmer, Ontario

36 B. Napier Simpson, Jr, Restoration Architect, Project Report, *Paisley Town Hall* (n.d.)

37 Hunter, 'Theatre Architecture in Canada,' 36

38 Historical Committee, *The Light of Other Days* (Gravenhurst: Municipal Corporation of Gravenhurst 1967), 40, 43

39 Letter received from Marian Fry, Gravenhurst Archives Committee, 19 February 1982

40 William Rowley Chadwick, *Drayton Opera House, Drayton, Ontario: A Pictorial Record* (n.p. 1977)

41 Frank Dougherty, local historian (1987), Meaford, Ontario

42 Orville Macke and L.W. (Curly) Wilson of St Marys

43 Margaret Rodger, 'Opera House Future Unsure at St. Marys,' Stratford *Beacon Herald*, 17 October 1972, 16

44 Wayne Faddon and others, *St. Thomas: 100 Years a City 1881–1981* (St Thomas: St Thomas Centennial Committee 1981), 84, 85

45 Marion McRae and Anthony Adamson, *Cornerstones of Order* (Toronto: Clarke-Irwin 1983)

46 Gordon and Helliwell's original drawings are in the Archives of Ontario. In india ink on vellum, they are superbly drawn, though now badly deteriorated.

47 Archives of Ontario, Photographs Acc. 10015, S16215

48 R. Thomas Orr as told to Mary Ellen Burt, Stratford-Perth Archives, Cy2.3 C2 58A

49 Archives of Ontario. Minutes of Council, City of Stratford 1898–99; meetings 20 June and 30 November 1898; meeting 5 August 1898

50 Stratford-Perth Archives, Stratford's Theatre Albert, 6y2.3 C72 67

51 John Pettigrew and Jamie Portman, *Stratford: The First Thirty Years* (Toronto: Macmillan 1985), vol I, 121.

52 Peter John Stokes, *Old Niagara on the Lake* (Toronto: University of Toronto Press, 1971)

53 Hilary Russell, *All That Glitters: A Memorial to Ottawa's Capitol Theatre and Its Predecessors*, Canadian Historic Site: Occasional Papers in Archaeology and History, No. 13 (Ottawa: National Historic Parks and Sites Branch, Parks Canada, Indian and Northern Affairs 1975), 47–8

54 Thanks are due to numerous librarians, archivists, municipal officials, architects, amateur and professional historians, and interested citizens, all of whom gave invaluable help in assembling the reference materials used in compiling this chapter.

8 Chronology: Theatre in Ontario to 1914

RICHARD PLANT

This chronology appears simple enough: merely a list of lightly annotated dates providing a number of impressions among which is a sense of the overall development of theatre in Ontario between the 1700s and 1914. As is inherent in the nature of chronologies, the dates and information can be taken as accurate to the extent they can be made so, given the nature and current state of the discipline. Scholars in the field now know that far more theatre occurred from the beginning of the nineteenth century than generally has been acknowledged. However, we are only starting to uncover and analyse in any comprehensive way the records of that activity. Some examples are worth citing.

We now have enough documentation to indicate that almost every Ontario community has an extensive theatre history. The information is tantalizing but incomplete and creates problems. Dates may have been discovered that indicate activity in a community but may not be highly significant in themselves. We may have a record, for example, that an actor performed in a particular town on a particular evening. Because no other records exist surrounding that event, or because we have not had time to do research on hundreds of communities, we cannot offer any further information. Is the individual date of each such performance worth including in the chronology? Certainly it is a place from which to start. Again, most people will agree that the opening of Toronto's Grand Opera House was important. The opening of Cardno Hall in Seaforth was equally important to its community. As many such details as possible are included here.

As might be expected, the amount of theatre activity discovered in the first four decades is far less than was true later in the century. By the 1850s there was so much going on in so many locations that years of research and countless pages could be filled with performance details for individual towns and, in many cases, even for individual theatres. To some extent, this fact suggests that one evening's entertainment at a small theatre in Toronto in 1880 is less important than an evening in 1810. Certainly the appearance of an acting troupe in a community at the beginning of the century was a momentous occasion – one not encouraged by all, yet none the less significant – whereas theatrical evenings came to be taken for granted in most centres late in the century. By omitting of necessity far more in the later decades, this chronology runs the risk of providing a disproportionately large representation of events from the early part of the century, a disproportion which should be taken into account by users of the survey.

Pre-1800

In the light of the record preserved in General Montcalm's diary of the composition and staging on 5 March 1759 of *Le Vieillard dupé* by troops at Fort Niagara (now in American territory), we can speculate that theatrical entertainments may have been held at other French posts, for example, at Fort Frontenac (later Kingston) in what is now Ontario. But from 1759 to 1800, as the British became established, the sparseness of their settlement, the small garrisons, and the nature of their concerns appear to have made theatre next to impossible. A mid-twentieth-century retrospective reference to theatricals in Kingston during the 1790s (*Whig Standard*, 3 August 1946) has not been substantiated. By the early 1800s balls and concerts were taking place in English Niagara, but no evidence has yet been found of theatrical activity in public. Evidence from a few years later in York (Toronto) indicates that play reading within the home was a common activity and might well have occurred in Niagara in these early times. It may be that Lieutenant-Governor John Graves Simcoe's dislike of his officers' involvement with the stage exerted an influence at a crucial time. François de la Rochefoucauld-Liancourt visited Upper Canada between 1795 and 1797 during Simcoe's governorship. What Rochefoucauld reported of Kingston (12 July 1795) appears to be true for all Upper Canada at the time: he lamented the absence of 'amusement' and that there was no 'well-informed man' or books to 'shorten the long lingering day.' But that situation changed quickly during the 1800s.

1800–1914

30 September 1800, York: Joseph Willcocks recorded in his diary that 'Mr Russell' provided home entertainment by reading aloud from *Gulliver's*

Travels. On 12 October he read from the fourth volume of *Udolpho* (presumably Mrs Radcliffe's novel, *The Mysteries of Udolpho*).

3 October 1800, York: Joseph Willcocks attended a 'Puppet Shew' – 'the performance was very indifferent.'

ca 1802, York: Willcocks recorded the visit of a 'learned pig.'

11 February 1809, York: *School for Scandal* performed in a ballroom (name not given) by a group of 'New York comic gentry.'

7 May 1810, York: Messrs Potter and Thompson from London, England, performed 'songs, recitations and ventriloquism' at Mr Miller's Assembly Room. According to the *Gazette* (12 May 1810), the gallery gave way on this occasion, but for the second performance (14 May), it was 'secured under the direction of an obliging Gentleman.'

13 September 1810, York: For the 'second and last time,' the 'company of comedians from Montreal' presented Home's *Douglas* and Macready's *The Village Lawyer*. The troupe was managed by James Douglas(s), son of David Douglass, builder of the Southwark Theatre in Philadelphia.

24 December 1811, Kingston: 'Assembly' at Walker's Hotel, 'dancing to commence at 7 o'clock'

28 April 1812, Kingston: 'A variety of surprising Performances … a grand display of new curiosities … upwards of 200 extraordinary feats' at Poncet's Inn

6 May 1812, Kingston: *The Doctor's Courtship* performed by visiting troupe at Poncet's 'large Room, which is fitted up for the purpose'

25 May 1812, York: 'Various curiosities' at O'Keefe's Assembly Room

1815, Niagara: Building of Town Hall

25 January 1816 – July 1817, Kingston: Kingston Amateur Theatre (garrison officers and a few gentlemen from the town) performed nearly thirty mainpieces and nearly thirty farces during this eighteen-month period.

22 January 1818, Niagara: *Rose and Nancy*, the first play printed in Ontario; text taken from Mary Leadbeater's *Cottage Dialogues among the Irish Peasantry* (Dublin 1811) and published in the Niagara *Gleaner*

10 June 1818, Kingston: Mr Kennedy of the Montreal theatre in 'songs' and 'recitations'

3 July 1818, Niagara: 'The Convention, a farce As now acting with great applause in Upper-Canada,' the first native play (anon.) published in Ontario (Niagara *Gleaner*)

8 September 1818 – mid-May 1819, Kingston: H.A. Williams took management of theatre. Among the performers were Mr and Mrs Frederick Brown (February 1819) and Mr Carpenter and Miss Moore (March/April).

3 November 1818, York: Gentlemen Amateurs performed *Douglas* and *Love-A-la-Mode*.

1818, York: Theodore Hatton in *Douglas* and *The Spoil'd Child*

9 July 1819, York: Mr Biven's benefit: *The Village Lawyer; Quack Medicine; The Wags of Windsor; Father Outwitted*

7 August 1819, Kingston: Mr and Mrs Baker and troupe opened season and stayed until 24 August 1819.

28 October 1819, Niagara: *Dialogue* (anon.) published in Niagara *Gleaner*.

20 November 1820, Kingston: Sale of the Kingston Amateur Theatre's theatrical properties; receipts given to the Female Benevolent Society for indigent sick

13 November 1821, York: Master Dixon in comic songs, recitations, and dancing at Snyder's Ballroom

30 September – 22 October 1824, York: Mr Archbold and troupe (including Mrs Archbold, Mrs Talbot, Messrs Talbot, Gilbert, Trowbridge, Davis, and Miss Allan) from Albany performed at Mr Phair's Assembly Room. Allan MacNab, later Sir Allan MacNab, also performed with this company.

24, 25 December 1824, York: Family theatricals at the Baldwins' home

December 1824, York: Mr Talbot and company opened at Schofield's Mansion House (some of the company still in York in March 1825).

19 February 1825, York: Mr Glaus(e) with his puppets, Mr Punch, slack-wire act, tumbling, paintings, and songs at Mr Frank's Hotel

10 March 1825, York: Mr Pemberton at the ballroom in Mr Frank's Hotel

6 October 1825, York: Mr Taylor, ventriloquist

15 December 1825, York: Gilbert, Trowbridge, and Davis announced their intention of erecting a temporary theatre at Frank's Hotel; company opened late in December and was kept in York by weather conditions; company still active in York on 21 January 1826. Mr and Mrs Sol Smith were with this troupe.

1825: Erie Canal opened officially for traffic, extending the New York / Albany circuit to Utica, Syracuse, Rochester, Buffalo, Hamilton, York, Cobourg, Belleville, Kingston, Brockville – the basis of a Great Lakes circuit.

February 1826, York: Amateurs held benefit for Mr Dwyer, elocution teacher.

7 April 1826, York: First recorded visit of a circus, Blanchard's 'Royal Circus'

29, 31 July, 1 August 1826, York: 'Grand Exhibition of Living Animals' at Snyder's Inn

3 August – 23 September 1826, Kingston: Mr and Mrs Emmanuel Judah from Montreal performed in a 'small but comfortable theatre erected in the rear of the Kingston Hotel.'

7 August 1826, York: Mr Blanchard's Royal Circus

25 August 1826, Kingston: 'Mr Blanchard having arrived last evening with his troupe in the steamboat "Niagara" from a tour through the upper parts of the province, he begs to announce to his friends and the public that he proceeds immediately to Hallowell and Belleville, and will return to re-open to this town on Monday 4 September next' (*Chronicle*).

Summer 1826, York: Menagerie and equestrian show at Snyder's Inn

October 1826, York: Mr and Mrs Emmanuel Judah gave performances at Frank's Hotel, 'where they fitted up a theatre.'

11 November 1826, York: Musical concert by Master Dixon

1826, Ancaster: Amateur Society formed

24 March 1827, Ancaster: The Gore Militia held a 'Greek Ball' at Burley's Hotel in aid of suffering Greeks.

1827, York: Resident circus under Bernard and Black; still in existence as late as 1833

23 February 1828, York: Presentation of acts 1 and 2 of Terence's *Adelphi* (in Latin) as part of exam at the Royal Grammar School

12 April – 13 June 1828, York: Mr Archbold and troupe in local theatre

4 June 1828, York: Mr Charles French murdered Mr Edward Nolan after attending the theatre; the anti-theatre faction used this connection as a springboard for attacking theatre activity. French was hanged on 20 October 1828.

16 June 1828, York: York Amateur Theatre performed *The Poor Gentleman* and *High Life below Stairs* at Frank's Hotel.

21, 23, 24 June 1828, Ancaster: Performances by an unnamed troupe of players (possibly Archbold's company)

23–28 June 1828, York: 'Grand Caravan of Living Animals' at the Steamboat Hotel

28 June 1828, Hamilton: First recorded theatrical performance in Hamilton occurred at the Burlington Hotel Ballroom. Vague references in later accounts (e.g., Hamilton *Herald*, 7 September 1907) to performances before 1825 at Price's tavern, corner of Wellington and King streets and to 'a small room on Lover's Lane' (Wellington Street) are not substantiated by any reliable sources.

19 August 1828, York: Wax figure exhibition of Bradley, the Yorkshire Giant

1 December 1828, London: Birth of Graves Simcoe Lee, who acted in London amateur productions, then went on to a significant professional career, including the writing of 'Fiddle, Faddle and Foozle' (unpublished) (see 9 April 1853), the first indigenous play on the Toronto stage

10 January 1829, Guelph: Announcement in the *Gore Gazette* of 'The Husking Bee, or Courtship in the Woods' (unpublished) to be staged by the amateurs at the Priory 'about the latter end of the month'

16 November 1829, Kingston: Amateurs of the 79th Cameron Highlanders and the naval detachment open in the 'New Theatre' fitted up in a stable behind Mrs Walker's Hotel. Season runs into summer 1830.

2 January 1830, Kingston: Attempt by many local notables, including several garrison army and navy officers, to gather funds to build a new theatre

23 January 1830, Kingston: The Rev. W.R. Payne wrote to the Kingston *Examiner* refusing a gift of money from theatre performances which was meant to be used for charitable assistance; letter publicized ongoing battle between anti-theatre and pro-theatre sectors of community. (Gift was only £1, a provocative gesture if not an outright insult.)

15 October 1830, Kingston: Messrs Gilbert and Trowbridge announced opening of a 'pretty little theatre in the large room under the *Patriot* office.' They gave eight productions between 15 October and 12 November.

28 October 1830, Fairport (Dresden): Escaped Kentucky slave Josiah Henson, prototype of Uncle Tom in Stowe's novel and its countless stage adaptations, entered Canada via underground railroad and settled in this community.

1830, St Thomas: Edward Ermatinger witnessed Mr Long's company at a local performance.

29 September 1831, York: Grand panoramic view of Bytown, painted by W.S. Hunter, on display

24 November – 1 December 1831, York: Mr McCleary presents G.A. Stevens's (?) 'Lecture on Heads.'

1831, York: The first Mechanics' Institute (MIs often used as theatres) established in Upper Canada.

31 May 1832, Brockville: Burgess and Black menagerie

7 June 1833, York: The 'fattest heifer in Upper Canada' on display

5, 9, 12 July 1833, York: Columbus, 'the best known elephant in North America' on display

late July 1833, York: J.E.T.C. Vaughan and company performed in hotel and aroused anti-theatre sector.

2 August 1833, York: J.E.T.C. Vaughan announced beginning of transformation of the Methodist Chapel, satirically referred to as the 'American brimstone building,' into a theatre. Apparently this theatre was never completed, although Vaughan arranged one performance in the location.

3 August 1833, York: The Kembles decided not to visit York because of the lack of a theatre.

4 August 1833, Hamilton: Board of Police passed a town by-law against public performances without permission of the board.

20 September 1833, York: Waugh Brothers opened York's Theatre Royal

with a Chinese Kaleidoscope and a panorama of the burning of Moscow; the theatre did not seem to have been completed at this time.

9 October 1833, York: Grand Mechanics Ball with proceeds donated to the 'theatre project'

late 1833, York: Mr and Mrs Charles Robert Thorne and company performed at the Steamboat Hotel and at Keatings British Coffee House.

7 March 1834, York: York incorporated as the City of Toronto

31 May 1834, Toronto: City created Bylaw 6 requiring theatres to have a licence for performances; a contributing factor was the cholera epidemic of recent years.

February 1835, Kingston: Mr and Mrs Ashley, formerly of the Gilbert and Trowbridge company, performed in Mr Meagher's Hall at the Wellington Inn.

18 March 1835, Kingston: Garrison Amateurs performed at 'Old Marine Hospital, Point Frederick.'

2 July 1835, Toronto: J.W.S. Hows gave dramatic readings from Shakespeare at City Hall. A menagerie was on display on the grounds of Government House.

14 October 1835, Kingston: Mr Gilmour performed at Mr Meagher's Hotel, Barrack Street.

October 1835, Toronto: Travelling flea circus

19 December 1835 to mid-January 1836, Toronto: Charles Thorne and company performed at the Exchange Coffee House.

1835, Hamilton: Engine House reportedly being used for performances and lectures (unsubstantiated reference in *Herald*, 7 September 1907).

7 January 1836, Kingston: 24th Garrison Amateurs failed to invite Dr Edward Barker, editor of *Whig*, to their performance. He responded by attacking their theatricals in his paper.

14 January 1836, Toronto: Advertisement appeared concerning building of new theatre.

10 February 1836, Kingston: Dr Edward Barker published his play, *The Bridegroom*, in the *Whig*.

March, August, September 1836, Kingston: Mr and Mrs Ashley with S. Dyke and company appeared at the Commercial Hotel.

March 1836, Toronto: Opening of the new 'Theatre Royal,' reportedly in a former carpentry shop, by Messrs Thorne and Meers and company. Joseph Proctor the star performer with this company. Theatre Royal burned in 1840.

4, 20 May 1836, Toronto: Performances by the Toronto Theatrical Amateurs in *The Rivals* with manager, B. Stow, as Mrs Malaprop. Audience became rowdy when Union Jack ripped up as a political protest.

July 1836, Toronto: Visit by menagerie with 4,200-lb unicorn (rhinoceros)

Hamilton, Engine House

2 August 1836, Toronto: Francis Bond Head became patron of Theatre Royal, first official patron holding a senior government post. The same evening a protester against Head's policies ripped up a British flag at the theatre.

24 September 1836, Kingston: Farewell to the 24th Amateurs, who turned over their theatrical stock to the S. Dyke company. Proceeds to charity

1836, Galt: Performances by the Galt amateurs

1836, Belleville: Circus performances

6 February 1837, Bytown (Ottawa): Garrison Amateurs of the 15th Regiment offered *The Village Lawyer*; first recorded performance in Bytown. Over the next months (8 February, 1 March, 3, 4 April) Garrison Amateurs staged further theatricals.

13 April – 2 May 1837, Kingston: Kingston Dramatic Amateurs with Mr and Mrs Ashley and help from several officers of the garrison offered a season of shows.

26 April 1837, Toronto: Messrs T.B. Russell and T.A. Lyne performed at the Theatre Royal.

12 June 1837, Hamilton: Mr (T.B.?) Russell, manager of the theatre (Engine House), successfully petitioned to have £2 licence-fee order rescinded.

12 August 1837, Toronto: Toronto Juvenile Thespian Society ambitiously opened a new theatre with *The Miller and His Men* and *Killing Time*. However, there are no further recorded performances of this group.

October 1837, Kingston: Local amateur company failed

1837, London: Anna Jameson recorded in her book, *Winter Studies and Summer Rambles in Canada*, that, despite being more vigorous and prosperous than any centres other than Toronto and Hamilton, London had, 'I fear, a good deal of drunkenness and profligacy; for though the people have work and wealth, they have neither education nor amusements.'

1837, Niagara: John Simpson published *Captain Plume's Courtship* and a *Dramatic Sketch* in his *Canadian Forget Me Not for 1837*.

1838, Toronto: David H. Mayne published *Simon Black* and *The Lake of Killearney by Moonlight* in his *Poems and Fragments*.

1838–9, London: Local Garrison Amateurs staged a number of theatricals.

19 June – 31 July 1839, Toronto: Hugh Scobie (Chrononhotonthologos, pseud.) published *Provincial Drama Called the Family Compact* in the *British Colonist*.

13 August – 7 September 1839, Toronto: Messrs Elsworth and Gwynne (Gwinne) at the second Theatre Royal aroused anti-American and anti-theatre sentiments. Charles Kemble Mason was with this company.

22 August 1839, St Catharines: Local newspaper (*Journal*) records a

'Disturbance at the theatre.'

23, 24 September 1839, Kingston: Miss Margaret Davenport, child phenomenon, and her parents, Mr and Mrs Thomas Davenport, performed at the Lambton House.

4–14 October 1839, Toronto: Ravel Brothers and company staged a variety of entertainments at the Theatre Royal.

1840, London: Officers of Colonel Talbot's garrison, under the name 'The Gentlemen Amateurs,' took over an uncompleted Methodist church and fitted it up as a theatre (eventually called the 'Theatre Royal'). Apparently previous performances had taken place in a barn or an empty warehouse. William Mercer Wilson, a Scottish-born resident of Simcoe and captain of the militia in the London area during the 1837 rebellion (eventually became a judge and the first Grand Master of the Grand Masonic Lodge of Canada) invited to perform in some of these.

28 April 1840, Hamilton: Performance by the Hamilton Gentlemen Amateurs in the second-storey theatre of the new Town Hall (built in 1839)

3, 4 July 1840, Kingston: National Circus from the city of New York

14 July 1840, Kingston: Messrs Powell and Hough and company at Meagher's rooms

24–28 July 1840, Toronto: National Circus from the city of New York

1–14 August 1840, Toronto: Powell and Hough and company at the City Hotel (formerly Steamboat Hotel)

17 August 1840, Toronto: Revision of by-laws resulted in 'An Act to Regulate Theatrical Performances and Other Exhibitions' by Council.

18, 19 August 1840, Kingston: National Circus from the city of New York

August 1840, Cobourg: Visit by New York City Zoological Institute and Menagerie

8, 9 September 1840, Kingston: Bowery Theatre of New York (circus) in open space near the Lambton House

December 1840, Toronto: Birth of Colin 'Cool' Burgess, a long-time, local, favourite black-face performer who had a successful career in the United States and Canada before returning to Toronto late in century. He originated and made famous the song 'Shoo Fly, Don't Bodder Me.' He died on 20 October, 1905.

1840, Toronto: Black population petitioned Toronto Council to refuse licences to circuses and menageries that allowed 'certain acts, and songs, such as Jim Crow and what they call other Negro characters.' Petitions repeated in 1841, 1842 and 1843 – all unsuccessfully.

6 February 1841, Sandwich: Birth of Arthur McKee Rankin, later a successful actor in the United States and Canada who starred in *The Danites* for over ten years

10 February 1841, Kingston: As part of Act of Union, Kingston became

Hugh Scobie, playwright and publisher

capital of the Province of Canada until 1844, when capital moved to Montreal.

29 April 1841, Hamilton: Amateur theatricals at Town Hall

September/October 1841, Toronto: Local amateur company performances

2, 3 September 1841, Kingston: Opening of Atheneum with 'Grand Dramatic Concert' by Mrs Fitzwilliam

19 October 1841, Toronto: New York Bowery Amphitheatre (circus including plays in its entertainment)

23 October 1841, Brockville: John Richardson published his farce, *The Miser Outwitted*, subsequently performed at the Queen's Theatre (London, England; Dublin?) on 10 May 1848.

29 October 1841, Kingston: Atheneum 'fitted up expressly for the evening' for the Total Abstinence Society entertainment.

1841, London: Opening of the Mechanics' Institute

January – April 1842, Kingston: Kingston Amateurs performed at Tête du Pont barracks.

April 1842, Kingston: Civilian Amateurs performed at Atheneum.

30 June 1842, Toronto: Misses Elliott and Fitzjames and company at the City Hotel Assembly Room

25–28 July 1842, Toronto: Great Western Amphitheatre company (two stage plays in their entertainments)

September 1842, Hamilton: Edwin Dean and W.S. Forrest Company at Town Hall.

19 September – 1 October 1842, Toronto: Edwin Dean and W.S. Forrest Company opened in City Hall, then transferred to 'New Theatre' at Deering's North American Hotel. The first recorded use of gaslight on a Toronto stage was in Deering's theatre.

27 September 1842, Toronto: Mrs Samuel Butler in 'Recitations and Dramatic Sketches' at City Hall

15 October – November 1842, Toronto: Panorama displayed at the Waterloo building

24 October 1842, Kingston: Edwin Dean and W.S. Forrest Company at the 'new' theatre (Theatre Royal?)

28 October 1842, London: Performance by garrison Gentlemen Amateurs

18 January – 18 April 1843, Toronto: Officers of the garrison under Captain D'Alton with Gentlemen Amateurs presented a season of eight bills at Theatre Royal, North American Hotel.

18 February 1843, London: Staging of two plays by the Gentlemen Amateurs 'cast with a discrimination as to the idiosyncrasy of the performers'

April – 3 June 1843, Kingston: Edwin Dean and W.S. Forrest Company at the Theatre Royal

17–19 July 1843, Toronto: Rockwell and Stone's Circus

19–27 July 1843, Toronto: Edwin Dean and W.S. Forrest Company at the Theatre Royal

22 July 1843, Hamilton: Gentlemen Amateurs performed at Town Hall for Mr Marsh's benefit.

Fall 1843, Galt: Galt Thespian Amateurs opened first of a number of seasons.

October 1843, London: Raymond, Rivers and Company (professionals) appeared at the Mechanics' Institute.

17 January 1844, London: London Theatrical Company (amateur) at the 'Garrison Theatre'

5 March 1844, Kingston: Amateurs of the Dockyard at the Theatre Royal

14 June 1844, Toronto: Gentlemen Amateurs from Hamilton at Deering's Theatre Royal

14 August – 6 September 1844, Kingston: Mr Rodney's 'company of comedians' at the Theatre Royal

21–28 August 1844, Kingston: Mr and Mrs Forbes joined Rodney's company at the Theatre Royal.

12 September 1844, Hamilton: James Robertson applied to Board of Police for permission to rent 'Theatre Royal,' corner of King William and Catherine streets (first mention of Theatre Royal by name). Company may have been Mr Rodney's, travelling from Kingston with plans of playing in Hamilton followed by two weeks in Toronto.

October 1844, London: Michael McGarry applied to civic authorities to stage a production.

December 1844, Kingston: Opening of City Hall, containing public hall with a stage (sometimes referred to as Theatre Royal in nineteenth century; in 1921 renamed Memorial Hall)

January 1845, Cobourg: Establishment of 'a well appointed Amateur Theatre and Company' by 'some young Gentlemen of the Town'

31 January – spring 1845, Kingston: Performances by the 14th Regiment

2 June 1845, Toronto: Mr Henry Phillips at Theatre Royal

4 June 1845, Hamilton: Mr Henry Phillips at Town Hall

June–July 1845, Kingston: Chapman and Hamilton Company at Theatre Royal

19 November 1845, Toronto: Toronto Amateur Theatrical Society formed

28 November 1845, Hamilton: Hamilton Theatrical Society opened season at Town Hall.

November 1845, London: Shakespeare Club formed in reorganization of Gentlemen Amateurs under Captain Cowley, by this time editor of the London *Times*.

12 January – 29 May 1846, Toronto: Mr Mirfield's Lyceum opened for its

first season by Toronto Amateur Society under Thomas Lennox, who had been active in Hamilton.

January 1846, London: Shakespeare Club opened in new year, prompting London *Times* to state: 'Perfection we don't expect. We are far from wishing to check their ardour ... [but] we advise them not to undertake too much at one time, rather apply themselves to become perfect in all they attempt.'

1 June 1846, Toronto: George Skerrett and company opened Mr Mirfield's Lyceum until 25 June, when they went to Hamilton Theatre Royal.

10 July 1846, Toronto: George Vandenhoff at the Old City Hall

10 July 1846, Hamilton: Hamilton Amateur Theatrical Society benefit for Mr John B. Harrison, lessee and manager of Theatre Royal

13 July 1846, Hamilton: Signors Valentine and Michael Angelo in 'Dialogues in Ventriloquism' at the Theatre Royal

14, 15 July 1846, Hamilton: Mr and Mrs Charles Hill and their children Rosalie and Barton (actors) and Robert (treasurer), at Theatre Royal. Following this engagement, they toured through Brantford, Paris, Galt, Guelph, London, Woodstock, Chatham, (returned to) Hamilton, and Toronto, before travelling east to Kingston and other local towns; also travelled into Michigan and New York State.

13 August 1846, Hamilton: Miss Mary Duff and company at Theatre Royal

20 August 1846, Hamilton: Mrs Gilbert, formerly Miss Mary Duff, 'the Siddons of the American Stage,' joined by Hamilton Amateur Theatrical Society.

27 August 1846, Woodstock: Visit by the Hill family

28 August 1846, Toronto: Mrs Gilbert gave 'readings' at the Lyceum.

2 September 1846, Galt: One of two performances at Mr Young's 'elegant new assembly room'

5, 8 September 1846, Chatham: Mr and Mrs Charles Hill and family, assisted by three local amateurs, performed at Theatre Royal.

2, 4 December 1846, Hamilton: Hamilton Amateur Theatrical Society opened a subscription season in the refurbished Theatre Royal; season ran 8, 15, January; 2, 9 February; 2, 9, 25 March; 9, 21 April, 1847.

18 December 1846, Toronto: Toronto and Hamilton Gentlemen Amateurs staged *Did You Ever Send Your Wife to Camberwell?* in slightly localized adaptation by T.P. Besnard (*Did You Ever Send Your Wife to the Falls?*) during a season that ran to 6 May 1847.

1846, London: First piece of original writing for London's stage appeared as 'prologue' for performance by Mr and Mrs Powell.

25 March 1847, Hamilton: Performance by the Amateurs of J.B. Harrison's *Comedy – The Battle of Life* adapted from Dickens

20 April 1847, Toronto: Aborted duel between actor Barnes and manager

Besnard raised anti-theatre outcry.

21 April 1847, Hamilton: Local Amateurs with Toronto Amateurs performed at the Theatre Royal.

11 May 1847, Hamilton: George Skerrett and company opened season at Theatre Royal with Charles Hill as stage manager and Mrs Hill as a leading performer.

12 May 1847, Hamilton: Skerrett's performance under the patronage of Sir Allan MacNab

24 May 1847, Toronto and Hamilton: George Skerrett opened at Mirfield's Lyceum in a season alternating weeks between the two cities until 2 July (Toronto) and 7 July (Hamilton). During the period he brought in stars such as James Wallack, Sr, and Dan Leonard.

1 June 1847, Kingston: John S. Potter Company at the Theatre Royal

5, 6, 7 July 1847, Kingston: George Skerrett and company with James Wallack, Sr, performed at the Theatre Royal. They were on their way to begin engagement at Montreal's new Theatre Royal.

26 October 1847, Hamilton: Amateurs held benefit for Mark Harrison, J.B. Harrison's brother.

17, 23 December 1847, Hamilton: Mr Llewellyn at Theatre Royal

3 January 1848, Hamilton: Mr Llewellyn, under the patronage of Sir Allan MacNab, at Theatre Royal

January 1848, Toronto: T.P. Besnard spent three days in jail for debt.

4 February 1848, Hamilton: Hamilton Amateur Theatrical Society with T.P. Besnard at Theatre Royal

17 March 1848, Toronto: Birth of Clara Morris (Morrison), taken as a child to the United States where her stage career led to reputation as 'queen of melodrama'

5 May 1848, Hamilton: Mrs Baker's benefit under Sir Allan MacNab's patronage

13 May 1848, Kingston: Announcement of Mr and Mrs Charles Hill's plans of a summer tour through Upper Canada

Spring 1848: T.P. Besnard's tour of Upper Canada; performances in Niagara, St Catharines, Port Hope, Cobourg, Toronto (30 May, Old City Hall; 11 July, Temperance Hall)

2 June 1848, Hamilton: Hamilton Amateur Theatrical Society held a benefit for Misses Tyrell 'for their valuable services in the Theatre during the winter.'

27 June 1848, Kingston: Last night of a short season by Mr and Mrs Charles Hill, who then went to Sackets Harbour and Watertown, New York, before returning to Kingston, 'as they ascend the upper part of the province by way of Belleville, Cobourg and Port Hope'

9, 10 August 1848, Cobourg: The Hills at the Globe Hotel

John Ritchie (or Ritchey), mid-nineteenth-century theatre owner

28 August – 1 September 1848, Toronto: George Skerrett and the 'Viennoise Children' at Old City Hall

6 September 1848, Hamilton: The Hills at Theatre Royal; they returned 29 September to 9 October

9 October 1848, Hamilton: Mrs Hill's benefit under patronage of president and members of Highland Society of Canada West

10 November 1848, Hamilton: Hamilton Amateur Theatrical Society opened season at the Theatre Royal; ran 2, 8, 22, 29 December.

28 December 1848, Toronto: Opening of Ritchie's Royal Lyceum with Philharmonic Society concert: first purpose-built theatre in Toronto; stood until destroyed by fire on 31 January 1874.

1848, St Catharines: Opening of Town Hall containing a large room with a stage

1848, Niagara-on-the-Lake: Completion of Court House (now used by the Shaw Festival)

9 January 1849, Kingston: The Hills returned to Theatre Royal after bad luck in Rochester, New York.

12 January 1849, Hamilton: Amateurs continued season at Theatre Royal; 6 February, 16 March; 10, 25, 27 April.

16 January 1849, Toronto: T.P. Besnard and Hamilton Amateurs offered first plays performed at Royal Lyceum; a season of four nights.

18 January 1849, Brockville; Brockville Thespians, with Mr and Mrs Charles Hill, opened at Mr Buell's 'Large Hall' equipped with the touring stock sold by the Hills.

15 February 1849, Toronto: T.P. Besnard and Hamilton Amateurs at Royal Lyceum for three nights

20–22 February 1849, Toronto: Toronto Colored Young Men's Amateur Theatrical Society at the Royal Lyceum for three nights

7 April 1849, Toronto: Great Fire destroyed heart of city.

16 April 1849, Toronto: Toronto Dramatic Society held benefit for family of a fire victim.

6, 8, 11 June 1849, Toronto: Hamilton and Toronto amateurs performed with Charles Kemble Mason

2 July 1849, Toronto: Benefit for Mrs Lyons and Miss Phillips at end of two weeks of 'Operatic Soirees in Full Costume'; followed by two more weeks

2 July 1849, Kingston: Mr and Mrs Charles Hill, Rosalie and Barton Hill (6 July), at Theatre Royal (to August)

4 July 1849, Hamilton: Miss Eliza Brienti's 'Operatic Soirees in Full Costume' at Theatre Royal

25 July 1849, Hamilton: benefit for Miss Anna Cruise with John Potter's company at Theatre Royal

26 July 1849, Hamilton: Benefit for Charles Kemble Mason with John
Potter's company at Theatre Royal; second-last night of engagement

2 August 1849, Toronto: John S. Potter and company, including Charles
Kemble Mason and local professional Mr Brown, opened season at
Royal Lyceum.

27 August 1849, Kingston: Benefit for the Hills under patronage of the
Hon. John A. Macdonald

July and August 1849, Toronto and Kingston: Another serious outbreak of
cholera. Noted Toronto professional actor Mr Brown died of cholera in
August and was buried in Potters' Field.

25 September 1849, Toronto: Charles Kemble Mason organized remaining
members of Potter's company and opened Royal Lyceum with the Hills.
Season ran until 21 October.

25 November 1849, Hamilton: Hamilton Amateur Theatrical Society
opened new subscription season at Theatre Royal; next performance on
18 December.

26 November 1849, Toronto: Mrs Charles Hill, 'professor and teacher
of Dancing and Calisthenics' opened 'Academy for Dancing and
Calisthenics,' a common method used by performers to supplement their
acting income. Mrs Hill offered instruction during stays in a number of
Ontario centres and seems to have had a strong influence on dance in
Ontario.

22 December 1849, Toronto: T.B. DeWalden, the Hills, and Toronto
Amateurs opened season which ran into May 1850 at Royal Lyceum.

1850s: Local railway lines began to be constructed and provided easier
access to interior of southern Ontario for theatrical touring.

2 January 1850, Hamilton: Local Amateurs continued season: 4, 22,
30 January, 12 February ('last time before Lent'(?)), 16 February,
7 March.

15 January 1850, Toronto: Local Amateurs held benefit for Mrs Charles
Hill.

Spring 1850: Charles and Rosalie Hill toured various small towns in
southern Ontario.

3, 8 April 1850, Hamilton: Local Amateurs offered performances additional
to subscription season.

6 April 1850, Barrie: Charles and Rosalie Hill for two nights at the
Queen's Arms Hotel

17–20 April 1850, Hamilton: Miss Mary Duff and Company (including
local J.B. Harrison on 19 April), at Theatre Royal

19 April 1850, Toronto: Toronto and Hamilton Amateurs and the Hills held
testimonial for Mr DeWalden at Royal Lyceum.

4 May 1850, Toronto: Benefit for Miss Mary Duff

5 May 1850, Hamilton: Mr DeWalden and the Hills at Theatre Royal for five nights

19 June 1850, Toronto: Fanny Kemble gave dramatic readings at new City Hall.

22 June 1850, Toronto: Benefit by local Amateurs for Mrs Charles Hill at Royal Lyceum

16 July 1850, Whitby: Charles Hill gave lecture at Scripture's Hotel.

25 July 1850, Peterborough: Charles and Rosalie Hill gave 'Monodramatic Lecture on the Influence of Music, Dancing and the Drama' at Oddfellows' Hall.

5–31 August 1850, Toronto: T.P. Besnard, supported by a new company, including Mrs Mossop (Mrs John Drew), opened at Royal Lyceum; announced no liquor would be sold on premises.

13 September 1850, Hamilton: Local Amateurs performed, followed by dances in costume by successful competitors of Highland Society.

9 October 1850, Hamilton: 'Third Night' by local Amateurs, Mr and Mrs Hill, Rosalie Hill, and 'distinguished Toronto Amateur'

21 October 1850, Toronto: Toronto and Hamilton Amateurs held benefit for Charles Hill.

23 December 1850, Hamilton: Local Amateurs at Theatre Royal

1850, Ottawa (Bytown): Amateur theatricals organized by William Pittman at Town Hall.

1850 ca, Peterborough: Opening of Hill's Music Hall, second floor of Market Building; remained until a fire in 1861.

1850, St Catharines: Opening of Academy of Music

January 1851, Kingston: Theatre Royal burned

23 January 1851, Hamilton: Newly formed Histrionic Society presented its first bill.

25 March 1851, Hamilton: Histrionic Society performed with Sir Allan MacNab and the mayor of Hamilton in the cast and J.B. Harrison as director.

1 April 1851, Toronto: The new St Lawrence Market and Hall opened officially with a lecture on slavery.

21 April – 19 June 1851, Toronto: T.P. Besnard, as manager, opened Royal Lyceum with a company including Mr and Mrs Charles Hill. Besnard introduced the Herons and the Nickinsons (see below) to Toronto during this season.

24 April, 8 May 1851, Hamilton: Histrionic Society offered its final entertainments including 'Readings in Costume' on both evenings.

14 May 1851, Toronto: Charles Dibdin Pitt starred with T.P. Besnard's company. Besnard then added Fanny Wallack to his cast.

9 June 1851, Toronto: John Heron (father), Mary Ann, Fanny, and Agnes

(daughters) made Toronto debut with Besnard's cast. The Herons became major contributors to Ontario theatre over the next thirty years.

17 June 1851, Toronto: John Nickinson and Charlotte (oldest daughter) made first Toronto appearance with Besnard's cast. John Nickinson and daughters, Charlotte (Mrs Daniel Morrison), Eliza (Mrs Charles Peters), Virginia (Mrs Owen Marlowe), and Isabella (Mrs Charles Walcot), in addition to son John, became an important family in the nineteenth-century theatre. They had an enormous impact on Toronto theatre in particular.

23 June 1851, Kingston: Under T.P. Besnard's management, Heron family appeared for one week at Court House.

25 July 1851, Ottawa (Bytown): Besnard's management took the Herons to Montreal and then to West Ward Market in Ottawa before return engagements in Kingston and Toronto (August and November), as well as performances in Hamilton, Brantford, Dundas, and London.

26 July – 2 August 1851, Toronto: Nickinsons returned to the Royal Lyceum.

8 September 1851, Kingston: T.P. Besnard had Sir William Don, a notoriously arrogant actor, arrested for breach of contract.

13 October 1851, Toronto: Dean family performances in 'New York Bloomer' costumes aroused protest from Torontonians, including many who did not go to the theatre.

21–23 October 1851, Toronto: Jenny Lind performed at St Lawrence Hall, with proceeds of first appearance given to the mayor for a Protestant orphans' home.

November 1851, London: Herons performed at Mechanics' Hall.

2 January – 24 February 1852, Toronto: T.P. Besnard opened new season at Royal Lyceum with heavy reliance on local amateurs.

12 April 1852, Toronto: John Nickinson and Company opened season of forty-two plays at Royal Lyceum under Besnard's management.

1, 2 July 1852, Toronto: Joe Pentland's Equestrian Troupe (in *Mazeppa*)

18 November 1852, Toronto: Toronto Dramatic Association opened season; last bill of plays was on 8 February 1853.

28 March 1853, Toronto: John Nickinson refurbished Royal Lyceum and opened with largest stage company yet seen in Toronto.

9 April 1853, Toronto: John Nickinson staged 'Fiddle, Faddle and Foozle,' a farce by Graves Simcoe Lee, an actor in the company. 'Fiddle, Faddle and Foozle' (unpublished) noted at time to be first indigenous play on Toronto stage.

11 June 1853, Toronto: Graves Simcoe Lee's *Saucy Kate* staged at the Royal Lyceum

8 September 1853, Toronto: John Nickinson opened second season at Royal

Graves Simcoe Lee (twenty-four years old), actor and author of the first
Upper Canadian play presented on a Toronto stage

Sir Allan MacNab (by Wyly Grier) amateur performer and patron

Lyceum. Between this date and 12 February 1859 Nickinson ran series of seasons at Royal Lyceum. His company invariably had his daughters Charlotte and Virginia among its members as well as Graves Simcoe Lee and often C.W. Couldock, T.D. Rice of Jim Crow fame, and Denman Thompson, famous as the author of *The Old Homestead*. Thompson married and spent several years in Toronto. Over the seasons Nickinson brought many stars in short engagements to head company.

22 September 1853, Hamilton: John Nickinson and his Royal Lyceum company opened new Royal Metropolitan Theatre. Until 1858, Nickinson continued to run seasons at the Hamilton theatre on same basis as at Toronto's Royal Lyceum.

29 October 1853, Hamilton: 'A new farce' (unnamed) by Graves Simcoe Lee staged by Nickinson's company

7 November 1853, Toronto: John Nickinson returned to Royal Lyceum and continued season alternating weeks between Toronto and Hamilton.

1853, London: First train arrived in London.

1853, St Catharines: George Primrose born; from age six months, lived in London, Ontario. Later became famous, particularly with Lew Dockstader, as minstrel performer; called one of the 'millionaires of minstrelsy' and often credited with originating the soft-shoe dance. Died in San Diego in 1919.

3 January 1854, Toronto: Daniel Morrison, editor of Toronto *Daily Leader* (subsequently of *British Colonist* to 1858), later husband of Charlotte Nickinson, began his reviewing of Toronto theatre scene.

13 January 1854, Toronto: John Nickinson's 'The Fortunes of War' (unpublished), an adaptation of a popular afterpiece, performed at Royal Lyceum.

20 April 1854, Kingston: Performance by 54th Regiment Amateurs at City Hall

15–29 June 1854, Hamilton: John Nickinson opened at Royal Metropolitan Theatre, playing on 15, 16, 18, 22, 26, 29 June.

11 September 1854, Hamilton: John Nickinson opened for 'very short time' at Royal Metropolitan Theatre.

27 September – 16 October 1854, Hamilton: John Nickinson ran a season, including several performances by Sir William Don, the 'eccentric comedian,' whose benefit was on 13 October.

10 November 1854, Hamilton: Farewell benefit for Mr Peter and Miss C. Ritchings with their operatic-drama company

13–20 November 1854, Hamilton: Sanford's New Orleans Opera Troupe in a variety of entertainments, including 'The Greatest Novelty of the Age' – seventy gifts given to patrons.

Graves Simcoe Lee at age seventy

1854, Toronto: Birth of John J. Griffin, later manager of huge Sells
   Brothers Circus and person who opened first movie house in Ontario
1854, Ottawa: Professional performers appear at Town Hall.
22 February 1855, Manchester, England: Birth of Ida Van Cortland (Emily
   Buckley), later star of the Tavernier touring company headed by Miss
   Van Cortland and her husband, Albert Taverner(ier); retired from stage
   in 1898.
21 March – 4 April 1855, Hamilton: John Nickinson returned to Royal
   Metropolitan Theatre. Season included Denman Thompson, William
   Davidge, Sr, as well as T.D. Rice in roles as various as Otello (sic) and
   Jim Crow.
9 May – 9 June 1855, Hamilton: John Nickinson returned to Royal Metropolitan Theatre.
13, 14 June 1855, Hamilton: Winchell's Drolleries ('40 odd characters') at
   Royal Metropolitan Theatre
July – 23 August 1855, Kingston: Stewart's New York Dramatic Company
16 October 1855, Hamilton: Signor Donetti's Celebrated Acting Monkeys,
   Dogs and Goats at Royal Metropolitan Theatre
20 November – 12 December 1855, Kingston: Laponte and Lefleur Company
28 December 1855, Toronto: Rosa Cook, fourteen-year-old performer at
   Royal Lyceum, died of burns when her costume caught fire from a stove
   in the wings.
December 1855 – January 1856, Kingston: Mrs Kimber performed with
   Garrison Amateurs.
1855, London: W.Y. Brunton's 'Varieties' opened.
1855, London: City Hall opened, containing 540-seat, multi-purpose hall
   with stage.
3 June 1856, London: Rehearsal of adaptation of John Richardson's novel
   Wacousta
July 1856, Toronto: James Wallack, Sr, appeared with John Nickinson and
   company.
29 July – 23 August 1856, Kingston: G.W. Johnson, Messrs Rogers and
   Wilson, and 'Mrs Macready' performed.
Summer 1856, Toronto: City refused to issue a performance licence to a
   visiting circus, which aroused public debate over the value of such
   entertainments.
4 October 1856, Ottawa: Opening of Her Majesty's Theatre
27 November 1856, Guelph: Announcement of imminent opening of
   Market Building with courtroom and adjoining committee rooms planned
   for occasional use as theatre and dressing-rooms, respectively
1856, London: Opening of Covent Garden Theatre

1856, Merrickville: Building of Town Hall with assembly hall

1856: First year any significant number of plays published in Ontario. The following titles appeared: the Rev. John Borland, *Dialogues Between Two Methodists*; Caroli Candidus (pseud.), *The Female Consistory of Brockville*; Alexander McLachlan, *Fate*, in his *Poems*; Charles Sangster, *Bertram and Lorenzo*, in his *The St Lawrence and the Saguenay and other poems*; Toots (pseud.), *The Meal Club Plot* and *The Two Elders*, in *The Two Elders and the Sequel The Meal Club Plot*.

February, June 1857, Kingston: John Nickinson and company in Kingston

July 1857, Toronto: George Holland appeared with John Nickinson and company.

21 July 1857, Toronto: Lola Montez appeared with Nickinson's company.

31 December 1857, Ottawa: Official announcement of Ottawa as new capital of Canada

1857, Galt: Opening of Town Hall with ballroom

1857, Stratford: Opening of Town Hall with second-storey opera house

19–21 January 1858, Toronto: Anonymous adaptation, *The Poor of Toronto, or The Great Money Panic of 1857*, performed at the Royal Lyceum.

19 April 1858, Toronto: Opening of 'New Concert Hall' by Denman Thompson, 'Cool' Burgess, and Patrick Redmond (ran for one season)

May 1858, Toronto: Matilda Heron appeared with Nickinson's company; small house for the actress notorious for playing such 'fallen' women as the heroine of *La Dame aux Caméllias*.

July 1858, Toronto: Charles Mathews, Sr, appeared with Nickinson and company.

August 1858, Kingston: Nickinson and company in Kingston

November 1858, Toronto: William Petrie, former manager of Royal Lyceum, opened City Theatre in Ontario Hall (ran for one season).

20 December 1858, Brockville: Opening of Town Hall containing second-storey hall with stage and gallery

1858, London: Robert McBride published *A Division Court and County Court Case* in his *Poems, Satirical and Sentimental*.

1858, Toronto: Opening of Crystal Palace designed by Sir Sandford Fleming

1 April 1859, St Catharines: Birth of Mike Shea, who, with his brother Jerry (b. 15 August 1864), later became a major force in vaudeville theatre operation

4 April 1859, Toronto: Virginia (Nickinson) and husband Owen Marlowe reopened Royal Lyceum using remaining members of John Nickinson's company, including Graves Simcoe Lee and Denman Thompson.

1 June 1859, Toronto: Miss Davenport (formerly child phenomenon)

appeared with Royal Lyceum company.

30 June 1859, Niagara Falls: Blondin's sensational tightrope crossings of the falls. In 1860 Guillermo Antonio Farini (Bill Hunt from Port Hope) emulated, even augmented, Blondin's crossings.

July 1859, Toronto: Barry Sullivan appeared with Royal Lyceum company.

11 August 1859, Kingston: Horton Rhys (Captain Morton Price) made his 'theatrical trip for a wager' visiting (in Ontario) Kingston, Belleville, Cobourg, Port Hope, Peterborough, Toronto, Hamilton, St Catharines, and Ottawa.

29 August 1859, Toronto: Royal Lyceum closed by the Marlowes.

2 November 1859, Toronto: Miss Elise De Courcy (of New York) opened Royal Lyceum. Poor business led to Charles T. Smith's taking over the operation in January 1860.

29 December 1859, Toronto: 'A New Local Farce by a Gentleman of the City, Mysteries of the Independent Order of Sons of Masonry' (unpublished) at Royal Lyceum, where the 'grips, signs and pass words' would be exposed

1859, Toronto: Debut of McKee Rankin with Amateur Dramatic Club at Apollo Theatre

February 1860, Toronto: Adah Isaacs Menken at Royal Lyceum

March 1860, Toronto: John Nickinson, returning to Toronto, took over Royal Lyceum, renaming it Prince of Wales Theatre, and ran a season until the end of the summer.

1860s, Toronto: Native Torontonian Allan Halford established acting career in local performances.

20 October 1860, Toronto: Mr and Mrs Sam Cowell at Royal Lyceum during North American tour which included Ottawa among other Canadian centres

23 November 1860, Camden East: Birth of Gilbert Parker, internationally famous novelist, whose stage adaptation of his novel *The Seats of the Mighty* was used by H. Beerbohm Tree on his second American tour and to open Her Majesty's Theatre in London, England (28 April 1897). Between 1883 and 1886 Parker taught elocution at Trinity College, Toronto, and at Queen's University, Kingston.

January–March 1861, Toronto: Toronto Dramatic Club season at Dramatic Hall (formerly Apollo)

12 April 1861, Toronto: J.Z. Little and Charles S. Porter set up company at Royal Lyceum with backing of James Fleming.

October 1861, Ottawa: James Fleming's Royal Lyceum company appeared in Ottawa.

1861, Toronto: Thomas D'Arcy McGee published *Sebastian or the Roman Martyr*.

10 January 1862, Belleville: Mr J.W. Younder gave concert at Coleman's Hall.

January 1862 – April 1863, Toronto: Henry Linden opened at Royal Lyceum with company including Graves Simcoe Lee.

May 1862, London: Garrison fitted up theatre for performances by non-commissioned officers and men.

30 May 1862, Belleville: Miss Mary Angus Cameron gave dramatic readings at Atheneum.

27 June 1862, Whitby: Birth of May Irwin, long-time star with Augustin Daly and Charles Frohman

June 1862, London: Civilian Dramatic Society (also known as London Amateur Dramatic Association) formed, using garrison company's stage and stock. (This company might, in fact, have consisted of both garrison officers and civilians.)

18 December 1862, Belleville: Belleville Dramatic Club at Atheneum in aid of Lancashire Relief Fund

2 January 1863, Belleville: Dramatic Club gave its only recorded performance of the year.

30 March 1863, Toronto: 'Toronto by Daylight and Dark, or Life in the Queen City' (unpublished adaptation of *New York As It Is*) performed at Royal Lyceum as 'local drama in 4 acts.'

June 1863, Kingston: La Rue's Great War Show, including 90,000 moving figures of soldiers, animals, and ships

22 October 1863, Belleville: General Tom Thumb and wife at Atheneum

October 1863, Kingston: 'New Theatre' in use (no date for opening yet located)

October 1863, Toronto: *The Brighter World Above* (anon.) published in *Canadian Quarterly Review and Family Magazine.*

Fall 1863, Toronto/London: Asa Macfarland took over Royal Lyceum for approximately three months before moving to London for short period.

18 November 1863, Hamilton: 'Pepper's Ghost,' one of the most famous in an era of stage illusions, used on the Grand Opera House stage. Dr Pepper had shown the illusion privately in London only on 24 December 1862, which indicates how quickly the Canadian stage could incorporate innovations.

23 November 1863, Belleville: Opening of Mr Neilson's 'New Hall'

1863–5, Kingston: Performances by Garrison Amateurs and John Townsend, former member of parliament in England who emigrated to North America and established career as professional actor-manager. With his family, most of whom performed, he toured extensively.

January–August 1864, Toronto: Royal Lyceum opened with variety of entertainments offered sporadically during this period.

Ottawa, Her Majesty's Theatre c. 1867

23 April 1864, Cobourg: St George's Society celebrated Shakespeare's 300th birthday with dinner, songs, and performance of Falstaff scenes by Grammar School principal.

April 1864, London: Three-day Shakespeare Festival

28 September 1864, London: Birth of Richard B. Harrison, son of escaped American slaves. He starred in *Green Pastures* and ended his career as a teacher of dramatics and elocution in a small college in North Carolina; apparently named after Edwin Booth, who performed *Richard III* in London during Harrison's mother's pregnancy.

3 October 1864 – June 1865, Toronto: Joseph C. Myers reopened Royal Lyceum with Virginia Marlowe (née Nickinson) and Isabella Walcot (née Nickinson).

1864, Meaford: Opening of Town Hall

1864, Guelph: Thorpe's Music Hall in use (no opening date yet located)

1864, Hamilton: George Washington Johnson published *The Columbiad, The Count's Bridge*, and *Grantly Granville; or the Hag of the Mountains* in his *Maple Leaves*.

June–September 1865, Ottawa: John Townsend established Ottawa Theatre Company, including members of his family, at Her Majesty's.

6 November 1865, Toronto: Harry Langdon opened Royal Lyceum, which was then taken over by Flora Myers.

25 November 1865, Toronto: Harry Langdon returned, broke into box office and stole day's receipts.

April 1865, Toronto: *Temperance Dialogue* (anon.) published in the *Canadian Quarterly Review and Family Magazine.*

16 February 1866, Belleville: Dr McLean of Kingston lectured at Marble Hall.

23 April 1866 – August 1867, Toronto: Joseph C. Myers opened Royal Lyceum.

8 May 1866, London: Hyman's Music Hall, containing second-storey theatre, opened with 'Grand Concert of Vocal and Instrumental Music.'

9 August 1866, Toronto: Joseph C. Myers began fall-winter Royal Lyceum season, a period during which he leased Mechanics' Hall in Hamilton and managed tours throughout Ontario.

28 September 1866, Belleville: Mr LaSalle of Kingston bought Atheneum with intention of converting it to skating rink and gymnasium.

19 October 1866, Belleville; Miss Julia Dyer and company performed at Neilson's Hall.

1866, Brantford: Opening of Ker's Music Hall

1866, Toronto: Thomas Bush published *Santiago.*

January 1867, Hamilton: Joseph C. Myers leased Mechanics' Hall.

February 1867, London: Garrison performance

26 March 1867, Toronto: *The Workingmen of Toronto* (localization of *The Workingmen of New York*) staged at Royal Lyceum

13 May 1867, Toronto: Joseph C. Myers produced sensational musical which had taken New York by storm, *The Black Crook*, at Royal Lyceum.

7 October 1867, Toronto: George Holman opened Royal Lyceum, where he remained manager until 1872. Holman and his very talented wife, Sallie, headed Holman Opera Company, major influence on theatre in southern Ontario throughout last three decades of 1800s.

31 October 1867, Belleville: 'Penny Readings' at Ontario Hall

1867, Bradford: Birth of Ambrose Joseph Small, later owner of large theatre circuit, including Toronto's Royal Alexandra and London and Kingston Grand Opera houses

1867, Guelph: Town Hall in use as theatre (no opening date yet located)

1867, Hamilton: Local amateur society performed.

1868, Kingston: Marietta Ravel and Laura Keene made appearances at Royal Lyceum.

3 May 1869, Hamilton: Birth of Ida Lewis, later famous as Julia Arthur

6 September 1869, Wolfe Island: Birth of James K. Hackett, who became noted American actor, associated especially with *The Prisoner of Zenda*.

9 November 1869, Cobourg: Birth of Leila Koerber, later famous as Marie Dressler

1869, London: Robert McBride published *Dialogue Between the Client and the Lambton Ghost on Going From Court* and *A Division Court and County Court Case* (second printing) in his *Poems, Satirical and Sentimental*.

1869, Kingston: Use of Ontario Hall as theatre while City Hall Theatre Royal being repaired

1869, Goderich: Use of Victoria Hall as theatre (no date for its opening yet located)

1860s, Lindsay: Some time during this decade Thomas Bradburn added wing containing a performance hall to Town Hall.

By 1870, theatrical activity was flourishing in large and small centres throughout Ontario, particularly Toronto. At the beginning of 1870 there were at least six different Toronto locations for performances: the Royal Lyceum managed by George Holman and nightly housing his own Opera Company with visiting stars; the Temperance Hall; the theatre in the New Fort; St Lawrence Hall; the Mechanics' Institute; and the Music Hall. The year saw the opening of the Prince of Wales Music Hall and Mr Palmer's Concert Hall as well as seasonal performances at the Agricultural Hall and the Horticultural Gardens. The following dates from the first week in January are examples of the entertainments available but far too numerous for this chronology. We would find a similar type of activity in other large centres; for example, in Ottawa, where Her Majesty's Theatre, the Rink Music Hall, and Gowan's Hall operated throughout 1870. Later in the decade the Grand Opera House and Gowan's Opera House opened, and performances began at Rideau Hall, the governor-general's residence.

1 January 1870, Toronto: Independent Order of Good Templars presented-two temperance dramas at Temperance Hall; this temperance society performed at intervals throughout the year.

1 January 1870, Toronto: Royal Lyceum continued nightly activities under George Holman with *The Oriental Spectacle of Cherry and Fair Star*.

4 January 1870, Toronto: Theatricals at New Fort by Officers of the Garrison to which 'a limited number of the public' was admitted. These theatricals continued throughout year, including special benefit (6 July) for native-born professional Allan Halford and guest star Lillie Lonsdale.

4 January 1870, Toronto: Evening of dramatic readings at Music Hall by Mr Richardson

Ottawa, *Dearest Mama* at Rideau Hall, February 1889; Lady Isobel Stanley, daughter of Baron Stanley of Preston, second from right

10–14 January 1870, Toronto: Lessons in elocution and dramatic readings by Mr Richard Lewis at Mechanics' Institute

18 February 1870, Toronto: Toronto Histrionic Club performed two plays at Temperance Hall.

4 October 1870, Toronto: Opening of Mr Palmer's Concert Hall

12 October 1870, Toronto: Opening of Prince of Wales Music Hall housing variety entertainments

24 October 1870, Belleville: Belleville Dramatic Society opened new Masonic Music Hall.

2 September 1871, Guelph: Birth of James Forbes, who went on to successful career as playwright in commercial theatre. Among his plays are *The Chorus Girl*, which he wrote for Rose Stahl and later became *The Chorus Lady* on Broadway, *The Travelling Salesman, The Show Shop, A Rich Man's Son, The Commuters,* and *A Woman of Today*.

18 September 1871, London: Opening of Mr Spettigue's third-floor Concert Hall (Dundas and Clarence streets); ceased use as theatre and concert hall in 1875.

1871, Hamilton: W.P. Wood (of Ancaster) published his *Minnie Trail, or the Woman of Wentworth, A Tragedy in Three Acts*.

Port Hope, Music Hall and St Lawrence Hotel

Port Hope, inaugural concert, 1871, Music Hall and St Lawrence Hotel

Hamilton, Garrick Club performance

1871, Ancaster: Construction of Ancaster Township Town Hall containing a small stage with a semi-circular proscenium arch

6 May 1872, Toronto: Highly respected Mrs Charlotte Morrison (née Nickinson) returned to Toronto stage: she had 'been induced to give a short series of standard dramatic performances' at Royal Lyceum. Mrs Morrison performed until 1 June, when she appeared with James Wallack.

26 August 1872, Toronto: 'New Royal Lyceum' (renovated Royal Lyceum) opened under new management and with subsequent change of management in January 1873 continued in operation until it burned on 30 January 1874.

28 January 1873, Toronto: William Carter's *Placida, the Christian Martyr* given amateur performance, and script subsequently published by Globe Printing.

13 March 1873, Ottawa: Lady Dufferin hosted her first Rideau Hall theatrical, establishing a practice which continued until the Dufferins left in 1878.

9 August 1873, Toronto: First part of anonymous playlet *Our Poet in the Council Chamber* published in *Grip*; second part appeared on 6 September 1873.

⊨GARRICK ❋ CLUB.⊨

Organized 18th June, 1875.   ·   ·   Incorporated 2nd Feb'y, 1881.

President.

Vice-President.   Sec'y and Treas.

Trustees.

H. A. MACKELCAN.   D. HERBERT BROWNE.   P. D. CRERAR.   R. STEWART   R. TASKER STEELE.

H. H. ROBERTSON.   P. M. BANKIER.   J. H. STUART.

6. No member shall be allowed to ballot for a candidate, or be permitted to vote on any occasion whatever, or enjoy any of the privileges of the Club, who has been in arrear for his annual subscription for six weeks.

10. Any member shall have the privilege of introducing a friend, resident elsewhere than in Hamilton, or within five miles thereof, for a period not exceeding two weeks, provided the name of such person (with the written recommendation of two members) has been sent to the Secretary, and submitted to and approved of by the Trustees, and the Secretary shall thereupon post up in the Reading Room the name of the person introduced, with the names of the members introducing him, and the date of such introduction, and the person so admitted shall thereafter for the period of the Club for two weeks, subject to such Rules as the Trustees may from time to time prescribe.

12. Any member shall have the privilege of introducing a friend into the Club, provided the name and residence of such friend, and the name of the member introducing him be first inscribed in the Visitors' Book.

15. The Club shall be open every day for the reception of members at 8 o'clock in the morning, and shall be closed and the lights extinguished at midnight; and no member shall be admitted into or remain in the Club after that hour on any pretence whatever, unless specially authorized by the Trustees.

17. No member shall take away from the Club, upon any pretence whatever, any newspaper, pamphlet, book, map or other article, the property of the Club.

18. All members are to pay their bills for every expense they may incur in the Club before they leave the building.

19. No member is on any account to bring a dog into the Club.

32. Any cause for complaint that may arise is to be notified by letter to the Secretary, who shall lay the same before the Trustees.

33. Unless authorized by the Trustees under this rule, no game shall on any account be played for money

except ecarte, whist, cribbage and euchre; nor shall dice be used in the Club, except at backgammon.

No higher stakes than ten cent points shall be played for at whist, nor shall any bet exceed one dollar.

The games of ecarte, whist, cribbage and euchre may be played for limited stakes, the limits to be fixed by the Trustees, who shall have power to fix the charges for cards and a limit to the hours during which cards may be played in the Club, and to make such Rules in respect thereof as circumstances may hereafter call for.

34. Any member wilfully infringing any rule of the Club, or any rule or regulation made by the Trustees, or being guilty of conduct unbecoming a gentleman, shall be liable to expulsion or to suspension from all the privileges of the Club for such time as the Trustees may determine, on a vote of two-thirds of the Trustees, subject to an appeal to a general meeting of the Club, to be called by the Secretary at the written request of the member expelled or suspended, within one fortnight after he has received notice of the expulsion or suspension.

Hamilton, Garrick Club charter

1 September 1873, Ottawa: Renovation of Gowan's Hall, which opened again on 22 September as Gowan's Opera House.

25 December 1873, London: George Holman opened refurbished Hyman's Music Hall as Holman Opera House.

1873, St Thomas: Grand Opera House (also known as Claris House) opened.

1873: Town halls with performance spaces opened in Millbrook (Cavan Township Hall) and Port Perry.

1873, Gananoque: Dufferin Hall, located over MacKenzie's Furniture Store and Undertaking Service, in operation as a theatre for performances by touring professionals. Kingston Garrison Amateurs performed here on visits.

1873, Hamilton: *French Chaos* by Andrew Ramsay printed in his *One Quiet Day, A Book of Prose and Poetry*

1873, Ottawa: Performance of Grant Seymour's *Bluebeard* and the anonymous 'Prince John John or Specific Scandal' (unpublished) at the Rink Music Hall

3, 10 January 1874, Ottawa: William Henry Fuller's play *The Unspecific Scandal* appeared in *Canadian Illustrated News* (published in Montreal). Fuller also brought play out in separate printing by Woodburn Press in Ottawa in 1874; however, the fact that the play had been registered under the copyright act in 1868, indicates an earlier writing.

14 March – 16 May 1874, Toronto: Anonymous play *Grip in Council* appeared over six issues of *Grip*.

2 May 1874, Ottawa: Performance of *Grip Among the Politicians* at Gowan's Opera House

11 May 1874, Toronto: Opening of the Queen's Theatre, which remained in operation until it burned on 23 April 1883.

19 June 1874, Hamilton: Official formation of Garrick Club. With some interruption in activity, this amateur theatre company has continued under original charter to present day, now as Hamilton Players Guild.

18 July 1874, Toronto: T.J. Herndon introduced first so-named vaudeville season.

8, 29 August 1874, Toronto: Anonymous play *The Canadian Club* appeared in *Grip*.

14 September 1874, Toronto: Royal Opera House (also known as Royal Theatre) opened, replacing Royal Lyceum, which had been destroyed by fire. Royal Opera House burned 8 February 1883.

21 September 1874, Toronto: Grand Opera House opened under management of Charlotte Morrison; opening is notable for one of first uses of electricity in a Canadian theatre: the Grand's huge gas chandelier was lighted by electricity. The Grand remained in operation until destroyed by fire on 29 November 1879 but was succeeded by new Grand Opera House only two months later.

9 November 1874, Toronto: First visit by Mrs F.S. Chanfrau

December 1874, Aylmer: Opening of Town Hall with performance space. In the 1890s this hall was renovated and was thereafter referred to as the Opera House.

1874, Ameliasburg: Opening of Township Hall and Masonic Lodge

1874, Niagara-on-the-Lake: Stamford Town Hall erected

1874, Toronto: Three anonymous playlets appeared in *Light for the Temperance Platform: The Crooked Tree*, *The Moderate Drinker*, and *The Pump and the Tavern*.

1 February 1875, Ottawa: Opening of Gowan's New Opera House (also known as Grand Opera House), which remained until destroyed by fire on 5 July 1913. Old Gowan's Opera House (Sparks Street) subsequently called St James Hall.

February 1875, Toronto: Charlotte Morrison introduced 'living statuary' entertainment at Grand Opera House.

Scene from *Canadian Illustrated News* (24 April 1875) of F.A. Dixon's *The Maire of St Brieux*

31 March 1875, Ottawa: Lady Dufferin attended the second performance of F.A. Dixon's comic opera *The Maire of St Brieux* in her theatre at Rideau Hall. 'The prima donna, Mrs Anglin, both sang and looked charmingly.' Later this same year, Dixon's *Maire* was published in Ottawa; first public performance took place on 25 March 1876. American edition published in Philadelphia in 1879.

Spring 1875: Eugene A. McDowell's first performances in Ontario. In Toronto, Mrs Morrison and C.W. Couldock in cast for Boucicault's *The Shaughraun*, the play from which McDowell took his company's name.

17 July 1875, Toronto: Anonymous *Mr Mackenzie at Buckingham* appeared in *Grip*. On 5 July 'Grip' (J.W. Bengough (?)) gave lecture at Toronto Grand Opera House as part of benefit for St Nicholas Home.

28 December 1875, Toronto: John Wilson Bengough presented his *Heads and Tails* at Shaftsbury Hall.

1875, Toronto: Publication of Frederick Augustus Dixon's play *Little Nobody*.

1875, Guelph: Drill Shed in use as theatre

1875, Peterborough: Opening of Thomas Bradburn's Opera House on second floor of Town Hall

1875, Oakwood: Construction of Mariposa Community Hall

1 January 1876, Ottawa: F.A. Dixon's *Little Nobody* staged as Lady Dufferin's New Year theatrical entertainment at Rideau Hall

17 March 1876, Ottawa: Canadian actor W.H. Brent's play *Shaullanah* staged by Ada Gray's company at Gowan's Opera House.

20 March 1876, Paisley: Opening of Paisley Town Hall containing an opera house on second floor

25 March 1876, Ottawa: First public performance of F.A. Dixon's *The Maire of St Brieux* occurred at Gowan's Opera House as benefit for its music composer, F.W. Mills.

3 April 1876, Ottawa: Birth of famous actress, Margaret Anglin, in speaker's chambers of House of Commons (father was Speaker of the House)

8 May 1876, Toronto: At Royal Opera House, spectacular production of *The Black Crook*

20 May 1876, Toronto: *The Happy Return*, anonymous playlet, appeared in *Grip*.

17 June 1876, Toronto: Anonymous playlet *Presbyterian General Assembly* appeared in *Grip*.

19 August 1876, Toronto: *John Bull and Jonathan*, anonymous playlet, appeared in *Grip*.

9 September 1876, Toronto: Anonymous playlet *Scene at Ottawa* appeared in *Grip*.

September 1876, Belleville: Building of Temperance Hall

7 October 1876, Toronto: Anonymous playlet *Short Drama* appeared in *Grip*.

21 October 1876, Toronto: Anonymous playlet *Scene – City Hall* appeared in *Grip*.

4 November 1876, Toronto: *The New Minister*, anonymous playlet, appeared in *Grip*.

1876, Demorestville: Construction of Sophiasburgh Township Hall containing a stage and proscenium arch

1876, Toronto: Publication of Nicholas Flood Davin's political satire *The Fair Grit; or the Advantages of Coalition*

1876, Toronto: Publication of Samuel James Watson's poetic drama *Ravlan* and his dramatic poem *The Legend of the Roses*

1876–7 ca, Christie Lake: R.W. (Bob) Marks reportedly entered entertainment business by joining King Kennedy, 'the Mysterious Hindu from the Bay of Bengal' in touring magic act.

1 January 1877, Ottawa: Performance of F.A. Dixon's *Maiden Mona the*

Mermaid at Rideau Hall as the Dufferins' New Year theatrical. Script published in Toronto in 1877.

29 January 1877, Toronto: Performance of St John Molyneaux's *The Revolt of the Commune* at Grand Opera House

19 February 1877, Toronto: Publication of Lucknow doctor John Hutchinson Garnier's poetic drama *Prince Pedro*

9 March 1877, Belleville: Opening of the Belleville Opera House (also known as Bull's Opera House). It burned on 2 April 1880.

14 July 1877, Toronto: Anonymous satire *This Fishery Commission at Halifax* appeared in *Grip*.

16 July 1877, Whitby: Opening of Hopkins' Music Hall

28 July 1877, Toronto: Anonymous satire *The Land of Liberty* appeared in *Grip*.

15 September 1877, Toronto: Anonymous satire *The Commissioner and the Injun* appeared in *Grip*.

21 September 1877, London: Opening of new Mechanics' Institute

15 December 1877, Seaforth: Opening of Cardno Hall

1877, Toronto: Debut at Grand Opera House of actor Henry Miller (British born; came to Canada at age fourteen); very successful career included starring in New York opposite Margaret Anglin in William Vaughn Moody's *The Great Divide*

1877(?), Watford: Birth of Franklin McLeay; promising career as actor cut short by his untimely death in England in 1900.

1877, Woodstock: New Methodist church used as theatre.

1 January 1878, Ottawa: Performance of F.A. Dixon's *Fifine, the Fisher-Maid; or, The Magic Shrimps* at Rideau Hall as the Dufferins' New Year theatrical. Script published in Ottawa during 1877.

4 March 1878, Toronto: McKee Rankin brought his most successful play, *The Danites* (première 1877 New York), to Toronto for first time.

28 March 1878, Toronto: Ida Van Cortland made her first appearance in significant professional role at Grand Opera House.

7 September 1878, Toronto: Anonymous satire *The Sweets of Office* appeared in *Grip*.

20 September 1878, London: Opening of Victoria Hall

28 September 1878, Belleville: Opening of Good Templars' Hall

7 December 1878, Toronto: Anonymous satire *Scene in Ottawa* appeared in *Grip*.

21 December 1878, Gananoque: Local Amateur Dramatic Society performed in Dufferin Hall; on 30 and 31 December performed in Farmersville and Westport.

6 January 1879, Kingston: Eugene A. McDowell and his Shaughraun Company star at opening of Martin's Opera House, first major theatre

built in Kingston. Remained in operation until 6 December 1898, when it was destroyed by fire, but was succeeded almost immediately by Kingston Grand Theatre.

18 January 1879, Toronto: Anonymous satire *Scene at Ottawa* appeared in *Grip*.

24 February 1879, Ottawa: Performance of F.A. Dixon's *A Masque Entitled 'Canada's Welcome'* at Grand Opera House; script had two printings in 1879.

8 March 1879, Toronto: Anonymous playlet *The Tribulations of N F D* appeared in *Grip*.

15 March 1879, Toronto: Anonymous satire *H.M. Canadian Ship Blunderbore* appeared in *Grip*.

17 March 1879, Toronto: Opening of Pavilion at Horticultural Gardens

20 March 1879, Toronto: Performance in *Henry V* of 'young and talented Canadian actor,' James Green

29 November 1879, Toronto: Fire destroyed Toronto Grand Opera House killing stage carpenter, his wife, and child.

1879, Woodstock: Town Hall in use as theatre

1879?, Christie Lake: R.W. (Bob) and Tom Marks made their first attempt at touring. In the 1890s, these brothers, with other members of their family, Mrs R.W. (May A. Bell), George, Joe, Alex, Ernie, and Mrs Ernie (Kitty), ran at least three companies touring Canada and United States.

187?, Prescott: *Extract From an Original and Unpublished Play, Lately Performed at the Prescott Municipal Amphitheatre!* satirizing the Prescott council, printed anonymously

9 February 1880, Toronto: New, larger Grand Opera House opened, replacing previous building which burned only seventy-two days before. This theatre stood until 1928.

23 February 1880, Ottawa: Eugene A. McDowell presented first Ontario production of William Henry Fuller's operetta *H.M.S. Parliament*, which McDowell had premièred at the Academy of Music in Montreal on 16 February. McDowell then took *Parliament* on national tour (Halifax to Winnipeg) including at least twenty-four Ontario centres. *Parliament* also published in 1880.

14 May 1880, Toronto: Joseph Jefferson, famous as Rip Van Winkle, made first appearance in Toronto.

17 July 1880, Toronto: Anonymous satire *The Senator's Sensitive Daughter* printed in *Grip*.

6 October 1880, St Marys: Opening of St Marys Opera House in three-storey, limestone building erected by Oddfellows

29 November 1880, Hamilton: Opening of Grand Opera House

The Marks Brothers' production of *At the Point of the Sword*, act 3

The Marks Brothers in a touring wagon

1880, Clinton: Opening of new Town Hall with auditorium and stage

21 February 1881, Toronto: Tommaso Salvini, great Italian tragedian, opened first engagement at Grand Opera House; returned in December 1882.

19 March 1881, Toronto: Sarah Bernhardt gave first Ontario performances (Grand Opera House). She had performed in Montreal in 1880 and came back to Ontario centres on eight later tours (1887, 1891, 1896, 1905, 1910, 1911, 1917).

2 July 1881, Toronto: C.P.M.'s (pseud.) *Lord Fitz Fraud*, satirizing Toronto society, appeared in *Grip*.

30 July 1881, Toronto: *Society Idyls* by C.P.M. (pseud.) appeared in *Grip*.

21 August 1881, Toronto: *Fair Rosamond*, an anonymous parody of Swinburne, printed in *Grip*.

8 September 1881, London: Opening of London Grand Opera House in Masonic Temple; burned on 23 February 1900.

31 October 1881, Brantford: Opening of Stratford's Opera House; burned on 1 January 1908.

14 November 1881, Toronto: Ernesto Rossi and an American company opened in engagement at Grand Opera House; included *Hamlet, Othello*, and *Romeo and Juliet* 'In Italian and English.'

10 December 1881, Toronto: First section of Jay Kayelle's *Underground Theology*, a satirical attack on free-thinkers, appeared in *Grip*. Remainder of the play appeared on 17 and 24 December.

1881, Toronto: *The Boycott*, anonymous dramatic satire of the farmer's boycott in Scotland, appeared in *Grip's Almanack*.

1881: Emma Wells Concert Company made first Marks Brothers Canadian theatrical tour.

17 January 1882, Toronto: First Toronto appearance of the famous Mlle Rhea; she starred in *Camille*.

4 February 1882, Toronto: *Innocent Bigamy* by C.P.M. (pseud.), parodying domestic melodrama, printed in *Grip*.

9 March 1882, Toronto: 'Young Canadian Elocutionist, Mrs Esther Owen-Flint' presented program of dramatic and dialect recitations at Grand Opera House.

25 May 1882, Toronto: 'Art Decoration,' first of Oscar Wilde's lectures at the Grand Opera House

7 October 1882, Toronto: Jay Kayelle's *Marmion*, satire on removal of immoral books from grammar schools, printed in *Grip*.

November 1882, Toronto: Anonymous parody of Shakespeare scenes appeared in *Acta Victoriana*.

1882, Toronto: *The Sweet Girl Graduate* by Sarah Anne Curzon, attacking discrimination against women at the University of Toronto, printed in *Grip-Sack*.

1882, Rat Portage (Kenora): Building of Gore's Hall; destroyed by fire in 1885.

1882, Toronto: *Mrs. Tactician's Triumph* by C.P.M. (pseud.) printed in *Grip-Sack* as 'tragedy of love and tobacco.'

1882, Toronto: C.F. Newcomb and J.M. Hanks's plays, *The Fireworshippers* and *Dermot McMurrough*, published.

1882, Toronto: *Socrates and Xantippe* printed anonymously in *Grip-Sack*.

1882: Ida Van Cortland and Albert Tavernier (Taverner) formed touring company. Over the years, Ida Van Cortland became one of country's leading performers as she toured throughout Canada and United States.

22 January 1883, Toronto: J.W. Bengough in his new lecture, *Caricature, The Funny Art*, at Royal Opera House

13 February 1883, Toronto: First Canadian appearance of Quebec-born Mme Albani (Emma Lajeunesse)

11 June 1883, Toronto: Opening of Harry Piper's Zoological Garden Theatre

9 August 1883, Toronto: Performance of *The Long Strike* at Zoological Gardens in benefit of Toronto telegraphers on strike

10 September 1883, Toronto: George Holman opened refurbished Adelaide Street Skating Rink as Holman Opera House.

28 November 1883, Toronto: Opening of Royal Museum (a 'dime museum'), later re-named Theatre Royal and People's Theatre.

1883, Belleville: Opening of Carmen's Opera House; eventually renamed Griffin; stood until 1933

1883, Toronto: J.W. Bengough's *Bunthorne Abroad; or, the Lass That Loved a Pirate* published; this parody using Gilbert and Sullivan's hero later performed in Hamilton (1886).

7–9 February 1884, Toronto: Performances at Grand Opera House of William McDonnell's *Marina, The Fisherman's Daughter*, operatic romance published in 1883 in Toronto.

16 February 1884, Toronto: *Labour and Capital*, 'conversation of the times' in which two Irish labourers discuss government grants and building of the railway, appeared in *Grip*.

21 February 1884, Toronto: Henry Irving and Ellen Terry gave first performances in Ontario.

28 April 1884, Toronto: Mme Helena Modjeska appeared at Grand Opera House.

23 June 1884, Toronto: George Holman opened the Theatre Royal.

5 July 1884, Toronto: *The Baron Bold and the Beauteous Maid*, 'old time melodrama' by Titus A. Drum (pseud.) parodying melodramatic theatre, printed in *Grip*.

Belleville, Carmen's Opera House, opened 1883

25 August 1884, Toronto: Opening of Mackie's Summer Theatre at
Hanlan's Point

December 1884, Toronto: Dion Boucicault's first performances in Toronto
(Grand Opera House)

22 December 1884, Toronto: Performance of W.H. Fuller's *Off to Egypt* at
Grand Opera House

1884, London: Opening of the Queen's Avenue Opera House

1884, Ottawa: F.A. Dixon's comic opera *Pipandor*, with music by S.F.
Harrison, published.

1884, Toronto: Elizabeth Jane (Sweetland) Thompson's *A Double Life*
published.

1884, Warkworth: Opening of Percy Township Hall containing balcony and
proscenium stage

12 January 1885, Toronto: *For Queen and Country*, by Torontonian John
A. Fraser, Jr, under his and Charlotte Morrison's direction, performed as
annual theatrical of the Queen's Own Rifles at Grand Opera House.

14 February 1885, Toronto: *The Tuggers and the Toll Gate* by Titus A.
Drum (pseud.), in which protesting farmers destroyed toll gate, printed
in *Grip*.

12 March 1885, Toronto: John A. Fraser, Jr's *For Queen and Country*
repeated at Grand Opera House.

26 March 1885, Hamilton: Julia Arthur made professional debut at Grand
Opera House.

9 May 1885, Toronto: Anonymous *Following Up a Clue*, a 'detectivish
reportorial operetta,' printed in *Grip*.

23 May 1885, Toronto: *Such Is Life* by Titus A. Drum (pseud.) appeared in
Grip.

26 June 1885, Toronto: *Ambition; or, Be Sure You Are Off With the Old
Hall Before You Are On With the New* by J.W.S. (pseud.), satirizing
decision to build new City Hall in Hamilton, appeared in *Grip*.

1 July 1885, Toronto: *Muddled* by John A. Fraser, Jr, staged at Grand
Opera House under patronage of Lieutenant-Governor and Mrs
Robinson.

15 September 1885, St Thomas: Death of Jumbo the elephant in train
accident

17 October 1885, Toronto: *The Mind Cure* by Titus A. Drum (pseud.)
appeared in *Grip*.

31 December 1885, London: *Louis Riel, or The Northwest Rebellion*
performed. May have been Clay Greene's play which was on tour and
appeared in Montreal and Toronto at the time.

5 January 1886, Toronto: Opening of Greene's *Louis Riel* at Grand Opera
House

30 August 1886, Toronto: Opening of Toronto Opera House; remained until destroyed by fire on 28 March 1903.

August 1886, Hamilton: J.W. Bengough's *Bunthorne Abroad; or, the Lass That Loved a Pirate* performed by Templeton Star Opera Company.

11 December 1886, Toronto: *Before and Behind the Curtain*, a 'political farce' concerning workers' and universal suffrage, by Titus A. Drum (pseud.), printed in *Grip*.

18 December 1886, Toronto: Anonymous farce, *The Popish Plot*, concerning religious interference in Ontario schools, printed in *Grip*.

1886, Toronto: Toronto Theatrical Mechanics' Benevolent Association founded.

1886, Toronto: *Chaos* (revised version) by Andrew Ramsay printed in *Muriel the Foundling, and Other Original Poems*.

23 February 1887, Toronto: Toronto Theatrical Mechanics' Benevolent Association held first annual social.

4 April 1887: *The Golden Giant* by McKee Rankin (and American Clay Greene) received première in New York.

1887, Cannington: Opening of Town Hall containing second-storey auditorium with balcony, proscenium, and stage

1887, Toronto: Sarah Anne Curzon's *Laura Secord, the Heroine of 1812*, containing also a reprint of *The Sweet Girl Graduate*, published.

1887, Toronto: Opening of Cyclorama Building at Front and York streets

1887, Toronto: Charles Mair's *Tecumseh* published; also appeared in a London, England, imprint in 1887.

March 1888, Toronto: *Local*, a short, anonymous, dramatic satire printed in *Acta Victoriana*.

1888, St Catharines: Opening of Opera House

3 January 1889, Petrolia: Opening of Victoria Hall

11 July 1889, Kingston: The military operetta *Leo, the Royal Cadet*, by George Frederick Cameron with music by Oscar Telgmann, given its first performance at Martin's Opera House; subsequently taken on national tour. Text also published in Kingston in 1889.

6 November 1889, Toronto: Opening of second Academy of Music; later known as the Princess and destroyed by fire in 1915

1889, St Catharines: Publication of James W. Keating's *The Shrievalty of Lynden*, which dramatizes incompetence and corruption around an innocent man about to be hanged.

1889, Kingston: Publication of Heinrich B. Telgmann's stock melodrama, *Against the World; or, Life in London*

1889, Toronto: Opening of Majestic Theatre, formerly Jacob and Sparrow's Theatre, refurbished by Small and Stair

188?, Hamilton: Publication of *Nina, or A Christmas in the Mediterranean*, a 'nautical comic operetta written for the Harmonic Club' by Thomas Herbert Chesnut

188?, Brockville: Publication of a Gilbert and Sullivan style operetta, *A Modern Romeo and Juliet*, 'Written for the Prescott Dramatic Club' by Ernest G. Longley

22 October 1890, Kingston: Performance by McKee Rankin of *The Canuck*, a play shaped around Jean Baptiste Cadeaux, a character McKee's brother George claimed to have invented. George, who wrote a novel, *Border Canucks*, and a play, *L'Habitant*, eventually sued McKee for $10,000 over this matter.

6 December 1890, Toronto: Opening of Robinson's Musee Theatre, a dime museum; later operated under variety of names: Moore's Musee Theatre, Crystal Theatre and Eden Musee, Bijou Theatre.

1890, Rat Portage (Kenora): Opening of Jacob Hose's Music Hall

1890, Wingham: Opening of Town Hall with assembly room and proscenium stage

1890?, Coldwater: Opening of Abbott's Hall

February 1891: Marie Tempest gave first Ontario performances.

13 May 1891, Kingston: Performance of McKee Rankin's *The Runaway Wife*

1891, Toronto: Publication of *The Capture of Detroit, 1812*, act IV of Charles Mair's *Tecumseh* in *Raise the Flag and Other Patriotic Canadian Songs and Poems*

4 June 1892, Toronto: Roly Rowan's (pseud.) satirical sketch of a women's suffrage meeting, *Woman Suffrage*, printed in *Grip*.

6 September 1892, Hamilton: Grand Opera House enlarged and refurbished.

June 1892, Goderich: Records indicate Grand Opera House and Temperance Hall in use for stage performances (no opening dates for these buildings located so far).

Fall 1892, Toronto: Principal Harold Nelson (Shaw) began to develop School of Elocution at Conservatory of Music into school of theatre arts.

28 December 1892, Fort William: Announcement concerning Town Hall (opening in early 1893?)

30? December 1892, Lindsay: Opening of Academy of Music

1892, Kingston: Performance of C.K. Dean's *Castles in the Air* by Harry Lindley and company

1892, Ottawa: *A Mad Philosopher* by John Henry Brown published in his *Poems: Lyrical and Dramatic*.

1892, St Marys: Opening of Town Hall with assembly room and proscenium stage

15, 16 December 1893, Galt: performance of Jean Newton McIlwraith's *The Days of the Year, or the Masque of the Months* at Town Hall

Rat Portage Dramatic Club.

Monday Evening December 30th. 1889.

With New Scenery and Accessories

TOM TAYLOR'S COMEDY

Founded on Charles de Bernard's novel of Le Gendre.

"Still Waters Run Deep."

⇒ CASTE. ⇐

Mr. Potter...............................	Mr. Jas. Robinson.
Capt. Hawksley..........................	Mr. Geo. Ross.
John Mildmay...................	Mr. Geo. Mitchell.
Dunbilk....................................	Mr. John Brown.
Markham......	Mr. A. Dunham
Langford...................	Mr. R. Morgan
Gimlet.....................	Mr. R. Hobbs
Jessop....	Mr. O. Anderson.
Mrs. Mildmay	Miss F. Henesy.
Mrs. Sternhold	Miss A. Cockrell.

Servants, Guests. Etc.

Orchestra under the direction of Mr. E. D. Maluish.

Admission, 25 Cents·

Reserved Seats 50 Cents at Campbell's Bookstore until 7 o'clock, p. m. Dec. 30th.

Doors open 7.30.   Curtain Rises 8.15 Sharp.

Rat Portage (Kenora) Dramatic Club, newspaper advertisement, 1889

1893, Embro: Opening of Embro Town Hall containing second-storey assembly room with balcony and proscenium stage

1893, Peterborough: Publication of Harry Lindley's melodrama *Chick, or Myrtle Ferns*

1893, Toronto: Mr Daniels opened the Auditorium in Shaftsbury Hall as a variety theatre.

29 May 1894, Toronto: Birth of Beatrice Lillie (Lady Robert Peel), who became well-known and admired actress throughout North America and Britain

5 November 1894, Guelph: Opening of Royal Opera House

1 December 1894, Toronto: First section of J.W. Bengough's 'farcical tragedy,' *The Edison Doll*, appeared in *Grip*; remaining parts published in succeeding four issues.

15 February 1895, Hamilton: First performances of *Ptarmigan; or, A Canadian Carnival*, Jean Newton McIlwraith's comic operetta, at Grand Opera House; music by noted local musician John E.P. Aldous; also published in 1895

Fall 1895: Julia Stuart brought her production of Ibsen's *A Doll's House* to Ontario, performing in a number of centres, including Ottawa, Brockville, Peterborough, Toronto (28 October), Guelph, Berlin (Kitchener), and Brantford. Mrs Minnie Maddern Fiske brought her production to Toronto on 21 February 1896.

26 November 1895, Orillia: Opening of Town Hall with second-storey opera house; heavily damaged by fire in 1915 but rebuilt over 1916–17

1895, Pickering: Publication of William E. Anderson's *A Roman Drama in Five Acts Entitled Leo and Venetia*

1895, Ottawa: Publication of William W. Campbell's plays *Mordred* and *Hildebrand*

1895, Rat Portage (Kenora): Opening of Louis Hilliard's Opera House and Hotel; badly damaged by fire on 19 May 1898; reopened in November 1898; became Joe Derry's Palace Theatre in 1914; destroyed by fire and rebuilt in 1924

30 August 1896, Toronto: Birth of Raymond Massey, whose distinguished acting career included a role as Abraham Lincoln with which he is invariably associated

31 August 1896, Toronto: Edison's Vitascope at Robinson's Musee Theatre makes first public showing of a film in Toronto.

8 September 1896, Berlin (Kitchener): Opening of the Berlin Opera House

1896, Toronto: Publication of William and Louisa Schubart's *Ludwig, the Emigrant*

1896, Kent Bridge: Publication of Edward Worth's burlesque of secret societies, *Worth's Burlesque Ritual*

1896: Ida Van Cortland retired from stage

19 March 1897, Kingston: Performance of McKee Rankin's *True to Life*

15 October 1897, Ottawa: Opening of the Russell Theatre; burned in 1901, rebuilt, then torn down in 1928

December 1897, Carleton Place: Opening of Town Hall containing second-storey assembly room with 250-seat balcony and proscenium stage

1897, Hastings: Opening of the Town Hall containing assembly room with balcony and proscenium stage

1897, Toronto: Under Ambrose J. Small's management, Robert Cummings formed first stock company to be established in Toronto in approximately twenty years.

1897, Walkerton: Opening of Town Hall containing Victoria Jubilee Hall, a second-storey theatre with large proscenium stage, fixed seating, and balcony on three walls

1897, Ottawa: Publication of William W. Campbell's poetic drama *Morning*

1897, Toronto: Publication of Catharine Nina Merritt's Loyalist history drama, *When George the Third Was King*

May 1898, Toronto: Publication of A.E. McFarlane's *The Beginning of the Scandal* in *Acta Victoriana*

23 May 1898, Hamilton: Thomas W. Keene taken ill on stage and died shortly after.

14 November 1898, Kenora (Rat Portage): Opening of rebuilt Hilliard's Opera House with performance by Harold Nelson (Shaw) and his company

21 November 1898, Toronto: Opening of Empire Theatre in what was formerly Temperance Hall

1898, Ottawa: Publication of F.A. Dixon's *The Episode of the Quarrel Between Titania and Oberon from Shakespeare's A Midsummer Night's Dream* with the text 'specially arranged for representation with the Mendelssohn music'

1898, Toronto: Publication of James B. MacKenzie's drama, *Thayendanegea*, concerning the heroism of Joseph Brant, war-chief of the Six Nations Indians

5 January 1899, Galt: Opening of Scott's Opera House

22 February 1899, Toronto: Public debate at Toronto Methodist church on 'Ethical Basis of the Current Drama'

4 September 1899, Toronto: Opening of Shea's Yonge Street Theatre

6 December 1899, Toronto: Stage presentation of New Brunswicker John Louis Carleton's 'Irish character' melodrama, *More Sinned Against Than Sinning*, at St Michael's College; published in New York and Chicago in 1883; received a number of productions throughout Canada and United States

Berlin (Kitchener), Opera House under the name Star Theatre, c. 1915

Carleton Place, 'Cake Walk' cast, the Kermess, c. 1902

1899, Perth: Nelson's Opera House in operation (no opening date yet located)

1899, Toronto: Publication of *The Battle of the Little Big Horn* and *Millions for Her*, two rhymed-verse melodramas by J. Duff Henderson, in his *Alvira Alias Orea*

1899, Toronto: Publication of Agnes Maule Machar's *The Winged Victory* in her *Lays of the True North*; also published in 1899 in London, England, and reprinted in Toronto 1902

29 January 1900, Stratford: Opening of new Stratford City Hall containing 800-seat auditorium with balcony and proscenium stage

5 March 1900, Toronto: Performance of Montreal playwright W.A. Tremayne's *The Dagger and the Cross*, starring Robert Bruce Mantell, at Royal Opera House

March 1900, London: Performance of Hal Newton Carlyle's *For Canada and Empire* at Grand Opera House

25 August 1900, Sault Ste Marie: First performance of L.O. Armstrong's *Hiawatha or Manabozho; An Ojibway Indian Play* at Garden River

Reserve. Descriptive notes and excerpts 'to be used as a libretto' published in 1900 in Boston and 1901 in Montreal.

1900, Toronto: Publication of *David and Abigail* by Archibald Lampman in *The Poems of Archibald Lampman*

4 January 1901, Stratford: Opening of Theatre Albert, now Avon Theatre operated by the Stratford Festival

12 March 1901, Gravenhurst: Opening of Opera House on second storey of Town Hall; now used as theatre by Muskoka Summer Festival

9 September 1901, London: Opening of new Grand Opera House

1901, Hamilton: Publication of Thomas W. Hand's *The Siege of Tientsin, and the Destruction of the Boxers' Stronghold by the Allied Forces*

1901, Toronto: Publication of Ernest Thompson Seton's *The Wild Animal Play for Children*, published in New York in 1900

14 January 1902, Kingston: Opening of Grand Opera House replacing Martin's Opera House, which had burned in 1898

10–12 March 1902, Toronto: Performances of *Paardeberg* by Royal Grenadiers, directed by 'H.N. Shaw' (otherwise known by stage name Harold Nelson) at Princess Theatre

24 May 1902, Hamilton: George Summers, formerly head of Summers Stock Company, opened Summers Mountain Playhouse; continued in seasonal operation until destroyed by fire on 21 December 1914.

February 1903, Toronto: Mrs Patrick Campbell brought *The Second Mrs Tanqueray* to Princess Theatre, a production that aroused moralists in the city.

10, 11 June 1903, Toronto: Ben Greet and his famous company of English Players presented *As You Like It* and *The Comedy of Errors* in the residence garden of University of Toronto; the first of several influential visits.

3 September 1903, Drayton: Opening of Drayton Town Hall containing second-storey auditorium with balcony and proscenium stage

September 1903: Edith Baker toured number of Ontario centres, including London, Berlin (Kitchener), Guelph, Chatham, Woodstock, Barrie, and Lindsay, with her production of Ibsen's *Ghosts*.

2 November 1903, Toronto: Opening of Majestic Theatre

1903, Bowmanville: Opening of Bowmanville Town Hall containing 500-seat theatre with balcony and proscenium stage

1903, Toronto: Publication of Arthur Stringer's *Sappho in Leucadia* in his *Hephaestus, Persephone at Etna and Sappho in Leucadia*; also published in 1903 in London, England

June 1904, London: Ben Greet presented outdoor productions of *As You Like It* and *A Midsummer Night's Dream* at University of Western Ontario.

George Summers as Rip Van Winkle

1904, London: C.W. Bennett opened London's first 'high class vaudeville' in Mechanics' Institute.

1904, Toronto: Ben Greet presented his *Shakespearean Pastorals* in the Dean's Gardens at the University of Toronto.

1904, Toronto: Devastating fire in heart of city brought about subsequent major changes in fire safety regulations in theatres.

1904, Toronto: Birth of Lois Landon, who began her stage career as an interpretive dancer and singer in 1919, went on to star with Vaughan Glaser Players, and married Glaser in 1927

1904, Ottawa: Publication of Francis Grey's *Sixteen-Ninety*, 'A Series of Historical Tableaux'

August 1905, Owen Sound: Harold Nelson (Shaw) presented *Faust*.

1905, Dundalk: Opening of Municipal Offices and Assembly Hall

March 1906, Toronto: Opening of Theatorium, first permanent movie house in Ontario. John Griffin, its owner, and son Peter opened five more 'nickelodeons' in Toronto within a year as the beginning of their large chain.

2–5 May 1906, Ottawa: Performance of W.A. Tremayne's *The Triumph of Betty* (co-written with Irving Hall) at Russell Theatre

May 1906: Ambrose J. Small elected president of Canadian Theatre Managers' Association

3 September 1906, Toronto: Incorporation of Margaret Eaton School of Literature and Expression, which began in 1901 and continued under different names to 1941

October 1906 – Feb 1907: C.W. Bennett opened theatres in London, Ottawa, Hamilton, and Montreal as the beginning of his Canadian Vaudeville Circuit.

1906, Peterborough: Opening of Rupert Bradburn's Grand Opera House

1906, Port Dover: Opening of Port Dover Town Hall containing on second and third floors a theatre with balcony and proscenium stage

1906, Sunderland: Opening of Brock Township Hall containing second-storey auditorium with balcony and proscenium stage

28 January – 2 February 1907, Ottawa: First of Governor-General Earl Grey's annual dramatic competitions (until 1911) held at Russell Theatre.

31 January 1907, Gananoque: Fire destroys Turner's Opera House; no date for construction found so far, but in operation as early as 1891.

18 February 1907, Toronto: Johnston Forbes-Robertson starred in Shaw's *Caesar and Cleopatra* at Princess Theatre.

April 1907, Toronto: Publication of C.N. and A.M. Williamson's *Motors That Pass in the Night* in *Canadian Magazine*

9 May 1907, Toronto: First of four performances of J.W. Bengough's *The*

Belle (Isabella May) Stevenson, Mrs George Summers and leading lady of his company

Breach of Promise Trial Bardwell vs Pickwick by Dickens Fellowship Company of Players. Subsequent performances occurred on 10, 15, and 28 May; script published in Toronto in 1907.

27 May 1907, Toronto: Herbert Kelcey and Effie Shannon starred in Shaw's *Widower's Houses*, five months before its first public performance in England. (It had been presented privately in 1892 at J.T. Grein's Independent Theatre.)

19 August 1907, Toronto: Opening of F.W. Stair's new Star Theatre (replacing old Star Theatre)

26 August 1907, Toronto: Opening of Royal Alexandra Theatre

9 December 1907, Toronto: Opening of Gayety Theatre

December 1907, Toronto: Publication of Charles Gordon Rodgers's *Out of the Past* in *Canadian Magazine*

1907, Owen Sound: Opening of Wonderland Theatre (vaudeville and movies)

1907, Ottawa: Publication of James E. Caldwell's *The Yellow Bag*

1907, Ottawa: Publication of F.G. Scott's *The Key of Life*; also published in Quebec in 1907.

February–March 1908: Jane Corcoran presented Ibsen's *Hedda Gabler* and *A Doll's House*, as well as lectures about Ibsen by Sarah Dunbar on tour of Ontario centres.

1908, Toronto: Opening of Arts and Letters Club

1908, Meaford: Opening of Meaford Town Hall and Opera House

1908, Toronto: Publication of William W. Campbell's *Poetical Tragedies*

1908, Toronto: Publication of J.M. Harper's *Champlain; A Drama in Three Acts*; also published in Quebec and went into three editions and had a 1909 American printing.

1908: Mme Alla Nazimova's first tour of Canada; visited Ontario centres.

April 1909, Toronto: Publication of A.R. Carman's *Easter Week at Rome* in *Canadian Magazine*

19 December 1909, Niagara Falls: Performance of Emma Seymour Carter's *Final Rehearsal* by Anglican Club

1 March 1910, Toronto: Mme Alla Nazimova starred in Ibsen's *A Doll's House* at Princess Theatre.

6 April 1910, Toronto: Performance of Catharine Nina Merritt's *A Little Leaven* at Royal Alexandra Theatre in annual Earl Grey competition. Dora Mavor (Moore) praised by adjudicator Hector Charlesworth in otherwise undistinguished show.

July–October 1910, Toronto: Publication of Arthur Stringer's *The Blot* in *Canadian Magazine*

Summer 1910, Niagara-on-the-Lake: Records show existence of Park Theatre, apparently a large tent

Ottawa, Family Theatre, 1910 (used briefly by Ottawa Little Theatre)

1 August 1910, Toronto: Opening of Shea's Victoria Street Theatre

10 December 1910, Toronto: First theatrical entertainment by Arts and Letters Club; directed by Roy Mitchell

December 1910 – March 1911, Toronto: Publication of Arthur Stringer's *The Firebrand* in *Canada Monthly*

1910: Maude Adams, famous in J.M. Barrie's *The Little Minister* and as Peter Pan, performed in number of Ontario centres.

1910, Ottawa: Dora Mavor Moore, first Canadian to attend England's (Royal) Academy of Dramatic Art, returned to Canada and joined stock company in this city.

February 1911, Hamilton: Anonymous *Val and Tyne* printed in *McMaster University Monthly*.

24 May 1911, Hamilton: Performance of George Summers's *The Man from Ottawa* at Summers Mountain Theatre

18 September 1911, Brockville: Opening of the 'New Theatre'

1911, Beaverton: Opening of Beaverton Town Hall containing auditorium with proscenium stage

1911, Omemee: Opening of Coronation Hall containing auditorium on its upper floor with balcony and proscenium stage

February–April, 1912, Toronto: Publication of Arthur Stringer's *The House of Oedipus* in *Canadian Magazine*

19 August 1912, Toronto: Shea's presented Thomas Edison's Kinetophone, first showing of talking-moving pictures in Toronto.

1912, Bethany: Opening of Manvers Township Hall with stage and proscenium arch

1912, Ottawa: Publication of Clara Anderson's *A Character Sketch Entertainment, Entitled Afternoon Tea in Friendly Village* and *An Old Time Ladies' Aid Business Meeting at Mohawk Crossroads*

11 April 1913, Hamilton: Performance at the Grand Opera House of *The Vermont Wood Dealer's Visit to Hamilton*, an 'original farce'

20 May 1913, Toronto: Performance of *Deborah* at Princess Theatre, which became focus of court proceedings over charges of indecency on the stage

15 November 1913, Ottawa: Formation of Ottawa Drama League (later Ottawa Little Theatre)

15 December 1913, Toronto: Opening of Loew's Yonge Street Theatre (downstairs), part of complex which soon also held Winter Garden

1913, Ottawa: Publication of Clara Anderson's *The Minister's Bride*

1913, Toronto: Publication of Stephen Leacock's *Behind the Beyond* in *Behind the Beyond and Other Contributions to Human Knowledge*, also published in London, England, in 1913

1913, Toronto: Formation of University of Toronto Players Club

1913–14: Formation of the British Canadian Theatrical Organization Society brought three British companies, John Martin-Harvey, Laurence Irving, and Eva Moore / Henry Esmond, to tour Canada as antidote to Americanization of Canadian stage.

16 February 1914, Toronto: Opening of Loew's Winter Garden Theatre, above the Yonge Street Theatre

1 April 1914, Ottawa: Performance of anonymous *Biblical Drama Esther* in oriental costumes at Russell Theatre

20 April 1914, Toronto: Visit by Abbey Theatre during which Toronto censorship board refused permission for their production of Shaw's *The Shewing Up of Blanco Posnet*

27 April 1914, Toronto: Opening of Shea's Hippodrome

1914: Sir John Martin-Harvey made first Canadian tour, starring with own company; includes many Ontario centres.

1914, Hamilton: Performance of James Forbes's *The Chorus Lady* by Temple Stock Company

1914, Toronto: Publication of J.E. Middleton's *Pilgrims and Strangers*

1914: New 'Doctrine and Discipline of the Methodist Church of Canada' relaxed Church's strict rules forbidding attendance at theatre.

Select Bibliography

RICHARD PLANT

Locations and Collections

Researchers will find a very large body of published and unpublished materials related to early Ontario theatre. A thorough study by Heather McCallum which also covers resources available for the twentieth century will be part of the second volume of *Early Stages*. The following selected list is designed to draw attention to particularly important reference works, articles, books, and theses useful for the period up to the First World War. Each is important in itself; together they serve as a guide to the types of resources available. The wide range of materials, such as playbills, manuscripts, business records, conventional publications, and the not-so-conventional, three-dimensional performance artefacts, exists in an equally wide range of places. Government repositories, in particular the National Archives of Canada, the National Library, and the Ontario Archives, have sizeable collections. Among the holdings of the Ontario Archives are extensive photographic records, the Horwood Architectural Drawings, and microfilm or microfiche copies of almost all existing Ontario newspapers. Municipalities, cities, towns, and villages normally have archives or less formal aggregations of valuable documents. Local or regional history museums represent another source, as do public libraries at these same levels. Two libraries, especially, should be cited: the Fine Arts section of the Metropolitan Toronto Library houses the largest theatre collection; Hamilton Central Library has special holdings on the Hamilton-Wentworth area. Universities also have significant resources: library collections and archives often with a regional focus. Outside Canada, several major repositories contain materials related to early Ontario theatre history. In the United States, important resources exist at the Billy Rose Theatre Collection of the New York Public Library, the Theatre Collection of the Museum of the City of New York, as well as Harvard and Brown universities. In England, the Theatre Museum at Covent Garden (part of the Victoria and Albert Museum) and the British Library have extensive holdings. This is to say nothing of the collections held by private individuals within and outside Ontario.

Bibliographies

Ball, John and Richard Plant, eds. *A Bibliography of Canadian Theatre History, 1583–1975.* Toronto: Playwrights Co-op 1976
– *A Bibliography of Canadian Theatre History: Supplement, 1975–76.* Toronto: Playwrights Press 1979
McCallum, Heather. Research Collections in Canadian Libraries: Vol II, *Special Studies*; Vol. I: *Theatre Resources in Canadian Collections.* Ottawa: National Library of Canada 1973
Wagner, Anton, ed. *The Brock Bibliography of Published Canadian Stage Plays in English, 1766–1978.* Toronto: Playwrights Press 1980

General

Armstrong, Frederick, H.A. Stevenson, and J.D. Wilson, eds. *Aspects of Nineteenth-Century Ontario.* Toronto: University of Toronto Press 1974
Aylmer Centennial History, 1862–1972. Aylmer: Rotary Club of Aylmer 1972
Baillie, Joan Parkhill. *Look at the Record.* Oakville: Mosaic Press 1985
Bonnycastle, Sir Richard. *The Canadas in 1841.* New York: Johnson Reprint 1968
Bumsted, J.M., ed. *Canadian History before Confederation.* Georgetown: Irwin-Dorsey 1979
Calvin, D.D. *A Saga of the St Lawrence.* Toronto: Ryerson 1945
Carter-Edwards, Dennis. *Garrison Life: The 89th Regiment at Fort Malden, 1841–1842.* Ottawa: Parks Canada, n.d.
Champion, Thomas Edward. *The Methodist Churches of Toronto.* Toronto: Rose 1899
City of Toronto Central Records and Archives. *Princess Theatre, Toronto* and *Shea's Hippodrome.* n.d.
Conant, Thomas. *Upper Canada Sketches.* Toronto: William Briggs 1898
Croft, Melba Morris. *Fourth Entrance to Huronia* (The History of Owen Sound). Owen Sound: Stan Brown 1980
Descriptive Catalogue of the Provincial Exhibition at Toronto, Sept. 1858. 2nd ed. Toronto 1858
Drayton. *Plan of Drayton Opera House.* Drayton. n.d.
– *Specification of Labor and Material Required in the Erection and Completion of a Two-Storey Brick Town Hall for the Town of Drayton.* Drayton 1902

Dufferin and Ava, Marchioness of. *My Canadian Journal, 1872–8*. London, England: John Murray 1891

Firth, Edith, ed. *The Town of York, 1793–1815*. Toronto: Champlain Society 1962

– *The Town of York, 1815–1834*. Toronto: Champlain Society 1966

Glazebrook, George P. de T. *Life in Ontario: A Social History*. Toronto: University of Toronto Press 1968

Gourlay, Robert. *A Statistical Account of Upper Canada*. London, England: Simpken and Marshall 1822

Guillet, Edwin Clarence. *Early Life in Upper Canada*. Toronto: Ontario Publishing, 1933. Reprint: Toronto: University of Toronto Press 1963

Henry, Walter. *Events in a Military Life*. London, England. 1843

Hubbard, Robert. *Rideau Hall*. Montreal: McGill-Queen's University Press 1977

London, University of Western Ontario, Weldon Library Regional Collection. *Durand Drawings*. London: Masonic Temple, n.d.

Lysons, General Sir Daniel. *Early Reminiscences*. London, England: John Murray 1896

Martyn, Lucy Booth. *The Face of Early Toronto: An Archival Record 1797–1936*. Toronto: Paget 1982

– *A View of Original Toronto, the Fabric of York circa 1834*. Toronto: Paget 1983

Masters, Donald Campbell. *The Rise of Toronto, 1850–1890*. Toronto: University of Toronto Press 1947

Matthews, H. *Oakville and the Sixteen: The History of an Ontario Port*. Toronto: University of Toronto Press 1953

Meaford. *Specification of the Material and Labour to be Used in the Construction of Town Hall, Meaford, Ont.*, According to Plans and Details Prepared by Ellis and Connery, Architects, Toronto, 7 July 1908

Morgan, Henry James. *Canadian Life in Town and Country*. London, England: George Newnes 1905

– *Canadian Men and Women of the Time*. Toronto: Briggs 1898

Mulvany, C. Pelham. 'Social Life in Toronto.' In *Toronto: Past and Present; A Handbook of the City*. Toronto: Caiger 1884. Reprint: Toronto: Reprint Press 1970

Ottawa: *Souvenir of Plays at Government House, Ottawa*. Ottawa: Durie 1878

Ontario Archives, Toronto. Gordon & Helliwell Architectural Drawings, n.d.; Horwood Architectural Drawings (1203) 1–5, 1916; Wm Kingsford Papers, Mu 1628; Penson Memoirs, Mu 2314; Theatre Plan Files, Series C-3, App F.

Paddon, Wayne, et al. *St Thomas: 100 Years a City 1881–1981*. St Thomas: Centennial Committee 1981

Petrolia. *Almanac and Directory*. Petrolia *Advertiser* 1888

Phelps, Edward. *Petrolia 1874–1974*. Petrolia: Petrolia Print and Litho Ltd 1974

Preston, Richard, ed. *Kingston before the War of 1812*. Toronto: Champlain Society 1959

Priddis, Harriet. 'Reminiscences of Mrs Gilbert Porte.' *London and Middlesex Historical Society Transactions, 1911–1912*, 4 (1913), 66–9

Robertson, John Ross. *Robertson's Landmarks of Toronto: A Collection of Historical Sketches*, First Series. Toronto: Robertson 1894

Rochefoucauld-Liancourt, Duc de la. *Travels through the United States of North America, the Country of the Iroquois and Upper Canada in the Years 1795, 1796 and 1797*, vol. 1. London: Phillips 1799

Scadding, Henry. *Toronto of Old*. Toronto: Adam, Stevenson & Co. 1873

Speisman, Stephen A. *The Jews of Toronto: A History to 1937*. Toronto: McClelland and Stewart 1979

Spurr, John W. 'The Kingston Garrison, 1815–1870.' *Historic Kingston* 20 (February 1972), 14–34

Taylor, Conyngham Crawford. *Toronto 'Called Back' from 1897 to 1847*. Toronto: Briggs 1897

Toronto, Metropolitan Toronto Public Library, Baldwin Room. *John Howard Drawings, Royal Lyceum Theatre*. ca 1849

Toronto, partial set of *John M. Lyle Drawings for Royal Alexandra Theatre*; some dated 1906. Located at offices of Allward and Gouinlock, Architects, Toronto

Tulchinsky, G., ed. *To Preserve and Defend: Essays on Kingston in the Nineteenth Century*. Montreal 1976

Walker, Frank Norman. *Sketches of Old Toronto*. Toronto: Longmans, 1965

West, Bruce. *Toronto*. Toronto: Doubleday 1967

Whitfield, Carol M. *Tommy Atkins: The British Soldier in Canada*. Ottawa: Parks Canada 1981

Wilson, L.W., et al. *Early St Marys: A History in Old Photographs From Its Founding to 1914*. Erin: Boston Mills 1981

Wingfield, Alexander. *The Hamilton Centennial, 1846–1946*. Hamilton: Centennial Committee 1946

Young, James. *Reminiscences of the Early History of Galt and the Settlement of Dumfries*. Toronto: Hunter Rose 1880.

Books and Articles on the Theatre

'The Academy Theatre, Lindsay.' Paper for Local Architectural Conservancy Committee (LACAC), n.d.

Angus, William. 'A Spirited Military Opera of 1889.' *Historic Kingston* 25 (March 1977), 37–44

Arrell, Douglas. 'Harold Nelson: The Early Years (c. 1865–1905).' *Theatre History of Canada / Histoire du théâtre au Canada* 1:2 (Fall 1980), 83–110

Baillie, Joan Parkhill. 'Looking for a Home: Having Survived in Toronto Since

1825, Opera Deserves a Suitable House.' *Opera Canada* 25 (Winter 1984), 15–19, 44

Bains, Y.S. 'Theatre and Society in Early Nineteenth-Century Toronto.' *Nineteenth Century Theatre Research* 3:2 (Autumn 1975), 83–95

Bossin, Hye. *Stars of David*. Toronto: *Jewish Standard* 1957

Brault, Lucien, 'Theatres.' In *Ottawa Old and New*. Ottawa: Historical Information Institute 1946

– 'Theatres.' In *Hull, 1800–1950*. Ottawa: Université d'Ottawa 1950

Brault, Lucien and John Leaning. *La Salle Academy: A Heritage Building in Black and White*. Ottawa: Ministry of State for Urban Affairs 1976

Brown, Mary M. 'Ambrose Small: A Ghost in Spite of Himself.' In L.W. Connolly, ed. *Theatrical Touring and Founding in North America*. Westport, Conn.: Greenwood Press 1982

– 'Pepper's Ghost is Tearing Its Hair: Ottawa Theatre in the 1870's.' *Theatre History in Canada / Histoire du théâtre au Canada*
4 (Fall 1983), 21–33

Brown, Mary M. and Natalie Rewa. 'Ottawa Calendar of Performance in the 1870's.' *Theatre History in Canada / Histoire du théâtre au Canada* 4 (Fall 1983), 134–91

Cahn, Julius. *Official Theatrical Guide*. New York: 1896 on. Title varies.

Campbell, Mrs William. 'Toronto Theatres in Old Days.' *Annual Report for the Year 1930*. Toronto: York Pioneer and Historical Society 1931

Charlesworth, Hector, *Candid Chronicles*. Toronto: Macmillan 1925

– *More Candid Chronicles*. Toronto: Macmillan 1928

Colgate, William. 'Toronto Theatres in the Eighties.' *Canadian Magazine* 57 (August 1921), 279–82

Conolly, Leonard W. 'The Man in the Green Goggles: Clergymen and Theatre Censorship (Toronto 1912–13).' *Theatre History in Canada / Histoire du théâtre au Canada* 1:2 (Fall 1980), 111–23

Crane, Howard C. 'New Princess Theatre.' *Construction* (February 1918), 63–7

Crisp, Freda. 'A Record of Music and Dance in Hamilton: 1845–1855.' Manuscript in possession of Freda Crisp

Edwards, Murray D. *A Stage in Our Past: English-Language Theatre in Eastern Canada from the 1790s to 1914*. Toronto: University of Toronto Press 1968

Fairfield, Robert Calvin. *Meaford Town Hall: Feasibility Report*. Meaford 1981

Fraser, Kathleen D.J. 'Theatre Management in the Nineteenth Century: Eugene A. McDowell in Canada, 1874–1891.' *Theatre History in Canada / Histoire du théâtre au Canada* 1 (Spring 1980), 39–54

Frazer, Robbin. 'Sixty Years of Memories: The Ottawa Little House.' *Performing Arts*. 10 (Summer 1973), 25

Fulks, Wayne. 'Albert Tavernier and the Guelph Opera House.' *Theatre History in Canada / Histoire du théâtre au Canada* 4 (Spring 1983), 41–56

Guillet, Edwin Clarence. 'Theatre.' In *Toronto from Trading Post to Great City.* Toronto: Ontario Publishing 1934

Ham, George H. *Reminiscences of a Raconteur Between the 40's and the 20's.* Toronto: Musson 1921

Hare, John and Ramon Hathorn.'Sarah Bernhardt's Visits to Canada: Dates and Repertory.' *Theatre History in Canada / Histoire du théâtre au Canada* 2 (Fall 1981), 93–116

Harrington, George M. 'Toronto and Its Early Theatrical Entertainments.' *Canadian Monthly* 8 (June 1882), 600–13

Hayter, Charles. 'Kingston in 1859: A Theatrical Perspective.' *Historic Kingston* 27 (January 1979), 26–41

Hector, John. 'Musical and Theatrical Reminiscences.' *Canadian Monthly and National Review* 8 (June 1882), 579–82

Hill and Borgal, Architects and Planners. 'Town Hall Clinton: A Plan for Restoration.' Goderich 1978

Hunter, Robert. 'Theatre Architecture in Canada: A Study of Pre-1920 Canadian Theatres.' Ottawa: Historic Sites and Monuments Board of Canada 1985

Kingston, Corporation of the City of. *Kingston City Hall.* 1974

Klinck, Carl F. 'Early Theatres in Waterloo County.' *Waterloo Historical Society, Thirty-ninth Annual Report* (May 1951), 14–17

Lennox, Lord William Pitt. *Plays, Players, and Playhouses at Home and Abroad,* vol. 2. London, England: Hurst and Blackett 1881

Lindsay, John C. *Turn Out the Lights before Leaving.* Erin: Boston Mills 1983

'Loews Yonge Street Theatre, Toronto.' *Construction* (April 1915), 133–43

Middleton, Jesse Edgar. 'Theatre.' In *Municipality of Toronto, a History.* Toronto: Dominion Publishing 1923

– 'Theatre.' In *Toronto's 100 Years.* Toronto: Toronto Centennial Committee 1934

Miller, Orlo. 'History of Theatre in London.' Manuscript, London, University of Western Ontario, Regional Archives, n.d.

– 'Old Opera Houses of Western Ontario.' *Opera Canada* (May 1964), 7–8

Nels, Juleus. 'Lady Dufferin's Amateur Theatricals.' *Canadian Drama / L'Art dramatique canadien* 11:1 (1985), 245–50

New, William H., ed. *Dramatists in Canada.* Vancouver: University of British Columbia Press 1972

O'Brien, Kevin. *Oscar Wilde in Canada.* Toronto: Personal Library 1982

O'Neill, Patrick B. 'Theatrical Activity at York (Toronto), 1793–1934.' *Canadian Speech Communications Journal* 6 (1974), 47–61

– 'Fiddle, Faddle and Foozle. The First Stage Production of a Canadian Play in Toronto.' *Canadian Drama / L'Art dramatique canadien* 3 (Spring 1977), 20–2

– 'A Note on Bains's Calendar of Theatrical Performances in Toronto, 1809–1828.' *Nineteenth Century Theatre Research* 5 (Autumn 1977), 115–17

– 'Reflections in a Cracked Mirror: Canadian Drama and World War I.' *Canadian Drama / L'Art dramatique canadien* 10:2 (1984), 207–17

Plant, Richard. 'The Toronto Lyceum: A Study of Early Canadian Theatre in Miniature.' *Nineteenth Century Theatre Research* 4:2 (Autumn 1976), 73–88

Reilly, P.F. and William R. Chadwick. *The Berlin Opera House 1896–1900.* Waterloo: University of Waterloo 1976

Rhys, Horton. *A Theatrical Trip for a Wager.* London: Charles Dudley (for the author), 1861. Reprint: Vancouver: Alcuin 1966; New York: Blom 1969

'Royal Alexandra Theatre.' *Construction* (November 1907), 37–43

Runtz, Ernest. 'Theatre Design and Construction.' In *The Stage Year Book.* London 1913

Russell, Hilary. *All That Glitters: A Memorial to Ottawa's Capitol Theatre and Its Predecessors.* Canadian Historic Sites: Occasional Papers in Archaeology and History, 13. Ottawa: National Historic Parks and Sites Branch, Parks Canada, Indian and Northern Affairs 1975

Russell, Matthew. 'The Stagestruck Queen on King Street.' *Mayfair* 28 (March 1954), 66, 68–9

Shortt, Mary. 'Homage to Toronto's Myth-Makers: Three Popular Traditions in Theatre History.' *Ontario History* 76 (September 1984), 255–72

– 'Touring Theatrical Families in Canada West: The Hills and the Herons.' *Ontario History* 74 (March 1982), 3–25

Spurr, John W. 'Theatre in Kingston, 1816–1870.' *Historic Kingston* 22 (March 1974), 37–55

Tait, Michael Strong. 'Playwrights in a Vacuum: English Canadian Drama in the Nineteenth Century.' *Canadian Literature* 16 (Spring 1963), 3–18. Reprinted in New, ed., *Dramatists in Canada*

'Theatricals at Rideau Hall.' *Canadian Monthly* 7 (April 1875), 374–5

The Toronto Theatres Season, 1904–05. Toronto: Murdock 1905

Thurston, Catharine. 'A Look at Early Toronto Theatre: 1860–1869.' *York Pioneer* 71 (Fall 1976), 22–6

Waldhauer, Erdmute. 'Martin's Opera House, Kingston: 1879–1898.' *Historic Kingston* 26 (March 1978), 29–37

– *Grand Theatre 1879–1979.* Kingston: Grand Theatre 1979

– 'The New Grand Opera House, 1902.' *Historic Kingston* 27 (March 1979), 42–52

Yeigh, Frank. 'Drama of Hiawatha or Mana-Bozho.' *Canadian Magazine* 17 (July 1901), 207–17

Theses

Aikens, James R. 'The Rival Operas: Toronto Theatre 1874–84.' PH D, University of Toronto 1975

Asher, Stanley. 'Play-Writing in Canada: A Historical Survey.' MA, University of Montreal 1962

Edwards, Murray Dallas. 'The English-Speaking Theatre in Canada 1820–1914.' PH D, Columbia University 1963

Filewod, Alan D. 'Melodrama and Patriotism: Charles Mair's Tecumseh.' MA, University of Alberta 1978

Fraser, Kathleen D.J. 'A History of the McDowell Theatre Company 1872–1893.' MA, University of Western Ontario 1978

– 'Theatrical Touring in Late Nineteenth-Century Canada: Ida Van Cortland and the Tavernier Company 1877–1896.' PH D, University of Western Ontario 1985

Hallett, Mary Elizabeth. 'The 4th Earl Grey as Governor General of Canada, 1904–1911' PH D, University of London 1974

Haynes, Nancy Jane. 'A History of the Royal Alexandra Theatre, Toronto, Ontario, Canada: 1914–1918.' PH D, University of Colorado 1973

Hines, Frances R. 'Concert Life in London, Ontario, 1870–1880.' M MUS, University of Western Ontario 1977

Howard, Mildred Langford. 'The Acting of Clara Morris.' PH D, University of Illinois 1956

Lenton, Gerald Bentley Bruce. 'The Development and Nature of Vaudeville in Toronto from 1899 to 1915.' PH D, University of Toronto 1983

O'Dell, Leslie Anne. 'Theatrical Events in Kingston, Ontario: 1879–1897.' PH D, University of Toronto 1982

O'Neill, Mora Diane Guthrie. 'A Partial History of the Royal Alexandra Theatre, Toronto, Ontario, 1907–1939.' PH D, Louisiana State University 1976

O'Neill, Patrick B. 'A History of Theatrical Activity in Toronto, Canada: From Its Beginnings to 1858.' PH D, Louisiana State University 1973

Plant, Richard. 'Leaving Home: A Thematic Study of Canadian Literature with Special Emphasis on Drama, 1606 to 1977.' PH D, University of Toronto 1979

Rewa, Natalie. 'Garrison and Amateur Theatricals in Quebec City and Kingston During the British Regime.' PH D, University of Toronto 1988

Scott, Robert Barry. 'A Study of Amateur Theatre in Toronto: 1900–1930.' MA, University of New Brunswick 1966

– 'A Study of English Canadian Dramatic Literature, 1900–1930.' PHIL M, University of Toronto 1969

Shortt, Mary. 'From *Douglas* to *The Black Crook*: A History of Toronto Theatre 1809–1874.' MA, University of Toronto 1977

Tait, Michael Strong. 'Studies in the Theatre and Drama of English Canada.' MA, University of Toronto 1963

Weiller, Georgette. 'Sara Bernhardt et Le Canada.' MA, University of Ottawa 1968

Illustration Credits

Metropolitan Toronto Public Library Board: Rideau Hall, theatricals in the ballroom (page 4); Rideau Hall, audience for private theatrical 1873 (4); *Toodles* 1873 (9); Sarah Anne Curzon (11); *Hiawatha* c. 1920 (13); *Hiawatha* in the drama of 1904 (15); playbill Toronto Dramatic Society 1859 (31); playbill Royal Lyceum 1856 (33); illustration of *H.M.S. Parliament* (40); Royal Lyceum depicted in a woodcut 1858 (42); John Nickinson (76); Silverland Theatre (124); Harold Nelson (132); Ida Van Cortland as Billie Piper (137); Van Cortland as Juliet (140); Van Cortland as Lucretia Borgia (142); *Toodles* 1862 (147); Fanny Reeves (148); Daniel Morrison and Charlotte Nickinson Morrison (151); Mrs Morrison's playbill 1876 (153); May A. Bell Marks Brothers' production of *Little Starlight* (158); May A. Bell as Little Starlight (159); Patrick Redmond (177); playbill of *Fun for the Million* 1858 (179); Colin 'Cool' Burgess (180); minstrel entertainments 1872 (182); Marie Dressler (208); pencil sketch of Royal Lyceum 1849 (219); ground plan of Royal Lyceum 1849 (220); auditorium of Grand Opera House 1875 (225); Princess Theatre ruins 1915 (226); Royal Alexandra Theatre interior 1907 (229); Royal Alexandra Theatre exterior 1913 (230); Hugh Scobie (298); John Ritchie (303); Graves Simcoe Lee at twenty-four (308); Sir Allan MacNab (309); Lee at seventy (311); Port Hope Music Hall and St Lawrence Hotel (320); inaugural concert 1871 (320); scene from *The Maire of St Brieux* (324); The Marks Brothers in a touring wagon (328); Marks Brothers' *At the Point of a Sword* (328); Belle Stevenson (343)

Queen's University Archives: *Leo, the Royal Cadet* 1915 (12); Kingston Memorial Hall after restoration 1974 (218); Princess Street showing the Grand Theatre c. 1936 (236)

National Archives of Canada: *Hiawatha* c 1920 NAC C-2685 (13); *Grand Mogul* 1908 NAC 29248 (110); Russell Theatre *Yeomen of the Guard* 1918 NAC X-5166 (243); Her Majesty's Theatre c 1867 NAC C-2145 (316); *Dearest Mama* at Rideau Hall 1889 NAC 27143 (319); 'Cake Walk' cast 1902 NAC C-88234 (339); Ottawa Family Theatre 1910 NAC 42686 (345)

Special Collections, Hamilton Public Library: *The Mikado* c 1900 (111); Kate Gunn
in *The Mikado* c 1896 (113); Roselle Knott (135); Julia Arthur as Hamlet (143);
Hamilton Town Hall (216); playbill from opening of Grand Opera House 1880
(239); Hamilton Grand Opera House (240); Hamilton Engine House (295);
Garrick Club performance (321)

London Room, London Public Libraries and Museums: two performers from
Holman Opera Company (126): Grand Opera House program decoration 1894–5
(129)

Metropolitan Toronto Public Library Board, courtesy William Chadwick; map of
touring routes (130)

Archives of Ontario: Hilliard Opera House (131); Toronto Grand Opera House c
1875 (224); Holman Opera House (232); London Masonic Temple and Grand
Opera House (233); Orillia Opera House (271)

Metropolitan Toronto Public Library Board and Norman Studio, Ottawa: Eugene A.
McDowell (147)

Lois Steen: Adelaide Secord (150)

Heritage Recording Services, Environment Canada, Parks: St Marys Town Hall
(244); Gravenhurst Opera House (252); Cardno Hall 1985 (266); Cardno Hall
interior (267); Lindsay, Academy Theatre (268); Academy Theatre interior (269)

Archives of Ontario / Town of Aylmer: Aylmer Town Hall and Opera House (245)

Robert Fairfield: Paisley Town Hall and Theatre 1981 (246); Clinton Opera House
stage (249); Petrolia's Victoria Hall (251); Meaford Opera House (257)

Kitchener-Waterloo *Record*: Drayton Town Hall and Opera House (253)

University of Waterloo Archives: theatre chair c. 1900 (255)

Peterborough Centennial Museum and Archives: Belcher's front elevation 1872
(259)

St Marys District Museum: Opera House interior 1884 (261); St Marys Opera
House 1884 (263)

St Marys *Journal Argus*: conversion of Opera House 1986–8 (265)

Stratford-Perth County Archives: Theatre Albert 1905 (275)

Niagara-on-the-Lake Historical Museum: amateur performance in the 1890s (278)

Thomas Fisher Rare Books Library, University of Toronto, courtesy of the Elgin
and Winter Garden Project: Winter Garden as it appeared opening night 1914
(280); Elgin Theatre auditorium 1915 (281); three shots of the Elgin and Winter
Garden complex (282); three shots of restoration work 1985 (283)

Players' Guild of Hamilton: Garrick Club charter (322)

Hastings County Historical Board: Belleville Opera House (331)

Lake of the Woods Museum, Kenora: Rat Portage Dramatic Club newspaper
advertisement 1889 (335)

Archives of Kitchener Public Library: Berlin Opera House c. 1915 (338)

Mrs Hazel Summers Kompass: George Summers (341)

Index

Abbey Theatre 346
Abbott's Hall (Coldwater) 334
A'Beckett, Gilbert Abbot (playwright), 61, 111
Abie's Irish Rose 107
Academy for Dancing and Calisthenics (Toronto) 305
Academy of Music. *See* Lindsay; Philadelphia; St Catharines; Toronto; Washington
Academy Theatre. *See* Chicago; Lindsay
acoustics 217, 258
acrobats/acrobatics 48, 166, 167, 172, 173, 174, 181, 185, 196, 202, 209
actor-managers 125–34, 144
actors, stage representations of 99
actresses 63, 67–8, 82, 97–8
Adam and Eve in Paradise (panorama) 168
Adam, brothers, style 276, 282
Adam, Graeme Mercer (writer) 36
Adams, Maude (actress) 160, 345
Adelaide Street Skating Rink (Toronto; later Holman Opera House) 225, 330
Adelphi (Terence) 292
Adrienne Lecouvreur (Scribe and Legouvé) 99, 156
advance agents/notices 55, 68–9, 75, 124–5

Adventures of Jimmy Brown 92
advertising 30, 55, 66, 67, 71, 124–5, 127–8, 196, 269
African Native Choir 155
Afternoon Tea at Friendly Village, A Character Sketch Entertainment, Entitled (Anderson) 346
afterpieces, 61, 64, 181, 187, 189
Against the World; or, Life in London (Telgmann), 333
Agricultural Hall (Toronto) 318
Aladdin and His Wonderful Lamp (Green) 273
Albani, Mme (Emma Lajeunesse) 330
Albany (NY) 125, 172
Albee, E.F. (vaudeville manager) 199, 205
albinos 176, 192, 193
alcohol 57, 74, 191, 192. *See also* drunkenness
Alcott, Louisa May 113
Aldous, John E.P. (musician/composer) 10, 336
Alhambra Theatre. *See* Chicago; Milwaukee
Alixe 145
Allan, Miss (actress) 291
Allan Gardens (Toronto) 228
Alvira Alias Orea (Henderson) 339

Amateur Dramatic Club (Toronto) 314
Amateur Dramatic Society (Gananoque)
326
amateur performers 32, 63, 64, 66,
114–15, 119, 120, 178, 183–4,
209. *See also* garrison theatre
Amateurs of the Dockyard (Kingston)
300
Amateurs of the Military Train (London, Ont.) 59
Amateur Society (Ancaster) 292
amateur theatre 6, 8, 10, 13, 14, 25,
26, 34, 41, 48–50, 52–89, 102,
108–9, 292; in Bytown 296; in
Chatham 301; in Cobourg 300; in
Galt 296, 300; in Guelph 292; in
Hamilton 216, 297, 299–306
passim, 317, 323; in Kingston 5,
56–7, 79–80, 84, 216, 290, 291,
293, 296, 299, 300; in Lindsay 270;
in London, Ont. 59, 61, 79, 81, 82,
292, 300, 315; in Niagara-on-the-
Lake 278; in Ottawa, 242, 306; in
Toronto 14, 48–9, 80, 81, 82, 186,
294, 299, 300–1, 304–7 *passim*,
314, 321. *See also* garrison theatre
Amateur Theatrical Society. *See*
Hamilton; Toronto
*Ambition; or, Be Sure You Are Off With
the Old Hall Before You Are On
With the New* ('J.W.S.') 332
Ameliasburg (Ont.), Township Hall and
Masonic Lodge 323
American Civil War, The (panorama)
168
amphitheatres 222
Ancaster (Ont.) 6, 292; Ancaster
Township Town Hall 321
Anderson, Clara (playwright) 346
Anderson, William E. (playwright) 336
Angelo, Michael and Valentine (ven-
triloquists) 301

Anglican Club (Niagara Falls) 344
Anglicans/Anglicanism 21, 24, 28,
56
Anglin, Margaret (actress) 144, 145,
160, 324, 325, 326
animals / animal acts 4, 5, 6, 30, 48,
102, 117, 123, 168, 171–2, 191,
290–93 *passim*, 312, 332; in variety
entertainment 174, 175–6, 190,
202, 204. *See also* menageries
Anna Christie (film; based on O'Neill's
play) 209
Ann Arbor (MI) 131
Anstead, William (theatre builder)
248
Antigone (Sophocles) 111
anti-theatre sentiments 92–3, 99, 293,
296, 301–2. *See also* moral at-
titudes/issues
Anti-Theatrical Prejudice, The (Barish)
92
Antony and Cleopatra (Shakespeare)
96, 144
'Apollo Crowned By the Muses'
(Lathrop) 241
Apollo Saloon and Concert Room
(Toronto) 186, 187
Apollo Theatre (Toronto; later Dramatic
Hall) 314
'Apple of My Eye, The' (minstrel
entertainment) *182*
Arabella (role of) 83
Archbold, Mr and Mrs (performers)
291, 292
architecture 19, 21, 28, 29–30, 45;
theatre 49, 214–87
Armless Wonder (freak) 193
Armstrong, L.O. (playwright) 10,
339–40
army officers: 25, 26, 54, 56–7, 85n1
(*see also* military); theatricals 52.
See also garrison theatre

Arnold, Matthew (poet/critic) 101, 118
Arrah-na-Pogue (Boucicault) 102, 141
art: and burlesque 193–4, 198; galleries
    191, 227; glass 242; sculpture 91.
    See also painting
Artaxaminous, King (role of) 65, 73
'Art Decoration' (Wilde) 329
Art Deco architectural style 258
Arthur, Julia (actress; née Ida Lewis)
    127, 134, 141–4, *143*, 332. *See
    also* Lewis, Ida
l'Article 47 (*The Louisiana Creole*)
    145
arts, public vs private 91
Arts and Letters Club (Toronto) 344,
    345
Arts and Letters Players (Toronto) 12
Ashley, Mr and Mrs A. (performers)
    80, 294, 296
assembly rooms 16, 26, 167, 290, 291,
    299, 334, 336, 337
Astley, Philip (circus founder) 172
As You Like It (Shakespeare) 42, 144,
    340
Athenaeum (Toronto) 187
Atheneum Theatre. *See* Belleville;
    Kingston
'atmospheric' interior decoration
    282
At the Point of a Sword (Castle) 328
attics 233
Auber, Daniel François Esprit (com-
    poser) 110
audiences 90–1, 93, 94, 105, 201–3;
    attendance 69–70; decorum 217;
    participation 181
Audley, Lady (role of) 101
Avenue Theatre (Louisville, KY)
    161n10
Avon Theatre. *See* Stratford
Aylmer (Ont.) 175; Town Hall and
    Opera House *245*, 245–7, 323

backstage accommodations 219, 223,
    225, 231–2, 234–5, 258–9
Bailey, G.F. (circus operator) 174, 175
Baker, Betsey (role of) 64
Baker, Edith (performer) 340
Baker, Mr and Mrs (performers) 291,
    307
balconies 219–83 *passim*
Baldwin family 291
Balfe, Michael (composer) 110–11
balladeers 48
ballet: dancers 194; dress 95; 'girls' 93
ballroom dances 181
ballrooms 218, 223, 273, 291, 313
balls 217, 250, 289
balustrades 227, 234, 247
bands: big 281; concerts 217; governor-
    general's 210. *See also* concerts
Bandmann, Daniel (theatre manager)
    141, 146
banisters 283
banquet rooms 227
Barbe-Bleau (Offenbach) 113
Barker, Edward (playwright) 294
Barnes, Mr (actor) 301
Barney Roddy's Tavern (York) 173
Barnum and Bailey Circus (Greatest
    Show on Earth) 174, 175, 210
Barnum, Phineas T. 184, 190–1, 193
Barnum's Menagerie and Museum 123
*Baron Bold and the Beauteous Maid,
    The* ('Titus A. Drum') 330
Baroque architectural style 223, 227,
    231
Barrack Room, The (Bayly) 82
Barrett, Lawrence (actor) 155
Barrett, Wilson (playwright) 141
Barrie (Ont.) 127, 163n14, 305, 340;
    Queen's Arms Hotel 305
Barrison, Mabel (vaudeville performer)
    209
Barrymore, Lionel 137

Barrymore, Mrs Lionel (née Doris Rankin), 136, 137
Barrymore family 136
Bass, Jonathan (freak) 192
Battle Creek (MI) Opera House 131
Battle of the Little Big Horn (Henderson) 339
Bayes, Nora (vaudeville performer) 201–2
Bayly, Thomas Haynes (playwright) 82
Bearded Lady (freak) 193
Beatrice (role of) 149
Beaux Arts architectural style 228
Beaverton Town Hall 345
Beban, George (movie star) 210
Becket (Tennyson) 143
Beecham, Sir Thomas (conductor) 111
Beecher, Henry Ward (lecturer) 118
Before and Behind the Curtain ('Titus A. Drum') 333
Beginning of the Scandal, The (McFarlane) 337
Behind the Beyond and Other Contributions to Human Knowledge (Leacock), 346
Belcher, John A. (architect) 260
belfries, 250, 264, 274
Bella Donna (Thompson) 160
Bell, Digby (vaudeville performer) 201
Belle Hélène, La (Offenbach) 113
Belleville (Ont.) 25, 38, 78, 128, 174, 175, 291, 292, 296, 302, 314, 315, 317; Atheneum 315, 317; Bull's Opera House 326; Carmen's Opera House (later the Griffin) 330, *331* Coleman's Hall 315; Good Templars' Hall 326; Marble Hall 317; Masonic Music Hall 184, 319; Neilson's Hall 317; Ontario Hall 317; Temperance Hall 325
Belleville Dramatic Club 315
Belleville Dramatic Society 319

Belleville Opera House (a.k.a. Bull's Opera House) 326
Bell, May A. (actress) *158, 159*, 160, 327
bells, cue 241; ringers 185
Bell Smith, F.M. (illustrator) 223
Bells, The (Lewis; adapted from Erckmann-Chatrian) 94, 98, 134
Benedict, Julius (composer) 111
benefit performances 13, 69, 77, 80, 81, 82, 141, 292; in Belleville 315; in Hamilton 300–5 *passim*, 310; in Kingston 305; in Toronto 108, *153*, 304–7 *passim*, 318, 324; in York 291; *See also* charitable causes
Bengough, John Wilson (playwright/editor) 10, 324, 330, 333, 336, 342, 344
Ben Greet's English Players 340
Ben Hur (Young; after novel by Wallace) 160, 264
Bennett, C.W. (vaudeville theatre manager) 207, 342
Benny, Jack (vaudeville performer) 200
Benson, Sir Frank R. (actor) 120, 160
Bergerat, Emile (playwright) 144
Berlin (Ont.; now Kitchener) 29, 47, 175, 336, 340. *See also* Kitchener, Opera House 336, *338*; Star Theatre *338*
Bernard and Black circus (York) 172–3, 292
Bernhardt, Sarah (actress) 49, 92, 100, 134, 154, 163*n*15, 329
Bernheim, Alfred (writer) 128
Bertram and Lorenzo (Sangster) 313
Besnard, T.P. (actor-manager) 80, 81, 301–, 304, 306–7
Bethany (Ont.), Manvers Township Hall 346
Betsey Baker (Morton) 64

B.F. Keith Exchange (vaudeville circuit) 199, 204–7 passim, 210
Bijou Theatre (Chicago, IL) 161n10
Bijou Theatre (Toronto). See Robinson's Musee Theatre (Toronto)
Billings, Josh (comic lecturer) 118
Billy Rose (Sims) 119
birds / aviaries 190, 191
Bishop, Henry Rowley (composer) 95
Biven, Mr (actor) 291
Black Crook, The (J. and H. Paulton) 93, 116, 117, 194, 317, 325
'Black Donnellys,' the 24
Black-Eyed Susan (Jerrold) 101
black-face performers/performances 114, 176, 181, 183, 297. See also minstrel shows
blacklisting 199, 204
blacks: performers/companies 114, 115, 180; community, opposition to minstrel shows 14, 176, 178, 297
Blackwell, W. (architect) 269
Blair, Eugenie (actress) 155, 156
Blanchard, George (circus operator) 172, 292
Blanchard, Kitty (Mrs McKee Rankin) 136, 137
Blanchard's 'Royal Circus' 172, 291
Bleak House (Dickens) 157
Blind Tom (pianist) 117
Blobbs, Tillie (role of) 209
Blondin (tightrope performer) 169, 314
Blot on the 'Scutcheon, A (Browning) 155
Blot, The (Stringer) 344
Bluebeard (Seymour) 322
Bohemian Girl, The (Balfe) 111, 155
Boito, Arrigo (composer) 110
Boker, George H. (playwright) 155
Bombastes Furioso (Rhodes) 65, 73, 77
booking practices 127–34, 199, 206
Booth, Agnes (actress) 149

Booth, Edwin (actor) 94, 316
Booth, Julius Brutus, Jr (actor) 149
Border Canucks, Our Friendly Relations (novel) (G.C. Rankin) 137, 334
Borland, Rev. John (playwright) 313
Boston 125, 144, 172, 340
Boucicault, Dion (actor/playwright) 65, 73, 101–2, 110, 111, 324
Bower, Frank (performer) 178
Bowery Theatre of New York (circus) 297
Bowes, Mr 68
Bowker, (playwright) 155
Bowmanville (Ont.) 175; Town Hall 340
Box and Cox (Morton) 71
boxes: orchestra 240; private 223, 252, 266, 269, 274; proscenium 221, 240; royal 229; theatrical 219, 221, 227, 231, 234, 235, 238, 242–3, 280, 283
boxing 188
box offices 231
Box (role of) 72
Boycott, The (Anon.) 329
Boyes, Sergeant (actor) 63
Boys' Home (Toronto) 56
Bradburn, Rupert (theatre owner) 261, 342
Bradburn, Thomas E. 260, 268, 318, 325
Bradburn's Grand Opera House. See Peterborough
Bradburn's Opera House. See Peterborough
Bradford (Ont.) 317
Bradley, the Yorkshire giant 292
Brampton (Ont.) 175
Brandenberger, Albert (theatre owner) 276, 277
Brantford (Ont.) 38, 47, 127, 163n14,

175, 301, 307, 336; Ker's Music Hall 317; Stratford's Opera House 329
Brant, Joseph (Six Nations Chief) 337
Breach of Promise Trial Bardwell vs Pickwick, The (Bengough) 342, 344
Breed of the Treshams, The ('John Rutherford,' pseud. of Evelyn Greenleaf Sutherland and Beulah Marie Dix) 160, 162n13
Brent, W.H. (actor/playwright) 325
Brett-James, Antony (writer) 55
Brewery Theatre (Kingston) 84
brick buildings, 232, 233, 246–50 *passim*, 254, 256, 258, 260, 262, 272, 273, 274, 276
Bridegroom, The (Barker) 294
Brienti, Eliza (performer) 304
Brigham Young's theatre 136
Brighter World Above, The (Anon.) 315
Britain: cultural influence of 3, 5, 6, 8, 10, 12, 13, 14, 18–26 *passim*, 32, 34, 35, 47, 48, 50; influence of, on theatre architecture 215
British Blondes 16–17, 194, 195
British and Canadian Theatrical Organization Society 10, 162n13, 346
British Museum Mr Wood's (York), 190
British Officer, The 54
Broadway productions 319
Broadway Theatre (New York) 136
Brock Township Hall (Sunderland) 342
Brockville (Ont.) 128, 172, 175, 291, 293, 299, 304, 334, 336; Mr Buell's 'Large Hall,' 304; New Theatre, 262, 345; Town Hall, 261–2, 313
Brockville Civic Auditorium 262
Brockville Thespians 304
brother acts 210
Brougham, John (playwright) 102
Brown brothers (vaudeville performers) Albert, Alex, Fred, Harry, Nelson, Tom, Will 209–10

Brown, Mr and Mrs Frederick (actors), 290
Brown, Jessie (role of) 149
Brown, J. Francis (architect) 254
Brown, John Henry (playwright/poet) 334
Brown, Mary M. (historian) 16, 25, 48
Brown, Mr (actor) 305
Browne, George (architect) 217
Browning, Robert (poet/playwright) 155
Brownlow, Lieutenant (actor) 73
Brunton, Mrs (amateur actress) 82
Brunton's Varieties (London, Ont.) 125
Brunton, W.Y. (actor-manager) 127, 312
Buckley, Emily. *See* Van Cortland, Ida
Buckstone, John Baldwin (playwright) 62
Buell's 'Large Hall' (Brockville), 304
Buffalo (NY) 127, 204, 206, 209, 291; Garden Theatre 205; Majestic Theatre 205; Seneca Theatre 205; Shea's Buffalo Theatre 205; Shea's Hippodrome 205
Bull's Opera House (Belleville Opera House) 326
Bulwer-Lytton, Lord (playwright) 96, 105
Bunthorne Abroad; or, the Lass That Loved a Pirate (Bengough) 10, 330, 333
Bunty Pulls the Strings (Sloane and Smith) 160
Burgess and Black menagerie 293
Burgess, Colin 'Cool' (minstrel performer) 122n5, 127, 178, *179, 180,* 185, 187, 297, 313
Burke, Horwood and White (architects) 273
burlesque: 115–17, 176, 186, 187–8, 190, 193–8; 'dirty' sketches in 116–17; houses/theatres 166, 189, 242; performers 119–20

burlesques 65, 66, 336
Burley's Hotel (Ancaster) 292
Burlington Hotel Ballroom (Hamilton) 292
Burnett, Frances Hodgson (novelist/playwright) 143
Burns, George (vaudeville performer) 200
'burnt cork' performers, *180. See also* black-face performers
Burt's New Theatre (Toledo, OH) 161*n*10
Bush, Thomas (playwright) 8, 317
Bushman, Francis X. (movie actor) 210
business, stage 97, 203
Business of the Theatre, The (Bernheim) 128
Butler, Mrs Samuel (performer) 299
Butler's Theatre (Kingston) 217
Byron, Henry James (playwright) 77, 94, 106–7
Byron, Lord (poet/playwright) 94
Bytown (later Ottawa) 25, 29, 296; Garrison Amateurs, 296; panorama of 168, 293. *See also* Ottawa
Byzantine architectural style 234

cabarets 198
Cadeux, Jean Baptiste (character) 137, 334
Caesar and Cleopatra (Shaw) 342
Caldecott, Randolph (illustrator) 103
Caldwell, James E. (playwright) 344
Camden East (Ont.) 314
Cameron, Con (midget) 193
Cameron, George Frederick (poet/playwright) 10, 36, 333
Cameron, Mary Agnes (performer) 315
Camille (Dumas *fils*) 100, 121, 134, 141, 145, 152, 154, 156, 329
Camille (role of) 100, 154
Campbell, Mrs Patrick (actress) 340

Campbell, William Wilfred (playwright/poet) 8, 47, 336, 337, 344
Canada and Its Provinces 47
Canada West (Upper Canada) 27–35
Canadian Club, The (Anon.) 323
Canadian Forget Me Not for 1837, The (Simpson) 8
Canadian Pacific Railway (CPR) 38, 43, 44, 127, 242
Canadian Theatre Manager's Association 342
Canadian Vaudeville Circuit 342
Cannington (Ont.), Town Hall 333
Canuck, a Play of Anglo-American Life, The (A.M. Rankin and F.C. Maeder) 137, 334
Captain Plume's Courtship (Simpson) 8, 296
Capture of Detroit, 1812, The (Mair) 334
Cardinal, The (L.N. Parker) 158
Cardno, John Alexander (theatre owner) 266–7
Cardno, Kenneth (theatre owner) 267
Cardno Hall (Seaforth) *266*, 266–8, *267*, 288, 326
Caricature, The Funny Art (Bengough) 330
Carleton, John Louis (playwright) 337, 339
Carleton Place (Ont.) *339*; Town Hall 337
Carlyle, Hal Newton (playwright) 339
Carlyle, Lady Isobel (role of) 101
Carman, A.R. (playwright) 344
Carmen (Bizet) 94
Carmen's Opera House (Belleville) 330, *331*
'Caroli Candidus' (pseudonymous playwright) 10, 32, 313
Carpenter, Mr (actor) 290

Carrere & Hastings (architects) 228
Carter, Emma Seymour (playwright) 344
Carter, Sir James (judge) 63
Carter, 'Jemmy' (female impersonator) 63
Carter, William (playwright) 321
Casino Theatre (Ottawa) 198
Caste (Robertson) 107
casting, 60–4
Castles in the Air (Dean) 334
catchpenny shows 90
Cavan Township Hall (Millbrook) 322
ceilings 217, 223, 234, 242, 247, 248, 254, 256, 258, 272, 276, 283; domes 221, 237, 274, 279; frescoed, 221, 223, 231, 240, 258
censors/censorship 12, 14, 48, 189, 197, 198, 204, 206, 346
Challener, Frederick (artist) 231, 235, 242
Champlain: A Drama in Three Acts (Harper) 344
chandeliers 234, 254, 264
Chanfrau, Mrs F.S. (performer) 323
change rooms 246. *See also* dressing-rooms
Chaos (Ramsay) 333
Chaplin, Charlie (vaudeville performer) 200
Chapman and Hamilton company 300
characters: in comedy 104, 106; in melodrama 95, 101; stereotyped 137
Character Sketch Entertainment, Entitled Afternoon Tea in Friendly Village, A (Anderson) 346
charades 54
Charge of the Light Brigade, The (Tennyson) 119
charitable causes, fund raising for 55–6, 67, 72, 75, 77, 79, 80, 87n35, 113, 114, 118, 120, 291,

293, 296. *See also* benefit performances
Charity (Gilbert) 41
charlatans 174
Charles O'Malley (Lever) 108
Charles the Second (J.H. Payne) 62, 65
Charlesworth, Hector (critic) 16, 105, 344
Charley's Aunt (Thomas) 109
chasers, movie 203, 242
Chatham (Ont.) 127, 157, 175, 183, 270, 301, 340; Theatre Royal 301
Chatterton, Johnny ('Seigneur Perugini') 125
Cheese, The (Jerome) 120
Chesnut, Thomas Herbert (playwright) 333–4
Cheyney, Mr Pierce, Jr (millionaire; husband of Julia Arthur), 144
Chicago (IL) 128, 161n10, 195, 209, 221, 337, 339
Chicago Symphony Orchestra 155
Chick, or Myrtle Ferns (Lindley) 336
child actors/performers 17n5, 176, 185, 192, 196, 297
children's shows 203–4
Chimes of Normandy, The / Les Cloches de Corneville (Planquette) 111, 113, 155
chimneys 247, 274
Chocolate Soldier, The (Straus/Stange) 165n44
choirs 157
choral societies 30
Chorus Girl, The (Forbes), 319
chorus: girls, 134; room 281
Chorus Lady, The (Forbes) 319, 346
Christie Lake (Ont.) 325, 327
'Chrononhotonthologos.' *See* Scobie, Hugh
Cibber, Colley (actor/playwright) 96, 154–5

Cigarette Maker's Romance, The
(Hannon; adapted from novel by
Crawford) 160, 162*n*13
Cincinnati (OH) 141, 161*n*10; Wood's
Theatre 145
Cinderella theme 107
cinema(s), 16, 48, 49, 261. *See also*
movie houses; movies; circles 219,
221; dress 69, 70, 222, 223, 234,
238, 240; family 69, 223, 242
circuits / circuit owners and managers
127–33, 197–8, 199, 204, 212*n*41
circus(es), 1, 5, 6, 12, 14, 123, 166,
170, 171, 172–6, 292, 294, 296,
297, 300, 310, 312, 399; and blacks
176, 178, 297; Mr Blanchard's
'Royal' 291; carnival elements in
175; 'European' 30; first 172–3,
291; freaks in 175, 192; and menageries 172, 173, 174; moral attitudes
towards 92, 173–4; and other
variety entertainment 172, 173, 187,
199
City Girls (vaudeville show) 204
City Hall. *See* Hamilton; Kingston;
London (Ont.); Stratford; Toronto
City Hall Theatre Royal (Kingston),
318
City Hotel (Toronto; formerly
Steamboat Hotel) 297, 299
City Theatre (Toronto) 313
Civic Square (Toronto) 280
Civilian Amateurs (Kingston) 299
Civilian Dramatic Society (London,
Ont.) 79, 315
Claris, George (theatre owner-manager)
265
Claris House. *See* St Thomas
Clarlase (role of) 82
Class/classes: lower 46, 186; middle
24, 47, 93; social 68, 70, 85*n*6, 186;
upper 21, 22, 23, 25, 32, 46, 48,

52, 58, 59, 99, 186; working 32, 38,
45, 46, 93, 186, 193, 199–200, *See
also* élite; garrisons; garrison
theatre
Classical Revival architectural style 278
Cleather, Captain (amateur actor) 64
Cleveland (OH) 145, 161*n*10
Cleveland Theatre (Cleveland, OH)
161*n*10
Cline, Maggie (vaudeville performer)
202
Clinton (Ont.), Town Hall and Opera
House 248–50, *249*, 252, 329
cloak spaces 231
*Cloches de Corneville, Les / The
Chimes of Normandy* (Planquette)
111, 113, 155
clock towers 250, 260, 267
clowning/clowns 172, 173, 196
Clytemnestra (role of) 144
Cobalt (Ont.) 45; Silverland Theatre
124
Cobourg (Ont.) 13, 28, 32–3, 173,
175, 207, 291, 297, 300, 302, 314,
316, 318; Globe Hotel 302; Opera
House 32; Town Hall 32; Victoria
College 13; Victoria Hall 214
Cohan, George M. (composer/actor/
playwright/producer) 205
Coldstream, Sir Charles (role of) 73
Coldwater (Ont.), Abbott's Hall 334
Coleman's Hall (Belleville) 315
Cole, W.W. (circus operator) 174
Cole's Museum, Hippodrome, and
Menagerie 174
Colleen Bawn, The (Boucicault) 102,
111, 139
College Banjo and Guitar Club 155
College of Music (Toronto) 14
Collier, William (playwright) 74
Collins, Wilkie (playwright) 100, 104,
145

Colman the younger, George
(playwright) 87n29, 103
Coloured Young Men's Amateur
Theatrical Society, the Toronto
14
Columbia Burlesque Circuit 197
Columbiad, The (G.W. Johnson) 316
'Columbus' (elephant) 6, 171, 293
columns, supporting/decorative 219,
221, 227, 231, 234, 238, 240, 264,
267, 284
comedians/comediennes 48, 63, 73,
181, 185, 203, 209, 290, 300
comedies 42, 62, 65, 66, 77, 78, 82,
83, 100, 114; of manners 10
comedy 24, 66, 93, 103–9, 119, 160,
209; musical 10, 48, 117, 144, 183,
185, 197, 209, 210. *See also* Old
Comedy
Comedy of Errors, The (Shakespeare)
340
Comedy – The Battle of Life (adapted
by J.B. Harrison) 301
comic: characters/roles 65, 181; dramas
115; extravaganza(s) 65; lecturers
118; monologues 180, 181; opera(s)
121, 242, 324 (*see also opéra
comique*); operetta(s) 333–4, 336;
sketches 114–15
Commercial Hotel (Kingston) 294
Commissioner and the Indian, The
(Anon.) 326
communication(s) 18, 19, 28, 30, 48,
50. *See also* telegraph; telephone
Commuters, The (Forbes) 319
concert: gardens 187; halls 111, 184,
185; 'numbers' 95; rooms, 187;
saloons, 166, 186–90, 194
concerts 49, 68, 155, 216, 217, 281,
292, 299, 304, 315, 317, 320. *See
also* music
Confusion (McKee Rankin) 137

Connor, Ralph (Charles William
Gordon; novelist) 47
Conservatory of Music (Toronto) 15,
334
control boards/booths 241, 258
Convention, The (Anon.) 68, 290
Cook, Rosa (performer) 312
Cooke, Richard (elocutionist) 119
Copp, Mary (role of) 62, 65
copyright (registration) 8, 163n21
Cora (role of) 145
Corcoran, Jane, 344
Cormon, Eugène (playwright) 96
'Cornichon' (pseudonym) 72–3
Cornwall (Ont.) 25, 175
Coronation Hall (Omemee) 345
corps dramatique 60–2, 67, 75, 87n26
Corsican Brothers, The (Boucicault;
adapted from Dumas) 97, 98, 121
Corsican Trap 97
Costume Drama 47, 96–9, 103, 104,
121
costumes 5, 12, 14, 56, 66, 67, 84,
117, 141, 143, 191, 194, 258, 346;
'fleshings' 96; 'New York Bloomer'
12, 307
*Cottage Dialogues among the Irish
Peasantry* (Leadbeater) 290
Couldock, C.W. (actor) 145, 149, 310,
324
Count of Monte Cristo, The (Dumas
père; adapted by Fechter) 102, 134,
144, 152, 157
Count's Bridge, The (G.W. Johnson)
316
Court House. *See* Kingston; Niagara-
on-the-Lake
Court House Green (York) 171
Court House Square (London, Ont.)
216
Covent Garden Theatre (London, Ont.)
312

Coward, Noel (actor/playwright/ composer) 98
Cowell, Mr and Mrs Sam (performers) 314
Cowley, Francis (playwright) 66
Cowley, Capt. Joseph (editor) 81, 300
'C.P.M.' (pseudonymous playwright) 329, 330
Crane, C. Howard (architect) 228
Crane, W.H. (actor) 125
Crawford, Isabella Valancy (poet) 36
Criterion Theatre (Chicago, IL) 161n10
Critic, The (Sheridan) 62
criticism/critics: dramatic 14, 16, 59, 71–5, 77; 155; literary 36
Crooked Tree (Anon.) 323
Crosman, Henrietta (actress) 158
Crow, Jim (character/role) 176, 178, 183, 297, 310, 312
Cruise, Anna, benefit for 304
Crystal Palace. See London (Eng.); Toronto
Crystal Theatre and Eden Musee (Toronto) See Robinson's Musee Theatre (Toronto)
Cummings, Robert (actor) 337
Cupid (role of) 270
cupolas 279
curio halls/shops 170, 193
curtains: act 231, asbestos 262; drop 181, 238, 264, 270, 272–3; house 234, 238, 240, 241, 267; stage 231. See also drop
Curzon, Sarah Anne (playwright) 10, 11, 329–30, 333
Cushing, Eliza (poet/playwright) 32
cyclists, trick 209
Cyclorama Building (Toronto) 169, 333
Cymbeline (role of) 143
Cynthia 144
Cyrano de Bergerac (Rostand) 144
Cyrano (role of) 144

D'Alton, Captain (actor) 65, 80, 88n38, 299
Dagger and the Cross, The (Tremayne) 158, 165n42 339
Dainty Dashing Polly Girls, The (vaudeville show) 204
Daly, Augustin (actor-manager) 145, 209, 315
Dame aux camélias, La (Dumas fils) 100, 313
dance 32, 48, 195, 305, 306; halls 103, 198
dancers 160, 183, 209, 342; wooden shoe 260
dances/dancing 13, 24, 58, 97, 167, 203, 290, 291; belly 195; buck and wing 181; and burlesque 194, 195–6; cake walk 181; 339; can-can 189; clog 181; cootch 195; girls, 95, 115; in minstrel shows 114, 180, 181, 183; soft-shoe 310; tap 181; and variety theatre 185, 188, 189; and vaudeville 203
dance of the seven veils 195–6
Daniels, Mr (theatre owner) 336
Danites, The (A.M. Rankin, Miller, and Fitzgerald) 136, 138, 139, 297, 326
Dan'l Druce 155
D'Arcy of the Guards 145
daredevil feats 169–70
Darktown Swells (minstrel show) 115
Daughter of the Regiment (Donizetti) 110
Davenport Brothers 117–18
Davenport, Fanny (actress) 139
Davenport, Margaret (child star/actress) 297, 313–14
Davenport, Mr and Mrs Thomas (performers) 297
David Abigail (Lampman) 340
David Copperfield (Dickens) 104
David Garrick (Tom Robertson) 99

Davidge, William, Sr (actor) 312
Davin, Nicholas Flood (playwright) 8, 10, 325
Davis, Mr (actor) 291
Days of the Year, or the Masque of the Months (McIlwraith) 334
Deacon Crankett 152
'dead-heads' 137
Dead Heart, The (Philip) 96
Deaf, Dumb, and Blind Institution (Toronto) 56
Dean, C.K. (playwright) 334
Dean, Edwin (actor-manager) 299, 300
Dean family 12, 307
Dean's Gardens (University of Toronto) 342
Dearest Mama (Gordon) 319
debates / debating clubs 6, 144, 167, 337
Deborah (Cheltnam) 157, 346
De Courcy, Elise (actress) 314
Deering, Mr (actor-manager / theatre owner) 65, 299, 300
De Forest's Hotel (York) 173
Dei Franchi brothers (roles of) 97
de Koven, Reginald (composer) 121
d'Ennery, Adolphe P. (playwright) 96, 111
Demorestville (Ont.), Sophiasburg Township Hall 325
Dermot McMurrough (Newcomb and Hanks) 330
Descriptive Catalogue of the Provincial Exhibition 186
Desdemona (role of) 141
Detroit (MI) 124, 127, 128, 131, 133, 161*n*10, 204, 206, 226, 235
Devil's Web, The 155
DeWalden, T.B. (actor) 305, 306
dialect: comedians 181; recitations, 329. *See also* elocution; recitations/reciters

dialogue 97, 98–9, 104, 110
Dialogue (Anon.) 291
Dialogue Between the Client and the Lambton Ghost on Going From Court (McBride) 318
Dialogues Between Two Methodists (Borland) 313
Dickens Fellowship Company of Players 344
Dick Mit Dree I's (burlesque) 115
Dickson Street (Galt) 273
Did You Ever Send Your Wife to Camberwell? (Coyne) 301
Did You Ever Send Your Wife to the Falls? (adapted by Besnard) 301
dime museums 12, 166, 190–3, 199
Dinner at Eight (film) 209
Disjointed Man (freak) 193
Division Court and County Court Case, A (McBride) 313, 318
Dixon, Frederick Augustus (playwright) 8, 10, 41, *324*, 324, 325–6, 327, 332, 337
Dixon, Master (performer) 167, 291, 292
Dobbs, Tommy (role of) 65
docks / dock space, scene 235, 258
Dockstader, Lew (minstrel manager) 183, 210
Dockyard, Amateurs of the (Kingston) 300
Doctor's Courtship, The 290
Dog of Montargis, The (trans. from German from a tale by George Sand) 102
Doll's House, A (Ibsen) 100, 336, 344
domes, ceiling 221, 237, 274, 279
Dominion of Canada 27; coat of arms 240, 241
Don Cézar de Bazan (d'Ennery and Dumanoir) 102, 111, 141

Donetti's Clebrated Acting Monkeys, Dogs and Goats 312

Donizetti, Gaetano (composer) 110

Don Pasquale (Donizetti) 110

Don, Sir William (actor) 307, 310

Dora (Tennyson) 141

Dorma, Caroline (role of) 87*n*29

Double Life, A (E.J. Thompson) 332

Douglas (Home) 5, 290, 291

Douglass, David (theatre builder) 290

Douglas(s), James (actor-manager) 290

Downie Street (Stratford) 274, 276

Downing, Robert (actor) 155, 156

drama 14, 200, 201; classical, 102; Ethiopian 115; modern 121; of modern life 99–100. *See also* Costume Drama

dramatic: clubs 41, 47 (*see also* amateur theatre); competitions 242, 244; festivals, amateur 49; poems 325; readings 13, 294, 306, 315, 318; recitations 329 (*see also* elocution; recitations/reciters); sketches 32, 299; verses 119

Dramatic Hall (Toronto; formerly Apollo Theatre) 314

Dramatic Sketch, A (Simpson), 8, 296

draperies 227, 279

Drayton (Ont.), Town Hall and Opera House *253*, *255*, 256, 258, 340

dress circles 69, 70, 222, 223, 234, 238, 240

dressing-rooms 225, 235, 238, 240, 256, 258, 267, 270, 272, 281

Dressler, Marie (vaudeville performer / film star; née Leila Koerber) 201, 207, *208*, 209, 270, 318

Dressler's Players, Marie 160

Drew, John (actor) 160

Drew, Mrs John (Mrs Mossop; actress) 306

Drew, Mrs Sydney (née Gladys Rankin) 136

Drew, Pride and Sackett's Museum (Toronto) 191

Drew's Company, Mrs 136

Drew family 136

Drill Shed (Guelph) 324

drinking establishments. *See* concert saloons; taverns

Drinkwater, John (poet) 118

Dr. Jekyll and Mr. Hyde (adapted from novel by Stevenson) 254

drop(s) 250; act 241; house 242; curtains, 181, 238, 264, 270, 272–3; scene(s), 41. *See also* curtains

'Drum, Titus A.' (pseudonymous playwright) 330, 332, 333

drunkenness 99, 101, 103. *See also* alcohol

dual roles 97

duels/duelling 97, 157, 301

Dufferin Hall (Gananoque) 322, 326

Dufferin, Lady 6, 144, 321, 324, 325–6

Dufferin, Lord 325–6

Duff, Mary (actress; later Mrs Gilbert) 301, 305

Duke of Meiningen's theatre company 157

Duke's Motto, The (Brougham) 102

Dumas *fils*, Alexandre (playwright) 100

Dumas *père*, Alexandre (novelist/ playwright) 102, 134, 144, 152, 157

'Dumbells,' the (entertainment troupe) 6

Dumb Girl of Genoa, The (Farrell) 102

Dunbar, Sarah (lecturer) 344

Duncan, Francis (writer) 57–8

Duncan, Lieutenant (actor) 64

Duncan, Sarah Jeannette (writer) 36, 47

Dundalk (Ont.), Municipal Offices and Assembly Hall 342
Dundreary, Lord (role of), 114
Dundreary Married and Done For 106
Duprez and Green (minstrel troupe) 178
Durand, George F. (architect) 233–5, 250
Dutch Act 181
dwarfs 185. *See also* midgets
Dwyer, Mr (elocution teacher) 13, 291
Dyer, Julia (actress) 317
Dyke's Theatre Company 67–8, 294, 296

Easter Week at Rome (Carman) 344
East Lynne (Oxenford and Palmer) 41, 101, 139, 160
Eberson, John (architect) 282
École des Beaux-Arts architectural style 228
Eden Musee, Crystal Theatre and (Toronto). *See* Robinson's Musee Theatre (Toronto)
Edison Doll, The (Bengough) 336
Edison, Thomas A. (inventor) 160, 346
education, 28; theatre in/and, 14, 17n6, 19
educational content 13–14, 168, 173, 190–3
Edwardian architectural style 227, 235, 238, 256, 276
82nd Regiment 77
83rd Regiment 58, 62, 65, 68, 80
Elaine (role of) 143
Electra (Euripides) 144
electric: control boards 241; lighting 38, 191, 223, 236, 238, 241, 254, 264, 270, 274, 283; moon 283; railways 46; streetcars, 38, 39, 46
electricity and hydroelectricity 14, 38–9, 44, 46, 241, 323
electroliers 242, 272

elephants 6, 92, 171, 174, 176, 204, 293, 332
elevators 45, 235, 282
Elgin Theatre (Toronto) *281, 282, 283, 284*
Eliot, George (novelist) 93
élite: gentry 53, 70, 77, 79, 82, 85n1; social/cultural 53–4, 69–70. *See also* class, upper
Elliott, Gertrude (actress) 160
Elliott, Miss (performer) 299
Ellis & Connery Architects 258
Ellsler, Effie (actress) 158
elocution/elocutionists 118–21, 123, 168, 329; training 13, 14, 133, 314, 319, 334. *See also* recitations/reciters
Elsworth, Mr (performer) 296
Eltinge, Julian (vaudeville performer) 201
Embro (Ont.), Town Hall 336
Emerson, Ralph Waldo (lecturer/poet/essayist) 32
Emma Wells Concert Company 329
Emmett, Dan (black-face performer) 178
Empire Theatre (Detroit, MI) 161n10
Empire Theatre (Toronto; formerly Temperance Hall) 337
Empire (Toronto; burlesque house) 198
Engaged (Gilbert) 108
Engine House (Hamilton) 294, *295*, 296
England 103, 106, 127, 170
English Vernacular Revival, 256
Enos (early stage name of Julia Arthur) 141. *See also* Lewis, Ida
entrance: halls 231; lobbies 242, 261; porches *245, 247*, 254
Episode of the Quarrel Between Titania and Oberon from Shakespeare's A Midsummer Night's Dream (Dixon), 337

'Equescurriculum, The' 174
equestrians/equestrian acts/shows 123, 172, 173, 174, 292
Erie Canal 5, 25, 291
Erie, Lake 20, 23, 127
Erlanger, Abraham (producer) 160
Ermatinger, Edward 123, 293
Ernani (Verdi) 110
Erring but Great-Hearted Woman character 101
erring child, the 102–3
Escaped Nun, the (Edith O'Gorman) 118
Esmond, Henry (actor-manager) 346
'Ethiopian Delineators' 176, 178. *See also* black-face performers
Esther, Biblical Drama (Anon.) 346
Ethiopian Harmonists (minstrel troupe) 178
Evil Eye, The (Almar) 241
Exchange Coffee House (Toronto) 294
Exeter (Ont.), Town Hall 250
Exhibition Grounds (Toronto) 176
exhibits, travelling 166, 168–71
Experiment: a Farce in One Act, The (Rankin) 134
exports/exporting 22, 23, 28–9, 36, 43
Extract from an Original and Unpublished Play, Lately Performed at the Prescott Municipal Amphitheatre (Anon.) 327
extravaganzas 65, 67, 187
Eytinge, Rose (actress) 152

façades 219, 231, 246, 247, 254, 276
Face in the Moonlight, The (Osborne) 157
Fag (role of) 64
Fair Grit; or the Advantages of Coalition, The (Davin) 10, 325

Fair Rosamond (Anon.) 329
fairs 176; agricultural 30
Falkland (role of) 64
'fallen women' 100, 313
Falstaff (role of) 96, 316
family: circles 69, 223, 242; entertainment, variety theatre as 198, 199, 200, 203–4, 206; variety 190, 193, 199, 212n41
Family Theatre (Ottawa) 345
Famous Players theatre circuit 206, 226
fan, skill with 97
Fanchon the Cricket 141
Fanny's First Play (Shaw) 165n44
farce(s) 5, 7, 16, 32, 42, 56, 57, 61, 62, 64, 65, 66, 68, 71, 74, 77, 84, 108–9, 144, 160, 277, 290, 299, 307, 310, 314, 333, 346
farcical tragedies 336
Farini, El Nino (performer) 170
Farini, Guillermo Antonio (Bill Hunt) (stunt performer) 169–70, 314
Farmersville (Ont.) 326
Farrell, J. (playwright) 102
fate, in melodrama 100
Fate (McLachlan) 313
Father Outwitted (trans. from Lope de Vega) 291
Faust (Goethe) 157, 158, 342
Faust (Gounod) 110, 117
Faversham, William (actor) 160, 159
feats of strength 118
Fechter, Charles, 102, 104, 117
Federal architecture. *See* Loyalist architecture
Felicia, or Woman's Love 152
Female Benevolent Society (Kingston) 67, 291
Female Consistory of Brockville, The (Caroli Candidus') 10, 32, 313
Female Drummer, The 276

female: impersonation 181; minstrel troupes 194–5; roles, 62–3, 72, 82, 87*n*29, 181
feminine arts on stage 97
Ferguson, John (theatre manager) 128
Ferguson, Peter (architect) 274
'Fiddle, Faddle, and Foozle' (Lee) 292, 307
Fielding, Major (actor) 62
Fifine, the Fishermaid; or, The Magic Shrimps (Dixon) 326
15th Regiment 296
54th Regiment 310
Fifth Avenue Theatre (New York; first) 145
fights, staged 97
Fille de Madam Angot, La (Lecocq and Byron) 110
film theatres. *See* movie houses/palaces
finales 181
Final Rehearsal (E.S. Carter) 344
Firebrand, The (Stringer) 345
fire engine houses / fire halls 249, 256, 261, 274
fire: escapes 252; prevention authorities 221, 250; safety regulations 342
fireproofed theatres 231
fires 215; in Belleville 326; in Brantford 329; in Brockville 262; in Galt 274; in Gananoque 342; in Hamilton 161*n*3, 340; in Kingston 217, 238, 306, 327, 340; in London (Ont.) 131, 235, 329; in Meaford 258; in Niagara 27; in Orillia 272, 273, 336; in Ottawa 242, 243, 323, 337; in Peterborough 260; in Rat Portage 330, 336; in St Thomas 265; in Stratford 275, 276; in Toronto 26, 34, 41, 221, 222, 226, 227, 228, 294, 304, 321, 323, 327, 333, 342
Fireworshippers, The (Newcomb and Hanks) 330

First Families of the Sierras, The Miller) 136
First Night, The (Wigan) 83
Fish Out of Water (Lunn) 64
Fiske, Harrison Gray (playwright) 157
Fiske, Minnie Maddern (actress/playwright) 145, 146, 157, 160, 226, 336
Fitch, Clyde (playwright) 144
Fitgig, Ceralia (role of) 62
Fitzball, Edward (playwright) 67
Fitzgerald, P.A. (actor/playwright) 136
Fitzjames, Miss (performer) 299
Fitzwilliam Island (Ont.) 137
Fitzwilliam, Mrs 299
flag, British 294, 296
flea circuses, travelling 12
Fleming, Sir Sandford (architect) 313
flimflam men 174
Flint, Adelaide (actress) *150*
Flock, E.W.M. (lawyer) 163*n*14
floor(s), 242; flat, 247, 248, 249, 251, 260, 264, 265, 267; raked/sloped, 227, 231, 251, 254, 258; temporary 223
Florence Co. W.J., 139
Florence, Mrs (actress) 106
Florence, W.J. (comedian) 106
fly: galleries 240, 270, 281; lofts 223, 236, 258; flying 235
folk literature 181; music 181
Following Up a Clue (anon.) 332
Fontenelle (H.G. and M.M. Fiske) 157
Fool's Revenge, The (Taylor) 94, 96
footlights 221, 222, 234
Forbes, James (playwright) 47, 319, 346
Forbes, Mr and Mrs (actors) 300
Forbes-Robertson, Sir Johnston (actor) 160, 342
For Canada and Empire (Carlyle) 339

foreign actors 134, 146–59. *See also*
   touring companies/productions
Forepaugh-Sells circus 175
For Queen and Country (Fraser) 332
Forrest, W.S., company 299, 300
Fortier, J.D. (decorator) 272
Fort Niagara 277, 289
'Fortunes of War, The' (Nickinson) 310
Fort William (Ont.) 44, 133; Town Hall
   133, 334
47th Regiment 56, 70, 71, 77, 78,
   81–2, 87*n*35
Foster, William 36
Fouché (role of) 97
14th Regiment 300
14th Street Theatre (New York),
   212*n*41
Fowler, Orson Squire
   (phrenologist/lecturer), 118
foyers 231
Fra Diavolo (Auber) 110
frame buildings 217, 218
Francesca da Rimini (Boker) 155
Franchi, Dei *See* Dei Franchi
francophone performers 156–7
Franklin, Irene (vaudeville performer)
   201, 202
Frank's Hotel (York) 123, 218, 291,
   292
Fraser, John A., Jr (playwright /
   director) 332
freaks 175, 191, 192–3
Frederic Lemaitre (Fitch) 144
Freemasons' Tavern (Kingston) 216
Free, Mickey (character) 169
French Chaos (Ramsay) 322
French, Charles (murderer) 292
French Empire architectural style 269
French, James (theatre manager) 221
French opera 110–11
French Renaissance architectural style
   231, 233, 260, 270

frescoed ceilings 221, 223, 231, 240
Friganza, Trixi (vaudeville performer)
   201
Frohman, Charles (manager, producer)
   144, 209, 315
frontier dramas 158
Frou-Frou (Meilhac and Halévy;
   transl. by Daly) 100, 121, 156
Fuller, William Henry (playwright) 8,
   40, 41, 323, 327, 332
fund raising 55–6

gables 264, 265
Gaiete Vaudeville Company 185, 199
galleries: art 191, 227; audience seating
   219, 221, 223, 226, 227, 231, 234,
   238; cross-over 280; fly 240, 270,
   280; rigging 270 240, 241, 248,
   269, 272
Galt (Ont.; now Cambridge) 163*n*14,
   175, 296, 300, 301; Scott's Opera
   House 273–4, 337; Town Hall 273;
   313, 334, 336; Young's Assembly
   Room 301
Galt Thespian Amateurs 300
gamblers and gambling, 60, 174
Gambrinus, King of Lager Beer 115
Gananoque (Ont.) 322; Amateur
   Dramatic Society 326; Dufferin Hall
   322, 326; Turner's Opera House 342
Garden River Reserve (Sault Ste Marie)
   10, 339–40
Garden Theatre. *See* Buffalo; New
   York
Gardiner, C.R. (circuit manager) 128
Garnier, John Hutchinson (playwright)
   326
Garrick Club. *See* Hamilton; Montreal
Garrison Amateurs. *See* Bytown;
   Kingston; London (Ont.); Toronto
garrison: entertainments 6, 14, 25;
   theatre 32, 52–89, 108–9, 123. *See*

also Bytown; Kingston; London (Ont.); Toronto; York

garrisons 20, 21–2, 289

Garrison Theatre (London) 300

Garrison Theatrical Club (Kingston) 78

Garside's Hotel (York) 173

Gascon, Jean (actor/director) 277

gas lighting 14, 30, 34, 221, 223, 264, 299, 340

Gayety Theatre (Toronto) 196, 197, 198, 344

Gentlemen Amateurs. *See* Hamilton: Kingston; London; Toronto; York

George Watson & Son (architects) 245–6

Georgia Minstrels (minstrel troupe) 178

Georgian architectural style 21, 258

Georgian Bay 27, 28, 44, 127

German, performances in 157

Gertrude (role of) 141

'G.F. Bailey's & Cos. Metropolitan Quadruple Combination,' 174

Ghent, Stephen (role of) 145

Ghosts (Ibsen) 121, 340

giants 193

Gilbert, Mr (actor-manager) 291, 293

Gilbert, Mrs (actress; née Mary Duff) 301, 305

Gilbert and Sullivan 8, 10, 113, 330

Gilbert and Trowbridge touring company 294

Gilbert, W.S. (playwright/librettist) 41, 106, 107–8, 113

Gilflory, Mrs (role of) 106

Gillis Theatre (Kansas City) 162n10

Gilmour, Mr (performer) 294

girl/'girlie' shows 117, 186

Glaser, Vaughan (actor-manager) 342

glass-blowing exhibitions 190, 191

Glaus(e), Mr (puppeteer) 291

glees 95

Glengarry School Days (Connor) 47

Globe Hotel (Cobourg) 302

Goderich (Ont.) 157–8; Grand Opera House 334; Temperance Hall 334; Victoria Hall 318

Godley, John 3, 5

gods, aisles/seating of the 231, 238, 242

Golden Age 16–17, 174–5

Golden, George Fuller (vaudeville performer) 201

Golden Giant, The (A.M. Rankin and Greene) 137, 333

Goldie Street (Paisley) 247

Goldoni, Carlo (playwright) 154

Goldsmith, Oliver (playwright) 103

Good Templars' Hall (Belleville) 326

Goodwin, Nat (actor) 160

Gordon & Helliwell, Architects 270

Gore Militia (Ancaster) 292

Gore's Hall (Rat Portage) 330

Gothic architectural style 273

Gothic Revival architectural style 262

Gouinlock, George W. (architect) 265

Gounod, Charles François (composer) 110

Government House (Ottawa) 41

Government House of Upper Canada (Toronto) 34, 294

Gowan's Hall (Ottawa) 318, 322

Gowan's New Opera House. *See* Ottawa

Gowan's (Old) Opera House. *See* Ottawa

Graham, Franklin (historian) 155

Grammar School (Cobourg) 316

'Grand Caravan of Living Animals' 171, 292

Grande Duchese de Gérolstein, La (Offenbach)

'Grand Exhibition of Living Animals' 171, 291

Grand Masonic Lodge of Canada 297

Grand Mechanics Ball (York) 294

Grand Mogul (Farnie) *110*
'Grand Olio Entertainment' 184
Grand Opera House Company 222
Grand Opera House. *See* Goderich;
  Hamilton; Kingston; London, (Ont.);
  Ottawa; Peterborough; St Louis; St
  Thomas; Toronto
Grand Rapids (MI) 139, 161*n*10
Grand Theatre. *See* Grand Rapids;
  Kingston; London(Ont.)
Granger, F.H. (artist) 219, 221
*Grantly Granville; or the Hag of the
  Mountains* (Johnson) 316
Gravenhurst (Ont.): Opera House *252*,
  254, 256, 284, 340; Town Hall 254,
  340
Gray, Ada (actress) 325
Gray, George (architect) 256
Great Divide, The (Moody) 145, 326
Greatest Show on Earth, (Ringling
  Brothers and) Barnum and Bailey's
  174, *175*
Great Lakes circuit 291
Great Northern Theatre (Chicago, IL)
  161*n*10
Great Slave Troupe of Jubilee Singers
  114
Great Western Amphitheatre company
  299
'Greek Ball' 292
Greeley, Horace (journalist) 32
Greenaway, Kate (illustrator) 103
Greene, Clay (American playwright)
  137, 332, 333
Green, James (actor) 327
Green Pastures (Connelly) 316
green room 225
Green Stockings 144
Greer, Sergeant (actor) 80
Greet, Ben (actor-manager) 340, 342
Grein's (J.T.) Independent Theatre
  (London, Eng.) 344

Grey, Francis (playwright) 342
Grey, Earl (governor-general) 6, 49,
  342, 344
Grier, Wylie (painter) 309
gridiron 231, 236, 280
Griffin, John J. (theatre manager)
  206–7, 310, 342
Griffin, Peter (movie-house owner) 342
Griffin Theatre. *See* Belleville; Stratford
Grip Among the Politicians (Anon.) 323
Grip in Council (Anon.) 323
'Grip' (J.W. Bengough(?); playwright/
  editor) 324
Grip-Sack 329–30
Grip (Toronto) 8, 137, 321, 323–7
  passim, 329, 330, 332, 333, 334,
  336
Grosvenor, Florence, benefit for 81
Group of Seven 47
Guelph (Ont.) 24, 29, 38, 123, 127,
  141, 175, 292, 319, 336, 340; Drill
  Shed 324; Market Building 312; the
  Priory 302; Royal Opera House 336;
  Thorpe's Music Hall 316; Town Hall
  317
guest artists 61, 146–52
Guillaume Tell (Rossini) 110
Gulliver's Travels (Swift) 289–90
Gunn, Kate (performer) *112*
'Guy Fawkes' (song) 75
Guy Mannering (adapted from novel by
  Scott) 157
Gwynne (Gwinne) Mr (performer), 296
gymnasia 317

Habberton, John (novelist) 114
L'Habitant (G.C. Rankin) 334
Hackett, James K. (actor / vaudeville
  performer) 201, 318
Halévy, Ludovic (playwright) 100
Halford, Allan (actor) 314, 318
Haller, Mrs (role of) 99–100

Hall, Irving (playwright) 342
Hall, Mrs Buchanan (poet/lecturer) 118
Hamilton (Ont.) 6, 10, 25, 28, 29, 38,
    39, 41, 45, 48, 70–1, 133, 141,
    178, 291, 293, 296, 301, 317, 337;
    amateur theatre in 216, 297,
    299–306 passim, 317, 323; Amateur
    Theatrical Society 301, 302, 304,
    305; animals / animal acts in 312;
    benefit performances in 300, 301,
    302, 304, 305, 310; and burlesque
    195, 197; Board of Police 300;
    Burlington Hotel Ballroom 292;
    circus(es) in 175; City Hall 332;
    Engine House 294, 295, 296;
    Garrick Club (now Hamilton Players
    Guild) 321, 322, 323; Gentlemen
    Amateurs 297, 300; Grand Opera
    House 10, 14, 41, 111, 131, 141,
    162n14, 197, 239, 240–1, 315,
    327, 332, 334, 336, 346; Histrionic
    Society 306; Mechanics' Hall 71;
    317; Pantages Theatre 200, 210;
    performances in 292, 299, 300, 301,
    307, 330, 346; performers from 112;
    plays published in 316, 319, 322,
    333–334, 336, 340, 345; Price's
    tavern, 292; resident stock com-
    panies in 146; Royal Metropolitan
    Theatre 161n3, 310, 312; Summers
    Mountain Playhouse 340; Summers
    Mountain Theatre 345; Templeton
    Star Opera Company 333; theatre
    facilities in 125, 131, 216, 216, 294,
    295, 297, 300; Theatre Royal 300,
    301, 302, 304, 305, 306; touring
    companies in 124, 125, 127, 128,
    155, 301, 314; Town Hall 216, 216,
    297, 299, 300; variety theatres in
    189; vaudeville in 204, 207, 342;
    ventriloquism in 301
Hamilton Amateurs 304, 305, 306;

Hamilton Amateur Theatrical Society
    300, 301, 302, 304, 305; Hamilton
    Theatrical Society 300
Hamilton Gentlemen Amateurs 297,
    300
Hamilton Players Guild 323
Hamlet (role of) 117, 130, 143, 143,
    154
Hamlet (Shakespeare) 94, 95, 119, 149,
    154, 155, 329
Hammond & Robinson (contractors)
    271–2
Hamper, Genevieve (actress) 95
Hampton Court 160
Hand, Thomas W. (playwright) 340
Hanks, J.M. (playwright) 330
Hanlan, Ned (vaudeville performer) 260
Hanlan's Point (Ont.), Mackie's
    Summer Theatre 332
Happy Return, The (anon.) 325
Harmonic Club (Hamilton?) 333–4
Harold Nelson Stock Company 14
Harper, J.M. (playwright) 344
Harrington, George (historian/diarist) 16
Harris, Amelia (diarist) 88n35
Harrison, J.B. (playwright) 301, 305,
    306
Harrison, Mark 302
Harrison, Richard B. (actor/teacher)
    316
Harrison, S.F. (composer) 332
Harriston (Ont.) 256; Town Hall 244
Harry Lorrequer (Lever) 108
Hastings (Ont.) Town Hall, 337
Hatton, Theodore (actor) 291
Hauk, Minnie (opera singer) 94
Haverly-Burgess Minstrels (minstrel
    troupe) 178
Haverly, J.H. (minstrel performer) 178
Haverly's Minstrels 183
Havlin's Theatre (St Louis, MO) 161n10
Havresac (role of) 76

Hazel Kirke (Mackaye) 102
Hazlewood, Nellie (early stage name of
    Julia Arthur, née Ida Lewis), 141,
    164*n*25. *See also* Lewis, Ida
Heads and Tails (Bengough) 324
heating, (theatres) 247, 260, 270
'Heaven Will Protect the Working Girl'
    (song) 207
Hedda Gabler (Ibsen) 344
Heir at Law, The (Colman the younger)
    87*n*29, 103
Helen's Babies (Habberton) 114
Henderson, J. Duff (playwright) 339
Henley, George (stage name of Arthur
    McKee Rankin) 136
Henry V (Shakespeare) 95, 327
Henry, Walter 87*n*35
Henson, Josiah (escaped slave) 293
*Hephaestus, Persephone at Etna and
    Sappho in Leucadia* (Stringer) 340
Herbert, Victor (composer) 117
Her Majesty's Theatre. *See* London
    (Ont.), Ottawa
Herndon, T.J. (theatre manager) 189,
    323
Herndon family (actors) 146
heroines 100, 113
Heron, Matilda (actress) 12, 100, 145,
    154, 313
Heron family 125, 306–7; Agnes,
    Fanny, Mary Ann (actresses) John
    (actor) 306–7; Bijou (actress) 145
Herrmann the Great (magician) 118
Heuck's Theatre (Cincinnati, OH)
    161*n*10
*Hiawatha or Manabozho; An Ojibway
    Indian Play* (Armstrong) 10, *13, 15,*
    339–40
Highland regiments 66
Highland Society 66, 306
Highland Society of Canada West
    (Hamilton) 304

High Life below Stairs (Townley) 292
High Park (Toronto) 176
High Victorian period 13, 35–42, 184
highways 46, 124. *See also*
    transportation
Hildebrand (Campbell) 336
Hill, Barton (performer) 301, 304
Hill, Charles (actor/manager/lecturer)
    301, 302, 305, 306
Hill, Mrs Charles (actress) 304, 305,
    306
Hill, Penny (theatre manager) 259–60
Hill, Robert (treasurer) 144
Hill, Rosalie (actress/lecturer) 304, 305,
    306
Hill family (actors) 305, 306
Hill's Music Hall (Peterborough)
    259–60, 306
Hill's Opera House (Ann Arbor, MI)
    131
Hilliard, Robert (stage star / vaudeville
    performer) 201
Hilliard's Opera House and Hotel (Rat
    Portage, now Kenora *131,* 133, 336,
    337
Hippodrome (New York) 236
Hippodrome, Shea's. *See* Buffalo;
    Toronto
historical: artifacts 190; dramas 337
    (*see also* Costume Drama); pageant
    plays 158; panoramas 168; romances
    47, 158; tableaux 342
Histrionic Society (Hamilton) 306
H.M. Canadian Ship Blunderbore
    (anon.) 327
H.M.S. Parliament (Fuller) 8, *40, 41,*
    327
H.M.S. Pinafore (Gilbert and Sullivan)
    126
Hoffman, Gertrude
    (burlesque/vaudeville performer)
    195, 196, 201

hoists 246
Holland, George (actor) 313
Holman, George (actor-manager) 34,
    125, 127, 233, 317, 318, 322,
    330
Holman, Sallie (Mrs George; amateur
    actress), 82, 233, 317
Holmans 146
Holman Opera Company, 125, 126,
    131, 317, 318
Holman Opera House. See London
    (Ont.), Toronto
Holmes, Sherlock (role of) 158
Holy City, or The Way of the Cross,
    The 158
Home, John (playwright) 5, 80
'home talent' shows 114–15
Honeymoon, or How to Rule a Wife,
    The (Tobin) 155
Hope, Bob (vaudeville performer) 200
Hopkins, George (theatre owner-
    builder), 248
Hopkins' Music Hall (Whitby), 248,
    326
Hopper, Edna Wallace (vaudeville
    performer) 201
Horseshoe Falls 169
Horticultural Gardens Pavilion
    (Toronto) 327
horticultural pavilions 184, 228, 318,
    327
Hose's Music Hall (Rat Portage; now
    Kenora) 334
hotels 26, 29, 65, 83, 125, 167, 171,
    176, 218, 240, 241, 291
Houdini (vaudeville performer) 201
Hough, Mr (performer) 297
house: curtains 234, 238, 240, 241,
    267; drop 242; lights 223, 231, 264,
    272
House of Oedipus, The (Stringer) 346
Hows, J.W.S. (performer) 294

Hughes, Lieut-Col. (military
    commander) 80
Hugo, Victor (novelist/playwright) 96,
    102
Hume, Wallace (architect) 221
humour, 109, 181. See also comedy
Hunchback, The (Knowles) 149
Hunt, Bill. See Farini, Guillermo
    Antonio
Hunter, W.S. (painter) 168, 293
Hunting, Percy (actor) 254
Hurlbut, Frank (carpenter) 254
'Husking Bee, or Courtship in the
    Woods, The' 292
Hyman's Music Hall (London, Ont.;
    later Holman Opera House) 317, 322

Ibsen, Henrik (playwright) 99, 121,
    336, 340, 344
Ici On Parle Français (Williams) 109
idiot savant 117
'I Don't Care' (song) 202
illusions 14, 315
immigrants 3, 13, 14, 20–4, 27–8, 35,
    38, 42–4, 46, 183, 199
Imogen (role of) 143
improvisation 181
Inchcape Bell, The (Fitzball) 67
independence of theatre companies/
    managers 127, 128– 162n13
Independent Order of Good Templars
    318
Indians, native 10, 20, 22, 46, 47, 119
ingenue roles 82
Ingomar the Barbarian (Lovell) 96,
    97–8, 116
Innocent Bigamy ('C.P.M.') 329
inns 26, 123–4, 186
In The Workhouse – Christmas Day
    119
inventions/discoveries 137, 170, 175,
    190, 203

Iphigenia (Euripides) 144
Irish: attitudes towards 114; caricatures 178; 'character' melodrama 337, 339; immigrants 23, 24, 27–8; stage representations of 102, 180, 337, 339
Irish Lion, The (Buckstone) 62
'Iron Mike.' *See* Shea, Michael
Irving, Sir Henry (actor-manager) 49, 93, 94, 109, 118, 134, 141, 143, 330
Irving, Laurence (actor-manager) 346
Irwin, Flora (vaudeville performer) 209
Irwin, May (vaudeville performer) 201, 207, 209, 315
Isabella (role of) 149
Is She a Woman (Collier) 74
Italian, performances in 154
Italian Renaissance architectural style 242
Italianate architectural style, 246
Ixion (burlesque show) 194

Jackson, Buckner (vaudeville performer) 209
Jackson, Stewart (vaudeville performer) 209
Jackson, T.D. (architect) 222
Jackson (MI) 141
Jacob Hose's Music Hall (Rat Portage) 334
Jacob, H.R. (theatre circuit manager) 128, 225
Jacob's (H.R.) Royal Museum and Novelty Company 191
Jacob and Sparrow's Opera House or Theatre (Toronto; later the Majestic Theatre) 225–6, 333
Jameson, Anna (author) 296
Janauschek, Mme Francesca Romanana Magdalena (actress) 155

Jane Eyre (adapted by Brougham) 41
Janis, Elsie (vaudeville performer) 201
Jarvie, Balilie Nicol (actor) 61
J.B. Lent's World Fair Leviathan Universal Living Exhibition 174
Jefferson, Joseph (actor) 327, 334
Jerome, J.K. (playwright/novelist) 119, 120
Jerrold, Douglas (playwright) 101
Jessica (role of) 63, 95
Jessie Brown, or the Siege of Lucknow (Boucicault) 101, 149
Jews, attitudes towards 114
John Bull and Jonathan (anon.) 325
John Gilpin (anon.) 103
Johnson, E. Pauline (poet) 47
Johnson, George Washington (playwright) 316
Johnson, G.W., performs in Kingston 312
Johnson's Minstrels 183
Jo Jo the Dog Faced Boy (freak) 192, 193
Jolson, Al (vaudeville performer) 186, 201, 202, 211
Jones, Henry Arthur (playwright) 155
Josephine 156–7
Josephine, Empress (role of) 143–4, 156–7
Joshua Whitcomb (Denman Thompson) 103
Joy Girl, The (film) 209
Judah, Mr and Mrs Emmanuel (performers) 16, 291, 292
jugglers/juggling 48, 173, 202, 203
Julia (role of) 149
Juliet (role of) *140*, 141, 143, 149, 151, 152
Julius Caesar (Shakespeare) 155, 160
Julius Cahn's Official Theatrical Guide 225, 227, 242, 243

Jumbo (elephant) 332
Juvenile Thespian Society, Toronto 296
'J.W.S.' (pseud. playwright) 332

Katherine and Petruchio (Garrick) 96
Kayelle, Jay (playwright) 329
Kean, Charles (actor) 95
Keatings British Coffee House (York) 294
Keaton, Buster (vaudeville performer) 200
Keene, Laura (actress) 317
Keene, Thomas W. (actor) 146, 154–5, 337
Keith, B.F. (vaudeville circuit owner) 199, 205. *See also* B.F. Keith Exchange
Kelcey, Herbert (actor) 158, 344
Kemble, Fanny (performer) 306
Kemble family 6, 293
Kennedy, King (magician) 325
Kennedy, Mr (performer) 290
Kenora (Ont.; formerly Rat Portage) 6, 44; Gore's Hall 330; Hilliard Opera House 337; Jacob Hose's Music Hall 334; Rat Portage Dramatic Club *335*
Kenworthy, Mr (ventriloquist) 167
Keogh, Lieutenant (amateur actor) 71, 74
Kermess, the (Carleton Place) *339*
Ker's Music Hall (Brantford) 317
Key of Life, The (Scott) 344
Killing Time (Morton) 296
Kimber, Mrs (actress) 312
Kinetophone 346
King, George W. (architect) 275
King Arthur (Carr) 143
King for a Day (Auber) 110
King John (Shakespeare) 96, 149
King's College (Toronto) 28
Kingston (Ont.) 3, 6, 10, *12*, 13, 16, 22–5 *passim*, 28, 29, 30, 38, 125, 133, 137, 168, 178, 289, 290, 291, 297, 299, 300, 305, 307, 313, 333, 334, 336; amateur theatre in 5, 56–7, 79–80, 84, 216, 290, 291 293, 296, 299, 300; Atheneum Theatre 217, 299; Butler's Theatre 217; circus(es) in 172, 175, 297; City Hall 70, 217, 300, 310, 318; Civilian Amateurs 299; Commercial Hotel 294; Court House 307; Female Benevolent Society 67, 291; Freemasons' Tavern 216; Garrison Amateurs 67, 83–4, 87n35, 294, 312, 315, 322; garrison theatre in 5, 52–3, 55–61 *passim*, 63–70 *passim*, 74, 77, 78, 81, 83–4, 85n3, 87n35, 216, 290, 293, 294, 296, 300, 310, 315; Garrison Theatrical Club 78; Gentlemen Amateurs, 66, 67, 216; Grand Opera House *12*, 127, 131, 162n14, 317, 340; Grand Theatre 238, 240, 284, 327; Lambton House 297; La Rue's Great War Show 315; Martin's Opera House, 163n20, *236*, 237–8, 326–7, 333, 340; Mr Meagher's Hall 294; Mr Meagher's Hotel 294; Meagher's rooms 297; Memorial Hall 215, 217, *218*, 300; Naval and Military Amateurs 56, 61, 65–7; Navy Dockyards 84; New Theatre 293, 300, 315; Ontario Hall 318; Poncet's Inn 290; Royal Lyceum 317; Tête du Pont barracks 216, 299; theatre facilities in 80–1, 83–4, 215, 216–17, *218*, *236*, 237–8, 291, 293, 299, 300; Theatre Royal 217, 299, 300, 302, 304, 306, 318; touring companies in 125, 127, 128, 291, 292, 294, 301, 312, 314; Town Hall 217; Mrs Walker's Hotel 293; Walker's Hotel 216, 290; Wellington Inn 294

Kingston Amateurs 299
Kingston Amateur Theatre 5, 56–7, 290, 291
Kingston Dramatic Amateurs 80, 296
Kingston Hotel 16, 58–9, 291
Kirby, William (poet; novelist) 32, 36
Kirke, Miller (role of) 102
Kismet or the Two Tangled Turks 242
Kitchener (Ont.; formerly Berlin) 29, 47
Klaw, Marc (producer) 160
Knight, Joseph (critic) 106
Knoll, Mr (cornetist) 191
Knott, Roselle (actress; later Mrs Ernest Shipman) *135*
Knowles, Sheridan (playwright) 96, 156
Knox Church (Galt) 273, 274
Koerber, Leila. *See* Dressler, Marie
Kotzebue, August F.F. von (playwright) 99–100

Labour and Capital 330
Lady Audley's Secret (adapted from novel by Braddon) 101, 222
Lady Clancarty (Taylor) 98–9
Lady Constance (role of), 149
Lady Lil (Marston) 156
Lady of Lyons, The (Bulwer-Lytton and Byron) 34, 96, 141, 149
Lady of Quality, A (Burnett) 143
Lajeunesse, Emma (Mme Albani) 330
Lake of Killearney by Moonlight (Mayne) 296
Lalor, George H. (architect) 240
Lalor and Martin (architects) 222
lambrequins 234
Lamb, Thomas W. (architect) 282–284
Lambton House (Kingston) 297
Lamert, Captain (actor) 73, 83
Lampman, Archibald (playwright/poet) 36, 340
Lancashire Relief Fund 315

Lancers, The (J.H. Payne) 66
Lancers, The (adapted by Miller) 145
landings, 248, 273
Land of Liberty, The (anon.) 326
Landon, Lois (dancer/singer/actress) 342
Lane, Henry (architect) 278
Langdon, Harry (theatre manager) 317
Langley, Mr (architect) 248
Lang, Mr (actor) 73
Langtry, Lillie (actress / vaudeville performer) 92, 201
language 103, 121, 195–6
lanterns, 221, 234, 247, 272, 279, 283
Laponte and Lefleur Company 312
La Rue's Great War Show 168, 315
LaSalle, Mr (theatre owner) 317
Lathrop, Francis (artist) 241
Latin, plays presented in 292
Lauder, Harry (vaudeville performer) 201
Laughing Water Festival (Meaford) *257*
Laura Secord, the Heroine of 1812 (Curzon) 333
Laurel, Stan (vaudeville performer) 200
Laurier (elephant) 176
lavatories 231, 250, 259
lawsuits, 163n21
Leach, Jonathan (actor) 74
Leacock, Stephen (author) 47, 346
Leadbeater, Mary (author) 290
leasing of theatres 133
Leavitt, Michael B. (theatre manager) 133–4, 194
lecture halls 184
'Lecture on Heads' (Stevens) 293
lecturers 118, 123, 168, 170, 175, 190, 203, 216
lectures 13, 30–1, 118, 167, 190, 191, 217, 260, 294, 306, 317, 324, 329, 330, 344. *See also* educational content

Lee, Graves Simcoe (actor/playwright) 8, 292, 307, *308*, 310, *311*, 313, 315
Le Gendre (de Bernard) *335*
Legend of the Roses, The (Watson) 325
legitimate theatre(s): and burlesque shows 193–6; and minstrel shows 176, 183; and movies 210, 284; and variety theatre 167, 184, 185; and vaudeville 200–1, 204, 207, 209, 210–11
Legouvé, Ernest (playwright) 99
Lemon, Mark (playwright) 111
Lempert, Leon (painter) 240
Lempert, Leon J., & Son, Architects 280
Lennox, Thomas (actor) 301
Lent, J.B. (circus operator) 174
Lent's Circus 175
Leo, the Royal Cadet (Cameron) 10, *12*, 333
Leonard, Dan (actor) 302
Lescarbot, Marc (poet/playwright) 10
Leslie, Emma (actress) 62
Lever, Charles (novelist) 108
Le Vieillard dupé 289
Lewis, Ella (child actress) 141
Lewis, Horace (actor) 139
Lewis, Ida (actress; stage names Nellie Hazlewood / Enos / Julia Arthur) 127, 134, 141–4, *143*, 164*n*25, 317, 332
Lewis, Lillian (actress) 156
Lewis, Portia (actress) 139
Lewis, Richard (elocutionist) 319
L'Habitant (George Rankin) 334
licences, performance 6, 173–4, 176, 178, 312
Life on the Stage (Morris) 145
Life in Wellington's Army (Brett-James) 55
lifts 281, 282. *See also* elevators
lighting 5, 14, 91, 168, 249, 258, 279;

electric 38, 223, 236, 238, 241, 254, 264, 270, 274, 283; gas 14, 30, 34, 221, 223, 264, 299, 340
light opera(s) 10, 111, 113, 155, 207. *See also opéra comique*
light-proof plugs 279
Light for the Temperance Platform 324
Lillie, Beatrice (Lady Robert Peel; actress) 336
Lily of Killarney, The (Benedict) 111
Lincoln, Abraham (role of) 336
Linden, Henry (actor) 315
Lind, Jenny (singer) 30, 307
Lindley, Harry (actor-manager/ playwright) 82, 146, *150*, 334, 336
Lindsay, Lieutenant (actor) 73
Lindsay (Ont.) 163*n*14, 270, 340; Academy of Music / Academy Theatre *268*, 268–70, *269*, 284, 334; Town Hall 268, 318
lion-tamers 172
literary and debating clubs/societies 6, 13, 47
Literary Garland 32
Little Egypt (burlesque dancer) 195
Little, J.Z. (actor-manager) 314
Little Co-ed, The 160
Little Em'ly (Rowe) 104
Little Eva (role of) 101
Little Hip (elephant) 204
Little Leaven, A (Merritt) 344
Little Minister, The (Barrie) 121, 345
Little Nobody (Dixon) 324, 325
Little Starlight (role of) *160*
'little theatre' 12–13, 49. *See also* amateur theatre
Little Toddlekins (Mathews) 109
Little Willy (role of) 101
Living Ossified Man, the, 192, 193
Living Picture 270
'living statuary' 189, 193–4, 195, 323

Llewellyn, Mr (performer) 302
Lloyd, Alice (vaudeville performer) 201
lobbies 242, 247, 249, 256, 262, 282
Local (Anon.) 333
Lockyear, Ensign (amateur actor), 71, 75
Loew, Marcus (theatre owner) 200, 282
Loew's theatres. *See* Toronto
Loew's vaudeville theatre syndicate, 199, 200, 210
lofts: fly 223, 236, 258; rigging 227, 235, 236, 240, 243, 258
Loftus, Cissie (vaudeville performer) 201
London (Eng.) 5, 17n6, 34, 42, 48, 154, 172, 189, 228, 230, 290, 299; Canadian-written plays published in 333, 339, 340, 346; Crystal Palace 228; Grein's (J.T.) Independent Theatre 344; Her Majesty's Theatre 314; Old Vic Theatre 17n6; Queen's Theatre 299
London (Ont.) 16, 23, 25, 29, 38, 39, 125, *126*, 146, 175, 296, 300, 301, 307, 310, 313, 316, 318, 332, 340; Amateur Club 61; amateur theatre in 59, 61, 79, 81, 82, 83, 292, 300; Brunton's Varieties 125; City Hall 312; Civilian Dramatic Society, 79, 315; Court House Square 216; Covent Garden Theatre 312; Garrison Amateurs 71, 74–5, 79, 296; Garrison Theatre 300; garrison theatre in 52, 53, 55, 57–65 *passim*, 68, 69, 71, 73–5, 77–8, 79, 81–2, 88n35, 296, 297, 299, 300, 315, 317; Gentlemen Amateurs 215, 297, 299, 300; Grand Opera House (first; in Masonic Temple, 1881–1900) *129*, 131, 152, 154, 155, 163n15, 252, 329, 339; Grand Opera House (New) (second; 1901–) 131, 133,

162n14, 163n15, 235–6, 317, 340; Grand Theatre 284; Holman Opera House 125, 131, *232*, 232–3, 322; Hyman's Music Hall 317; Mechanics' Hall 233, Mechanics' Institute 216, 299, 300, 326, 342; Music Hall 232; Queen's Avenue Opera House 332; Shakespeare Club 81, 215–16, 300, 301; Shakespeare Festival 316; Mr Spettigue's Concert Hall 319; Tecumseh House Hotel 155; theatre facilities in 83, 131, 215–16, 232–6, 286n24, 297; Theatre London 160; Theatre Royal 83, 125, 297; touring companies in 127, 128, 152, 162n13, 300, 301, 340; University of Western Ontario 340; and variety shows 312; and vaudeville 207, 342; Victoria Hall 326
London Amateur Dramatic Association 315. *See also* Civilian Dramatic Society, London.
London Amateurs / London Amateur Theatricals 82, 83
London Assurance (Boucicault) 65
London Theatrical Company 215–16
London Comedy Company 125
London Electric Company 236
Longley, Ernest G. (playwright) 334
Long, Mr (actor) 123, 293
Long Strike, The (Boucicault) 330
Lonsdale, Lillie, benefit for 318
Lord Fitz Fraud ('C.P.M.') 329
Lorenzo (role of) 95
Lorne, Marquess of 10
Louis XI (role of) 97
Louise, Princess 10
Louis Riel, or The Northwest Rebillion (Greene) 332
Love-A-la-Mode (Macklin) 290
Lovell, Maria (playwright) 96

Lowery, Colonel (theatre patron) 71
Loyalist architectural style 21
Loyalist history dramas 337
Lucia di Lammermoor (Donizetti) 110
Lucretia Borgia (adapted from Victor
Hugo) 141; (role of) *142*
Ludwig, the Emigrant (Schubart and
Schubart) 336
Lunn, Joseph (playwright) 64
Lyceum, Mr Mirfield's (Toronto)
300–1, 302
Lyceum Theatre. *See* Cincinnati; Cleve-
land; Detroit; Toledo; Toronto
Lyle, John MacIntosh (architect) 228,
230, 231
Lyne, T.A. (performer) 296
Lyons, Mrs, benefit for 304
lyric-stage productions 276
lyric theatre 281
Lysons, General Sir Daniel (female
impersonator) 62

*Mabel Heath, or The Farmer's
Daughter* 141
McArdle, Edward A. (vaudeville
theatre manager) 206
McAuliffe, J. (theatre owner) 232
Macbeth (Shakespeare) 95, 145, 155,
157
McBride, Robert (playwright) 313, 318
McCleary, Mr (performer) 173, 293
McCullough, Mr (actor) 154
Macdonald, Hon. John A. (theatre
patron) 305
McDonnell, William (playwright) 330
McDowell, Eugene A. (actor-manager)
8, 17n5, 127, 137, 141, 146, 147,
254, 324, 326–7
McDowell, Mrs Eugene A. (Fanny
Reeves) *145*
Macfarland, Asa (theatre manager) 315
McFarlane, A.E. (playwright) 337

McGarry, Michael (producer) 300
McGee, Thomas D'Arcy (playwright)
314
Machar, Agnes Maule (playwright) 339
McIlwraith, Jean Newton (playwright)
10, 334, 336
McIntyre and Heath (vaudeville
performers) 201
Mackaye, Steele (playwright) 102
McKay, William (contractor) 254
MacKenzie, James B. (playwright) 337
Mackenzie, William Lyon 3
Mackie's Summer Theatre (Hanlan's
Point, Toronto) 332
McLachlan, Alexander (playwright) 313
McLean, Dr (lecturer) 317
McLeay, Franklin (actor) 326
McMullen, Rowland (stunt participant)
170
MacNab, Sir Allan (actor / theatre
patron) 291, 302, 306, *309*
Macready, Mrs (performer) 312
Macready, William Charles
(playwright) 5, 290
Madeleine Morel (Bandmann) 145
Madison Square Theatre (New York) 145
Mad Philosopher, A (Brown) 334
Maeder, F.C. (actor/playwright) 137
magic/magicians 49, 118, 123, 166,
185, 202, 325
Maiden Mona the Mermaid (Dixon)
325–6
Maid and the Money, The (musical)
204
Mair, Charles (playwright) 8, 36, 41,
333, 334
Maire of St Brieux, The (Dixon) 324,
324, 325
Majestic Music Hall (Toronto) 202
Majestic Theatre. *See* Buffalo,
Stratford, Toronto
Makepeace, Stanley (architect) 282

managers, theatre 127–34
Managers' New Exchange 128
Man and Superman (Shaw) 160
Mandolin Quintette 155
Man from Ottawa, The (Summers),
   345
Maniac Lover, The (Wilks) 102
Manitoulin Island (Ont.), 44, 137
Mansart, François (architect) 233
Mansfield, Richard (actor) 144
Mantell, Robert Bruce (actor) 95, 145,
   146, 155, 157, 160, 339
Manvers Township Hall (Bethany) 346
Man and Wife (Collins) 145
Maple Leaves (Johnson) 316
Marble Hall (Belleville) 317
Margaret Eaton School of Literature
   and Expression (Toronto) 17n6, 342
Marguerite (role of) 157
Marina, The Fisherman's Daughter
   (McDonnell) 330
marine masques 10
Marionettes, The (Reece and McArdle)
   160
Mariposa Community Hall (Oakwood)
   325
Maritana (role of) 141
Maritana (Wallace) 111
Market Building. *See* Guelph;
   Peterborough; York
markets / market buildings 187, 215
Markham (Ont.) 175
Marks, Alex (actor) 327
Marks, Ernie (actor) 327
Marks, Mrs Ernie (Kitty) (actress)
   327
Marks, George (actor) 327
Marks, Joe (actor) 327
Marks, May A. Bell (Mrs R.W.
   (actress) *159*, 327; Stock Company
   158, 160
Marks, R.W. (Bob) (actor) 325, 327

Marks, Tom (actor) 327
Marks Brothers (touring company) 48,
   127, 327, *328*, 329
Marlowe, Julia (actress) 160
Marlowe, Owen (actor-manager) 313,
   314
Marlowe, Mrs Owen (née Virginia
   Nickinson; actress) 149, 307, 310,
   313, 314, 316
Marmion (Kayelle) 329
Marriage of Convenience, A (Gundy;
   adapted from Dumas) 162n13
Marshall, William (actor-manager) 125,
   127, 146
Marsh, Mr, benefit for 300
Marston, Lawrence (playwright) 156
Martin, William (theatre owner) 127,
   237
Martin-Harvey, Sir John (actor-
   manager) 127, 158, 160, 162n13
   346
Martin's Opera House. *See* Kingston
Marx Brothers (vaudeville/film
   performers) 200
Mary of Magdalen (adapted from
   Hebbel) 226
Mary Stuart (adapted from Schiller) 157
Mascotte, La (Farnie and Reece) 155
Masks and Faces (Taylor) 99
Mason, Charles Kemble (actor) 296,
   304, 305
masonic halls/lodges 5, 30, 297
Masonic Lodge (Ameliasburg) 323
Masonic Music Hall (Belleville) 184,
   319
Masonic Temple (London, Ont.) 233.
   See also Grand Opera House
   (London, Ont.)
masques 10
*Masque Entitled 'Canada's Welcome',
   A* (Dixon) 327
Massey, Raymond (actor) 336

Massey Hall (Toronto) 49, 214
Mathews, C.J. (playwright and actor)
  73, 109
Mathews, Charles, Sr (actor) 313
Matthews, Captain John (radical
  reformer) 26
matinées 197, 203, 209
Maude, Cyril (actor) 160
Maxwell (one-eyed fiddler) 26
May, Isabella (Belle Stevenson; Mrs
  George Summers; actress) 343
Mayne, David H. (playwright) 296
Mazeppa (Lord Byron) 117, 194, 307
Meaford (Ont.), Town Hall and Opera
  House 257, 258–9, 284, 316, 344
Meagher's: Hall (Kingston) 294; Hotel
  294; rooms 297
Mean Club Plot, The ('Toots') 313
mechanics' halls 125
Mechanics' Hall. *See* Hamilton,
  London (Ont.)
mechanics' institutes 6, 13, 30, 293
Mechanics' Institute. *See* London
  (Ont.); Toronto; York
Meddle, Mack (role of) 65
Medea (Euripides) 144
Meers, Mr, touring company 294
Mefistofele (Boito) 110
Meilhac, Henri (playwright) 100
Mellish, Fred (architect) 273, 274
melodrama 93–4, 100–3, 104, 110,
  121, 144, 145, 149, 226, 329, 330,
  333; Costume Drama as 97, 98; and
  dime museums 191; and elocutionists
  119; parodies of 329, 330; plot in 101;
  and Shakespeare 95–6
melodramas 16, 32, 42, 48, 49, 65, 66,
  111, 302, 336, 337, 339
Memorial Hall (Kingston; earlier Town
  Hall / City Hall / Theatre Royal) 215,
  217, 218, 300
menageries 14, 30, 166, 171–2, 173,

  174, 176, 178, 184, 191, 192, 292,
  293, 294, 297
Mendelssohn, Felix (composer) 111,
  157, 337
Mendelssohn Choir 47
Menken, Adah Isaacs (actress) 194, 314
men-only entertainments 118, 187, 197
Mephisto (role of) 157
Mercedes (role of) 144
Merchant of Venice, The (Shakespeare)
  63, 95, 155, 160
Merrick, Mercy (role of) 145
Merrickville (Ont.) Town Hall, 312
Merritt, Catherine Nina (playwright)
  337, 344
Merry Wives of Windsor, The
  (Shakespeare) 96
mesmerists 118
Methodist Chapel (York) 293
Methodists/Methodism 20, 24, 28, 32,
  48, 297, 326, 337, 346
Metropolitan Dramatic Association
  (Ottawa) 242
Metropolitan Opera House (New York)
  241
mezzanines 267
Middleman, The (Jones) 155–6
Middleton, J.E. (playwright) 58, 346
midgets 123, 185, 193. *See also* Nutt,
  Commodore; Stratton, Charles S.;
  Thumb, General Tom
Midland (Ont.) touring companies in 127
Midsummer Night's Dream, A
  (Shakespeare) 95–6, 149, 340
Mignon (Thomas) 110
Mikado, The (Gilbert and Sullivan),
  performed in Hamilton *111, 112,* 113
Mildmay, Mrs (role of) 82
military: band(s) 10, 17n5, 43, 52, 68,
  71 *see also* regimental band(s));
  officers/personnel 20, 21, 23, 25, 26,
  32, 52–84, 85n1, 85n6, 86n8, 86n17;

theatre/theatricals (*see* garrison theatre)
Military Orphan Asylum (Quebec City) 87*n*35
Military Train Corps 61
militia 22, 35, 77, 88*n*39, 292, 297
Millbrook (Ont.), Cavan Township Hall 322
Miller, Henry (actor) 144, 145, 326
Miller, Joaquin (novelist) 136
Miller, Mr (tavern owner), 290
Miller, Orlo (theatre historian), 83
Miller and His Men, The (Pocock) 87*n*29, 296
Miller's Assembly Room (York) 290
'Millionaires of Minstrelsy' 183
Millions for Her (Henderson) 339
Mills, Charles (architect) 240, 241
Mills, F.W. (composer) 325
Millward, Jessie (stage star / vaudeville performer) 201
Milwaukee (WI) 162*n*10
Mimico (Ont.) 209
Min and Bill (film) 209
Mind Cure, The ('Titus A. Drum') 332
mind-readers 202
miniature figures, moving 168
Minister's Bride, The (Anderson), 346
Minneapolis (MO) 137
Minnie Trail, or the Woman of Wentworth, A Tragedy in Three Acts (Wood), 319
minstrel: performers 172, 187, 188, 210, 310; shows 34, 42, 48, 114–15, 166, 176–84, *182*, 187, 194–5, 199
Miraculous Child character 101
Mirvish family 232
miscegenation 102
Miser Outwitted (Richardson) 299
Miss Multon 145 (anon.)
Mister Interlocutor (role of), 114, 115, 181

Mr Mirfield's Lyceum (Toronto) 300–1, 302
Mitchell, Roy (director), 345
Moderate Drinker, The 323
modernism, architectural style 228, 230
modern life, drama of 49, 99–100
Modern Romeo and Luliet, A (Longley) 334
Modjeska, (Mme) Helena (actress) 42, 99, 139, 145, 330
Molyneaux, St John (playwright) 326
Moncrieff, William Thomas (playwright) 66, 98
Money (Bulwer-Lytton) 105
monologues 108, 180
Montagu, H.J. (actor) 108
Montcalm, General Louis-Joseph de (military commander) 289
Montez, Lola (actress) 313
Montreal, (Que.) 3, 5, 6, 25, 28, 32, 54, 60, 67, 75, 85*n*7, 124, 137, 157, 162*n*14, 172, 230, 299, 307, 332; Academy of Music 327; circus(es) in 172; Garrick Club 88*n*47; plays published in 323, 340; playwrights from 339; resident stock companies in 146; Shakespeare Dramatic and Literary Club 88*n*47; Theatre Royal 302; touring companies in/from 128, 290, 291; and vaudeville 206, 207, 342
Moodie, Susanna (author) 32
Moody, William Vaughn (poet/playwright) 145, 326
'Moon Hath Raised Her Lamp Above, The' (aria) 111
Moore, Dora Mavor (actress) 17*n*6, 344, 345
Moore, Eva (actress-manager) 346
Moore, Miss (actress) 290
Moore's Musee Theatre (Toronto). *See* Robinson's Musee Theatre (Toronto)

Moorish architectural style 223
moral attitudes/issues 12, 48, 49, 50, 56,
    78, 100, 292, 329, 340, 346 and bur-
    lesque 194, 195–6, 198; and circuses
    92, 173–4; and comedy 104–8; and
    Costume Drama 98–9; and dime
    museums 190–1; and melodrama
    102–3; and *opéra bouffe* 113; and
    theatre 92–4, 196; and variety theatre
    167, 188–90; and vaudeville 92. *See
    also* anti-theatre sentiments;
    indecency; religion
Mordred (Campbell) 336
More Sinned Against Than Sinning
    (Carleton) 337
More Than Queen (Bergerat) 144
Morgan, Joe (role of) 101
Morning (Campbell) 337
Morris (Morrison), Clara (actress) 145,
    154, 302
Morrison, Mrs Daniel (née Charlotte
    Nickinson; actress-manager), 14, 98,
    106, 107, *151*, 152, 193, 307, 321,
    323, 332; and Grand Opera House
    (Toronto) 139, 145, 146, 149–52,
    153, 222, 320
Morrison, Daniel (editor/critic) 14, *151*,
    310
Morrison, Lewis (actor) 158
Morton, J.M. (playwright) 64, 71
Morton, Sam and Kitty (variety-
    vaudeville performers) 185
Mossop, Mrs (Mrs John Drew; actress)
    306
Mother and Son (Mellon) 157
motion picture houses. *See* movie
    houses; movie palaces
motion pictures. *See* movies
Motors That Pass in the Night
    (Williamson and Williamson) 342
Mountebank shows 173
Mountford's Museum (Toronto) 191

moustaches 95, 108
movie:houses 90–1, 199, 206–7, 215,
    238, 262, 279, 306, 312, 342, 344;
    palaces 49, 279, 282; projection booth
    280. *See also* cinema(s).
movies 169, 206, 226, 242, 277, 336,
    346; and legitimate theatre(s) 210,
    266, 284; and touring companies 133,
    134, 157, 160; and variety theatre
    169, 193, 198, 200, 203, 210–11;
    and vaudeville 198, 210–11. *See also*
    cinema(s)
movie theatres. *See* movie houses
moving figures 315
*Moving Panorama of England, Ireland
    and Scotland, A* (panorama) 168
Mr Mackenzie at Buckingham (Anon.)
    324
Mrs. Tactician's Triumph ('C.P.M.')
    330
Mrs. Wiggans (Allingham) 66
Muddled (Fraser) 332
Mulock, Cawthra (theatre owner) 228,
    230, 231
Mulvany, Pelham (historian) 16
murals 235, 242
*Muriel the Foundling, and Other
    Original Poems* (Ramsay) 333
Murphy's Minstrels 183
Musee Theatre (Toronto) 191–3, 334
museums 170, 173, 175; dime 12, 166,
    190–3
music 16, 19, 24, 26, 32, 47, 49, 52, 60,
    74, 77, 87n26, 98, 111, 136, 155,
    336. *See also* concerts
musical: accompaniment 214; and choral
    societies 30; comedy/comedies 10,
    48, 117, 144, 185, 197, 198, 209,
    210; revues, 185–6, 210–11; satire
    41; score 97
Musical and Dramatic Competition,
    Governor-General Earl Grey's 6

musicals 49, 66, 116–17, 158, 204,
   230, 317, 325
music halls 187
Music Hall. *See* London (Ont.); Port
   Hope; Toronto
musicians 30, 57, 68, 117, 123, *177*,
   188, 192
musicians' rooms 281
Muskoka (Ont.) 44, 139
Muskoka Summer Festival 340
Mutt and Jeff in Panama 160
Myers, Flora (theatre manager) 317
Myers, Joseph C. (theatre manager) 316,
   317
'Mysteries of the Independent Order of
   Sons of Masonry' (Anon.) 314
Mysteries of Udolpho, The (Scribe) 290

Nabob for an Hour, A (Poole) 62, 64
'Naked Lady, The' (Menken) 194
Nannary, William (manager) 139
Napanee (Ont.) 175
Napoleon 144, 157
Napoleonic era 156–7; Wars 21, 23
Napoleonic Wars, The (panorama) 168
Nathan, George Jean (critic) 116
National Circus (New York) 297
Naval and Military Amateurs (Kingston)
   56, 61, 65–7
Navy Dockyards (Kingston) 84
navy officers/personnel 25, 55, 56–7
Nazimova, Alla (actress) 160, 344
negro(es) 114, 117, 181, 183. *See also*
   blacks; minstrel shows
Neilson, Adelaide (actress) 149, 151–2
Neilson's Hall (Belleville) 317
Nelson, Harold. *See* Shaw, Harold
   Nelson
Nelson's Opera House (Perth) 339
Newark (Ont.; now Niagara-on-the-
   Lake) 277
Newcomb, C.F. (playwright) 330

New Concert Hall (Toronto) 313
New Fort (Toronto) 318
New Grand Opera House (London, Ont.)
   235–6
New Magdalen, The (Collins) 100, 141,
   145
New Minister, The (Anon.) 325
New Princess Theatre (Toronto) 228
newspapers 5, 14, 16, 28, 30, 44, 49,
   58, 59, 124, 125. *See also* reviews
newsreels 203
New Theatre. *See* Brockville; Kingston;
   Toronto
New York As It Is 315
'New York Bloomer' costume 12, 307
New York Bowery Amphitheatre 299
New York City 25, 28, 34, 42, 48, 75,
   103, 128, 189, 228, 297; Broadway
   Theatre 136; and burlesque 194, 195;
   Canadians perform in 137, 141, 144,
   145, 146; Canadian-written plays
   performed in 137, 333; Canadian-
   written plays published in 337, 339,
   340; circus(es) in 172; Fifth Avenue
   Theatre (first) 145; 14th Street
   Theatre 212*n*41; Garden Theatre 144;
   Hippodrome 236; Madison Square
   Theatre 145; Metropolitan Opera
   House 241; Orpheum Theatre 209;
   Park Theatre 167; touring companies/
   performers from 125, 228, 230, 290,
   291, 326; and vaudeville 205, 206,
   207, 209
New York City Zoological Institute and
   Menagerie 297
New York (state) 5, 20, 21, 25, 209, 301
Niagara Court House (Niagara-on-the-
   Lake) 227, 278–80, 304
Niagara Falls (Ont.) 29, 46, 124, 170–1;
   Anglican Club 344; front 170; stunts
   at 169–70, 314
Niagara (Ont.; now Niagara-on-the-

Lake) 3, 5, 6, 8, 20, 22, 25, 39, 68,
124, 277, 290, 291, 296, 302, 389;
Town Hall 290
Niagara-on-the-Lake (Ont.) 242, 277,
278; Court House 277, 278–80, 304;
North Hall 278; Park Theatre 344;
Stamford Town Hall 323
Niagara River 28, 277
Niagara (steamboat) 292
nickelodeons 206, 342. *See also* movie
houses
Nickel Theatre (Ottawa) 242
Nickinson, Charlotte 14, 146, 307, 310.
See also Morrison, Mrs Daniel
Nickinson, Eliza (Mrs Charles Peters)
307
Nickinson, Isabella (Mrs Charles
Walcot) 125, 307, 316
Nickinson, John (actor-manager) 8, 12,
34, 75, 76, 82, 88*n*39, 125, 127, 146,
310; performs/tours 125, 307, 310,
312, 313 and Royal Lyceum
(Toronto) 221, 307, 310, 314 and
Royal Metropolitan Theatre
(Hamilton) 310, 312
Nickinson, John (son) 307
Nickinson, Virginia (Mrs Owen Mar-
lowe) 149, 307, 310, 313, 314, 316
Nickinson family 306, 307
night clubs 198
Nightingale Ethiopian Serenaders
(minstrel troupe) 178
*Nina, or A Christmas in the
Mediterranean* (Chesnut) 333–4
Nipigon (Ont.) 133
Nolan, Edward (murder victim) 292
Nolan, Sergeant (amateur stage manager)
65
non-English speaking theatre 16
North American Hotel (Toronto) 65,
299
North Bay (Ont.) 38, 44, 127, 163*n*14

northern Ontario 43, 44–5, 47
North Hall (Niagara-on-the-Lake) 279
North Square Street (Galt) 273
Norwood, Robert (playwright) 8
Norworth, Jack (vaudeville performer)
201, 211
No Thoroughfare (Dickens and Collins)
104
novelties / novelty acts 181, 189, 190
nudity 194, 198
Nutt, Commodore (midget) 118, 185

Oakwood (Ont.), Mariposa Community
Hall 325
Oberon (role of) 96
O'Brien's 4 Great Shows Consolidated
174
O'Connor sisters (vaudeville performers)
209
Octoroon, The (Boucicault) 101–2
Oddfellows 262, 264, 327
Oddfellows' Hall (Peterborough) 306
Offenbach, Jacques (composer) 113
officer corps. *See* military
officers/personnel
Off to Egypt (Fuller) 332
O'Flaherty, Biddy (character) 169–70
O'Gorman, Edith ('the Escaped Nun';
lecturer) 118
O'Keefe, John (playwright) 103
O'Keefe's Assembly Room (York) 16,
290
Old City Hall (Toronto) 294, 299, 301,
302, 304
Old Comedy 103–4
Old Gooseberry (Williams) 109
Old Guard, The (Boucicault) 76
Old Homestead, The (Thompson)
102–3, 160, 180, 310
Old Marine Hospital (Point Frederick)
58, 294
Old Time Ladies' Aid Business Meeting

at Mohawk Crossroads, An (Anderson) 346
Old Vic Theatre (London, Eng.) 17*n*6
olio 181, 184, 187, 197
Oliver and Sewell Contractors 274
Oliver Twist (Dickens) 136
Omemee (Ont.), Coronation Hall 345
Omnibus, The (Pocock) 65
O'Neill, Eugene (playwright) 102
O'Neill, James (actor) 102, 127, 134, 144, 152, 155, 157
O'Neill, Nance (actress) 137
O'Neill, Patrick (theatre historian) 168
one-man shows 118
One Night in A Bar Room (minstrel show sketch) 115
One Quiet Day, A Book of Prose and Poetry (Ramsay) 322
Only a Farmer's Daughter (Barnes and Levick) 121
Only a Halfpenny (Oxenford) 71
Only Man, The 162*n*13
Only Way, The (Wills; adaptation of *A Tale of Two Cities*) 158, 160
Ontario Arts Student League 47
Ontario College of Art 47
Ontario Dramatic Club 7
Ontario Hall. See Belleville; Kingston
Ontario, Lake 20, 25, 127
open-air/outdoor productions 144, 340, 342
opéra bouffé 113
opera chairs 221, 223, 234, 238, 254, 264
opéra comique 110. *See also* comic opera; light opera
opera houses 6, 12, 17, 32, 41, 215, 243–61, 268, 274, 313; audiences in 91, 94. *See also* Grand Opera House; town halls
Opera House. *See* Belleville; Cobourg; Gananoque; Gravenhurst; Meaford;

Orillia; Ottawa; Peterborough; Rat Portage; St Catharines; St Marys
opera(s): comic, 121, 242, 323; light, 10, 111, 113, 155, 207. *See also opéra comique*
opera(s)/opera companies, 34, 94, 100, 109–13, 200, 201, 203, 310. *See also* Holman Opera Company
operatic romances, 330
'Operatic Soirees in Full Costume,' 304
operetta(s) 113, 165*n*44, 327, 332, 334; comic 333–4, 336; military 333
Ophelia (role of) 141, 149
Orangemen 23, 28
Orangeville (Ont.) 170
orchestra: boxes 240; enclosures, 252; pit(s) 221, 222, 234, 238, 274, 276, 281; seating 226, 227, 231, 242, 252, 256, 258, 266, 269, 272, 274, 280; stalls 223
orchestra-level foyers 231
orchestra(s) 172, 173, 188
organs 281
Oriental Spectacle of Cherry and Fair Star, The 318
Orillia (Ont.) 127, 163*n*14; Opera House 270–3, 271, 284; Town Hall and Market Building 270, 336
'ornamental staff' 274
Orphans' Home (Toronto) 56
Orphée aux Enfers (Offenbach) 113
Orpheum Exchange (vaudeville circuit) 199
Orpheum Theatre (New York) 209
Osgoode Hall (Toronto) 29
Othello (role of) 312
Othello (Shakespeare) 95, 329
Ottawa (Ont.) 8, 10, 14, 25, 29, 32, 38, 39, 41, 45, 47, 141, 145, 175, 178, 210, 242, 313, 325; amateur theatre in 242, 306; Casino Theatre 198; Confederation Square 243; Family

Theatre *345*; Government House 41; Gowan's Hall, 318, 322; Gowan's New Opera House 323 (*see also* Grand Opera House); Gowan's (Old) Opera House (later St James Hall) 318, 322, 323, 325; Grand Opera House 10, 41, 242, 318, 323, 327; Her Majesty's Theatre 125, 242, 312, *316*, 317, 318; House of Commons 325; Metropolitan Dramatic Association 242; Nickel Theatre 242; Opera House 128; plays published in 323, 324, 326, 327, 332, 334, 336, 337, 342, 344, 346; resident stock companies in 146, 345; Rideau Hall 4, 144, 318, *319*, 321, 324, 325–6; Rink Music Hall 318, 322; Russell Hotel 242; Russell Theatre 131, 241–3, *243*, 337, 342, 346; St James Hall (formerly Gowan's Opera House) 323; theatre facilities in 241–243, *243*; touring companies in 127, 128, 157, 314, 336; Town Hall 241, 306, 312; and variety theatre 189, 195, 197, 199, 204, 207, 242, 342; West Ward Market 307

Ottawa Drama League (later Ottawa Little Theatre) 13, *345*, 346

Ottawa Theatre Company 317

Our American Cousin (Taylor) 106, 134

Our Boys (Byron) 94, 106–7

Our Poet in the Council Chamber (Anon.) 321

Ours (Robertson) 107

outdoor / open-air productions 144, 340, 342

Out of the Past (Rodgers) 344

Owen-Flint, Esther (elocutionist) 119, 329

Owen Sound (Ont.) 342, 344; Wonderland Theatre 344

Oxenford, John (playwright) 71

Paardeberg 340

Pacific Scandal 35, 41

pageant plays / pageants 10, 158

painting 47, 91, 170; scenery 47, 62, 83, 270

paintings 168, 190, 283, 291. *See also* panoramas

Paisley Ontario, Town Hall and Opera House *246*, 247–8, 325

Palladian architectural style 232

Palmer, A.M. (manager) 141, 145

Palmer's Concert Hall (Toronto) 318, 319

Panorama of Jerusalem, The (panorama) 168

panorama(s) 117, 166, 168–9, 293, 299

Pantages Theatre. *See* Hamilton; Toronto

Pantages vaudeville syndicate 199

pantomime(s) 172, 187, 273

Paradise Lost (Milton) 168

'Paris by Moonlight' (variety afterpiece) 189

Parisian architectural style 223

Parker, A.J. (circus operator) 173

Parker, Gilbert (novelist) 41, 47, 314

Parker, Louis N. (playwright) 158

Park Theatre. *See* New York; Niagara-on-the-Lake

parodies/parody 10, 41, 119–20, 194, 329, 330

parquette(s) 69, 70, 221, 222, 223, 234, 238, 240, 269, 274

Parthenia (role of) 97–8

Passing Shows, The 185, 198

Passing of the Third-Floor Back, The (Jerome) 120

Pastor, Tony (vaudeville manager) 185, 209, 212*n*41

Patient Penelope, or the Return of Ulysses (Cowley and Williams) 66

patronage, theatrical 6, 25, 52, 55, 70, 77–84, 88n47, 296
Patterson, Tom (founder of Stratford Festival), 276
Pauline (role of) 149, 152
Pavlova, Anna (dancer) 160
Paxton, Joseph (architect) 160
Payne, John Howard (playwright) 62, 65
Payne, Rev. W.R., 56, 293
Peg O' My Heart (Manners) 107
Pemberton, Mr (performer) 291
'Penny Readings' 317
Pentland's Equestrian Troupe 307
People's Dime Museum (Toronto) 191
'People's Hipposoonamadon' 174
People's Theatre (Toronto; originally Royal Museum; later Theatre Royal) 330
Pepper, Dr (illusionist) 315
'Pepper's Ghost' illusion 14, 315
Percy (Ont.) 175
Percy Township Hall (Warkworth) 332
performance: anxiety 74; licences, 6, 173–4, 176, 178, 312
Périchole, La (Offenbach) 113
period drama. *See* Costume Drama
Perry's Peerless Players 160
Perth (Ont.) 175; Nelson's Opera House 339
Perugini, Seigneur (Johnny Chatterton) 125
Peterborough (Ont.) 23, 32, 133, 269, 314, 336; Grand Opera House, Rupert Bradburn's 162n14, *259*, 261, 342, Hill's Music Hall 259–60, 306; Market Building 259, 306; Oddfellows' Hall 306; Opera House, Thomas Bradburn's 260–1, 325; Town Hall, 324–5
Peter Pan (Barrie) 160
Peter Pan (role of) 345

Peters, Mrs Charles (née Eliza Nickinson) 307
Petrie, William (theatre owner) 313
Petrolia (Ont.) 41, 250; Victoria Hall 250–2, *251*, 254, 333
Phair's Assembly Room (York) 291
Phantom Lady (freak) 193
Philadelphia (PA) 125, 139, 172, 324; Academy of Music 236; Southwark Theatre 290
Philharmonic Society (Toronto) 304
Philip, Watts (playwright) 96
Phillips, Sergeant (female impersonator) 62
Phillips, Henry (performer) 300
Phillips, Miss, benefit for 304
Pickford, Mary (film star) 226
Picton Amateur Operatic Company *110*
Pilgrims and Strangers (Middleton) 346
Pinafore (Gilbert and Sullivan) 8
Pinero, Sir Arthur Wing (playwright) 121
Pipandor (Dixon) 332
Piper, Billie (role of) *138*
Piper, Harry (zoo/theatre owner) 175–6, 330
Pique (Daly) 139
Pitou, Augustus (actor-manager) 125, 127, 128
Pitt, Charles Dibdin (actor) 306
Pittman, William (amateur producer) 306
Place of Truth, The (Gilbert) 108
Placida, the Christian Martyr (Carter) 321
Planquette, Robert (composer) 111, 113
playlets 8, 172, 323, 325, 327
playwrights/playwriting, 6, 8, 48, 49, 307. *See also* individual names
Plot and Passion (Taylor), 96, 97
Pocock, Isaac (playwright) 65, 87n29
Poems: Lyrical and Dramatic (Brown), 334

Poems of Archibald Lampman, The 340

Poems and Fragments (Mayne) 296

Poems (McLachlan) 313

Poems, Satirical and Sentimental
  (McBride) 313, 318

Poetical Tragedies (Campbell) 47, 344

poetic: drama 10, 32, 47, 326, 337;
  justice 93, 100

poetry 32, 36, 47, 91, 95; dramatic 325;
  reading (verse speaking) 118–21

poets 118

police 137, 195, 196, 204, 300

Policeman's Benefit Fund 197

political: farce, 333; protests, 294, 296;
  satire, 325

politics 5, 8, 9, 10, 12, 22–3, 24, 26,
  27, 28, 35, 36, 37, 43

Pollyanna (film) 226

Poncet's Inn (Kingston) 290

Poole, John (playwright) 62

Poor Gentleman, The (Colman) 292

*Poor of Toronto, or The Great Money
  Panic of 1857, The* (Anon.) 313

Popish Plot, The (Anon.) 333

population: composition of 3, 20, 21, 23,
  24, 35, 39, 43–4; growth of 18, 19,
  21, 24, 25, 29, 45, 53, 78, 88n43,
  166; shifts in 37, 38, 43. *See also*
  rural depopulation; urbanization

porches 272; entrance 245, 247, 254

Portal, Mr (female impersonator) 62

Port Dover (Ont.) Town Hall 342

Porte, Mrs Gilbert (writer) 58, 215

Porter, Charles S. (actor-manager) 314

Port Hope (Ont.) 128, 170, 175, 183,
  302, 314; Music Hall 320; St
  Lawrence Hotel 320

Portia (role of) 63, 95, 141

Port Perry (Ont.) 175; Town Hall 322

Potter, John S. (actor-manager), 302,
  304, 305

Potter, Mr (performer) 167, 290

Potters' Field (Toronto), 305

poverty, comic approach to 105

Powell, Mr (performer) 297, 301

Powell, Mrs (actress) 301

Powell, Harry J. (architect) 276

Power & Son (architects) 237

Power's Theatre (Grand Rapids, MI)
  161n10

Pratt, William W. (playwright) 101

Presbyterian General Assembly (Anon.)
  325

Prescott (Ont.) 175, 327

Prescott Dramatic Club 334

Prescott Municipal Amphitheatre 327

Price, Captain Morton (Horton Rhys)
  314

Price's tavern (Hamilton) 292

Primrose, George (minstrel/vaudeville
  performer) 183, 210, 310

'Prince John John or Specific Scandal'
  (Anon.) 8, 322

Prince Pedro (Garnier) 326

Prince of Pilsen, The (musical) 204

Princesse de Trébizonde, La (Offenbach)
  113

Princess Theatre. *See* Toronto

Prince of Wales (Albert Edward), 170,
  191

Prince of Wales Music Hall (Toronto)
  318, 319

Prince of Wales Theatre (Toronto;
  formerly Royal Lyceum) 314

Priory, the (Guelph) 292

Prisoner of Zenda, The (Rose; adapted
  from novel by Hope) 121, 318

Private Secretary, The (Hawtrey;
  adapted from von Moser) 109

Proctor, George (architect) 249

Proctor, Joseph (actor) 294

professional theatre companies. *See*
  resident stock companies; touring
  companies

Progressive Burlesque Circuit 197
prologues 68
prompters 72, 74
properties 61, 67, 79, 256, 291
property rooms, 225, 258
proscenium: 219, 234, 235, 238, *244*,
    250, 252, 266, 280, 283, 284, 333;
    arches 222, 223, 227, 236, 240,
    241, 249, 258, 267, 276, 321, 325,
    346; boxes, 221, 240; murals, 235;
    openings 231, 236, 238, 241, 243,
    247, 252, 254, 256, 258, 264; stages
    332, 334, 336, 337, 339, 342, 345
*Provincial Drama Called the Family
    Compact* (Scobie) 8, 296
'Psyche's Dream' (ceiling design) 242
Ptarmigan; or, A Canadian Carnival
    (McIlwraith) 10, 336
public relations 92–3
published drama, 5–6, 8–9, 10, 32,
    290, 291, 294, 296, 299, 313, 316,
    318, 319, 324–7 *passim*, 332,
    333–4, 336, 337, 339, 340, 342,
    344, 345, 346
Pump and the Tavern, The (Anon.)
    324
Punch, Mr (character) 291
Punch and Judy show 192
puppetry / puppet shows 166, 167, 192,
    290, 291
puritanism 92, 101, 168, 186, 190. *See
    also* anti-theatre sentiments; moral
    attitudes/issues
'Push and Pluck, the' 269
Pygmalion and Galatea (Gilbert) 108,
    141

Quack Medicine 291
Quebec City 28, 87*n*33, 172; Military
    Orphan Asylum 87*n*35
Queen Anne architectural style 240
Queen's Arms Hotel (Barrie) 305

Queen's Avenue Opera House (London,
    Ont.) 332
Queen's Own Rifles (Toronto) 332
Queen's Square (Galt) 273, 274
Queen's Theatre. *See* London (Eng.);
    Toronto
Queenston limestone 278
Queen's University (Kingston) 28, 314
Quo Vadis (Stange; adapted from novel
    by Sienkiewicz) 157

racetracks 5, 134
racism 14, 114–16, 176, 178, 297
Radcliffe, Ann (novelist) 290
Radcliffe, Colonel (theatre patron) 55
railways 19, 27, 35, 38, 39, 43, 44–5,
    46, 53, 124, 160, 175, 310;
    influence of 6, 12, 28–9, 32, 33,
    37, 41, 127, 244–5, 305; 'picnic
    trains' 39
*Raise the Flag and Other Patriotic
    Canadian Songs and Poems* (Mair)
    334
Raising the Wind (Kenney) 109
Ramsay, Andrew (playwright) 322, 333
Ranch Queen, The 160
Randolph, Lady (role of) 80
Rankin, Arthur (McKee's father; MP;
    showman) 134
Rankin, Arthur McKee (actor/play-
    wright) 8, 47, 134–9, 163*n*21, 297,
    314, 326, 333, 334, 337
Rankin, Doris (Mrs Lionel Barrymore)
    136, 137
Rankin, George Cameron
    (novelist/playwright) 163*n*21, 334
Rankin, Gladys (Mrs Sydney Drew)
    136
Rastus (role of) 115
Rat Portage (Ont.; now Kenora) 6, 133;
    Gore's Hall 330; Hilliard Opera
    House 133; Jacob Hose's Music Hall

334; Joe Derry's Palace Theatre 336;
Louis Hilliard's Opera House and
Hotel *131*, 336
Rat Portage Dramatic Club *335*
Ravel Brothers (performers) 297
Ravel, Marietta (performer) 317
Ravina (role of) 87*n*29
Ravlan (Watson) 325
Raymond, Rivers and Company (actors)
300
RCMP 6
Read, Charles J. (architect) 228
reading(s) 5, 8, 10, 47, 91; of plays,
289–90; societies, 13, 14; *See also*
dramatic readings; literary and
debating clubs/societies; newspapers;
novels
Rebellion of 1837 26, 297
recitals 217
recitations/reciters 118–21, 167, 168,
173, 290, 291, 299, 329
'Red Head' (song) 202
Red Mill Theatre (formerly the
Theatorium; Toronto) 206
Redmond, Patrick (performer / theatre
manager) *177*, 178, *179*, 189–90,
313
Red Stocking Female Minstrel
Company 195
Reeves, Fanny (Mrs Eugene A.
McDowell) *145*
Regent Theatre (Toronto) 226
regimental: band(s) 52, 53, 60, 69, 77,
80, 87*n*26, 108–9 (*see also* military
bands); players 60–2; theatricals
(*see* garrison theatre)
regional circuit, independent 128, 130,
133
rehearsals 72, 74, 97, 108, 139
reinforced concrete construction 231,
264
religion, 3, 12, 24, 50, 78, 92–3,

167–8, 333. *See also* moral
attitudes/issues; and specific
denominations
Renaissance architectural style 223,
231, 233, 242, 260, 270
Renfrew (Ont.) 24, 127, 163*n*14
Mme Rentz's Female Minstrels 194,
195
resident: amateur minstrel troupes,
183–4; circuses 292
resident stock companies 6, 12, 48, 59,
63, 78, 146, 149–54, 184, 196; in
Hamilton 48, 146; in Kingston 63,
69, 78, 80, 84; in London (Ont.) 63,
78; in Ottawa 146, 345; in Toronto
34, 53, 77, 78, 80, 82, 94, 139,
146, 149–52, 232, 337
Restoration drama 98
reviews 30, 59; of garrison theatre 59,
60–3, 64, 65–6, 67–77, 83;
literary 36
Revolt of the Commune, The
(Molyneaux) 326
revues 116, 185–6, 198
Rhea, Mlle Hortense (actress) 154, 155,
156–7, 329
Rhodes, William Barnes (playwright) 65
Rhys, Horton (Captain Morton Price)
314
Rice, Thomas D. (black-face performer)
176, 178, 310, 312
Richard II (Shakespeare) 96
Richard III (Shakespeare) 26, 96, 115,
151, 154–5, 316
Richardson, John (novelist/playwright)
8, 299, 312
Richardson, Mr (performer) 318
Richelieu (Bulwer-Lytton) 96, 155, 242
Richelieu, Cardinal (role of) 97, 155
Rich Man's Son, A (Forbes) 319
Ricketts, John Bill (circus manager)
172; circus 5

Rideau Hall (Ottawa) *4*, 6, 8, 144, 318,
    319, 321, 324, 325–6
rigging: gallery 270; loft(s)/system(s)
    227, 235, 236, 240, 243, 258
Rignold, George (actor) 95
Riley and Woods (variety-vaudeville
    performers) 185
Ringling Brothers and Barnum and
    Bailey's Greatest Show on Earth 175
Ringling Brothers Circus 174, 175
Rink Music Hall (Ottawa) 318, 322
Rip Van Winkle (Boucicault) 134, 136
Rip Van Winkle (role of) 327, *341*
Ristori, Adelaide 154
Ritchie (Ritchey), John (theatre owner)
    218, *303*
Ritchie's Royal Lyceum (Toronto). *See*
    Toronto, Royal Lyceum
Ritchings, Miss C. (performer) 310
Ritchings, Peter (performer) 310
Rivals, The (Sheridan) 58, 103, 294
Rivers, Mr (performer) 300
*River Thames and the City of London,
    The* (panorama) 168
RKO-Radio Pictures of Canada 206
road companies. *See* touring companies
Robertson, James (theatre manager) 300
Robertson, John Ross (publisher) 16,
    218
Robertson, T.W. (playwright) 99, 106,
    107
Robin Hood (de Koven) 121, 155
Robinson, Mr (actor) 68
Robinson's Musee Theatre (Toronto;
    later Moore's Musee Theatre; Crystal
    Theatre and Eden Musee; Bijou
    Theatre) 334, 336
Rob Roy, or Auld Lang Syne
    (adaptation of novel by Scott) 61, 66
Rochefoucauld-Liancourt, François de
    la 289
Rochester, or King Charles the

Second's Merry Days (Moncrieff)
    98, 121
Rochester (NY) 26, 136, 291, 304
Rockwell and Stone's circus 300
Rodgers, Charles Gordon (playwright)
    344
Rodney, Mr (actor-manager) 300
Rogers, Mr (performer) 312
Roi s'amuse, Le (Hugo) 96
*Roman Drama in Five Acts Entitled Leo
    and Venetia, A* (Anderson) 336
Romanesque architectural style 256
Roman Italian architectural style
    261
romantic: actors 97; architectural style,
    275
romanticism, 93–4, 111, 113
Romeo Creek (Stratford) 276
Romeo and Juliet (Shakespeare) 42,
    329
Romeo (lion) 176
Romeo (role of) 154
Rome and Watertown Railway 127
roofs: 254; trusses 249, 252
rope-walkers 172. *See also* slack-rope
    acts/artists; tightrope performers
Rosalind (role of) 149, 152
Rosamund (role of) 143
Rose of Castile, The (Balfe) 110
Rosedale (Wallack) 17n5
Rose and Nancy (Leadbeater) 290
Rose, the Raving Wild Girl 193
Rossi, Ernesto (actor) 154, 157, 329
Rossini, Giacomo (composer) 110
Rowan, Roly (pseudonymous
    playwright) 334
Rowe, George Fawcett (actor) 104
Roxanne (role of) 144
Royal Academy of Dramatic Art
    (England) 17n6, 345
Royal Achievement of Arms 231
Royal Alexandra Theatre (Toronto).

See Toronto
Royal Artillery 60–1, 64, 65, 80
Royal Canadian Academy 47
Royal Canadian Rifles 75
Royal Circus, Mr Blanchard's 172, 291
Royal Circus (Bernard and Black's; York) 172–3
Royal Grammar School (York) 292
Royal Grenadiers 340
Royal Lyceum. *See* Kingston; Toronto
Royal Metropolitan Theatre (Hamilton) 125, 161*n*3, 310, 312
Royal Museum (Toronto; later Theatre Royal and People's Theatre) 330
Royal Navy 53, 81, 83–4
Royal Opera House. *See* Guelph; Toronto
Rumfustian Inamorato (Walker) 65
Rumfustian (role of) 65
Runaway Wife, The (McKee Rankin) 137, 334
Runnymede Public Library (Toronto) 228, 230
Rupert of Hentzau (Hope) 121
rural: areas/society 21, 23, 28, 36–7, 39, 43, 45, 46; depopulation 37, 38, 43 (*see also* urbanization); life, 102–3, 243–5; melodrama 121; sketches 103
Russell, Annie (actress) 160
Russell, Lillian (actress) 49
Russell, Mr (performer) 289–90
Russell, Mr (theatre manager) 296
Russell, T.B. (actor) 296
Russell Hotel (Ottawa) 242
Russell Theatre. *See* Ottawa
Ruthven, Guy (role of) 67
Ruy Blas (Hugo) 102

Sackets Harbour (NY) 302
St Catharines (Ont.) 124, 128, 163*n*14,
175, 183, 204, 277, 279, 296–7, 302, 310, 313, 314, 333; Academy of Music 306; Opera House 333; Town Hall 277, 304
St George's Society (Cobourg) 316
St James Hall (Ottawa; formerly Gowan's Opera House) 323
Saint Joan (Shaw) 144
St Lawrence Hall (Toronto) 29, 30, 214, 278, 307, 318
St Lawrence Hotel (Port Hope) *320*
St Lawrence Market and Hall (Toronto) 13, 306
St Lawrence River 20, 23, 25, 27, 28, 29, 127
St Lawrence and the Saguenay and other poems, The (Sangster) 313
St Louis (MO) 161*n*10
St Marys (Ont.) 157, 175, 184; Opera House, 262, *262*, *263*, 264–5, *265*, 327; Town Hall 265, 334
St Marys Milling Co. 264
St Michael's College (Toronto) 337
St Patrick's Day 102, 145
St Thomas (Ont.) 127, 131, 133, 175, 245, 293, 332; Grand Opera House (Claris House) 162*n*14, 265, 322; Town Hall 265
Salomé dance 195–6
saloons 103, 166, 176, 186–90, 198, 205
Salt Lake City (UT), 136
Salvini, Tommaso (actor) 95, 329
Sandwell, B.K. (editor) 10
Sandwich (Ont.) 134, 297
Sanford's New Orleans Opera Troupe 310
Sangster, Charles (playwright) 8, 32, 313
Santiago (Bush) 317
Sappho in Leucadia (Stringer) 340
Sarnia (Ont.) 28, 163*n*14

satire 8, 10, 32, 41, 325, 326, 327, 329, 332, 333, 334
Saucy Kate (Lee) 307
Sault Ste Marie (Ont.) 10, *13, 15,* 39, 44, 127, 160, 339–40
Scadding, Henry (historian) 16
Scarlet Pimpernel, The (Orczy and Barstow) 98
scene: changes 61; docks, 235; dock space 258; equipment 227, 241; flats 241; flown 241
Scene at Ottawa (playlet; Anon.) 325
Scene at Ottawa (satire; Anon.) 327
Scene – City Hall (Anon.) 325
Scene in Ottawa (Anon.) 326
scenery 5, 10, 14, 41, 57, 61, 66, 67–8, 83, 84, 133, 157, 222, 223, 240, 248, 270, 272, 274; counterweighted 236; horizontally tracked 252; and minstrel shows 181; painting 47, 62, 83, 270; and Shakespeare 95, 144, 149; stock 243. *See also* stage setting
Schofield's Mansion House (York) 291
School of Elocution (Toronto) 14, 334
'Schoolmaster of Bottle Flat, The' (Anon.) 136
schools 3, 12, 24, 50, 78, 333
School for Scandal, The (Sheridan) 5, 103, 146, 290
School (Robertson) 107
Schubart, William and Louisa (playwrights) 336
scientific discoveries/inventions 137, 170, 175, 190, 203
Scobie, Hugh (playwright/publisher; pseudonym; 'Chrononhotonthologos') 8, 296, *297*
Scotland/Scots 13, 20, 24, 27, 108, 114, 329
Scott, Clement (critic/playwright/poet) 108, 120–1, 141

Scott, F.G. (playwright) 344
Scott, John (theatre owner) 273
Scott, Sir Walter (novelist) 61
Scott, William Fry (structural engineer) 228
Scott-Siddons, Mrs (elocutionist) 119
Scott's Opera House (Galt) 273–4, 337
Scribe, Eugène (playwright) 99
Scripture's Hotel (Whitby) 306
Seaforth (Ont.), Cardno Hall *266,* 266–8, *267,* 288, 326
Seaman, Julia (actress) 117
seating, theatrical, capacity / descriptions of 166, 215–82 *passim*; gods 231, 238, 242; loge 281; risers 227, 234, 238, 279; sofa 221. *See also* opera chairs
Seats of the Mighty, The (Parker) 314
Sebastian or the Roman Martyr (McGee) 314
Second Mrs. Tanqueray, The (Pinero) 121, 340
Secord, Adelaide (née Flint; actress) *150*
Secord, Laura (heroine) 10
Secret Warrant, A (Tremayne) 165*n*42
Sells Brothers Circus 206, 310, 312
Selwyn, Edgar (playwright) 47
Senator's Sensitive Daughter, The (Anon.) 327
Seneca Theatre (Buffalo) 205
sentimentality, and Old Comedy 103–4
'serenaders,' 185. *See also* singers
servants (roles of) 60, 64
Seton, Ernest Thompson (playwright/novelist) 340
sets 14, 16, 158, 252, 258; fixed 252, 258
setting, in Costume Drama 97–9
Seven Sisters, The (Almar) 145
17th Regiment 61, 62, 66, 81, 82
71st Highlanders 77

79th Queen's Own Cameron
  Highlanders 66, 80, 84, 293
sex: and burlesque 195, 198; as theme
  105, 109, 113
Seymour, Grant (playwright) 322
Seymour, Walter (actor) 158
Shaftsbury Hall (Toronto) 214, 324,
  336
Shakespeare, William 32, 34, 65–6,
  81, 115, 119, 141, 143, 157, 222,
  329; plays performed in Cobourg
  316, 340; Kingston 63; London
  (Ont.) 340; New York 144; Ontario
  95–6, 127, 144, 146, 154–5, 157,
  158; Ottawa 337; Sault Ste Marie
  158; Toronto 41, 42, 145, 149,
  151–2, 294, 327, 329, 340; York
  26, 123
Shakespearean Pastorals 342
Shakespearean Saloon (Toronto) 187
Shakespeare Club (London, Ont.) 81,
  215–6, 300, 301
Shakespeare Dramatic and Literary
  Club (Montreal) 88n47
Shakespeare Festival (London, Ont.)
  316
Shannon, Effie (actress) 344
Sharpley, Sam (minstrel performer)
  178, 180
sharp-shooting exhibits 118
Shaughraun, The (Boucicault) 102, 324
Shaughraun, the (role of) 147
Shaughraun Company 145, 324,
  326–7. See also McDowell, Eugene
  A.
Shaullanah (Brent) 325
Shaw, George Bernard (playwright)
  159, 342, 346
Shaw, Harold Nelson (actor-manager)
  14, 130, 133, 334, 337, 340, 342
Shaw, Mary (actress) 82–3
Shaw Festival 279, 280, 304

Shea, Jerry (theatre owner) 205–6,
  207, 209, 313
Shea, Michael (Mike) (theatre owner)
  204–5, 206, 207, 313
Shea Amusement Company 205,
  279–80
Shea's theatres. See Buffalo and
  Toronto
Shenandoah (Howard) 144
Sheppard, O.B. (theatre manager) 227
Sheridan, Richard Brinsley (playwright)
  5, 32, 34, 62, 103, 104
She Stoops to Conquer (Goldsmith) 81,
  103, 160
Shewing Up of Blanco Posnet, The
  (Shaw) 346
Shipman, Ernest (film producer) 135
Shipman, Mrs Ernest (actress; née
  Roselle Knott) 135
'Shoo Fly, Don't Bodder Me' (song)
  297
Short Drama (Anon.) 325
Show Shop, The (Forbes) 319
Shrievalty of Lynden, The (Keating) 333
Shubert Brothers (theatre owners) 210
Shylock (role of) 95
Siamese twins 193
Siddall, J.W. (architect) 275
Siddons, J.H. (lecturer-humorist) 119
Siddons, Sarah (actress) 119, 301
side shows, circus 175, 176
Siege of Algiers, The 123
Siege of Lucknow, The 101, 149
Siege of Tientsin, and the Destruction
  of the Boxers' Stronghold by the
  Allied Forces, The (Hand) 340
Siegrist and Zafretta French and
  Spanish Troupe 174
siffleuses 119
sight-lines 231, 234, 243, 252
Signor Donetti's Celebrated Acting
  Monkeys, Dogs and Goats 312

Silver King, The (Jones) 101
Silverland Theatre (Cobalt) *124*
Simcoe, John Graves (lieutenant-
    governor) 5, 6, 289
Simcoe (Ont.) 175, 297
Simon Black (Mayne) 296
Simpson, John (playwright) 8, 296
Sims, George R. (poet) 119
sing-alongs 181, 202
singers/singing 30, 114–15, 183, 187,
    188, 201, 202–3, 342; plants 202.
    See also musicals; opera(s);
    operetta(s); song(s)
Singla, Etienne (composer) 98
Sir John (elephant) 176
sister acts 209
Sister Mary (Scott and Barrett) 141
Sister Mary (role of) 141
six-brother act 210
Six Nations Indians 337
six-sister act 209–10
Sixteen-Ninety (Grey) 342
60th Regiment 55
62nd Regiment 58, 69, 82
63rd Regiment 61, 69, 75–6, 79,
    88*n*35
66th Regiment 87*n*35
skating rinks 225, 317, 330
Skeleton Dude (freak) 193
Skerrett, George (actor-manager) 125,
    301, 302, 304
sketches 32, 103, 114, 115–17, 180
Skinner, Otis (actor-manager) 155
Sky Pilot (Connor) 47
slack-rope acts/artists 173, 291
slang expressions in dialogue 105–6
slavery 13, 34, 102, 115, 293, 306;
    songs/spirituals 114. *See also*
    abolitionism
Slote, Hon. Bardwell (role of) 105, 106
Small, Ambrose Joseph (theatre
    owner/manager) 127, 131, 133–4,
    207, 235, 238, 265–6, 317, 333,
    337, 342
Smith, Charles T. (theatre manager) 314
Smith, Mr (glass blower) 190
Smith, Sergeant George (actor) 61–2
Smith, Mrs Solomon (actress) 291
Smith, Solomon (actor) 124, 291
Smith, S. (painter), 83
smoking/smoking-rooms 196, 231
snobbery, in low comedy 107
Snyder's Ballroom (York), 167, 291
Snyder's Inn (York) 171, 291, 292
Society Idyls ('C.P.M.') 329
Socrates and Xantippe (Anon.), 330
soft-shoe dance 310
song(s) 32, 48, 75, 167, 290, 291, 297,
    316; arias 111; and burlesque shows
    187; and circuses 173; in minstrel
    shows 114–15, 176, 180, 181, 183;
    in musical shows 117; and specialty
    shows 185; spirituals 114; and
    vaudeville 202, 204, 207, 209
Sophiasburg Township Hall
    (Demorestville) 325
Sophocles (playwright) 111
Sothern, Edward 82
Sothern, E.A. (actor) 106, 134, 160
Sothern, E.H. (actor) 160
soubrette, 74
sounding boards 241, 242
sound reflection 243
Southwark Theatre (Philadelphia) 290
souvenir stands 170
Spackman, John (actor-manager) 125,
    127
Sparling, James (builder) 258
sparring exhibitions 188
Sparrow, J.R. (theatre manager) 225
speaking tubes 241
spear carriers (roles of) 60
special effects 42, 157, 168
specialty acts 181, 185, 187, 188, 197

spectacles 42, 54
Spectre Bridegroom, The (Moncrieff) 66
Spettigue's Concert Hall. *See* London, Ont.
spin-offs 106
spirit world demonstrations 118
Spoil'd Child, The (Bickerstaff) 291
Spurr, John (historian) 16, 60, 81
stage: apron 234, 250, 267, 274; business 97, 203; coaches 124; curtains 231; descriptions of 220–84 *passim*; equipment 227; furniture 158; stagehouses 262, 276; illusions: 'Pepper's Ghost' 14, 315; 'Irishmen' 24; language 98–9 (*see also* dialogue; tushery); lighting 258, 279; managers/management 65, 74; peninsula 279; sets 14, 16
Stahl, Rose (actress) 319
Stair, E.D. (theatre/circuit manager) 131, 133, 226, 333
Stair, Fred W. (theatre manager) 196, 197–8, 344
stairs 218, 221–83 *passim*
Stamford Town Hall (Niagara-on-the-Lake) 324
Stanley, Lady Isobel (actress) *319*
star attractions/performers 95, 96, 108, 134–52, 184, 186, 192–93, 200–3, 204, 207–11
Star Burlesque House (Toronto) 196, 197–8
Star Theatre. *See* Berlin, Toronto
Steamboat Hotel. *See* York
steamboats 19, 23, 25, 39, 124
Steger, Jules (vaudeville performer) 201
Steinberg, Saul (artist) 252
stereotyped characters, 137, 181, 183
Stevens, G.A. (lecturer) 293
Stevenson, Belle (Isabella May; Mrs George Summers) *343*

Stewart's New York Dramatic Company 312
Still Waters run Deep (Taylor) 77, 82, *335*
stock: companies: joint, 269; houses 226; melodrama 333; resident (*see* resident stock companies); scenery 243; summer 48
Stone, Victor (vaudeville performer) 209
Story of a Soldier's Life, The (Wolseley) 54
Stow, B. (actor-manager) 294
Stowe, Harriet Beecher (novelist) 293
Stranger, The (Kotzebue) 99–100
Stratford (Ont.) 163*n*14, 175, 313; Avon Theatre (formerly Theatre Albert) *275*, 276–7, 284, 340; City Hall 274, 275–6, 339; Griffin Theatre 276; Majestic Theatre 276; Romeo Creek 276; Theatre Albert (*see* Avon Theatre); Third Stage Theatre 279; Town Hall 274–5, 276, 313
Stratford Festival 276
Stratford Minstrel Troupe 184
Stratford-on-Avon Players 160
Stratford's Opera House. *See* Brantford
Stratton, Charles S. (midget) 185
Straus, Oscar (composer) 165*n*44
strength, feats of 118
Stringer, Arthur (playwright) 340, 344, 345, 346
strip-tease 198
strolling companies 168. *See also* wandering players
Stuart, D. (piper) 66
Stuart, Julia (actress) 336
subscriptions: and garrison theatre 59, 60, 87; library 5
Such Is Life ('Titus A. Drum') 332
Sudbury (Ont.) 44, 127, 163*n*14

Suffering Servant character 101
Suffolk, Duke of (role of) 158
suffrage 333, 334
Sullivan, Barry (actor) 151, 314
Summers, George H. (actor-manager/
    playwright) 48, 340, *341*, 345
Summers, Mrs George (Isabella May /
    Belle Stevenson) *343*
Summers Mountain Playhouse
    (Hamilton) 340
Summers Mountain Theatre (Hamilton)
    345
Summers Stock Company 340
Sunday School Circuit 174
Sunderland (Ont.), Brock Township
    Hall 342
sunlight, auditorium, 223
Sunshine Sketches of a Little Town
    (Leacock) 47
supporting actors 97–8
Sutherland, Mr and Mrs (actors) 63
Sweet Girl Graduate, The (Curzon) 10,
    329–30, 333
Sweethearts (Gilbert) 108
Sweetland, Elizabeth Jane (Elizabeth
    Jane Thompson; playwright) 332
Sweets of Office, The (Anon.) 326
Swinburne, A.C. (poet/critic) 329
Swiss Bell Ringers 118
Switchell, Sample (role of) 101
Sword of the King, The (MacDonald)
    158
swordsmanship 97
Sylvester, Anne (role of) 145
Sylvie and Bruno (Carroll) 92

tableaux: historical 342; vivants (living
    statuary) 189, 193–4, 195, 334
Tabor, Alan (actor) 185
Talbot, Mr and Mrs (actors) 291
'talent' shows (amateur) 114–15
Tale of Two Cities, A (Dickens) 158

talking-moving pictures 346. *See also*
    movies
Taming of the Shrew, The
    (Shakespeare) 96, 123
Tanguay, Eva (vaudeville performer)
    201, 202
Tanhouser Co. 160
Tavernier Company 139, 312
Tavernier-Lewis New York Comedy
    Company 139
Tavernier (né Taverner), Albert (actor-
    manager) 14, 127, 134, 139, 141,
    155, 330
taverns 5, 39, 123–4, 167, 170, 171,
    186
Taylor, C.C. (historian) 16
Taylor, Mr (theatre manager) 128
Taylor, Mr (ventriloquist) 291
Taylor, Tom (playwright) 77, 96,
    98–9, 106, 335
Tears, Idle Tears (Scott) 108
Teazle, Lady (role of) 146
technical contributions 14, 66–7
technological change 18, 19, 37–9, 44
Tecumseh House Hotel (London, Ont.)
    155
Tecumseh (Mair) 41, 333, 334
television 90–1, 200, 211, 284
Telgmann, Heinrich B. (playwright) 333
Telgmann, Oscar (composer) 10, 333
Temperance Dialogue (Anon.) 317
Temperance Hall. *See* Belleville;
    Goderich; Toronto
temperance: lecturers 123; societies 13,
    318
Temperance Plays, 101
Tempest, Marie (performer) 334
Temple Stock Company 346
Templeton Star Opera Company 10,
    333
Ten Nights in a Bar Room (adapted by
    Pratt from Arthur's novel), 101

Tennyson, Alfred, Lord
(poet/playwright) 141
Terence (Roman poet/playwright) 292
Terrapin. (*See* Toronto)
Terry, Ellen (actress) 49, 93, 330
Tête du Pont barracks (Kingston) 216,
299
Thayendanegea (MacKenzie) 337
Theatorium. *See* Toronto
Theatre Albert. *See* Stratford
theatre buildings/facilities 6, 26, 32,
39, 41, 83–4, 125, 146, 199, 200,
214–87; in Hamilton 125, 131, *216*,
216, 294, *295*, 297, 300; in
Kingston 80–1, 83–4, 215, 216–7,
218, *236*, 237–8, 291, 293, 299,
300; in London (Ont.) 83, 131,
215–16, 232–6, 286*n*24, 297; in
Ottawa 241–3, *243*; in small towns /
rural areas 243–61; in Toronto 131,
166, 214, 218–32, 294, 296, 304,
318; in York 218, 291, 293–4
Le Théâtre du Nouveau Monde 277
Theatre London (London, Ont.) 160
Theatre Managers' Club (Toronto) 206
Theatre Royal. *See* Chatham; Hamilton;
Kingston; London (Ont.); Montreal;
Toronto; York
Theatre, The (magazine) 120–1
Third Stage theatre (Stratford) 279
13th Hussars 77
30th Regiment 56, 66, 70, 73, 82, 83
This Fishery Commission at Halifax
(Anon.) 326
Thomas, (Charles Louis) Ambrose
(composer) 110
Thomas, William (architect) 278
Thompson, Denman (actor/playwright)
102–3, 122*n*5, 125, 127, 160, 178,
187, 310, 312, 313
Thompson, Elizabeth Jane (Elizabeth
Jane Sweetland; playwright) 332

Thompson, Lydia, and her British
Blondes 194
Thompson, Mr (actor) 167, 290
Thorne, Mr and Mrs Charles Robert
(actors) 294
Thorpe's Music Hall (Guelph) 316
Three Farces by Molière 277
Three Students, The (Sachs) 145
'Throw Him Down, McClusky' (song)
202
Thumb, General Tom (midget) 118,
123, 184–5, 315
Thumb, Mrs Tom (Lavinia Warren)
118, 315
Ticket-of-Leave Man, The (Taylor) 101
tightrope performers / funambulists
169–70, 314
Tillie's Nightmare 159, 207
Tilly, Vesta (vaudeville performer) 201
Timothy to the Rescue (Byron) 77
Tobin Mr (actor) 155
Tom Cobb (Gilbert) 108
Toodles The (Raymond) 7
Tool, J.H., & Sons (carpenter-builders)
272
Toole, John L. (actor) 107, 149
'Toots' (pseudonymous playwright) 313
To Prescott and Back for Five Shillings
(adapted from Morton) 242
Tories/Toryism 22, 26, 28. *See* also
conservatives/conservatism
Toronto (Ont.) 8, 9, 12, 13, 25–6, 28,
29–30, 34–5, 36, 39, 41–2, 43,
45, 94, 103, 133, 145, 178, 270,
273, 274, 277, 278, 280, 289, 294,
297, 336, 337; Academy for
Dancing and Calisthenics 305;
Academy of Music (second; later
known as the Princess) 226, 333;
Agricultural Hall 318; Allan Gardens
228; Amateur Dramatic Club 314;
amateur theatre in 14, 48–9, 80, 81,

82, 186, 294, 299, 300, 301, 304–7
passim, 314, 321; Amateur
Theatrical Society 80, 300; animals /
animal acts in 294; anti-theatre
sentiments in 301–2, Apollo Saloon
and Concert Room 186, 187; Apollo
Theatre 314; Arts and Letters Club
344, 345; Arts and Letters Players
12–13; Athenaeum (concert saloon)
187; benefit performance(s) in 108,
153, 304–7 *passim*, 318, 324; Bijou
Theatre 334; and burlesque 195,
196, 197–8; censorship in 346;
circus(es) in 173–4, 175, 297, 299,
300; City Hall, new 306; City Hall,
Old 294, 299, 301, 302, 304; City
Hotel 297, 299; City Theatre (in
Ontario Hall) 313; Civic Square 281;
College of Music 14; Conservatory
of Music 15, 334; Crystal Palace
313; Crystal Theatre and Eden
Musee 334; Cyclorama Building
169, 333; dime museums in 334;
Dramatic Hall 314; dramatic
readings in 294, 306, 318; Drew,
Pride and Sackett's Museum 191;
Eden Musee 334; Elgin Theatre *281,
282, 283*, 284; Empire (burlesque
house) 198; Empire Theatre
(formerly Temperance Hall) 337;
Exchange Coffee House 294;
Exhibition Grounds 176; first
indigenous play staged in 292, 307;
first public showing of film in 336;
first talking-moving pictures shown
(1912) 346; Garrison Amateurs 56,
83; garrison theatre in 52, 53, 55,
56, 57, 59, 61–6 *passim*, 69–74
passim, 77, 78, 87*n*35, 299, 318;
Gayety Theatre 196, 197, 198, 344;
Gentlemen Amateurs 81, 299;
Government House 34, 294; Grand

Opera House (first) 29, 41, 94, 106,
108, 117, 127, 146, 149–52, *153*,
222–5, *224, 225*, 288, 323, 326,
327; Grand Opera House (second)
41–2, 49, 94, 98, 118, 131, 139,
162*n*14, 225, 227, 323, 327, 329,
330, 332; Great Fire of 1849 304;
Harry Piper's Zoological Garden
Theatre 330; High Park 176;
Horticultural Gardens and Pavilion
228, 318, 327; H.R. Jacob's Royal
Museum and Novelty Company 191;
Jacob and Sparrow's Theatre (later
the Majestic Theatre) 333; Loew's
Uptown 200; Loew's Winter Garden
49, 200, *280*, 281–4, 346; Loew's
Yonge Street Theatre 281–2, 346;
Lyceum Theatre, 180, 188–9, 220;
Lyceum, Toronto 34; Mackie's
Summer Theatre (Hanlan's Point)
332; Majestic Music Hall 202;
Majestic Theatre 340; Majestic
Theatre (formerly Jacob and
Sparrow's Theatre) 333; Massey Hall
49, 214; Mechanics' Institute 318,
319; minstrel troupes in 176, 178,
180; Mr Mirfield's Lyceum 300–1,
302; Moore's Musee Theatre 334;
Mountford's Museum 191; movie
houses in 206; Musee Theatre
191–2, 193, 334; Music Hall 318;
New Concert Hall 313; New Fort
(theatre in) 318; New Princess
Theatre 228; New Theatre 299; nickelodeons in 206, 342; North
American Hotel 65, 299; Ontario
Hall 313; Mr Palmer's Concert Hall
318, 319; panoramas in 168, 299;
Pantages Theatre 200, 210, 284;
People's Dime Museum 191;
performances in 289, 300, 302, 307;
plays published in 296, 314, 315,

317, 321, 323–27 *passim*, 329, 330, 333, 334, 336, 337, 339, 340, 342, 344, 346; Princess Theatre (formerly the Academy of Music) 49, 131, 204, 225, *226*, 226–8, 310, 340, 342, 344, 346; Prince of Wales Music Hall 318, 319; Prince of Wales Theatre (formerly Royal Lyceum) 314; Provincial Hall 9; Queen's Theatre 41, 189, 222, 323; Red Mill theatre (formerly the Theatorium) 206; Regent Theatre 226; resident stock companies in 80, 139, 146, 149–52, 232, 337; Robinson's Musee Theatre 334; Royal Alexandra Theatre 49, 196, 210, 221, 225, 228–32, *229*, *230*, 230, 236, 281, 284, 317, 344; Royal Lyceum 8, 14, 34–5, 41, *42*, 70, 82, 125, 178, 218–21, *219*, *220*, 304–7 *passim*, 310, 312, 313, 314, 317, 318, 321, 323; Royal Opera House / Royal Theatre (formerly Royal Lyceum) 41, 118, 195, 197, 221–2, 323, 325, 330, 339; Runnymede Public Library 228, 230; St Lawrence Hall 29, 30, 214, 278, 307, 318; St Lawrence Market and Hall, 13, 306; School of Elocution 14, 334; Shaftsbury Hall 214, 324, 336; Shakespearean Saloon 187; Shea's Hippodrome 16–17, 200, 205, 206, 210, 279, 280, 346; Shea's Toronto Theatre 201, 206; Shea's Victoria Street Theatre 49, 201, 205, 206, 345; Shea's Yonge Street Theatre 337; Shea vaudeville theatres 200, 202; Star Burlesque House 196, 198; Star Theatre 344; Temperance Hall (later the Empire Theatre) 302, 318, 319, 337; Terrapin (concert saloon) 185, 187;

Theatorium (later Red Mill Theatre) 206, 342; theatre facilities in 131, 166, 214, 218–32, 294, 304, 318; Theatre Royal (first) (*see* York, Theatre Royal); Theatre Royal (fourth) 330; Theatre Royal (second) 26, 34, 294, 296, 297; Theatre Royal (third; in North American Hotel) 65, 299, 300; touring companies in 124, 125, 128, 152, 294, 296, 297, 301, 314, 336; University of Toronto Players Club 346; Varieties Saloon 180, 187; variety shows in 184, 222; variety theatres in 180, 187, 222, 336; vaudeville in 166, 200–6 *passim*, 323; Zoological Gardens 330; zoos in 175–6
Toronto Amateurs 305, 306
Toronto Amateur Society 301
Toronto Amateur Theatrical Society 80, 300
Toronto Anti-Slavery Society 34
Toronto Coloured Young Men's Amateur Theatrical Society 14, 304
Toronto Conservatory of Music 14, 47
'Toronto by Daylight and Dark, or Life in the Queen City,' 315
Toronto Dramatic Association 307
Toronto Dramatic Club 81, 314
Toronto Dramatic Society *31*, 304
Toronto Histrionic Club 319
Toronto Juvenile Thespian Society 296
Toronto Lyceum 34
Toronto Opera House 131, 133, 225–6, 333
Toronto Symphony Orchestra 47
Toronto Theatre, Shea's 201
Toronto Theatrical Amateurs 294
Toronto Theatrical Mechanics' Benevolent Association 333
Toronto University Glee Club 155

Total Abstinence Society (Kingston) 299
touring companies/productions 5, 6, 8,
    10, 14, 19, 25–6, 32, 34, 41, 42,
    48, 67, 75, 77, 123–65, 178, 184,
    196–7, 231–2, 234–5, 289, 291,
    292, 305; American 26, 48, 49, 53,
    90, 94, 125, 127–33, 137, 162n13,
    167, 290, 291, 329, 346; British 48,
    49, 90, 94, 125, 127, 128, 134,
    162n13, 290, 346; Canadian 48, 80,
    90, 125, 127, 136–41, 290, 301,
    302, 327, 330; European 127, 167;
    Irish 125
touring: houses 231–2, 234–5; routes
    130 town halls 125, 169, 184, 185,
    215, 243–61
Town Hall. See Ancaster; Beaverton;
    Bowmanville; Brockville;
    Cannington; Carleton Place;
    Cobourg; Embro; Exeter; Fort
    William; Galt; Gravenhurst; Guelph;
    Hamilton; Harriston; Hastings;
    Kingston; Lindsay; Merrickville;
    Millbrook; Niagara; Niagara-on-the-
    Lake; Ottawa; Paisley; Port Dover;
    Port Perry; St Catharines; St Marys;
    St Thomas; Stratford; Walkerton;
    Wingham; Woodstock
Town Hall and Market Building
    (Orillia) 270, 336
Town Hall and Opera House. See
    Aylmer; Clinton; Drayton; Meaford;
    Paisley; Peterborough
towns 21, 25, 38, 43, 45, 46. See also
    individual towns
Townsend, John (actor-manager) 81,
    125, 127, 141, 315, 317
Townsend, Stephen (playwright) 143
Township Hall. See Ameliasburg;
    Warkworth; Demorestville
Tracy and Durand (architects) 233
tragedians 99, 155, 329

tragedy 48, 65–6, 93–4, 111, 319,
    330, 336
Tragedy of Douglas, The (Home) 80,
    290, 291
Traill, Catharine Parr (writer) (author)
    32
trains 159; picnic 39. See also railways
Traito, Albert (painter) 270
trampoline 202
Trans-Canada Theatres Ltd 162n14
transportation 19, 25, 28, 30, 124–5,
    160. See also mass transit; railways;
    steamboats
trapeze acts 170, 173
traps: cellars 281; spring 235; stage
    243, 274, 280
travelling companies/productions. See
    touring companies/productions
Travelling Salesman, The (Forbes) 319
Traviata, La (Verdi) 100
Tree, Ellen (actress) 95
Tree, H. Beerbohm (actor) 314
Tremayne, W.A. (playwright) 8, 157,
    158, 339, 342
Trenton (Ont.) 163n14, 175
Trinity College 314
Tripp, Charles ('the Armless Wonder')
    193
Trip To Coontown, A (mintrel show)
    115
Triumph of Betty, The (Tremayne and
    Hall) 342
'Triumph of Drama, The' (mural) 242
Trovatore, Il (Verdi) 66, 110
Trowbridge, Mr (actor-manager) 291,
    293
True to Life (McKee Rankin) 137, 337
try-outs 209
Tucker, Sophie (vaudeville performer)
    200
Tudor, Mary (role of) 158
Tugboat Annie (film), 209

Tuggers and the Toll Gate, The ('Titus A. Drum'), 332
Tully, Kivas (architect) 227, 278
tumbling acts 291
Turnbull, Quarter Master Sergeant (actor) 80
Turned Head, The (A'Beckett) 61
Turner's Opera House (Gananoque) 342
Tuscan architectural style 217
tushery 98–9. *See also* dialogue; stage language
Twelfth Night (Shakespeare) 41, 96, 144
Twelve Temptations, The 117
24th Garrison Amateurs 294, 296
24th Regiment 58–9, 60, 67–8, 75, 80
Two-Bodied India Boy (freak) 193
Two Bonnycastles, The (Morton) 71
Two Elders, The ('Toots') 313
Two Elders and the Sequel the Meal Club Plot, The ('Toots') 313
Two-headed Boy (freak) 193
Two Off-Uns (burlesque) 115
Two Orphans, The (d'Ennery and Cormon) 96, 115, 139, 141, 146
Tyrell, Misses, benefit for 302

Uncle Dick's Darling (Byron) 107
Uncle Tom (role of) 101
Uncle Tom's Cabin (adapted from novel by Stowe) 8, 34, 100–1, 183, 293
Underground Railroad Company, The (Rice) 183
Underground Theology (Kayelle) 329
'unicorns' 171–2, 192, 294
Union Station (Toronto) 228
United States: Canadian-written plays published in 344; anti-American sentiments 296; cultural influence of 5, 8, 10, 12, 14, 18–19, 22, 26, 32, 34, 35, 47, 48, 50; fear of 10,

20; influence on theatre architecture 215
University of California 144
University College 29, 111
University of Toronto 10, 13, 28, 111, 314, 329–30, 340, 342
University of Toronto Players Club 346
University of Western Ontario 340
Unrepentant and Resourceful Villainess character 101
Unspecific Scandal, The (Fuller) 8, 41, 323
Upper Canada College (Toronto) 136, 230
urbanization / urban society 18, 19, 23, 25, 29–30, 36–9, 43–6, 50, 53, 57, 102–3, 183, 199–200; population 184, 186
Used Up (Boucicault and Mathews), 73, 109

Val and Tyne (Anon.) 345
'Van Amburgh and Co.'s Great Golden Menagerie' 74
Van Amburgh, Isaac (lion-tamer) 172, 174
Van Cortland (Courtland), Ida (née Emily Buckley; later Mrs Albert Tavernier) 14, 134, *138*, 139–41, *140*, *142*, 155, 312, 326, 330, 337
Vandenhoff, George (performer) 301
Van Studdiford, Grace (stage star / vaudeville performer) 201
Varieties Saloon (Toronto) 180
variety: combinations, 185, 201; family 193, 199, 212n41; resorts, 186–7 (*see also* concert saloons); shows 41, 48, 181, 184–90, 192, 199, 200–1, 222, 297, 310, 312; syndicates 10, 12; theatre(s) 16, 123, 166–213, 222, 336. *See also* acrobats/ acrobatics; burlesque; dime

museums; magic; minstrel shows; panoramas; puppetry; vaudeville
vaudeville 48, 49, 189, 198–211; airplane on stage 203; audiences 201–3; big time 204, 205, 206, 209, 210–4; booking practices 199, 206–7; and burlesque 105, 197, 198; circuits, 199, 204, 212n41; and circus(es) 199; and dime museums 190, 199; and legitimate theatre 200–1, 204, 207, 209, 210–11; in London (Ont.) 207, 342; managers, 204–7; and minstrel shows 114, 176, 183, 199; moral attitudes toward 92; and movies / movie theatres 198, 206–7, 210–11; and musicals 204; in Ottawa 199; in Owen Sound 344; in Peterborough 260, 261; and radio 200, 211; small time 206–7; in Stratford 276; in Toronto 166, 200–6 passim, 323; and touring companies 133, 134, 157; and variety shows 185
Vaudeville Managers' Protection Association 205
vaudeville theatres 199, 200, 215, 313; architecture of 279, 280–4; in Ottawa 242; in Toronto 166, 200, 205–6, 207, 210, 279, 280, 281–4, 282, 283
Vaughan Glaser Players 342
Vaughan, J.E.T.C. (actor-manager) 293
Venetian Masque 95
ventilation in buildings, 223, 234, 241, 270, 274
ventriloquism 167, 290, 291, 301
'Venus and Attendants Meeting Adonis and Eros' (fresco) 231
Verdi, Giuseppe (composer) 110
Vermont Wood Dealer's Visit to Hamilton (adapted from Logan's Vermont Wool-Dealer) 346

Vernacular Revival, English architectural style 256
Verne, Olga (actress) 157
vestibules 223, 231, 273
Victoria College (Cobourg) 13, 28, 170
Victoria Hall. See Cobourg; Goderich; London (Ont.); Petrolia
Victoria Jubilee Hall (Walkerton) 337
Victorian: architectural style 267, 275; attitudes 99, 100, 108, 113, 154, 198, 200 (see also moral attitudes/issues); civic architecture 249
Victoria Street Theatre, Shea's. See Toronto
Victoria, Vesta (vaudeville performer) 201, 202
'Viennoise Children' 304
Vieth Frederick Harris D. (diarist) 63, 64, 82, 86n23
Village Lawyer, The (Macready) 5, 290, 291, 296
villains/villainesses 97, 101, 102, 155
Viola (role of) 152
Virginia Minstrels 178, 184
Virginia (role of) 156
Virginius (Knowles) 96, 156
virtuoso mode of performing 94, 95
Vision of the Heavens, The (panorama) 168
Vitascope 336
voice: lessons 144, 145; projection 73–4
von Mueller, Count (military aide), 170

Wacousta (Richardson) 312
Wags of Windsor, The (Anon.) 291
'Waiting at the Church' (song) 202
waiting-rooms 231
Walcot, Charles (actor) 125
Walcot, Isabella (Mrs Charles; née Nickinson) 125, 307, 316

Walker, C.E. (playwright) 65
Walker's Hotel. *See* Kingston
Walkerton (Ont.): Town Hall 337;
    Victoria Jubilee Hall 337
Wallace, Vincent (composer) 111
Wallack, Fanny (actress) 306
Wallack, James (actor) 321
Wallack, James (Sr) (actor) 302, 312
Wallbrook, Jimmy (vaudeville
    performer) 260
Waller, Lewis (actor) 134, 162*n*13
wandering players 166, 167–8
War of 1812 21, 22, 25, 26, 52, 277
Ward, Artemus (comic lecturer) 118
wardrobe stock 67–8. *See also*
    costumes
Warkworth (Ont.) Percy Township Hall
    443
Warren, Elfin Minnie (midget) 118
Warren, Lavinia (Mrs Tom Thumb)
    118, 315
'Washing Up' (minstrel entertainment)
    182
Waterloo building (Toronto) 299
Watertown (NY) 302
Watford (Ont.) 326
Watson, Samuel James (playwright)
    325
Waugh Brothers (actors) 293–4
waxwork figures 191, 192, 292
Way Down East (Thompson) 103
Weeks and Smyth (architects) 262
Welland (Ont.) 277
Welland Canal 277
Wellington, Duke of (patron) 55
Wellington Grey and Bruce Railway
    256
Wellington Inn (Kingston) 294
Wentworth, Colonel 68
Wesleyans / the Wesleys 6, 24, 93
West, Billy (minstrel performer) 183
western: frontier dramas 158;

settlement/development 35, 36, 38,
    43, 44, 45
West, Madeline (role of) 144
Westport (Ont.) 326
West Ward Market (Ottawa) 307
Wheeler's Opera House (Toledo, OH)
    131
'wheels' (burlesque circuits) 197, 198
When George the Third Was King
    (Merritt) 337
When Knighthood Was in Flower
    (Kester; adapted from Mayor's
    novel) 121, 158
'When Other Lips' (aria) 111
Whitby (Ont.) 175, 209, 315; circus(es)
    in 175; Hopkins' Music Hall 248,
    326; Scripture's Hotel 306
Whitcomb, Joshua (role of) 180
White, Porter J. (actor) 157
White's Serenaders (minstrel troupe)
    178
Whitlock, Billy (minstrel performer)
    178, 184
Whitman, Walt (poet) 39
Whitney, C.J. (theatre/circuit manager)
    128, 131, 133, 228, 235
Whitney Grand Theatre (Detroit, MI)
    161*n*10
Widower's Houses (Shaw) 344
Wigan, Alfred (translator) 83
Wilbur, A.R. (manager) 141
Wilbur, Clarence (vaudeville performer)
    209
Wild Animal Play for Children, The
    (Seton) 340
Wilde, Oscar, lectures 118, 329
Wild Oats (O'Keefe) 103
Wilks, T.E. (playwright) 102
Willard, E.S. (actor) 155–6, 158
Willcocks, Joseph (diarist), 167,
    289–90
Williamsburg (Ont.) 175

Williams, H.A. (theatre manager) 290
Williams, M. (playwright) 66
Williamson, A.M. (playwright) 342
Williamson, C.N. (playwright) 342
Willy, Little (role of) 101
Wilson, L.W. (Curly) 264
Wilson, Mr (performer) 312
Wilson, William Mercer (actor/diarist)
    81, 297
Wiltshire Regiment (62nd Regiment) 57
Winchell's Drolleries 312
Windermere, Lady (role of) 141
Windham, Lt-Gen. Sir Charles (theatre
    patron) 55
windlasses 274
windows 247, 248, 249, 254, 262, 264,
    273, 279
Windsor (Ont.) 29, 45
Winged Victory, The (Machar) 339
Wingham (Ont.), Town Hall 334
Winnipeg (Man.) 8, 327
Winter Garden Passing Shows, The
    186, 198
Winter Garden Theatre, Loew's. See
    Toronto
Winter Studies and Summer Rambles in
    Canada (Jameson) 296
Wizard of the Nile, The (Herbert) 117
W.J. Florence Co. 139
Woffington, Peg (role of) 99
Wolfe Island (Ont.) 318
Wolseley, Colonel Garnet 54
Woman Suffrage ('Roly Rowan') 334
Woman of Today, A (Forbes) 319
Woman in White, The (Collins) 100
Woman With A Past (role of) 121
Wombwell's Royal English Menagerie
    174
women: as actresses 63; and burlesque
    193–4, 196, 197, 198; discrimina-
    tion against 329–30; in dramatic
    verse 120; as elocutionists 119; in

Gilbert and Sullivan operettas 113;
    in male roles 117, 194; as matinée
    audiences 203; in melodrama 101,
    102, 103; problems of, as dramatic
    theme 100; roles in garrison produc-
    tions 62–3, 82, 87n29; and tableaux
    vivants / living statuary 193–4; and
    theatre advertising 196; and variety
    theatre 188–9; and vaudeville 203
'Women of Mumbles Head, The'
    (Clement Scott) 120–1
Wonderland Theatre (Owen Sound) 344
Woodburn Press 323
Wood, Colonel (architect) 235
Wood, W.P. (playwright) 319
Wood's British Museum (York) 190
Woodstock (Ont.) 127, 131, 193, 175,
    301, 326, 340; Town Hall, 327
Woolf, Benjamin E. (playwright)
    105–6
Wooster, Thomas (contractor) 246
Workingmen of New York, The (Anon.)
    317
Workingmen of Toronto, The (Anon.)
    317
World's Fair (Chicago) 195
Worth, Edward (playwright) 336
Worth's Burlesque Ritual (Worth) 336
Wurlitzer organ 280

'Yankee Doodle' 26
Yellow Bag, The (Caldwell) 344
'Yes, Let Me Like a Soldier Fall' (aria)
    111
Yiddish theatre 44
Yonge Street Theatre, Loew's (Toronto)
    346
Yonge Street Theatre, Shea's (Toronto)
    337
Yorick's Love (adapted from the
    Spanish by Howells) 155
York (now Toronto) 5, 6, 13, 16, 20,

21, 22, 25–26, 53, 277, 289–94;
amateur theatre in 292; animal acts
in 291, 292, 293; Barney Roddy's
Tavern 173; benefit performances in
291; Bernard and Black circus
172–3, 292; circus(es) in 172–3,
291, 292; concerts in 292; Court
House Green 171; De Forest's Hotel
173; Frank's Hotel 123, 218, 291,
292; garrison theatre in 52, 53;
George Garside's Hotel 173;
Gentlemen Amateurs 290; home
entertainment in 289–90, 291;
Keatings British Coffee House 294;
'learned pigs' in 4, 290; Mechanics'
Institute 293; menageries in 171;
Methodist Chapel (theatre) 293;
O'Keefe's Assembly Room 16, 290;
panoramas in 168, 293; Phair's
Assembly Room 291; play reading in
289; puppet shows in 167, 290, 291;
reading aloud in 289–90;
Schofield's Mansion House 291;
Snyder's Ballroom 167, 291;
Snyder's Inn 171, 291, 292;
Steamboat Hotel (later City Hotel)
171, 292, 294; taverns and beer
shops in 167; theatre
buildings/facilities in 218, 291,
293–4; Theatre Royal 26, 293–4;
touring companies/productions in
290, 291, 294; wax figure
exhibitions in 292; Mr Wood's
British Museum, 190. *See also*
Toronto
York Amateur Theatre 292
York circus 173
Yorkshire Giant 292
Yorkville 30, 39
Younder, J.W. (performer) 315
Young and Cawsey (contractors) 275
Young, James (historian/diarist) 16

Young's 'assembly room' (Galt) 301
Yum-Yum (role of) 113

Zacharias' Funeral (ministrel show
sketch) 115
Ziegfeld Folies, The 185, 198
zoological gardens / zoos 171, 175–6
Zoological Gardens (Toronto) 330
Zoological Institute 172

THE ONTARIO HISTORICAL STUDIES SERIES

Peter Oliver, *G. Howard Ferguson: Ontario Tory* (1977)

J.M.S. Careless, ed., *The Pre-Confederation Premiers: Ontario Government Leaders, 1841–1867* (1980)

Charles W. Humphries, *'Honest Enough to Be Bold': The Life and Times of Sir James Pliny Whitney* (1985)

Charles M. Johnston, *E.C. Drury: Agrarian Idealist* (1986)

A.K. McDougall, *John P. Robarts: His Life and Government* (1986)

Roger Graham, *Old Man Ontario: Leslie M. Frost* (1990)

Joseph Schull, *Ontario since 1867* (McClelland and Stewart 1978)

Joseph Schull, *L'Ontario depuis 1867* (McClelland and Stewart 1987)

Olga B. Bishop, Barbara I. Irwin, Clara G. Miller, eds., *Bibliography of Ontario History, 1867–1976: Cultural, Economic, Political, Social* 2 volumes (1980)

Christopher Armstrong, *The Politics of Federalism: Ontario's Relations with the Federal Government, 1867–1942* (1981)

David Gagan, *Hopeful Travellers: Families, Land and Social Change in Mid-Victorian Peel County, Canada West* (1981)

Robert M. Stamp, *The Schools of Ontario, 1876–1976* (1982)

R. Louis Gentilcore and C. Grant Head, *Ontario's History in Maps* (1984)

K.J. Rea, *The Prosperous Years: The Economic History of Ontario, 1939–1975* (1985)

Ian M. Drummond, *Progress without Planning: The Economic History of Ontario from Confederation to the Second World War* (1987)

John Webster Grant, *A Profusion of Spires: Religion in Nineteenth-Century Ontario* (1988)

Susan E. Houston and Alison Prentice, *Schooling and Scholars in Nineteenth-Century Ontario* (1988)

Ann Saddlemyer, ed., *Early Stages: Theatre in Ontario, 1800–1914* (1990)